Sense and Semblance

AN ANATOMY OF SUPERFICIALITY IN MODERN SOCIETY

REMINGTON NORMAN

2007
FOUNTHILL

First Published in 2007
by
FOUNTHILL
Tisbury, Wiltshire SP36RH, England

A CIP catalogue record for this book
is available from the British Library

© 2007 Remington Norman

www.founthill.com

ISBN 978-0-9555176-0-0

Cover design by Tadpole Design, Cape Town, South Africa

Typographic design and layout by
G.J. du Toit Fine Typography, Hout Bay, South Africa

Printed in Cape Town, South Africa by Mills Litho

CONTENTS

INTRODUCTION

'How great is the number of those in whose minds no source of
thought has ever been opened, in whose life no consequence of thought
is ever discovered; who have learned nothing upon which they can
reflect; who have neither seen nor felt any thing which could leave its
traces on the memory … and yet are supposed to be thinking beings'

Dr Samuel Johnson: (1758)

The problem

We live in an increasingly schizophrenic world. While material innovation
and scientific advance fuelled by remarkable intellectual achievement have
transformed western societies in a couple of generations, the concomitant
increase in personal freedom and well-being have spawned a shallow mindset
which prefers appearance to reality, surface to depth, and readily embraces
the desires, fashions and whims of popular mass culture. Presentation and
show now dominate public lives and private thought. Personal and social life
is awash with superficiality—obsessed with 'feel good', 'lifestyle' and social
status—and the fashionable expectation of unrestricted liberty has led to an
over-sensitivity to the rights and sensibilities of the individual at the expense
of wider society. A disproportionate emphasis on the present has reinforced
a reluctance to look behind events or ideas or to tackle what is detailed or
challenging. The more entrenched this perspective becomes, the stronger
is the disposition to regard the superficial as a barometer of value and the
greater its influence on the government of decision and action.

Superficiality has facilitated mediocrity, whether in what we buy or
consume, listen to or see, or are invited to believe. While this is unfortunate
in itself, what is worse is that mediocrity is routinely accepted as excellence.
The apotheosis of these trends is the cult of celebrity which diverts focus from
serious debate and distorts priorities towards the facile opinions, behaviour
and concerns of its hollow sub-culture.

Superficiality has quietly seeped into everyday life at many levels. The
trend is very evident and its consequences damaging. For most it passes for
normality, failing to appreciate how shallow the world around them has
become; others, seeing the damage, despair. Immediacy and 'feel good' displace

clear thought, any doubts being assuaged by the misconceived notion that
"The world works well enough, so why change it?" As this mindset becomes
the norm—the way life is—its impact is lessened; rather like living with
everyday violence in a sink housing-estate or a black African township you
become inured to it. The fact is that, while many are busy chasing a chimerical,
idealised, 'lifestyle', superficiality has corroded genuine quality of life.

The argument of this book is that until these realities are recognised there
is negligible chance of stopping, let alone reversing, the trend. This requires
hard-edged, dispassionate thinking, free of obfuscation and sentimentality.

This message is profoundly uncomfortable—especially for those who
benefit from the culture of superficiality or who prefer to conduct their lives
on sentiment rather than reality. People understandably reject the notion that
their own arrangements are less than perfect, but that is the inevitable diagnosis for a culture which fails to see where it is going, or if it does, chooses
to ignore the problems in the misguided belief that somehow 'it'll all come
right'.

Superficiality particularly suits cults and trendy social movements which,
in many cases, achieve penetration through a potent mix of moral indignation
and populism, often based on a few deceptively simple propositions. They
prefer to avoid searching analysis and strive to deflect attempts at rigorous
scrutiny of their beliefs. Logic has always been a particular difficulty for ideologies; it puts obstacles in the path of otherwise appealing ideas and has an
inconvenient habit of exposing intellectual sham.

This book is concerned with both the moral and social pathology of
superficiality. It pulls no punches in addressing the problems and is not written
to provide easy answers or balsamic consolation.

Symptoms

The superficial, in the sense I wish to discuss it, concerns our preoccupation
with Image—with what is obvious, shallow and illusory—at the expense
of Reality (the contrasts are further discussed in Chapter 1). It takes no great
genius to understand that it is the Reality, not the Image, which ultimately
determines how things are and which should therefore occupy our attention. Yet, we are routinely seduced by show or persuaded by facile argument
and intellectual sophistry. In the superficial society, the overwhelming tendency is to think, interpret, evaluate and decide on the basis of appearance.
This instinctive acquiescence is in part gullibility and in part laziness. On the

one hand, trust disposes us to accept impressions or opinions at face value; on the other, even when we recognise the possibility of a disparity between Appearance and Reality, we shirk the intellectual effort necessary to validate our impressions. This is analogous to constructing our universe from mirror images; these are only as true as the mirror producing them and, as we have no way of determining, from the images alone, how true they are, to arrive at a reliable assessment it makes sense to study the mirror itself.

Sometimes the Image conveniently matches the Reality, but it is their divergence which creates problems for governments, societies and businesses. At a personal level, the implications of failing to deal in reality are no less serious: this is not merely a dividend of our passive acceptance of whatever is presented to us, but is often reflected in an active striving to project an Image which we believe will promote our interests or enhance our social status. Image deceptions are not always blatant and it is the subtler and more insidious which cause greatest problems. As this book suggests, vigilance and an intelligent focus are essential.

The effects of superficiality

It is in human nature to court pleasant stimulation and avoid inconvenience, so it is natural that we willingly accept whatever promises least effort — the short-cut, the quick fix. This opens the door to a world conducted on appearance and deceit, where social progress is a function of impression rather than merit.

This is no less true of political, corporate and international affairs. Businesses are prey to slick, jargon-laden, management nostrums, superficially impressive but based on insecure foundations. Corporations are distracted by external pressures for greater social responsibility on the basis of populist arguments which a little straight thinking shows to be unsound. Corrupt nations trade on distorted images of competence and tolerance, while the western model of universal (American-style) democracy, rights without responsibilities, a litigious victim culture and rampant consumerism is foisted unquestioningly on the world.

Modern political life is in the grip of Image manipulation and skilful marketing. Public figures now perform for the media and even the most important of political issues may be decided on personalities and trivialities, rather than on extended discussion. Public debate, even on major issues, is conducted at the most superficial level — half-truth, hyperbole, melodramatic appeal, sound-bite and slogan—driven more often than not by media skills than by credible argument. The issues themselves often have marginal influence on the outcome.

These trends have been nourished by intellectual deficiency and a media explosion which, coupled with greater choice and the ready availability of on-demand entertainment, have shortened attention spans and encouraged moral and intellectual laziness. We flit from one thing to another, unwilling to tackle anything which does not immediately capture our interest, and when it does, in no great depth. A predilection for entertainment—sport, reality television, pop idols, computer games and psychotherapy and its derivatives (especially in the USA)—has turned these into surrogate religions and destroyed the taste for more serious and effortful pursuits. Priorities are more likely to be determined by personal inclination than by any dispassionate assessment of what matters or should concern us. In consequence, we are readily short-changed by the media, duped by advertising, and vulnerable to any half plausible proposition. In a world rich in diversity, we make much of the process of choosing between minimally differing alternatives and scrabble round examining various styles of veneer oblivious to the rotting supports beneath. There is urgent need for a more systematically critical attitude, at every level, but even this is of limited use unless we have the disposition to ask the right questions and the capacity to evaluate the answers.

The roots of superficiality

These are complex—in part evolutionary, in part social and structural. Falling educational standards have contributed, as has the increasing misuse of language to spin and distort the truth. Deceits and half-truths escape notice if played to audiences which lack the motivation to challenge them. Sentimentality—the replacement of hard truths, blame and shame with sentiment—has also been a significant influence. In particular, spurious love disguised as 'caring' substitutes for discipline with children and people are encouraged to see themselves as victims rather than relying on their own resources. Sentimentality turns behaviour that was traditionally the province of personal responsibility into the deterministic result of state or others' failings. The more society fragments and offloads personal obligations and moral responsibilities onto its institutions, the greater its de-moralisation and the less are individuals resourceful in their own interest as their self-reliance atrophies.

Much of this—both the superficiality itself and our willingness to accept it—is due to what I call the marginalisation of wisdom. This is largely a consequence of the progressive liberal iconoclasm of the 1960s and on, which infected a generation and de-railed education. Rejecting what was regarded as essential, traditional, wisdom—not so much the wisdom of knowledge, though this is part of it, but the accumulated wisdom of sensitivity and experience—opened the door to much pseudery and questionable expertise. Public gullibility has allowed these to take hold; they have unseated wisdom and instinctual judgement in many areas and together with an unhealthy emphasis on the individual rather than the community, have stripped societies of their collective force and of the sanctions and cohesion they once had. Obsession with the morally sacrosanct idea of 'freedom of the individual' and the explosion of rights and entitlements divested of countervailing responsibilities, have been particularly damaging—creating destructive imbalances which extend beyond the family into the wider social sphere.

It is tempting to see this as Gresham's Law in full spate: mediocrity driving out excellence. There is a noticeable lack of confidence to discern good from bad, the facile from the serious, contrived cleverness from genuine wisdom or stuff from nonsense. Even when they can, people find themselves intimidated from saying so by convention or political correctness. Our appreciation of genuine worth, as opposed to 'flash', has steadily eroded as we become increasingly mesmerised by the inconsequential and ephemeral—in particular, cheapened media, shallow argument and vacuous celebrity. Value tends to be equated with whatever is found to be superficially attractive or with what most captures people's fickle attention.

Why should any of this matter?

The facile answer is to point out that western societies enjoy higher standards of living, greater choice, more, and more varied, leisure, better healthcare and longer life expectancy than ever before—so what is there to worry about? Plenty. If one looks at the reality beneath this superficially satisfactory image one finds that, despite increasing material prosperity, people report themselves to be more discontented than ever, societies and families are fragmenting, businesses face pressures unrelated to their proper responsibilities and politicians are widely disrespected and distrusted. Nations are being held to ransom by un-elected groups bent on furthering agendas related to the environment and religion, to eradicating elites and to smashing capitalism. To much of this activity, the targets involved have no effective response. In many countries, social order is breaking down under the influence of drugs, alcohol, crime, personal abuse, intolerance and other forms of anti-social behaviour. In desperation, governments scratch at the surface with ever more stringent laws and regulations in the hope of improving the situation. Meanwhile, much of the moral glue that held societies together, effectively, for centuries has been jettisoned, often with political assistance, in favour of illusory freedoms and contentious rights, which provide little durable benefit either to the individuals on whom they devolve or to the wider community. In the name of inclusivity, we seem to have lost the collective resolve to respond robustly to political correctness, loutishness or sheer stupidity. Multi-culturalism and the emerging power of different ethnicities and religions have undermined social and political convictions to the point where even the most basic and long-held moral principles are now open to question. In many societies there is now palpable tension between the desire for equality and the demand to maximise individual freedom as a precondition of unfettered expression of individuality. Until we recognise and challenge this rampant superficiality we will fail to restore collective identity and with it the will to respond with conviction to many serious threats to personal, social and national life.

To the reader

This is not a philosophy book, nor a book about philosophy, but a look at the issues relating to superficiality from a philosophical and sociological standpoint. It is necessarily detailed and closely argued, but is not written with academics or professionals in mind, rather for the general reader: someone who is sufficiently interested to be prepared to delve beneath the surface for better understanding. The ideas and concepts involved come from philosophy, sociology and psychology, and these are the perspectives which underlie this work.

I wish to anticipate, and defuse, one particular threat to the theme of this book—namely that it is no more than an elaborate reworking of the idea that the world is going to the dogs. This belief, forcefully expressed by successive older generations and equally forcefully ridiculed by successive younger ones, conflates two separate ideas: first that morals themselves have become more relaxed—the usual examples are sexual permissiveness and a decline in behaviour and respect—and second, that morality itself, whether or not its principles have altered, is increasingly less regarded and adhered to.

Whether specific social changes amount to moral degeneration is arguable and the belief that they do is easily criticised, because specific evidence is largely subjective and thus hard to pin down. The usual, and reasonable, sally is that change is not necessarily degenerative. The value society or individuals put on change is of no particular concern to this book, nor is the de-moralisation of society I refer to central to its thesis, which is that whatever moral and social change there has been are a symptom of other, more fundamental problems now facing civilised societies. The fact of change is beyond dispute—behaviour which would have been considered outrageous and censured even a generation ago is now accepted without comment, and toleration appears to amount to an unlimited moral and social licence. The interesting questions are not what particular value you put on such changes, but why they have happened and what the trends portend. If there has been moral degeneration, it is probably better understood as an erosion of virtue than as specific behaviours, but this is not a matter argued here. My contention is that a variety of influences—poor education and media output in particular—have led to diminished intellectual skills which encourage superficiality and discourage the pursuit of deeper truths and explanations. Part of the problem with the preoccupation with surface is that much of what are in fact moral problems are now considered as social issues. This is a convenient intellectual sleight of hand to avoid addressing more profound, but uncomfortable, realities. Thus culpability and shame become excusability, and true toleration is usurped by incessant talk of equality and multi-culturalism. No one is threatened by this process and a semblance of order is maintained. Such deceit is a prime symptom of more durable damage to individuals and societies inflicted by superficiality. It is these phenomena and their inter-relationships that this book sets out to expose and explain. If the world is indeed going to the dogs, it is not because of free love or public drunkenness *per se* but because of what these say about social values and public policy. To suggest, therefore, that this book is merely a serial complaint against social degeneration is both a misrepresentation and a facile caricature of its argument: a good example, in fact, of the very superficiality I wish to expose.

Philosophers are often caricatured as hair-splitters and as incapable of giving useful advice. This is to misunderstand the nature of philosophy, which is primarily to refine and clarify issues by teasing out their inherent complexities. Looking to a philosopher for practical prescriptions is akin to expecting a coffee machine to produce meat pies. The charge of hair-splitting is less wide of the mark: hairs need to be split, but this activity is not undertaken mindlessly, nor simply to demonstrate mental dexterity, but to illuminate areas where there is genuine conceptual confusion. The philosopher's art is, in part, recognising which particular hairs are worth splitting.

This is the antithesis of unthinking superficiality which leads life on an entirely different plane. Here there is no interest in splitting hairs or in hairs in general, but an endless tinkering with the hairstyle, in the hope of transient satisfaction. In this, as in so much in the cosmetic culture, the Image supplants the Reality. It is the futility of this approach that this book is delighted to expose.

CHAPTER 1
DISTORTING REALITY

'Beware lest you lose the substance by grasping at the shadow'
'The Dog and the Shadow', Aesop's Fables

'There is no reality except the one contained within us. That is why so
many people live such an unreal life. They take the Images outside them
for reality and never allow the world within to assert itself'
Hermann Hesse, Demian, 1919

An essential prerequisite of understanding superficiality and what it means
to say that societies are becoming increasingly conditioned by it is to spell
out the different aspects of reality and examine what can be contrasted with
them. In normal usage, reality is opposed to illusion or appearance and its
contraries may be combined into the concept of Image — which fuses what
is presented to us, either by our senses or through language, and opposes it
to the underlying realities. What matters here is not a precise determination
of the opposites of reality, rather to understand that what is often taken for
real is illusion, mere appearance either by chance or design, and that failing
to recognise the existence and influence of such false correspondence can
cause important damage.

Image is a concept suffused with distinct references and complex subtle-
ties; in its most common sense, we contrast it with what we regard as reality — what we see, hear, feel or taste. The external world plays tricks on our
senses that alter perspective and distort what we take for reality, so we must
live with the fact that there is no simple correlation between sensory information and what we make of it. Where something more than a straightforward
response is required, for example when we evaluate personalities or situations, individual people often interpret 'the same' signals very differently. So
the relationship between Image and Reality is blurred. Such fallibility causes
confusion and fuzziness and provides opportunities for others to exploit this
looseness for their own ends.

In another, derivative sense, often related to personality and public life,
Image is critical to approval and success. The Image manipulation industry is
pervasive and influential, deploying its arts to distract attention from realities

that are unpalatable or, for diverse reasons, we seek to hide. For example, the demands of acceptability mean that much public discourse is dumbed-down and sanitised with the specific aim of avoiding alienating anyone. Political and personal behaviour is frequently driven by the twin ideals of 'inclusivity' and 'politically correctness' which are presented as both desirable and uncontroversial. The reality is that they are neither, and the latter, in particular, is constantly derided. While there may, on occasion, be genuine difficulty in finding ways to strike a balance between the demands of reality and the need to respect feelings and sentiment, this is slender justification for universal proscription. Such sentimentalised image management compromises policy-making which leads in turn to bad decisions and long-term social problems.

At a more intimate, individual level, most people like to project a good personal image. This seems to matter, to a greater or lesser extent, to every social human being living beyond the basic level of survival. How we are seen appears to trump any concern as to what we really are, and usually reflects an underlying restlessness and tension. Much personal image projection is based on the perceived importance of wealth, yet there seems to be little recognition of two incontrovertible facts: first, that the obvious markers of success—money, status etc—have no permanent relationship to underlying character, except possibly to disguise it, and are therefore no reliable basis for judgement, and second, that wealth-related trappings change nothing of importance in core personality.

Superficiality is driven by image, appearance and illusion, and it is these that enable it to seep so effectively into so many areas of our lives. As a prelude to better understanding these mechanisms, this chapter sets out their nuances and discusses their principal differences. In broad terms, Image has two main references: first, in its opposition to Reality and in this, Image deals with the patina of things—what we observe on the surface. It is in this sense that people are often criticised for focusing on appearance to the detriment of substance. Here we need to distinguish between three types of distortion:

1. We perceive signals correctly and interpret them correctly—but they are false. A simple example is a distorting mirror which gives the impression that a person is perhaps taller or thinner than they actually are.
2. We misinterpret signals we receive, either by simply misreading or else by putting weight on them that they will not bear. For example, people driving expensive cars are generally taken as wealthy—which, is prob-

ably their intention — whereas it is entirely possible that the car is borrowed, or bought on credit, or even stolen or that there is no wealth behind this single, prominent, asset.

3. Image distortion is deliberately designed to deceive. For example, in some parts of the Middle East, attractive women in night clubs are in fact men and not all Rolex watches are made by Rolex. Here, we perceive and interpret signals correctly, but they have been manipulated to fool us: appearance leads us to one conclusion, when the reality is quite the opposite. Out and out impostors are not always benign: the trade in fake drugs, which either contain little or none of the active ingredient, or worse, are positively harmful, is significant and even dangerous, particularly where it is impossible for anyone but a specialist to distinguish the fake from the authentic.

Philosophers have long recognised problems related to Image; in particular, to what extent there is a Reality beyond perception. Plato was led to postulate 'universals' to account for the fact that we have no solid evidence of an independent reality, and others, notably Bishop Berkeley, maintained the more extreme empiricist position that there is no external reality, but rather that what we take as solid objects are mere collections of sensory data particular to an individual. The — equally extreme — consequence of this theory is that so-called physical objects cease to exist in any meaningful sense when nobody is observing them, so the house simply disappears when we leave it. In fact, to be strictly correct, an object cannot properly be said to disappear at all as it is only there when it is actually being perceived. The logical upshot of all this is that we have no irrefragable way of proving that an object continues to exist when no-one is sensing it, although sending a remote controlled bomb to demolish it and then returning to view the ruins, makes a strong, if expensive, case for supposing that it does.

In the second, derivative sense, Image refers to an obsession with appearance in general; with our own image, and, by extension, perception of people, goods, services, companies, governments, etc. It is generally true that most people want to be thought well of by their neighbours and community; however, in striving to achieve this, the impression given is frequently much different from that intended. People are notoriously bad at evaluating their own personas. Most of us would undoubtedly call ourselves considerate, caring, flexible, good listeners, generous, etc.— would that we were! Also, we are generally insensitive to our own signals—e.g. from body language and verbal style—either because we ignore them altogether or else because we are insufficiently attuned to the feedback we receive to enabling us to re-score our transmissions to achieve the desired end. Irving Goffman, the American social psychologist, discussed this in some depth (cf. *The Presentation of Self in Everyday Life*) and on the basis of his research distinguished between the signals we 'give' and those we 'give off'. One set are intentional, the other not. For example, I may think that my telephone manner is friendly whilst in fact it comes over as brusque and aggressive, or that I am being charming when in fact I am perceived as oozing obsequiousness.

From an apparent obsession with the patina of things derives the notion of *spin*—which uses deliberate omission or distortion to cast negative events in a more positive light. This distracts the focus away from the reality, and thereby avoids confronting inconvenient issues head-on. This image manipulation has become a front-line weapon for nations, politicians and organisations in reacting to problems or working to shape events in an environment which demands greater and faster public accountability.

The complexities of the relationship between Image and Reality are well illustrated by considering the most basic level of information processing—human perception. Any disjunction between raw sensory perception and that involved in personal and social assessment is more a matter of subject matter rather than of conceptual difference, and the broad similarities make the comparison worthwhile. If, as individuals, we consider perception at all, we probably think of it as a simple response to a simple stimulus: we see a car, hear a sound, touch a table or smell a rat and in each case, the relationship is that of subject (us) to object (what is perceived). In fact, the process is considerably more complex than any straight forward one-to-one relationship. Identical physical stimuli can produce different responses in different people, and dissimilar stimuli can produce similar responses. An extreme and dramatic example of the complexities of mapping external onto internal 'reality' is the phenomenon of synaesthesia—where stimuli delivered to one sense produce responses in another (one of the more common cases is where colours are perceived as sounds). Studying the senses gives valuable insights into the logic involved in understanding even the most basic perceptual tasks and emphasises the pitfalls of taking an over-simplified view of the relationship between Image and Reality.

Our senses are the primary organs through which we construct our image of the external world. The ears and eyes, for example, are constantly bombarded by a vast amount of information in the form of mechanical (ears) or photic (eyes) impulses — from which we select and integrate into a meaningful whole, whilst the proprioceptive and vestibular systems (often overlooked in discussion of the senses) supply our sense of position and of movement and balance respectively. Processing this information is not as simple as it might seem, as common attributes frequently applied to objects — e.g. colourful, solid, moving, loud, before, after, or three-dimensional — are interpretative qualities not possessed directly by the primary information itself.

The senses do not function independently but are highly interlinked, with the vestibular system at the heart of the arrangements, co-ordinating information from other senses. In this respect, it has primacy over the other senses, in that it influences much of what we do and governs aspects of audition, proprioception, vision, muscle tone and balance. When it is working as it should, it behaves as a rapid-reaction system constantly adjusting to reflect incoming stimuli and so to maintain equilibrium.

It is tempting to think of the human perceptual system as unidirectional transmission of information from primary receptors through the higher brain cortex to response, with what we loosely call 'perception' somewhere in between. In fact the process is far from passive: the brain is an enclosed system — impervious to light and other direct sensory input and itself incapable of direct perception; it has therefore to construct what we term the real world from the neural signals (small electrical impulses) it receives. To achieve this speedily, without being overwhelmed, requires efficient, active selection to prioritise to what is useful and to ignore or discard what is not. The precise mechanisms are still unclear, but it is likely that part of the process involves the use of predictive hypotheses (this is the theory of the perceptual psychologist Richard Gregory; cf. R. Gregory, *Eye and Brain*) that are cumulative and also sensitive to our particular needs and environment. It is maladaptive to make distinctions which have no obvious survival value for us — e.g. Africans have no use for the Eskimo's multiple concepts of snow, nor teetotallers for the fine distinctions of professional wine-tasters. In this sense, the interpretive system must act intelligently and this is no less the case for personal or social evaluation.

Some problems are fundamental. Take, for example, the perception of colour: both Locke and Newton postulated that light itself was colourless; so how is it that our minds manage to evoke a vast range of colours? Perhaps this is something that we acquire with our brains—i.e. colour sense is 'hard-wired' in—or perhaps it is something that is part of innate inheritance in the way perception just happens to work. It is likely that what we, as advanced evolutionary examples of neural networks, start with reflects what has been found to have survival value over centuries of evolution. Susan Greenfield has set out an understanding of *mind* and *consciousness* in which *plasticity* plays an important role. She argues that the 'personalisation of the physical brain is driven not so much by genes as by individual experiences', a model which might well apply to higher order emotion and social perception (Susan Greenfield, *The Private Life of the Brain*).

The perceptual analogy is pertinent to understanding personal social behaviour. Perception involves at least two distinct processes: first the recognition of what is important and the filtering out of unwanted information; second, the use of stored data to construct 'reality' from sensory input. It is the brain's use of experience to create strategies for perceiving, in a broader sense, that leaves it open to deception and allows Image to misrepresent Reality. Common visual illusions are simple illustrations of this phenomenon—these range from distortion of normal images (e.g. distorting mirrors) to impossible images (e.g. the ever-descending staircase), and even to illusory movement from a static image or contrary motion (e.g. the Doppler Effect). The more complex phenomena of 3D vision and stereoscopic sound require the integration of subtle temporal and spatial information received from eyes and ears. Neurologists are discovering that simple inputs pass through a number of synaptic way-stations on their way to the brain's repository of intelligence (the cortex) and are subject to a variety of influences and transformations as they are processed. In short, we don't simply receive information, *we actively construct it*. Perception is very much the creature of circumstance: a single stimulus may be perceived as one thing in one context and something completely different in another. Our senses tend to deliver what we expect to see, hear etc. in a given situation and this emphasises the constructive and interpretive role individuals play in the processing of sensory and other information.

Whilst we generally regard the physical world as true to the image we have of it, philosophers have, for centuries, asked 'What is it really like?', and propounded theories which try to make sense of both Image and Reality. It is clear that the relationship is not straightforward, as the power of illusion demonstrates—magicians would be much less fascinating if they actually cut people in two. In fact, theorising about what is *really* out there or what the world is *really* like is of limited interest. People must live by practicalities, and for most normal purposes it is convenient to assume that physical objects exist independently of our perceiving them. What needs emphasis is that in general we *construct*, rather than *perceive* reality—whatever the philosophical status of solid objects—and it is this gap which creates the possibility of deception. The critical question, therefore, is how we handle discrepancies that arise between one sense and another—in other words, how we recognise and deal with conflicting or inconclusive information.

Our senses are not merely called upon to order and help us navigate our universe, although at the level of objects and temporal and spatial relationships this is what we rely on them for. Above these primary levels there lie secondary qualities, which require more detailed knowledge and interpretation. For example, there is no direct correspondence between an X-ray plate and what it shows. To diagnose fractures, dislocations, tumours and general abnormalities requires specialist knowledge—first, how the picture illustrates the anatomy, second, what counts as 'normal', and thirdly, what deviations from this normality amount to abnormality. In this instance, judgements are experiential in a deeper sense than those of whether or not there is a table in the room and what its qualities are. Interpreting X-ray plates is closer to evaluating personalities and more complex images than to saying that someone is bald or has a wooden leg.

The structures and processes of sensory imaging thus have compelling, if more abstracted and less obviously referential, parallels in the broader world of personal and social Image. Whilst most people have no difficulty correctly describing a square of primary colour, where there exists a strong correspondence between stimulus and response, they are likely to give a variety of accounts of inherently more complex signals involving a heavier interpretive load—e.g. social behaviour, manners, motives, personality traits. Here, problems frequently arise from the fact that any given presentation is likely to be interpreted differently by people who pick up different signals—or, perhaps more accurately, different aspects of 'the same' signal. This makes it difficult to talk of identity when it comes to dealing with personal displays and raises the somewhat abstruse philosophical question (not to be further discussed here) of whether two people looking at an object or scene actually perceive the same thing. The main difficulty with saying that they don't is that it removes much of the 'absolute' or 'concrete' external world and thereby renders perception at best subjective or at worst solipsistic.

For present purposes it is sufficient to note that images and impressions are highly constructed and that what we perceive or focus on is conditioned by our interests and background (this in turn is partly the product of our cultural shaping). The matter of Image thus becomes of prime importance in how we discuss the world around us and events within it.

If there are difficulties with simple physical signals—e.g. colours and sounds—the problems of evaluating personality and social signals, which do not readily map onto anything that might be called reality, are more complex. As with physical signals, we construct and interpret what we see and hear of behaviour to fashion profiles of other people. This is a far from easy task, as the interpretive element in personality evaluation is considerably greater than that required to describe inanimate objects. It is the perceptual 'gappiness' between a signal and an individual response to it, that enables us to influence others to accept a chosen image, and this same gappiness which makes such assessments so fluid and, indeed, so personal. There is not much anyone could do to convince a non-colour-blind person that a red square is in fact green; however, there is much that can be done to convince your neighbour that you are friendly or trustworthy.

There is also the added difficulty that signals themselves are far from absolute. Whilst there is a strong element of certainty that a red object will elicit a 'red' perception, the cues and signals used to convey personal information vary from person to person and are strongly individual. Behaviour that one person considers suitable to convey the impression of friendliness may not be felt suitable by another—and neither's cue may be so interpreted by a recipient. Even if the signal is appropriate, it has to be transmitted—and this can fail for a variety of reasons. There are four possible permutations: an appropriate signal incorrectly transmitted, an inappropriate signal correctly transmitted, an inappropriate signal incorrectly transmitted, or an appropriate signal correctly transmitted.

To all this must be added the complication of context. Signals rarely arrive singly, but generally appear in clusters which require further evaluation for significance and relative importance. Even if the signal is appropriate and correctly transmitted, its interpretation is likely to depend as much upon the circumstances of its usage as on the signal itself, so even an appropriate and correctly transmitted signal may fail to achieve the desired result. Take again the man who intends his expensive car to convey the image of wealth: the car is only an appropriate signal to those who realise it is an expensive car. Even those who know this may regard that type of car as indicating 'flash' wealth—showing off—and so the positive Image is tarnished with a negative taint. Even if the car and the wealth are established, the driver may dress in such a way as to suggest lack of substance or dependability—once again compromising the desired image. If there is a significant dissonance between the signal and the perceived 'norm', then a fundamental decision must be made as to what is to be relied on. A teenager driving a Ferrari is more likely to arouse suspicion than admiration. Such a fragile information system suggests that personal images are difficult to create. They are also hard to sustain, even briefly, and can rarely be permanently altered by deliberate manipulation.

The development of Personal Image and the thinking behind it, are discussed in greater detail in Chapter 5 (Class, Elites and Status), but it is worth noting here that, at the personal level in particular, Image feeds on insecurity. Generally people who are genuinely secure—quiet self-confidence rather than blustering or studious extraversion—are less in need of, or concerned with, self-image than those who are fundamentally insecure. The insecure rely on exaggerated, value-obvious, trappings—large cigars, exotic cars, high-status companions—to bolster self-image and personal esteem. It is instructive (and often amusing) to watch the behaviour of 'important' people who are fundamentally insecure; their language, body language and general demeanour betray them at practically every step, particularly if they try to shore up their status with incongruent props, dominating conversation or clumsy posturing.

Try as people may to create and sustain their ideal self-image, such images are generally earned, not manufactured. Positive images, in particular, are consequences of continuity, rather than something that can be successfully manipulated, and are swiftly compromised by inappropriate behaviour. An image is an amalgam of factors, which accumulate and evolve over time. Some people appear not to care about their own image ('take me as you find me') nor, by implication, are concerned themselves with the posturing of anyone else. This unconcern may, of course, hide a very real preoccupation with self-image or social esteem, but in general genuinely high-status people have no need of contrivance to reinforce their standing. In fact, overt concern with image often conflicts with claims to status.

The uncomfortable reality is that, in seeking to consciously alter your image, you can only go so far. Deliberate deception will achieve a short-term impact, but true personality will inevitably show through — it's impossible to keep up an act indefinitely and it's in unguarded moments and through untrained signals that true character is expressed: 'No mortal can keep a secret. If his lips are silent, he chatters away with his finger tips; betrayal oozes out of him at every pore'. (Sigmund Freud, *Dora: An Analysis of a Case of Hysteria*)

A more complex, yet no less essential, element of striving for Image is susceptibility to the fake. Fakes abound — whether as skilfully presented personalities, products or services or as trust which turns out to be misplaced. There is a growing culture of fakery, which works in two senses: firstly, the figurative sense, which leads people to take the easy option, rather than doing the work necessary to achieve a given goal; secondly, in the literal sense, where something is simply not what it is claimed to be. Both appeal to our readiness to accept a low-cost alternative. The difference is that literal fakes, whilst not the real article, may do the job they are supposed to — fake Rolex watches still, presumably, tell the time — whilst figurative fakes do not deliver at all.

Wealthy societies are willingly seduced by the culture of fakery. Consumer choice has made it possible to have cheap replicas of practically everything, and the rise of the celebrity culture has led people to prefer tacky look-alikes to simpler, but genuine, alternatives. Food has been grown and selected to look perfect, but this is often achieved at the expense of flavour and purity. Sophisticated marketing has conditioned us to accept mediocrity at many levels and to a certain extent blunted our critical faculties. Under the banner of increasing choice, supermarkets fill their shelves with standardised products whilst squeezing out traditional, high quality suppliers who produce either in small quantities or offer unusual or rare varieties. It has been estimated that we eat around 10–12 basic species of food, versus the 100–120 of a century ago (David Boyle, *Authenticity*, 2003). The image of greater choice often founders on the reality of less.

This is certainly the case with 'short-cut' faking. Appeals to indolence offer solutions which remove most of the need for effort: The more extreme offerings of the weight control and fitness industries are compelling examples of the genre. We are seduced by the idea of instantly delivery and that this is compatible with high quality and minimum personal effort. The literal aspect of faking works on a poorly developed sense of true value, which allows us to be easily taken in by appearance. An interesting angle on this is that many faked artefacts require detailed, expert analysis to distinguish them from the original, yet fetch a fraction of the price, so authenticity, rather than mere appearance, has quantifiable added cash value. Nonetheless, people's unwillingness or incapacity to examine value or question authenticity is a powerful component of quality of life in many of its social and non-social aspects. We are particularly susceptible to misreading at the personal level: people who look and behave confidently are frequently taken at face value and esteemed credible and right-thinking. Inchoate thoughts or defective opinions delivered authoritatively are all too often taken as sound irrespective of their intrinsic merit.

Faking often operates on a basis of sentimentality. At a personal level this refers to the practice of blotting out whatever we find unpalatable; we either avoid or deny the reality. We know the extent to which we must work to achieve our goals, but realising that this is uncomfortable and time-consuming, prefer to accept the blandishments of those who offer the short cut and the quick fix. Sit in your vibrating armchair, eating chocolates, and the weight will drop off. Listen to a tape while you sleep, and you can learn a language in a few weeks. These 'results without effort' prescriptions are delusions, and the stock-in-trade of fakers and conmen, who profit massively from our eagerness to escape the demanding realities of effort. We are conditioned to judge by the look of things and the claims made for them and in doing so suspend rational judgement in favour of attractive superficiality. The same is true of personal responsibility: we are all too ready to transfer our real burdens onto others, encouraged by those who tell us that misfortunes are not really our fault, but due to 'the system' and thus beyond our control.

A particularly damaging aspect of sentimentality is the denial that human beings have a natural capacity for evil. We want a world in which people are responsible, kind and generally virtuous, and there is a strong disposition, against powerful contrary evidence, to believe in universal natal goodness. The fashionable view is that all that needs doing to achieve this is to put in place appropriate systems; on this model, failings are readily attributed to a faulty or badly applied system, rather than recognising that people have a natural capacity for evil for which they must bear responsibility. It is sentimentalising of the worst kind to think that you can change human nature simply by changing systems of social regulation.

A disturbing by-product of sentimentality has been a rise in populism. In Athenian society the opinion of the majority was equated with the truth, but in today's more open societies there is little justification for supposing that what is popular is either worthy or right. In fact, popular opinion, taken as 'common-sense', in its normal meaning of sound judgement, is often defective; the opinions of the *demos* are all too often facile and illogical and much of what passes for common-sense is superficial — both ill-informed and counter-factual. At other times, common-sense appears to desert us as we are too easily seduced into believing agenda-driven nonsense: e.g. that foetuses have souls or that vegetables feel pain. Too often, reality is held to ransom by extremists in pursuit of contentious goals.

This is not to say that all image-making and manipulation is dishonest. Far from it. There is no dishonesty in emphasising one's strengths or in trumpeting the virtues of a genuinely useful product. The pressing problem for individuals and societies is to recognise fakes at every level; for this, it is necessary to be aware of the tricks and stratagems of the fakers, to sharpen wits to a sufficient extent to detect the signals which distinguish the honest from the dishonest, and to evaluate information as dispassionately as possible. It's also important to recognise the difference between those who try to assess reality but misread it (e.g. Neville Chamberlain during the Munich crisis — transfixed in a pacifist's dream) and those who can't be bothered to even try.

The image we have of people or organisations is however not just based on signals that are either correctly or incorrectly read, but from a base that is built up over time. This introduces a critical overlay to personal judgements which colours incoming signals and also enables us to short-circuit the evaluation process: *trust*. Trust is a not symmetrical; it takes time to accumulate but is easily destroyed. Once the seeds of distrust are sown, they are hard to eradicate; this is as true of governments as it is at a more intimate personal or social level. Few aspects of our lives are immune from its influence: the learned professions can suffer from a lack of trust as much as weather forecasts and marriages. One advantage of media globalisation is that breaches of trust less easily swept under the carpet. If people or organisations set themselves up as trustworthy, then they must live up to that claim and be constantly tested against it. Information received from untrustworthy sources is downgraded in value by comparison with similar signals from trustworthy ones. Trust goes beyond concrete achievement and measurable performance although specific performance warranties are now an accepted element of contractual negotiations. Where these are not available, trust alone is considered an inadequate safeguard.

In the public sphere in particular, reality is often distorted by the perceived need and desire to be 'all inclusive'. This encompasses what has come to be known as Political Correctness, although its scope is wider than that. Dumbing-down presentations and diluting political policies to meet the reality of the poor intellect and catchpenny aspirations of many voters, combines with the perceived need to sanitise political messages to avoid alienating anyone, in particular volatile minorities. This produces an almost pathological reluctance to saying anything which is in any way contentious, more particularly if it is also intellectually challenging. Appeasement is considered preferable to honest debate or confronting difficult issues. Such sentimentality is corrosive. In Britain, for example, politicians have decreed that everyone of appropriate age should have access to higher education, which both pleases the equal opportunities lobby and is considered politically correct. However, among those whose job it is to deliver on this promise it is widely recognised that many would-be students are wholly unsuited either by intellect or disposition to the rigours of academic discipline. This dogmatic egalitarianism has led to the dilution of degree qualifications and along the way put centres of excel-lence under unwarranted pressure to distort admissions criteria to bring in more students from the less academically able, the socially disadvantaged and ethnic minorities.

Political Correctness is an Image hallmark of western moder-nity—embracing all races, sexual orientations and religions. In its relentless zeal for inclusiveness, it traduces values, corrupts good sense, and entrains heavy social and economic costs. Too often, the approach to political reform is not driven, as one might think it properly should be, by considerations of whether what is being proposed will improve anything, but by how much it will contribute to those involved being seen as progressive and modern. The frustration and inertia of politics leads those involved to resort to image manipulation and spin to convince people of their progressive credentials. Politicians effectively engage in sleight of hand by publicly espousing popu-list ideals, whilst in reality trying to do something entirely different. Police departments may believe that criminals are more likely to come from lower socio-economic groups and terrorist crime from particular ethnic minorities. However, it is unacceptable to admit such assumptions, even less so to act upon them, because to do either would be taken by minority leaders as unjus-tifiable discrimination. In the end, it is the Politically Correct Image which supervenes. This is a reflection of the hegemony of Image and the underlying fragility of politics in general and multi-ethnic societies in particular.

Political Correctness also constrains law-making. The belief that by changing the Image one can turn bad to good, undesirable into desirable, has influenced lawmakers throughout the world and society, to the extent that its fabric is determined by its laws. The prevailing logic in many countries — both dictatorships and democracies — is that by using the law to change or limit behaviour, one somehow changes underlying attitudes (e.g. on race, religion, or disability). At a less exalted level, television makeover programmes carry the sub-plot that by showing people how something should be done, how a negative aspect of their lives can be changed (e.g. eating habits, personal behaviour, or home tidiness) one thereby turns them into better people. This facile prescriptiveness ignores the fact that behaviour patterns are essentially products of beliefs and culture, and that such reactive changes are rarely more than superficial. A good example is the failure of rehabilitation to significantly reduce recidivism rates in many crime categories. Over half of British prisoners re-offend within two years of release (Architectural Review, October 2003) and in the USA the rate of recidivism is 60%. Other studies show either a neutral or even negative correlation between rehabilitation and recidivism (Cognitive-Behavioural Treatment Review, Vol. 14, 1–3), although there is disagreement on how recidivism is properly measured (M. Maltz, *Recidivism*, 2001). The reality is that rehabilitation is principally designed to suppress inappropriate behaviour and regarded simply as 'a cost-effective form of crime prevention' (www.going-straight.com) rather than as changing attitudes and beliefs.

The arts of Image are also widely deployed to distract people from matters they might find unpalatable; not only from the more obviously upsetting (e.g. the detail of war) but also from the intellectually distasteful, such as dishonesty and malfeasance, which many would prefer to ignore. This recognises a growing reluctance to face up to reality and its implications, for which spin and sentimentality provide a convenient refuge.

The difficulty, a genuine one for any supposedly civilised society, is to find ways of balancing the demands of reality with the need to respect feelings and sentiment. This is equally true in routine social behaviour whereby, for example, one avoids saying what is patently true to spare the feelings of others. It is easy to step from the largely desirable habit of self-censorship to maintain civilised behaviour and the social fabric, to the undesirable practice of concealing or distorting facts for political or ideological ends. Those who exploit the evident gaps between Image and Reality to persuade, fake or deceive usually seek to rationalise their actions on the basis that ends justify means. Unfortunately, this is rarely the case. Understanding the workings of Image manipulation is an essential pre-requisite to undermining the malign aspects of its influence and to promoting a stable environment in which diversity, excellence, creativity and genuine social cohesion can flourish.

CHAPTER 2

VANISHING WISDOM

'It is the province of knowledge to speak and the
privilege of wisdom to listen'
Oliver Wendell Holmes Sr., The Poet at the Breakfast Table, 1872

'It is better to have wisdom without learning, than to have learning
without wisdom'
C.C. Cotton, Lacon, 1825

'The errors of a wise man make your rule, rather than the perfections of
a fool'
William Blake, On Art and Artists

'There is no great concurrence between learning and wisdom'
Sir Francis Bacon

The culture of superficiality has diverse sources and, as the following chapters elaborate, many different faces. Among its most insidious facilitators is the marginalisation of wisdom, which has led to the substitution of simplicity for complexity and soft options for more rigorous discipline. Among its notable dividends are the abandonment of traditional manners and social sanctions, the emasculation of public debate to a level where appearance matters more than substance, and the rise in sentimentality — whereby misplaced sentiment and superficial affection have displaced shame and blame and corroded the ethic of personal responsibility.

It is neither disingenuous nor unduly patronising to note that difficulty is now avoided in many areas — intellectual, domestic, religious, work — and replaced by the soft option. We no longer expect to wait for anything or to think problems through for ourselves other than in the most superficial manner. This is not just a subtle shift of emphasis but a fundamental change in our approach to life and its pleasures and problems. The social glue of a common morality has been jettisoned in the face of the unstoppable onslaught brought about by the demands of individual sensitivities, priorities and appetites.

This in part reflects diminishing self-reliance, in part the desire to avoid difficulty. The signs are everywhere: in personal life, traditional wisdom has been replaced by 'experts' who advise people how to behave, dress and eat, what to buy, and much else. In education, classical texts and traditional values have all but been abandoned to modern, less demanding alternatives; in society, technical expertise is now esteemed above wisdom and sound judgement; and in much of sport (both amateur and professional) the 'noble amateur', who loved the game for itself, has been replaced by professionals motivated largely by financial considerations and the need to win at all costs. In general, a presumption of integrity has weakened to the point at which it is necessary to rely on ever more sophisticated technology to detect and trap miscreants. Where cheating was once seen as a degradation of honour, it is now regarded as 'fair game' provided you can get away with it. In many areas of human endeavour, sustained effort is no longer seen as necessary for success—there is enough dimtottic, know-nothing celebrity to confirm that—and the rewards of patience and perseverance have been sidelined in favour of instant gratification. It is one thing to be dismissive of respectability and the traditional virtues, quite another to expect a life of effortless indolence.

The shift has been stealthy, but discernible. A couple of generations ago in most developed countries and at all levels of society, there existed clear parameters of acceptable behaviour underpinned by a shared moral consciousness. Even in relatively poor areas, conduct was ruled, strictly, by an entrenched set of customs, backed by sanctions for transgressors. These extended beyond basic manners to speech and general comportment and were grounded in strong, if unspoken, sentiments of respect both for the community in which you lived and for your family, friends and neighbours.

Such a framework of largely unwritten wisdom encompassed values, norms and customs, and was an essential cohesive element of a community's social structure. This wisdom has all but disappeared. Across much of society, manners are considered distinctly old-fashioned and the values which sustained them inappropriate to modern living. People now consider they are entitled to express themselves in whatever way they find most congenial—dress, gesture, speech, etc.—and regard any restraints as both arbitrary and unreasonable. Customs have adapted to embrace this change. What was lost in the impatience to remove limits on behaviour were the rights and sensibilities of others who now feel threatened and offended by aggression, intemperate language, indecency and disregard for privacy. The mass media, whose influence rose in parallel with the rebirth of the individual, saw an opportunity to extend its franchise and adapted its output, first to reflect, then to sustain, the new ethos.

One can debate the causes of this shift in attitude, which are clearly multi-factorial. Undoubtedly, the spread of affluence and the ready availability of credit post-1945 and general technological change have played significant roles. The former gave ordinary people hitherto unknown purchasing power, matched by an array of goods to spend it on. Technological change contributed, both by providing the consumer boom with a greater variety of merchandise — particularly cars and electronics — and also by fuelling people's aspirations to acquire the latest model, fashion item or invention.

With this scramble to possess came an equally potent urge to be seen to possess. This was a powerful lever in changing relatively introverted and circumscribed community structures. As people became more mobile and more openly sociable, what you had — or did not have — rather than what you were soon became the yardstick for judgement and the principal determinant of status. Societies whose cohesion was hitherto maintained to a large extent by recognised and broadly shared moral values were progressively undermined by these trends, and the deeper values of morality were soon usurped by the cult of possession. How you came by the money to buy or the fact that you were mired in credit as a result, did not signify; what mattered, was that you bought, owned, consumed and displayed.

The political and social imperatives directing people towards this Utopian vision of the future had no place for what were seen as outdated views of the past. The wisdom of the Ancients was regarded as irrelevant to modern living, and not to be modern — and thus 'with it' and 'progressive' — was considered a solecism. The concomitant rise in liberalism meant that many accepted values were stigmatised as old-fashioned and rejected, along with much of the traditions of literature and art which sustained them. The wisdom of the great classical texts, the Bible and much else, has been variously eroded, sidelined, devalued or casuistically deconstructed.

There seems slender justification for rejecting wisdom, accumulated over centuries and across many cultures. This wisdom is not to be equated with expertise or with any specific cannon of knowledge; it is rather an indefinable corpus of evolved experience and values inextricably linked to the broad art of living. Taking the evidence of history, one might reasonably regard such wisdom as particularly valuable, having withstood centuries of trial and evolution to provide a resilient store of accumulated prescription and practice that transcended societal differences. It delivered messages that are as near as one is likely to get to universality in the human condition. After all, collective consciousness both seeks to reflect the realities of the present world and to provide continuity with the past—in A. H. Halsey's phrase it 'carries the past into the future'. Yet, in a matter of 40–50 years it became worthless history. Blown by a strongly iconoclastic wind, few sought to question the authority of this wisdom—which would have been a difficult debate to win—preferring to diminish its impact by impugning it as out of date. What mattered was the future, and anything seen as retrospective was *ipso facto* consigned to intellectual oblivion. In an era of post-war euphoria and personal liberation, this shift in mindset was easily accomplished.

These factors continue to influence society. What progressive intellectuals really dislike is that these truths and edicts sit uncomfortably with the modern outlook. In particular they dovetail poorly with the shift in balance from broad equality between the demands of society and those of its members, to today's dominance of the requirements of the individual. It seems almost impossible for modern man, obsessed by the notion of a creative clean sheet, as it were, to comprehend that, as Brecht recognised 'mixing one's wines may be a mistake, but old and new wisdom mix admirably'. Societies, largely by virtue of their co-operative nature, gave their members a place in the system by way of their role, skills and status and thus an element of identity. This is now seen by some as an unacceptable restrictiveness and a constraint on individual development. Doctrinaire egalitarians see any such categorisation as offensive and seek to break down the social order which produced it.

Abandoning the fine discriminations of accumulated wisdom effectively removes a fundamental support from society and increases the likelihood of disorder and fragmentation, both of which are now very evident in many western societies. To question a particular rule or policy may be reasonable and resulting revisions are likely to have minimal impact on social cohesion. To question the entire enterprise is another matter altogether—and to the extent that this has happened as a result of liberal or so-called 'progressive' ideologies has deprived societies of an essential anchor for setting and enforcing its rules and values. Without these latter, the maintenance of civilised society becomes more problematic and governments then resort to law and regulation to deal with ever more detailed minutiae of personal conduct. The progress of this reformist agenda was accelerated by the effects of significant immigration into Britain and America which, as numbers increased needed to turn multi-ethnic societies into multi-cultural ones. The former can be made to work, but the latter not, unless the different religious and ethnic communities are persuaded to ignore minor differences and to accept a shared moral and social code. The reality is that persistent difficulties over allegiance and religious requirements have turned the cosy image of well integrated multi-culturalism into lawlessness, tribal strife, and dissent, often papered over with a thin veneer of 'getting along'.

The truths and values of traditional wisdom are not spelt out in simple epithets or crisp 'one-liners', but rather require receptive intelligence, study and effort to extract and assimilate. Wisdom, as one author put it, is not just words 'to the wise', it is 'words for the wise'—the implication being that a certain intelligence and endeavour are prerequisites for attaining it. The traffic is not all one way: the seeker after wisdom is himself changed by the quest. Wisdom was definitely not intended for everyone. Plato was appalled at the idea that written ideas would roam freely about and possibly fall into hands that had no business with them. Writing turns up everywhere; it does not select its readers. It would, for example, be irresponsible to allow arguments for universal suffrage or egalitarian democracy to fall into the hands of slaves. There is also the fact that written words (unlike speeches) can do nothing to prevent or correct misunderstanding and misinterpretation. Even live speeches are compromised if they are broadcast, as the audience has no chance to question the speaker or clear up misunderstandings. (The discourse of Plato and Socrates on this matter is well commentated by Kieran O'Hara in *Trust: From Socrates to Spin*)

The globalisation of written and spoken information has made information and discourse almost universally available. It is arguable that this is not always a good thing, as people with low intellect grasp only the bits they are able or prepared to understand, and then use these to promulgate distorted or incomplete views. The implication is that currency of the more potentially 'dangerous' propositions and truths should be restricted to those who are capable of understanding and responding sensitively. Developing public policy needs intellectual precision and, given this is a restricted attainment, is probably better achieved by being removed from popular democracy. This is not to suggest that popular mass movements are necessarily misguided, but rather that there is a clear role for intellectual elites in developed societies. This is an unashamedly elitist argument which recognises that bad intellectual currency often drives out good and thereby creates problems. It is also an argument which needs divorcing from its inevitable moral overtones.

Whilst the history is clear, it is less apparent why, in the clamour for personal liberation, and the prevailing politically convenient Lot-like attitude to looking backwards, no attempt was made to explain why the accumulated wisdom of the past was defective and should be rejected. One does not have to look far for an explanation. Traditional wisdom takes as axiomatic that some people are not equipped for it either intellectually or morally; not only is this divisive, it also implies a fundamental human inequality which is, in effect, a class division. This assault on classes and categorisation is fundamental to neo-liberal thinking as is the abolition of elites, and such wisdom is unashamedly elitist. Recognising differences in native intelligence, for example, is anti-egalitarian and many consider this divisive. The implicit assumption is that all inequalities are inequitable and generally result in undesirable consequences; this is, of course, far from being the case. The reality that wisdom requires intelligence and effort and that not all are guaranteed of attaining it are profoundly distasteful ideas to those who regard all as equal, if not in achievement, then in potential. It is hardly surprising therefore, that liberal ideology should seek to marginalise it.

Wisdom also reminds us that we are far from perfect. It demands that we work on our imperfections, at least to subdue, or at best to eradicate their worst aspects, otherwise we are likely to suffer for them. It was partly to remove the extremes of impulse and individuality and to make social life tolerably pleasant for everyone that traditional education was structured as it was and that manners evolved and became so effective — despite the over-elaborate (and often delightful) excesses of the 18th and 19th Centuries. Subduing imperfections sits ill with a modern *laissez-faire* ethos, dedicated to the principles of least effort and unfettered liberty.

This decline in manners evinces a marked change in attitude to the place of the individual in society and to social behaviour in general. Manners, once a non-negotiable and inviolable part of community life, are now considered old-fashioned, outmoded, *passé* — unnecessary restrictions on the pursuit of personal fulfilment. Even to mention the word, let alone with any hint of approbation, brands one as a 'has-been'. Yet manners were part of the glue which maintained smooth social functioning for centuries, and it is entirely plausible to argue from a sociological perspective that the decline in quality of social life and personal responsibility has tracked, *pari passu*, that in manners.

Nor, lest anyone attempt to cast the issue in class terms, should it be believed that manners were an upper class preserve which social elites sought to impose on an unwilling majority. They pervaded society at every level—and moreover gave social values to the working-class who, often having little else, relied upon manners for self-respect and personal dignity and fiercely enforced decent behaviour in their communities. 'Manners Makyth Man' is a timeless reminder that personal desires have at times to be toned down, or sometimes even suppressed altogether, in the cause of social cohesion and that material poverty does not imply moral poverty.

It is as much the attitudes which lie behind behaviour as the erosion of manners themselves which should concern us. Nowadays, it is seen as entirely reasonable to ask "Why should I?" not drop litter, not swear, show regard for older, less able people, etc. Most examples one can think of—and there are many—demonstrate an over-riding concern for 'self'. This is a fundamental plank of the progressive platform which argues that self-expression is an entitlement which must not be curtailed. This is nothing short of logical sleight of hand, in that it confounds the widely held (and reasonable) view that everyone has the right to their opinion or to behave as they wish with the (unreasonable) proposition that puts all opinions or behaviour, however shallow or offensive, on an equal footing. In this philosophy absurd nonsense shares equal esteem with perceptive enquiry and rudeness with seemly conduct. It is on such grounds that children confront their parents, pupils their teachers, and everyone authority. What value has the voice of the grandparent, or the experience of the teacher, when met with such individualism? 'Why should I listen to you?" is the liberated individual's refrain. As we push forward the frontiers of individuality and the quest for novelty, authority is out, self-expression in. It is on such ground that unreasoned dissent treads on normal respect, and reasoned dissent confronts oppressive or dictatorial authority.

Societies everywhere are poorer for the demise of mannerly customs and behaviour—doubters need look no further than the welter of contemporary legislation and regulation designed to fill the gaps left by their absence—and increasingly resort to the law to replace proper education both in telling people what they should not do and then dealing with them when they transgress. Many feel that the former is best handled by good manners, the latter by social custom. The populist programme has it that manners and social customs impose unwarranted restraints on individuality. Whilst this has superficial plausibility, the reality is in fact the opposite, in that the constraints implied in a base of mutually shared values and expectations remove uncertainty from the framework of social interaction. Whilst manners have survived in residual form—and only then in sections of society where the social values behind them are supported by schools and the family—it is clear that they have done so at the expense of their normative force, which is now considerably reduced. Coarseness, offensive behaviour, and disrespect for the rights and sensibilities of others are rife, and consideration and mannerly behaviour, at least in public, is diminishing. This is not to say that these new standards are widely accepted; they are not. People may have come to regard them as the norm but many privately despair at the lack of action to eradicate excesses, and indict politicians of all persuasions, who are seen as fearful and supine, for their unconvincing token efforts to promote reasonable behaviour, and then only at minimum levels.

In this context, it is worth noting that, while violent and other serious crime and headline crime rates attract most public attention, it is the quotidian incivilities and misdemeanours which have a constant and more durable impact. These form no part of reported crime figures, but being much more closely woven into people's daily existence, are an ever-present and greatly resented source of irritation. Many now feel threatened in public places they once regarded as safe territory.

Failure to maintain the unspoken creed of manners means that the rituals which provided informal regulation of much potentially harmful behaviour (e.g. of promiscuity and the excessive consumption of alcohol) have had to be replaced by formal codes of conduct or laws, with appropriate sanctions attached. As these are only invoked in the most serious cases, much offence which would hitherto have been defused by appropriate manners or social sanctions now either goes unremedied or else ends up in the courts. The impression of greatly increased official interference in people's lives, which is widely resented, comes largely from the greater need for regulation to deal publicly with behaviour that was formerly the private province of family or community sanction. This is not an improvement.

Gone also are the dress codes of post-war days (look at films of daily life or sporting events in the 1950s and early 1960s to find suits, collars, ties and hats or caps as almost a uniform)—to be replaced, certainly by more colourful, comfortable clothes, but by no accompanying code of hygiene, decency or appropriateness. The 'anything goes—wear what you feel like' has removed dress conformity from all but a few formal social settings. Dress is used to further convey the doctrine of personal liberation. Young—and, distressingly, not so young—people dress in grunge style, or in quasi-military or other explicitly intimidating garb. This is an extension of unrestricted self-expression, the message being 'I can wear what I want', 'I am fit / healthy' or 'Don't mess with me'; the implicit threat in such defiance of conformity is often all too clear. In this, 'respect for things becomes as alien as respect for persons' (Bryan Wilson, *Gentility Recalled*, Foreword, Social Affairs Unit, 1996)

Nor is there any longer sanction for inappropriate dress in places where you might expect a degree of respect for the occasion or for others—for example, in restaurants and theatres. Social disdain and aggressive individualism are particularly noticeable at the top end of the income scale: those who can afford expensive restaurants or top-price opera seats feel no need for any minimum standard of dress. They clearly believe that their wealth (or perhaps their self-imagined high social status) detaches them from any requirement to take notice of accepted behaviour or account of others' sensibilities. No *noblesse oblige* here: 'I'm paying, so I decide' is the attitude. In many cases the reality probably boils down to the even less appealing: 'I can't be bothered and, in any case, I'm not interested in what anyone else thinks'. The distinction between 'freedom to' and 'freedom from' cuts no ice with such people, and the places they infect lack the gumption to make the point on behalf of their other clients by turning them away. The facile riposte is that formality is unnecessary and borders on regimentation. This misses the point that dress codes are not judged on necessity but symbolise a culture of courtesy to others in public places. There is a fine line between informality and discourteousness.

The erosion of manners and appropriate conduct is matched by a parallel diminution in respect. The rise of egalitarianism with its creed of universal equality, irrespective of birth, endowment, talent or social circumstances, is taken as entailing the belief that 'I'm as good as you'. It is a short step from deciding that we are all of equal worth, to rejecting demands to show respect to anyone. Children object to behaving in ways which seem to them deferential, often to people for whom they genuinely (and often justifiably) have little respect. In this, they fail to appreciate is that public respect and respectful behaviour do not necessarily signify private respect or approbation, but are merely forms of mannerly conduct designed to facilitate personal intercourse and promote social harmony.

The converse is that even where respect is justified, it is not always granted. It is reasonable to expect genuine respect to be earned, but once it has, it should be recognised. Forced elimination of differences erodes rather than enhances social cohesion and the 'equal worth' philosophy has wiped the respect slate clean to the extent that social hierarchies are no longer valued or even recognised. Highly trained professionals and those in high-value public positions are regularly patronised and derided. Doctors and emergency workers are assaulted (mainly because they either refuse, or are unable, to provide what someone demands) and their authority is ignored. Equality of humanity is a lowest-common-denominator basis of social intercourse; but, as societies grow in sophistication, it is to be expected that socially important skills differences should be recognised and valued. It is clear that much erosion of authority reflects frustration and distrust and to the extent that these are merited, is self-inflicted. Given the widening educational divide, those at the bottom of the intellectual scale seek to devalue achievement in others in order to maintain the fiction of complete equality and their own social status. There is also the brutal fact that if you think people don't care about you, you are unlikely to respect or defer to them.

Respect must be distinguished from respectfulness. The social importance of respectful behaviour is that is recognises individual entitlements—and signals mutual reciprocity. Disrespectful behaviour vitiates that mutuality and invites disrespectful behaviour in return. Behaving respectfully is no more than a social grace and has nothing to do with respecting people as individuals or for their achievements or position in, or value to, society. People who behave with disrespect fail to make this distinction and thereby demonstrate their misunderstanding of the way society works. The message they send is one of social indifference, yet these people are often the first to complain when their own rights are transgressed. The general disdain for social forms is further evidence of our self-absorption and introversion—we lack sympathy and therefore become out of touch with the needs of others and of society in general. The selfish and arrogant behaviour of many public figures—celebrities in particular—reinforces the impression that others matter little to them, especially when they interfere with their pursuit of self-interest and self-aggrandisement.

These social trends are hardly consonant with the image of civilised society; nor indeed are they in any credible sense progressive. Determining why people feel entitled to behave in these ways and what social and psychological factors motivate slovenly dress, unbecoming manners and the extremes of impatience which result in road rage, verbal aggression and the like should provide valuable insights for sociologists and social psychologists, but is outside the scope of this book. What can be said is that aberrant behaviour reflects, in part, the widely felt need to destroy what the social revolutionaries of the 1960s saw as unjustified inequalities and their desire to free themselves from what continues to be represented as the chains of subservience. Disrespectful behaviour with no real prospect of sanction is a means of non-verbally expressing one or more of the following sentiments: 'I don't care a damn'; 'I am independent'; 'I'm as good as you'; 'No-one can tell me what to do'. Such cocking-a-snook is puerile and achieves nothing beyond, perhaps, a degree of transient self-satisfaction for the perpetrator. Those who deliberately flout society's expectations must either feel uncomfortable with themselves or else are too self-indulgent to care or too thick-skinned to notice.

It is paradoxical that whilst people feel themselves more liberated from social convention than ever, they are becoming more dependent on society for welfare and support in times of crisis. In fact, the loosening of social constraints may produce a feeling of freedom at one level, but this is illusory. The reality is that social constraints and social codes liberate rather than enslave, in the sense that they provide a common framework in which freedom can flourish. But as a peg upon which to hang revolution, 'liberation' from social constraint succeeded handsomely.

The causes of social self-indulgence are complex, but some explanation can be found in the increase in the importance of technical competence which has shadowed the decline in moral consensus. Nowadays, it is skills, knowledge and contractual competence, rather than personal qualities, that define people and upon which reliance is placed for attributions of value or status. As Bryan Wilson noted, 'Reliance on technical competence reduces dependence on personal goodwill, inherent grace, gestures of respect, and hence the self-esteem that looks for confirmation in the esteem of others' (op.cit.).

There is no doubt that anti-social behaviour and attitudes are now entrenched and that they have significance beyond the superficial level of any irritation they may cause. However, though bad manners and disrespect may be what the public has resigned itself to expecting, it is mistaken to confound the average with the norm; and these trends are far from the norm. Making social policy under pressure often leads to this confusion. The typical argument generally runs: since a significant majority are ill-educated, lack morals or are poorly socialised, then this is what society must accept and around which it must structure itself. It is not beyond imagination to see that basing social expectations on anything but the more established foundations is a recipe for trouble. This is not, as many would perhaps have it, old-fashioned moralising, rather an observation on the undesirability of making social policy at the behest of one cultural group or another. Society's norms and expectations should be based on the general interest, not on what a vociferous minority, or even the majority, do or want. In many communities, clubs and groups, codes of behaviour continue to be valued and respected (and indeed, rigorously enforced) and there would appear to be an increasing weariness with lack of consideration and social selfishness. The mentality that sustains them is one further dividend of the marginalisation of wisdom.

The supersession of the modern intellectual has accelerated the devaluation of wisdom traditionally vested in old age. In earlier times, the skills you were taught at school or college stood you in good stead—possibly with a few adaptations—for the duration of your working life. The rapid pace of technological change has meant that skills are soon obsolete—technologies themselves are routinely superseded as are practices within any given discipline (think of car maintenance or computing). Retraining several times during a career is normal nowadays, as is the view that retirees have little value to society as they are no longer technically competent. Unfortunately, along with the obsolescence of their technical expertise has come the obsolescence of their value elsewhere; a technical has-been is also considered a moral has-been and the older citizen is no longer regarded as a source of accumulated wisdom. Grandpa's store of good sense has been thrown out with his bath water.

The future—or at least that envisaged by the intelligentsia of the early twenty-first century—is dominated by expertise, which, if not the enemy of wisdom, is antithetical to it. Looking for solutions to life's problems (as opposed to purely technical questions), one has the choice of consulting an expert or relying on the accumulated wisdom of generations of family, friends and other well-documented and well-trodden paths for advice. It is often an unenviable choice for those having to make it—does one raise one's children by the book, as it were, or by the prescriptions of grandma's accumulated wisdom, often dressed up as 'common sense'?

The experts have an advantage, in that they offer their wares in well-illustrated books, multi-media, and on the internet. Permanently accessible, slick presentations, usually backed by high sounding-qualifications and professorial plaudits, are peppered with plenty of convoluted jargon to gild the image. They are designed to be seen as both independent and academically respectable and therefore, by implication, well-founded.

To satisfy demand (and even to stimulate it) a legion of 'experts' has sprung up to deal with the difficulties of everything from child-rearing, deficient 'lifestyles' and dating, to handling bereavement and redundancy. Beneath the hype, many of these disciplines lack academic rigour, but in so far as they help people overcome their problems they can be said to possess a veneer of respectability, even if their prescriptions are often no more than common sense or traditional wisdom re-packaged in quasi-academic language.

This flowering of 'expertise' gives rise to several problems, the greatest of which is that more often than not disagreement on what should be done in any particular case (a glance through a few child-rearing books reveals diametrically opposed views on how to tackle unruly behaviour). This lack of unanimity leaves people confused, and instead of reverting to the tenets of received wisdom, they fall back on their instincts, which are often unsound. Many of these 'how to' pundits rely on the questionable assumption that one theory fits all, which is manifestly not the case when dealing with individuals. (Accepting that people are individuals and therefore require individual consideration in some circumstances is distinct from the individualism that sees itself as transcending the collective interests and demands of society). Given a shared line of genetic inheritance and the common personality traits that tend to accompany it, it is more likely that collective family wisdom can better help solve the family problems of both adults and children than the perforce impersonal prescriptions of books and DVDs. Naturally, this relies on received family wisdom being well-founded. Having the dysfunctional counselled by the deranged or deluded is likely to be counter-productive.

What has this social de-moralisation (= erosion of morality, not depression) to do with superficiality? A great deal, if one considers how changes in accepted (though not necessarily acceptable) behaviour have led people towards the superficial. If people are encouraged to rely on 'expertise' for what traditionally they dealt with from their own inner resources, it is hardly surprising that they increasingly look to outside agencies when things go wrong. This has repercussions: firstly, the emergence of a spreading culture of blame and the litigiousness which followed it (discussed further in Chapter 7), and secondly, the belief that 'if the experts are wrong, how can I be to blame'? If the expert you consult gives bad advice or you fail to implement the prescription handed down, then you may not properly be held accountable for the consequences. People therefore see the expert as a convenient route to absolution from many of their personal and social responsibilities.

Public policies in developed countries have long encouraged people to look to the state to sort out their problems. Apart from the tax burden of funding these responsibilities — and the bloated bureaucracies invariably required to deliver them — it is fair to ask whether people are being genuinely helped by removing individual accountability in this wholesale fashion. For one thing, it has spawned an undesirable culture of entitlement and, more seriously, has radically undermined self-reliance, one of the bastions of traditional wisdom. People left to their own resources can do much, and in so doing, develop their own experience and wisdom which stand them in good stead for the future. This is not to suggest that the state does not have a role to play, rather that indiscriminate mass provision is misguided.

The 'future is bright — grab it' ethos changed the prevailing ethic from abstinence to conspicuous consumption — from the ascetic to the unashamedly hedonistic. People saw the New Jerusalem and wanted it, not tomorrow when they could perhaps better afford it, but today, and on easy credit. Instant availability of everything from automatic waste-disposal units to exotic holidays snapped the traditional 'save then spend' ethic, and contraception weakened restraint in other moral spheres. Jesus Saves, Moses Invests, but Mankind unashamedly spends. This is not to say that goods, holidays, or contraception are undesirable; rather that the attitudes which their ready access encouraged has contributed significantly to the de-moralisation of society and to the demise of the traditional virtues and much of the wisdom which went with them. The prevailing belief is that happiness is instantly available, provided you can muster enough cash.

These cultural shifts, and the practical changes which accompanied them, bred a strong dependency culture nurtured by many governments under the general heading of 'welfare'. The legion of counsellors that attends modern warfare or a natural disaster eloquently testifies to this. One must, however, distinguish fields of expertise that don't undermine traditional Wisdom, from the more questionable disciplines that do. The former — reputable expertise — is only sustainable by development and continuous enrichment in their fields of knowledge; the latter largely reside in, but are not confined to, the provinces of the politics, sport and society and tend to borrow heavily from the social sciences and classical psychotherapy. Knowledge and rigorous scientific discipline characterise the one, but are often absent from the other.

The wisdom that is being marginalised, and which I wish to defend, is not to be easily had from books. Books indeed contain wisdom, but their precepts have to be skilfully applied, and that requires judgement. The bar to universality is that this wisdom is difficult; indeed, being far from obvious, it transcends the superficial, and resides in sensitivity of judgement and the ability to look beyond immediate experience.

One consequence of marginalising wisdom is that the values of such experience and judgement have been abandoned in many spheres—the learned professions being a notable exception—and particularly in the sphere of public policy, which, in most modern democracies, is dominated by spin and sound-bite. Politicians no longer succeed by quiet commitment to doing what they believe to be right by their constituents and their country, but by outsmarting opposition with flashier presentations and slicker media skills. They no longer sell sound policies or good government, but their own image, and it is by that yardstick that they are generally judged—unless of course, by mischance or mismanagement their policies fail spectacularly. Differences between political parties narrow with increasing reluctance to commit to unpopular policies, however desirable. Short-termism governs much polit-ical thinking and the resulting policies amount to little more than political sticking-plaster—popular, essentially palliative, patches which contribute little to the long-term public good.

Indeed, public policies in developed societies pander wilfully to the new *mores*. They are specifically formulated to deal with image problems—tol-erance, racial and religious discrimination in particular, rather than with the underlying causes of overblown sensibilities. This is sharply illustrated by the phenomenon known as Political Correctness (already discussed to a limited extent in the preceding chapter, and also in the context of language [Chapter 3] and politics [Chapter 11]). At its core is the belief that laws should be put in place to suppress language or behaviour that might conceivably offend any identifiable sector of society. One consequence is that people have formed themselves into special interest groups and used public over-sensitivity to Political Correctness to influence law-making, shape policy or sanitise public discourse to meet their particular concerns. For example, the considerable reluctance to discuss openly subjects perfectly acceptable in themselves—for example, racial or religious issues—springs from fear of a backlash from inter-ested groups who find it politically expedient to brand legitimate discussion of race as racism, and to ignore the manifest difference between targeting crimi-nals who happen to be, for example, Muslims, and attacking Muslims or their religion *en bloc*. Thus serious debate is either curtailed or never gets underway.

Those who don't belong to an identifiable pressure group tend to fare badly in the distribution of rights and entitlements.

Political Correctness is little more than crude social engineering in pursuit of attitude change. Although it is ineffective at producing anything more than a superficial level of conformity — as if, by scratching away the rash, you are curing the underlying disease — it dangerously compromises wisdom. Apart from the questionable desirability of pandering to what is often no more than opportunism, the uncritical pursuit of PC loses sight of some essential questions:

1. How far is it desirable to formulate public policy on the basis that someone might be offended (by, for example, 'black sheep' — in the USA the nursery rhyme has become, 'Baa Baa grey sheep')?
2. Are people actually affronted by what it is proposed to outlaw?
3. To what extent is it reasonable for anyone to take offence at X or Y?
4. Even if there is proven likelihood of giving offence, is it justified to legislate to appease private sensibilities that, in many cases, are apparently so insecure and fragile that they would be offended — e.g. by such trivialities as Baa Baa Black Sheep?

The goal of controlling 'inappropriate' behaviour often conveniently ignores the attitudes and general intellectual background that produced it and this is being skilfully exploited by pressure groups, to their advantage. Wisdom requires a balanced attitude and that account should be taken of appropriate perspective and reasonableness in such matters. Political Correctness ensures that it rarely is.

Striving to suppress sentiments or allow unconventional behaviour because some group takes offence, in pursuit of an image of tolerance or empathy, is often itself offensive (for example, the wearing of religious dress or emblems in schools or outlawing language indicating age or obesity). It is also likely to mire societies in lengthy and ultimately irresolvable wrangling about whether one is trying to control motives, actions or language. Do you prosecute words or actions — or both — or indeed, reporting or broadcasting any of these and, at what level of gravity does words or actions become unlawful? Do they have to give actual offence, or merely be likely to give offence? What constitutes, for instance, religious hatred or incitement to hatred, advocating terrorism or glorifying terrorism? Not all expressions of dislike betoken hate, and not all expressions of hate are necessarily offensive. It may give offence to suggest that a certain belief or creed is muddle-headed or anti-social, but is this sufficient reason for suppressing the sentiment? Too often, limits of acceptable criticism are set at zero, while those who claim to be offended at any negative or mildly irreverent sentiment are all too ready to castigate the values of their host society.

To accept the concerns of fragile sensibilities as sufficient reason for regulation is to accede to the proposition that the sentimental and rigidly self-righteous should take precedence over the rational. This leaves the well-being of societies vulnerable to the whims of intellectual fashion and the dictates of irrational extremism. It may be necessary for laws to deal with extremes of language or behaviour, but the only viable and sustainable route to eradicating the symptoms is to identify and tackle the causes. This means both educating those who give offence to better understand the effect of their behaviour and the reciprocity involved in tolerance, and also educating those who unreasonably take offence to react less sensitively and to accept and defuse criticism. Less rashness and greater rationality are what is needed, not increasing regulation.

If wisdom is to be restored, it has to once again become a cherished part of our acquired inheritance, and this is best done through sound schooling. In Britain and the USA, education at all levels has been party to the marginalisation of wisdom, and there is a growing feeling that policy and practices need changing. (A nearly successful attempt to remove evolutionary theory from the curriculum of American schools and replace it with the unsubstantiated theory of 'Intelligent Design', was finally shown up as an attempt to replace non-theistic with theistic teaching. Here, it is not principally the crude attempt at religious indoctrination that is disturbing, but the idea that children should be denied the opportunity of acquaintance of one of science's most powerful theories). Nonetheless, it would be unrealistic to expect rapid results and societies will have to live with the detritus of two generations of misguided education. Teaching is still infected with education theory formulated by modernisers who vehemently dislike the classics and anything smacking of traditional wisdom (see Chapter 9). In education, being 'forward looking' has a suitably progressive ring about it, but one which on closer examination is found to be hollow.

The mental capacity for wisdom comes from inculcating an intelligent approach to life and to dealing constructively with mistakes and misfortune. Knowledge, by contrast, tends to come as information, shorn of all the mistakes made on the way there—implicit in Karl Popper's recognition that knowledge advances by refutation, not just blind conjecture. The implication is that mistakes, and the lessons they bring, are critical to successful advancement and there is every reason to suppose that this applies equally to the acquisition of wisdom.

The progressive, neo-liberal movement is anti-elitist, and resents the traditions which sustain conventional wisdom. Its disciples are impatient and see only marginal value for the effort required to attain such wisdom. Thus modern wisdom—easy access for everyone—comes in ready packages: lifestyle books and simple prescriptions—superficialities which all can understand. The fact that their educational theories have generally failed to improve things, either for individuals or for societies—rather, the reverse—does not dampen their reformist zeal or actuate them to question their philosophy.

The modernist ethos has also infected the arts. Artists (often highly talented) have elected to forgo the traditions of their craft for absurd flights of abstract self-expression, of which dirty linen, embalmed sheep and piles of bricks are well-discussed examples. They forget—or ignore?—the fact that art has purpose beyond mere self-indulgence: it should uplift those who see, read or hear it. 'One will search in vain for release in modern art: for the aesthetic dimension in art, or for any attempt to elevate or gladden the spirit' (Anthea S. Leoussi, *Appreciating the Arts*, in *The War on Wisdom*, 2003). In the name of self-expression art has too often descended into a creative gutter of poor taste and self-indulgent output, largely devoid of intellectual or artistic merit. The public—led by critics and the art elite who are either unable, or afraid, to call it as it is—have been duped into uncritical acquiescence. It is noteworthy that the exhibitions which attract most visitors are those of traditional, representational art and artefacts, the exceptions being offerings of modern artists which are either pornographic or can be billed as 'shocking'. The pity is that many talented artists have squandered their undoubted gifts in this twisted cause.

The decay of many ancient crafts and languages throughout the world is also fall-out from the marginalisation of wisdom. These skills and customs were repositories of great wisdom and centuries of irreplaceable experience, handed down through generations; all part of the vanishing global cultural tapestry. For example, the San peoples of Namibia, Botswana and South Africa roamed the deserts for centuries, leaving a legacy of fascinating and evocative cave painting, and accumulating a great store of wisdom along their way.

Skilful use of plants kept them naturally healthy and resilient and enabled them to conserve food supplies and protect themselves from the sun. Isolated from modern civilisation, it took the needs of today's western health-care industry for San to realise what they had and to unlock its considerable value. This is not an argument for unrestricted preservation, rather recognition that wisdom may be sought, and found, in a variety of unlikely places.

The marginalisation of wisdom was strongly influenced by the student uprisings of the 1960s and 1970s. Whilst those protests may not have achieved their stated aim of overthrowing the establishment and the social order in Europe and America, their influence has been insidious and far-reaching. It has resulted in at least one notable expression of the classless society, namely the cult of celebrity. According to this, personal or social worth is determined by a scale which equates talent with the ability to attract attention, rather than on the traditional basis of the value of any contribution made. Whether this is considered progress or not is a matter of personal judgement. What is clear is that this distorted yardstick of merit has percolated through every level of society and changed both the aspirations of individuals and their idea of what matters in general. It becomes difficult to sustain a credible system of social or intellectual value when genuine wisdom is replaced by uncritical vacuity.

That wisdom has been marginalised is beyond doubt. What has replaced it is an undiscriminating insistence on progress at all costs from a perspective which is firmly fixed on the present and the future. Every change is hailed as progress, but it is by no means obvious that this 'new wisdom' is delivering progress in any sense that makes it worthwhile. Neither *more* nor *faster* mean *better*. We are overwhelmed with choice and possibility, with diverse distractions and entertainments, but it is doubtful whether our lives are genuinely richer for them. Indeed, there is increasing research evidence to suggest that, despite all the material advantages of the 21st century, people living in affluent societies are discontented and mal-adjusted to their circumstances. Jane Austen's heroines, who lacked many of the conveniences we take for granted, saw their chief preoccupation as finding a husband; yet, in their settled and predictable social milieu, they were probably more content and fulfilled than most young women facing the unpredictability, challenges and stresses of modern living, and beyond doubt much better equipped to cope with its problems and vicissitudes.

The extraordinary technical changes of recent decades have delivered much of undoubted value, but technical proficiency should not be confused either with progress or with wisdom. Technology relies on science, which tends to produce uniformity. Wisdom is not scientific but courts and reflects diversity. It also provides a bulwark against conspiracy theories, which work by collecting facts to support a predetermined conclusion. The twisted logic of much anti-western thought results from such a process. The underlying assumption is that there is no such thing as objective truth. Such unchallenged relativism makes it difficult to answer those who see no difference in principle between war and suicide bombings, or those who see the west as politically anti-Muslim. This is the opposite of the western empirical tradition and scientific methodology which marshals the facts available to it and then uses them to deduce conclusions on an objective and, as far as possible, non-prejudicial basis.

Wisdom is compatible with both science and with progress. These are not alternatives between which we must choose, but a challenge to societies to produce people who are both technically competent and intellectually flexible. Rigidity is the enemy of wisdom, which sits above the strict laws and methods of science, because only with wisdom can one make the moral choices which have become an increasingly frequent concomitant of scientific discovery. The marginalisation of wisdom is both corrosive and retrogressive. As long as societies are dominated by those who belittle the value of wisdom, its erosion will continue to the detriment of sound judgment and social cohesion.

CHAPTER 3

THE DEVALUATION OF LANGUAGE

'The great enemy of clear language is insincerity. When there is a
gap between one's real and one's declared aims, one turns as it were
instinctively to long words and exhausted idioms, like a cuttlefish
squirting out ink'
George Orwell, Shooting an Elephant (1950)

'The English language is in a bad way, but it is generally assumed that
we cannot by conscious action do anything about it. Our civilization is
decadent, and our language—so the argument runs—must inevitably
share in the general collapse.'
George Orwell, Politics and the English Language (1946)

In an important sense, the structure of a society is determined by the way it communicates. Not only do changing means and habits of communication alter relationships and influence attitudes, but the terms in which we communicate reflect collective intelligence and mould social progress. Beyond its central communicative role, language also has formidable creative power. If pictures are the shock troops of the information age, then language is its handmaiden.

The communications revolution and the proliferation of media have resulted in people reading less serious content than they were fifty years ago—books, political manifestos, essays and general argument. Information now arrives via the sound-bite, attention-grabbing headline and TV news-clip, all of which have facilitated a marked shortening of attention span and a diminished quality of argument. So, whilst media output has expanded, serious debate has contracted. Both have contributed significantly to the devaluation of language.

This chapter is not principally a review of the decline of language; rather, a discussion of its misuse to further the projection of Image, to distort reality and to manipulate opinion and sentiment, and how it has been devalued in the process. Language plays a central role in civilised life, both as a tool of expression and as a weapon of persuasion, and its misuse has nourished many of the attitudes which underpin today's veneer culture.

For all these reasons, clear and well-understood language is critical to social development. How it is used influences both understanding and the way we think; an elaborate, shared vocabulary makes for expressive diversity, imaginative richness and developed thought. Language not only describes events — it is also capable of creating them. The impact that the communications revolution has brought to bear on language has been dramatic and by and large acted against its positive development. The creative potential of language has been bent to the needs of image making, distorted for political ends, reduced to meaningless slogans and buzz words by relentless advertising and attenuated for the sake of expediency by semi-literate youth punching out text messages on mobile phones. Such is the damage done that the concise use of language to express clear ideas in normal discourse is a rapidly vanishing luxury; much language is now woolly or senseless — used for impact rather than for information — and constant vigilance is required to detect spin or to flush out ambiguity or hidden meaning.

The trend towards linguistic simplicity has been fuelled by failing education systems. Those who lack the intellectual capacity to express themselves cogently find their participation in society is thereby limited; their inability to understand moderately complex language or evaluate sustained argument forces those seeking to explain a decision or put across information either to ignore a significant proportion of their audience or else to puree their message into an easily digestible form with a concomitant sacrifice of detail. In such an intellectual vacuum, people are easy prey to persuasion and moral dependency, to their own, and often society's, disadvantage.

Language is the principal tool of communication, decision-making and argument. Words have many roles: they reflect the world we live in, are the most convenient and efficient means to describe things and events, and are central to conveying impressions and feelings. However, they are not themselves material things, events, impressions and feelings, but the medium through which these are transmitted. It is the imperfections of this interface which provide the facility for exploitation and distortion.

If willingness to massage language creates useful opportunities for the less scrupulous, it is also true that failure to identify and weed out what is disingenuous and superficial puts individuals and organisations at a disadvantage. Image manipulation tends to ensure that people who make the running are those able to produce the most persuasive pitch irrespective of the value or veracity of its content; committees frequently decide at the behest of the loudest, most assertive or demagogic member, leaving those with less political sharpness—and often a more useful contribution—to languish in the background. As Charles Dickens observed, 'Blustering assertion goes for proof half over the world'.

Language is well equipped for its principal task of delivering information and conveying sentiment. Rolling refinement and the addition of new words and expressions keep it alive and flexible to its purpose. The metaphor 'living language' is apt—language must evolve to reflect the prevailing circumstances; however, change is only positive to the extent that it enhances the power of expression. Many recent trends (in English) have been changes in style and usage rather than in productive evolution, more designed to accommodate the requirements of instant communication than for expressive versatility. There is a school of thought that eschews prescription where language is concerned and countenances anything, providing it is understood. It may be, to turn George Sampson's 1925 opinion on its head, that 'no serious damage is done to national tradition if a boy is permitted to say "Us'll hit he" instead of "I'll hit him", but there is, for some of us, an inbuilt revulsion to savaging common usage in this way'. (George Sampson, 1925, quoted in J. Honey, *Language is Power*, p 168). In general, the destruction of syntactical and grammatical conventions frustrates effective communication.

Laxity of language generally betokens laxity of thought and linguistic imprecision compromises clear argument and unambiguous comprehension. The relatively recent increase in swearing, for example, suggests not so much an increase in intemperance but a loosening in toleration and, above all, a paucity of vocabulary; a footballer who says 'fuck' more than one hundred times in a broadcast match, may possibly be giving vent to his feelings without the time to formulate complete sentences; but when he repeats the performance in everyday conversation, it is more likely that he is somewhat short of a more sophisticated expressive vocabulary. Whether either the expletives or the deficit matter is another question, but it is impossible to escape the conclusion that this kind of language is yet another unfortunate dividend of 'progressive' education which values self-expression more than correct—or at least conventional—usage.

Language, like any tool, can be misused, and misuse—beyond mere lapses in grammar or syntax—comes in many forms. Whether deliberately or not, clarity and precision are regularly ditched for obfuscation and words are used to distort meaning and to convey false impressions. This is possible because language is not used *in vacuo* but in context, which influences both its meaning and significance. How something is said or written is not neutral: the style in which an idea or thought is expressed affects what is being expressed, and the same words uttered by different people in one context, or the same person in different contexts, may convey entirely different meanings depending on the circumstances. Meaning is not confined to a literal correspondence between words and ideas. The choice and use of words also has a moral component which endows them with significance over and above their literal meaning: a subtle 'meta-language' enables us to convey innuendo, unstated implications, attitudes and moral messages. Non-linguistic facets of language — choice of words, richness of vocabulary and use of grammar and syntax — often reveal finely nuanced personal and social information.

Increasing linguistic misuse and imprecision have blurred the relationship between words and the world. This has happened because the lynch-pin of linguistic usage, integrity, has been steadily eroded. The more the meaning of words is determined by the user, rather than by accepted convention, the greater the loss of their communicative value. This is true both when words are detached from their common referents and also where inappropriate or over-use robs them of their emotive force.

The language of the financial industry, in particular, has been plundered to suggest that other, very different, sorts of operations should be conducted and evaluated along similar lines. It is now fashionable for managers to talk of welfare recipients, housing applicants and others cared for by public services as 'customers' and to use the terminology of 'product development', 'output' and general accounting to describe what happens to them. Whilst there is an obvious need for sound management and accounting in such organisations, it is a nonsensical distortion of reality to call prisoners, hospital patients or welfare recipients 'customers' of anything, least of all a government service. Being a customer implies the privilege of choice and the right to refuse a service and take 'custom' elsewhere — neither of which applies to prisoners, patients in public hospitals, or tax-payers.

In an age in which mediocrity, skilfully packaged, all too readily passes for what is acceptable, even what is excellent, manipulating language has become a convenient means of sustaining a false image and inflated sense of vitality and enthusiasm, which promotes intellectual mediocrity. Academia and the arts, in particular, routinely employ jargon and gobbledygook to conceal intellectual shallowness or to convey an impression of academic respectability where none is warranted. This has obvious survival value in cash-strapped, competitive environments where deliberately obscure language can be used to impress one's peers, supporters, grant-givers, etc, who are understandably reluctant to admit to ignorance. The psychological tactic relies on the idea that the less people are able to understand, the deeper and cleverer they may think you are. Fortunately, things are changing. Time was, if you didn't understand something you felt unable to deride it as nonsense. Now, if something is incomprehensible, unless it emanates from an irreproachable source, the chances are that it will be considered suspect. There is a growing impatience with the kind of language that verges on pseudery and, in an increasingly irreverent world, an easy preparedness to condemn the incomprehensible or pretentious. Unfortunately, such carpet-bombing is indiscriminate: the good is often castigated with the bad as pretentiousness is suspected in anything that is not readily understood.

As it is, language — which probably started as a crude means of conveying simple descriptive and emotive information — remains the most powerful communication medium we have. During its development, it has been put to an expanding variety of uses: as well as being the conveyor of knowledge and emotion, it is the chief enabler of diplomacy and politics and an essential armament of the advertising industry. It is hardly surprising that in this process of evolution and refinement it has fallen prey to misuse.

It is tempting to assume that there is a straightforward correspondence between words and objects. If there were, it would be a relatively simple matter to relate descriptions to language and thus identify incorrect usage. The nature of the relationship between language and reality is complex and has kept philosophers and linguists occupied for centuries. A principal concern, which reflects the main philosophical debate, is to what extent language actively creates reality rather than merely describing it. From this came the separation of a word's connotation (in general terms, its meaning) from its denotation (what it referred to). This distinction generated decades of discussion among philosophers on the problem of what words were supposed to denote when they had no obvious referents (e.g. abstract words, mental concepts or non-referential terms — for example, 'The present King of France'). This debate was abstruse and convoluted, and ultimately inconclusive and somewhat irrelevant — typical of academia paddling furiously in its own backwater. What emerged from it of practical value, to be particularly noted here, was the realisation of the loose nature of the relationship between words and things, events, sensations and feelings. It is this which, at a more superficial level, allows the exploitation of language in the cause of image-peddling.

This exploitation is pervasive, often insidious, and takes many different forms. What makes language so versatile and, by the same token, so vulnerable is the fact that with usage and changing circumstances words themselves acquire 'baggage' in the form of emotional accretions which alter their significance (though not their literal meaning). They cannot therefore be considered as neutral, colourless tokens which map easily on to the world and to whatever we take as reality. Much has been made of the need to strip language of unjustified connotations to establish a value-neutral basis for scientific and other discourse — particularly in the social sciences. In this prospectus, words are simply pieces of a jigsaw, to be fitted into their correct place on the board, and have no further significance. Many consider this a doomed quest outside the limited confines of academic research: firstly because, through usage, words have acquired adjuncts which cannot be eradicated and secondly because it makes no sense to divorce language from reality in this way. This hasn't stopped people trying — particularly sociologists, who have a clear need for descriptive and explanatory language that is free of the evaluative and contextual overtones of any given era or social system. To some extent this has been achieved in the sciences by tying words to specific referents, but for everyday usage the only route to value-neutral discourse would be a completely new language set. This is entirely possible, but it would not be long before, through usage, its elements attracted their own emotive attachments. In any case, it is far from clear that such a programme, even if it could be achieved, would be desirable. Fine language, with all its imperfections of nuance and imprecision is, like fine wine or great music, part of the pleasure and richness of living.

Linguistic neutrality is broadly unachievable — except perhaps in a few recondite areas of science or mathematics — because it requires both that words have tightly restricted, unambiguous denotations, and also that they do not have discretionary, non-verbal, components or values beyond their immediate referents. The desire for value-neutrality must also cope with the reality that, super-imposed, as it were, on words themselves is the context of their usage. This encompasses grammar and syntax, intonation, pronunciation, emphasis — in short, the way they are strung together — to which must be added expression, gesture and body language and the general social situation in which they are uttered, heard, written or read. All are capable of distorting literal meaning. This is the life which language has — the complete language package. Because it carries much more information within an utterance or written sentence than mere words, shorn of linguistic accretions, it is difficult to map onto the requirements of value-neutrality.

It is precisely these accretions which make language such a powerful ally of image-makers and spinners. As tools, words can be used with precision and clarity; as weapons, they can also be used to distract and confuse. The failings of language are often the consequence of low intelligence or paucity of vocabulary—unwitting failings which are not entirely unconnected. They are often also the result of insincerity or the deliberate exploitation of language in support of a political or other agenda. A considered choice of words promotes a false impression: for example, governments invariably talk of 'investing government money'—a phrase which carries positive over-tones of using funds, prudently, to generate a return. This is a multiple delu-sion: firstly, governments have no money beyond that raised by taxation, and secondly, their expenditure rarely has anything to do with investment in the normal meaning of that word. The reality is that governments *spend* (which often means *waste*) *taxpayers'* money—which is something entirely different. European Union bureaucrats being well aware of the widespread dislike of the erosion of national sovereignties resulting from the transfer of national powers to EU officials and institutions, deftly replaced the word 'power' with 'competence'—which is less controversial and takes some of the heat from an otherwise unpalatable reality.

Public pronouncements—of politics and business in particular—often rely on the power of words, chosen less for the sake of their meaning than to create a favourable aura. Unpicking such utterances is instructive (and even amusing), often revealing them to contain little of substance—phraseology cobbled together and spiced with plenty of positive buzz phrases, which expresses no clearly defined thoughts. In a classic, much-quoted, put-down a US Senator (McAdoo) described the speeches of President Warren Harding: they 'leave the impression of an army of pompous phrases moving over the landscape in search of an idea. Sometimes these meandering words would actually capture a strag-gling thought and bear it triumphantly, a prisoner in their midst, until it died of servitude and overwork'. In a similar vein, the British journalist Malcolm Muggeridge referred to the worthless use of language: 'using this non-language, these drooling non-sentences conveying non-thoughts, propounding non-fears and offering non-hopes ... lost forever in the media's great slag-heaps' (M. Muggeridge, *Chronicles of Wasted Time*, Vol 1).

The language we use carries a powerful personal image component, as its supra-linguistic significance provides a good indication of our personality. For instance, those who invariably focus on negatives and the less attractive side of people or events say much about their own character, as do their tone and choice of words about their moods, beliefs and attitudes. Since, in living language, words are written or spoken by people (rather than being generated by computers), they also carry moral significance. Using language inappropriately is potentially as dangerous as the indiscriminate use of a sledgehammer. We are as much responsible for the impact of our language and for its foreseeable consequences as we are for our physical actions. Indeed, where they are deliberately used to produce an effect, words amount to actions. Apart from extreme cases which justify suits for libel, slander or incitement, this moral responsibility is less and less recognised or subject to sanction. An apparently increased willingness to tolerate personally offensive or harmful language (abuse, swearing etc.) combined with what many see as oversensitivity to politically incorrect language reinforces the view that preservation of individual freedom of expression trumps respect for others and general social obligations, except perhaps where these might offend defined groups or minorities.

Language has been noticeably devalued over the last few decades. To a significant extent, this devaluation has followed the rise of mass media, the expansion of advertising and a decline in public literacy and in general media and educational standards. In many spheres, words have been replaced by images — we read and write less and view more. Spoken language in particular has continued to deteriorate, both through progressive reduction in personal vocabularies and through increased use of slang and distortion of meaning. Thus both the role and value of language has changed.

Society has tacitly condoned this devaluation and correct usage is increasingly seen as unnecessary and old-fashioned. This has happened in two different ways: firstly, language itself is being destroyed — e.g. by neutralising its meaning or by giving words different connotations; secondly, by using language itself as a means of subverting or distorting reality. Part of the blame for the success of linguistic exploitation must lie with the public, for whom the mushrooming of choice and improvements in electronic technology have gifted the ability to switch rapidly from one thing to another — mental multi-tasking, as it were. In a time-poor world, as long as the language used conveys the required message grammatical precision and integrity of vocabulary are regarded as irrelevant.

This borders on linguistic 'Humpty-Dumptyism': when it comes to spelling, grammar and syntax the rule is that anything goes, however sloppy, as long as it works. Linguistic expediency leaves little room for beauty or precision — so it is not surprising that personal and social difficulties are often the result of misunderstanding language.

Increased choice and demands on leisure time have eroded attention spans to the point at which people are unwilling to listen to or read lengthy or complex argument. They are impatient for the dividend — the pay-off: that is, the proposition that the argument is designed to support. This means that the message is determined by the conclusion, and is not — as it can only be — validated by the steps by which it has been reached. That a conclusion may not follow from the premises, or that an incorrect conclusion may be drawn from a perfectly logical chain of reasoning, is not considered relevant. What matters is the end product: the speaker or writer's viewpoint on that particular issue. So panache or presentation rather than plausibility often determine whether or not we are persuaded. To that extent that it succeeds, the medium has usurped the message.

Some of the worst depredations of language are perpetrated by the Image industry. One only has to look at the evolution of advertising slogans or newspaper headlines for examples of how language has been devalued. Constraints of time and space demand an economy with words, so advertisers and the media resort to shock-tactics to capture our attention and see repetitive hyperbole as a suitable means of achieving this. The facile and mindless repetition of superlatives in the pursuit of advertising impact has emasculated them to the point at which they no longer have real meaning or emotive force. Meanwhile, the news media have drained the emotive force from much of the language of despair and tragedy both by over-use and by use in inappropriate contexts — for example, as descriptions of relatively ordinary occurrences. We no longer react to 'wonderful', 'fantastic' or 'incredible' in a way that bears any relation to their literal meaning or status as superlatives, nor are we much moved by 'terrible', 'disastrous' or 'tragic'. These shock words have become no more than verbal prods to stimulate us or to capture our interest, whilst their essential significance is vitiated by the mundane situations to which they are routinely applied. (The marketing industry has followed suit: for example, for years the French apple grading system only recognised three levels of quality: excellent, super and extra super; even today, many food grading systems are based on purely cosmetic criteria, not on quality or flavour). This amounts to an abuse of language. We have cried 'Wolf!' on superlatives and many other words to the point that they have been stripped of their significance.

Excoriating words of content by depriving them of their emotive impact not only neutralises our normal responses but also impoverishes language itself, by reducing the available stock of expressive vocabulary. Few words now remain to convey genuine superlatives, whether of tragedy, wonder or achievement. The advertising industry, having exhausted its supply of viable superlatives by rendering them meaningless, is now obliged to turn to so-called 'lifestyle' benefits (which might, but usually don't, attach to their products) or to use stronger language or other means (e.g. sexual innuendo) to stimulate interest. Even though few are deceived into accepting the Image as Reality, using words as mere attention-seeking prods, to temporarily stimulate or arouse, is to misuse and degrade language.

The interests of linguistic integrity demand that we retain the link between words and the world. We rely on language for literal meaning as well as for effect. The further these links are blurred, the greater the inadequacy of language to persuade, to convey stronger feelings or to arouse genuine emotions. When words lose their efficacy, people may turn to more aggressive, even physical, means to achieve their ends. Conversely, Hitler's oratorical, rabble-rousing skills relied on a potent combination of emotion and language, where the emotive context rather than the literal meaning of the words used produced the desired results. Modern evangelists use much the same techniques.

If the effect of mass advertising and the media in pursuit of Image has been to strip meaning from words by over-use, those who misuse language in pursuit of ideologies and political agendas operate differently — by subtle distortion of meaning. This also strikes at the requirement for integrity in the use of language — that is, that words are reliable and have known value — which is destroyed by usage which negates that value or divorces words from their true referents. The requirement for language to be flexible is entirely compatible with that of integrity. Exploiting language for political ends make argument difficult, if not impossible. At the limit, two people using the same word intending different meanings are not using the same word at all. This reduces arguments about serious issues to confrontations about semantics and undermines communication. Suicide bombers are 'martyrs' to their supporters, 'murderers' to their opponents; abortion is 'murder' to one camp, 'the exercising of individual freedom of choice' to another. Debate on these issues then becomes argument between those who see themselves as upholders of religious tolerance and choice, and those who see themselves as guardians of life. It is easy to see that tarring those who perform abortions as 'killers' escalates the argument beyond the fundamental issues. The question of whether, and on what grounds, abortion or suicide bombing might be justified becomes mired in a sea of sterile emotive, semantic claim and counterclaim. This is often the case with discussion of important issues and makes exchanges unproductive — and irritating.

A decline in adult literacy means that children are leaving school (and even higher education) with limited vocabularies and poor communication skills. Their reduced vocabularies, in particular, have accelerated the devaluation of language. One might easily conclude from listening to today's youth in the USA and Britain that the sole adjectives of approbation and disapprobation are 'awesome' (extraordinary), 'obscene' (extra-ordinary, wonderful), 'gross' (extraordinary, definitely not wonderful) and 'wicked' (excellent); the advanced class might perhaps include 'cool', and 'dire' — both idiotic forms of emphasis — in their personal lexicons, but there is often depressingly little further refinement. Such word inflation allows literal meaning to be usurped by slack emotive exclamation, to everyone's disadvantage. Lazy language is what many people want — they can't be bothered, even if they have the skills, to use words properly, let alone construct whole sentences. The single-word sentence and the SMS, embellished or not with smileys, bid fair to accelerate the decline of prose, and probably poetry as well. Taking truncated language as the norm makes life more difficult for those who aspire to better speech and writing, especially when that norm is considered as a yardstick and used to berate those who dislike ugly and sloppy usage and strive to promote linguistic refinement.

Language adapts to needs — this is understandable and reasonable. Societies coin new words for new situations and objects, and for ideas that matter to them. It is well-known that the Eskimos have evolved a multiplicity of words to describe different snow types; this has obvious survival value in a climate in which, wisely, snow is not just 'snow'. In marking significant differences, language relies on repeatability so that to each variation there corresponds a particular word or phrase. One Eskimo may argue with another about whether the snow outside his front door is of type A or type B, but there is no argument about which word refers to which type. In such aspects, language closely mirrors reality and retains its intended reference.

In other situations, where new words are not so easily mapped on to objects, they create their own linguistic headaches. The medical profession is adept at coining new syndromes to describe and compartmentalise patterns of disease or behaviour. This has obvious value for patients who tend to feel instantly better if their symptoms are identified as this or that syndrome and take comfort in the knowledge that the doctor 'knows what is wrong' with them. However, the value is less clear for practitioners, trying to take the step from codifying a syndrome to validating it as a genuine entity rather than a haphazard cluster of symptoms, by identifying a causal chain and thereby enabling the development of an effective treatment. The new 'diseases' consequent on the trauma's of war, grief and occupation are particularly difficult as these appear to be psychosomatic—part psychological and part physical. Are they real diseases rather than just broad patterns of symptoms grouped together for diagnostic purposes? Moreover, which manifestations do you treat—the psychological or the somatic? As with the subsequently observable effects of theoretically deduced sub-atomic particles, it is reasonable to ask whether these syndromes represent real discoveries or are merely classificatory conveniences.

As well as situations in which professionals might argue as to whether a new word in fact corresponds to an independent reality, it is equally possible to imagine the opposite situation, in which language actually manipulates, or even creates, reality. In *1984*, George Orwell propounded 'Newspeak' as the official language of his fictional totalitarian state. By limiting the permissible words and phrases to those the leaders found acceptable, and enforcing conformity by fear, Newspeak was designed to diminish rather than to extend the range of possible thought and thereby eradicate thoughts that were considered unsuitable. Today's ruling elites believe that imposing such limitations will create the state they want by confine citizens to docile thoughts and appropriate attitudes. The obvious flaw in these arrangements is that suppressing the expression of undesirable thoughts does not, of itself, either eradicate the thoughts themselves or alter the attitudes which inspired them.

Politicians are obviously not convinced of this. They see it as an easy and desirable extension of such fictional manipulation to use language itself to mould thought. The general proposition is that if you command the language in which debate is conducted, then you are in a much stronger position to command the debate itself; in other words, to the extent that you define language, you can manipulate, if not control, thoughts and attitudes.

It is true that language has no life independent of those who use it—although there is a fascinating debate to be had about whether the absence of a word prevents the use of a concept. However, in the right hands—and indeed in the wrong ones—it is a powerful instrument. In social and political life, language is employed to argue, persuade and motivate. One can point to historic speeches which have swayed nations, shaken governments and altered the course of wars. In these instances, language has been deployed to convey or to change sentiment, often for the common good. In contrast to such great political oratory, in the modern political world too many speeches are no more than 'sound banquets'—fine-sounding, even moving language which, like healthy salads or Chinese take-aways, briefly nourish and sate but rapidly evaporate with the passage of time, into so much evanescent gas. This is because words, by themselves, 'butter no parsnips'—they merely signal attitudes and intentions; it is also, and more importantly, because words are too rarely (at least in public affairs) matched by actions.

Language is routinely called upon to distort reality and manipulate attitudes. Its most potent manifestations are in *spin, dumbing down, jargon, political correctness* and *sentimentality*.

SPIN

Although spin has existed in one form or another for centuries, its recent refinement is a by-product of the media revolution. It may be defined as the art of massaging communication to put a particular gloss on facts or events, and encompasses a wide range of manipulation from the simple expedients of exaggeration, generalisation and using loaded terms to disguise a lack of substance, to the less appetising habit of omitting salient facts. In general, spin works by focusing attention on style as a mask for insubstantiality. It relies for its potency on incongruity—on leaving a gap between what is said and reality—which deliberately provides a convenient conduit for misinterpretation. These are the twin tracks of double-speak and double-think. One can distinguish two principal ruses: using words to imply something that is not justified (*suggestio falsi*) and delivering only part of the truth (*suppressio veri*). Politicians, in particular, have refined the art of being 'economical with the truth' to the point that what is left out of their utterances is sometimes more important than what is put into them. British Prime Minister Harold Wilson memorably told the British public the day after sterling had been devalued that 'the pound ... in your pocket, purse, or bank' had not altered in value.

Possibly not physically, but all but the severely intellectually impaired realised that its purchasing power had indeed diminished and with it their standard of living. The remark was seen as a sly, if not downright misleading, ploy to finesse an unpalatable reality. That sleight of language provoked one commentator to remark that had Mr Wilson been captain of the ill-fated Titanic, he would have informed his passengers that he had stopped to take on ice. 'When Councilman Rogers was asked whether he had any evidence of police brutality in the community, he replied, truthfully, "There isn't any I have seen". He had, however, received several verbal accounts of police brutality from his constituents.' This statement may have been a truthful, but in its emphasis on the word 'seen' it effectively deceives the listener. President Clinton's emphatic denial, "I did not have sex with that woman", was of a similar genre — a crude attempt to re-define sex to exclude fellatio.

In legitimising spin, the media and advertising industries have much to answer for. Spin caters particularly to the needs of politics and business and has become highly sophisticated. Oversimplification, sloganising and economy with the truth are its stock-in-trade and accepted parts of the spin-doctor's armoury. Selective quotation and telling half a story in the cause of brevity, or to reinforce an argument, allow relevant information to be omitted in pursuit of an ulterior motive. The reader or listener is thus left to infer what is meant by skilfully drafted language or judicious omission, which may or may not square with the facts or the normal meaning of the words used. The art of formulating language to hint at one implication while using words which suggest another is well-practised in media, political and business circles. The difference between today and yesterday is that then, when something was unclear or misunderstood, you usually made an effort to correct or clarify; now, you strenuously defend it.

Spin is therefore a valuable political and social tool and, given its ability not just to distort the truth but also to create it, facilitates the ultimate deception. It is not that those who spin invariably disbelieve what they are saying. For instance, those who advocated going to war against Iraq in 2003 were apparently sincere in their belief in the danger of the threat from that regime. But the main protagonists spun so much of the slender evidence of that threat that they — and eventually their electorates — came to accept as reality what was no better than supposition.

The creative use of statistics to conceal reality is a derivative branch of spin, as is the use of repetition, on the grounds that, given sufficient frequency, whatever is repeated will be taken as true. There are various well-documented ways in which numbers can be used to deceive or to emphasise a point. Statistical fallacies are legion and range from the Biased Sample fallacy, through the Confusion of Correlation and Causation fallacy and the Misuse of Averages fallacy, to the Volvo fallacy and the Texas Sharpshooter fallacy. This last comes from a fictitious Texas 'sharpshooter' who fires a shot into a wall, then draws a bull's-eye around the bullet hole. In doing so he makes it appear as though, with a totally random shot, he has performed a highly non-random act. In normal target practice, the bull's-eye defines a region of significance, and there's a low probability of hitting it by firing in a random direction. However, when the region of significance is determined after the event has occurred, any outcome at all can be made to appear spectacularly improbable. To take a more concrete example: the statement that 'thirty percent of doctors smoke brand X' suggests both that doctors smoke and that those who do, smoke brand X. This statistic is misleading, in that it is impossible to validate what is being suggested without knowing what percentage of doctors, overall, smoke, and whether it is thirty percent of these, or of the totality of doctors, who smoke brand X; and, of those who smoke, whether they only smoke brand X. Background information, which is not disclosed, is often as important as what is.

Not surprisingly, politicians take advantage of the potential in statistical ambiguity: for instance, waiting lists and waiting times for consultations or operations in British public hospitals are frequently reported as declining, which suggests that the service is improving. In fact, the reality is often that administrators are either refusing to put people on the lists or only admitting non-urgent cases, so more can be dealt with in a given time, thus reducing both list sizes and waiting time. The use of statistics as spin is sometimes unsubtle to the point of crudeness. The statement that "The Prime Minister has set an interesting and historic precedent in the House; if you lie to the House 49 per cent of the time, that is OK because the 'totality' of it is that he spoke the truth". (British MP Michael Fabricant on Tony Blair, circa 2003). Disregarding the questionable grammar, this makes the point that statistics may be used to gloss over the fact of serial lying.

The substitution of style for substance has been greatly facilitated by the decline in education. The trend away from detailed, closely reasoned, argument which can be analysed, questioned, tested and thereby verified or falsified means that opinion formers now have to make their case and put over their ideas in brief interviews or short newspaper pieces. Here, what counts is not detail but impression, and a punchy one-liner or snappy slogan is what works best. Electorates have become used to the ten or thirty second product commercial and expect their politics and social ideas to arrive in similarly attenuated packages. As in much else, a bad thought delivered authoritatively is readily accepted as sound.

The art — or should it be the science? — of persuasion relies heavily on spinning. Proponents will argue that spinning is no more than making the best case for whatever it is you are supporting. Indeed, but there is a point at which editing amounts to distortion, and to the extent that spin know-ingly involves selective evidence and deliberate omission of material which, if included, might vitiate the conclusion or point to an entirely different one, makes it no better that unrefined deceit. It might be argued that people have become so cynical and habituated to spin that they are now de-sensitised and effectively immune. Indeed, the results of overt spinning nowadays are likely to be counter-productive, but this is no justification for doing it in the first place. Disreputable methods only spread discontent and disrespect, so system-atic deception is not a prudent long-term tactic.

The urge to spin comes not only from the desire to disguise the unpal-atable but also from the need to create substance from what is effectively window-dressing, to turn wind into water (many political 'initiatives' fall into this category), or else from a calculated, more sinister desire to avoid telling the truth. It is arguably not spin itself which causes most damage, rather the implication that this is normal practice and an acceptable way of conducting business. The fluid nature of truth means that, skilfully told, it often amounts to the most compelling lie of all.

DUMBING-DOWN

Dumbing-down is a relatively new phenomenon not just new jargon. It refers to the removal of intellectual content from material — mainly in broadcasting, news reporting and entertainment — to render it more intel-ligible, and thus more attractive, to those likely to view, read or listen to it. It encompasses not only the avoidance of difficult subjects, but presenting those that are treated in ways that exclude what is deemed to be above the target recipients' intellectual level. There is a healthy market for people who are happy to read the digest rather than the book, the abstract rather than the article, easy paraphrase rather than more demanding original. In the broadcast media this is spun as 'giving people what they want'; the reality it that it is a crude means of boosting audience ratings, and thereby — for commercial enterprises — advertising revenue.

In recent times, dumbing-down might be said to have begun with the appearance, in 1961 of the New Testament 'translation' of the New English Bible (completed in 1970). Hailed as a landmark for Christianity, this aimed to bring the Scripture closer to 20th century congregations and to facilitate Christian teaching by adapting Biblical language to suit the modern idiom. The NEB is perhaps easier to read than the Authorised Version, but this facility has been achieved at the sacrifice of meaning — not literal meaning but spiritual significance. The well-loved and mellifluous, albeit archaic, phraseology of the original is replaced by language of more current coinage. For example: 'quickly' becomes 'be quick about it', and much of the beauty of the older language, which derived principally from its resonance and rhythm, has been lost. The result has little of the mysterious, inspirational or uplifting qualities of the King James Version — and in places it reads like a badly drafted government document. The Christmas Story, with which even agnostics are broadly familiar, is a good example: 'Now in this same district there were shepherds out in the fields, keeping watch through the night over their flock, when suddenly there stood before them an angel of the Lord, and the splendour of the Lord shone round them. They were terror struck, but the Angel said "Do not be afraid, I have good news for you: there is great joy coming to the whole people … and on earth his peace for men on whom his favour rests". Much of this — as Ian Robinson (*The Survival of English*, 1973) points out — breaks fundamental rules of grammar and syntax, but it is the crude phraseology and ambiguity which destroys the beauty of the original. As he suggests, some might also irreverently enquire whether there is to be no peace for those on whom God's favour does not rest, or is there peace for all men, because his favour rests on them? Perhaps this is a deliberate trap for the shepherds!

The perceived success of the NEB percolated through to liturgy and worship and encouraged the Anglican authorities to bring hymns and sermons 'up to date'. A modern version of the Book of Common Prayer followed shortly after the NEB seeking to bring the liturgy closer to congregations. Thus it is that the rituals of marriage and burial have been shorn of much of the resonant mystical aura of the original texts. These services now bear more obvious relation to the realities of the modern world. Thus, marriage is not so much a union of hearts, minds and bodies, rather a signing ceremony for a contract that is more likely than not to be broken, with a strong whiff of social services looking over the happy couple's shoulders to ascertain their likely requirements for housing, health and general benefit. Pre-nuptial agreements reinforce the contractual theme. Even burial cannot escape the language reformation, and seems now more an exercise in waste-disposal than a sensitive ritual of farewell, complete with canned music as the coffin slides through a trap door into the municipal gas oven—at a decently solemn speed, compatibly mindful of the need to 'process' those waiting outside, in the crowded timetable of the 9–5 working day of a cost-conscious municipal crematorium.

What proponents of modern liturgy conveniently ignore is that that the language and rhythm of traditional Christian texts is an integral part of its message—and indeed its appeal. The stated purpose of revising the Bible and Liturgy was to modernise the Anglican Church and thereby make it more relevant to the age. The result, greatly accelerated by the concomitant 'modernisation' of hymns, guitar-strumming vicars, and 'happy-clappy' neighbour-hugging rituals, is worship filled with sickening sentimentality and folksy phrases about being 'nice', and treating the environment and other people 'nicely'—sentiment carried through with the extension of many Churches into glorified social clubs, complete with modern music and sermons stuffed with topical, jokey references to last night's sitcom episode, bland inclusivity and exhortations to be 'cool' and not 'stressed out'. The chief consequence of this banal attempt at relevance has been the alienation of many who were nurtured on the poetic and evocative language of traditional liturgy, and who see the new version as pandering to catchpenny for no discernible benefit. Now the principle of modernisation has been established, there will no doubt be a clamour for the interval between updates to be reduced from the current 300 years.

There is an important difference between bringing something up to date because its references are odd or inappropriate (e.g. rebasing money in modern equivalents to make the scale of a transaction more evident in plays or novels), and changing it for marketing purposes. The motives behind the New English Bible and Book of Common Prayer were presented as benefits for congregations when, in fact, they were no more than misguided marketing exercises—which, in fact, failed.

Dumbing down affects broadcast language and culture as well as what is written. As presentational styles have become more relaxed, language has become more colloquial and less rigorous. Slang has usurped Standard English and truncated idiom has replaced complete sentences. This urge to make audiences feel that they are being entertained rather than informed has turned news bulletins and documentary programmes into 'shows', whilst presenters of many of these programmes shout and gesticulate to keep the attention of their fickle, and apparently easily bored, audience. Meanwhile, news is read in short antiphonal sentences, often by newsreaders sitting on the edge of their desks or roaming the studio to give the impression of informality—a style deemed appropriate even to serious output. No longer can the careful use of language alone be relied upon for information and emphasis—graphic gesture and extreme voice modulation are also considered essential.

It is noticeable that those who front broadcast programmes today are becoming ever closer in social manner and persona to their audiences. This is deliberate—an attempt to make elites appear as ordinary people; to sustain the image of 'inclusivity' and make audiences feel more comfortable with an intelligence level that closely matches their own. Gone are the days when broadcasters were chosen from the upper end of the social and intellectual spectrum, and programmes were pitched at well above average intelligence. In the desire to bring broadcasting closer to the mean intellect of its audience, 'in' are vulgarity, slang and loose language, 'out' are long words, extended sentences and anything intellectually challenging. Such dumbed-down output is not complete argument elucidated for a less intelligent audience, but emasculated argument shorn of essential nuance and detail. The difference is akin to that between opera 'highlights' and the whole or an abridged book and the original. They are not equivalent either in fact or value.

The usual riposte to complaints about weak or misused language is that you have to make language relevant to the age and that, in any case, Standard English is an anachronism (they might add, but don't, 'in multicultural societies, many of whose citizens barely speak it anyway'). The justification of maintaining Standard English and received usage and pronunciation has been the subject of long debate in linguistic sociological circles. Multi-racial societies have brought a plethora of new words, accents and usage to countries which already had many regional dialects to absorb. The easy way out, both for those using language publicly and for those on the receiving end of public press and public utterances, was to abandon correct usage and rationalise the 'anything goes' rule which has now become *de facto* policy, at least in the mainstream of the English-speaking world. As with morality, it should not be difficult to understand that having an accepted, immutable kernel of usage makes it easier, not more difficult, to incorporate changes in style and vocabulary, demanded by contemporary discourse.

Parallel to this runs another debate: whether or not all languages are equal. Is Pidgin English equal to Standard English, or French or Spanish or Urdu? Some contend that all languages are equal, none more or less worth than another. This implies that all languages are equally capable of all necessary description and conceptual nuance. But does this mean 'actually'—i.e. as currently constituted—or 'potentially' capable of such expression? The former is definitely contentious, the latter probably tautologous.

The idea that all languages and dialects within a given language are equally valid and capable of an equal range of expression constitutes one of the principal pressures to abandon Standard English. Researchers—notably in the USA in the 1970s (Labov)—sought to prove that non-standard language was just as concept- and argument-rich as standard language. Until recently this was received wisdom in linguistic circles, but doubt has been cast on the validity of the research. Reviewing the research, one expert concluded that to describe all languages as equal is an hypothesis based on 'questionable premises and ... a triumph of ideological confidence over empirical knowledge'. (John Honey, *The Power of Language*).

The insistence on the superiority of standard language is regarded by some as linguistic imperialism designed to entrench the international standing of a particular language and to create cultural inequalities between that language and others. Some construe it as a sinister plot to enhance the power of a particular social elite, by which they presumably mean those who have received a good education. Liberals and counter-culture socialists make much of pluralism and cultural diversity, of which language is but one facet. What gets lost in these quasi-political wranglings is an answer to why public debate should be conducted at the lowest intellectual level, without any attempt to specify the supposed disadvantages of insisting on precise and received usage. In today's world, to ask such questions implies unwelcome criticism of education systems and, worse, that poor linguistic and comprehension skills indicate intellectual deficiency—an egregious offence against political correctness.

In countries with significant immigrant populations—particularly Britain and America—it is felt by some that imposing English as a language is authoritarian and deprives people of part of their cultural roots. The political Image is that of fashionable 'inclusiveness'; the social Reality is that to allow people to continue to speak and write only their own language puts them at a significant disadvantage when it comes to jobs and makes true integration less likely. As Newt Gingrich (*To Renew America*, 1995) puts it, 'Not learning a new language is risking their future by clinging to the past'. He adds that 'bilingualism suits community leaders because it keeps their voters/supporters isolated from the rest of the community/society. Multi-culturalism keeps people tied to the past—old habits and traditions. Immigrants need to make a sharp, psychological break with the past, immersing themselves in the culture and economic system that is going to be their home' (ibid.). Castigating the requirement for standard usage (in whatever language) as linguistic imperialism—or worse, as oppression—is nonsensical clap-trap; if anything, the opposite is true—a common structured language base empowers rather than disadvantages.

The debate over Standard English is further complicated by the fact that social acceptability is tied in part to educational competence, and this is indelibly reflected in language usage. There are interesting parallels between language hierarchy and social position in that (a) highly developed languages have both wider vocabularies and greater expressive capability, especially of the abstract, and that (b) social hierarchy is reflected in linguistic refinement. The latter happens in two main ways: firstly, richness and variety of vocabulary tend to parallel intelligence and educational attainment and thus to reflect it; secondly, language in general encodes a system of values. The linkage may possibly be less secure now than thirty years ago but it remains the case that an amalgam of vocabulary, accent, grammar and idiom are powerful indicators of social status, if not always of intellect.

Whilst some people feel that to confer privileged status on any particular accent or language usage is inappropriate for an increasingly egalitarian society, there remains a general respect for the more evolved and advanced forms of literacy. The continuing premium put on occupational ability remains tied to educational competence and this cannot be divorced from an evolved vocabulary and precise linguistic usage, although this has more to do with the desire for expressive precision and less with social correctness than those who advocate 'anything goes' might think.

Highly evolved languages are capable of expressing fine nuances of observation, feeling and argument—necessary for all sorts of occupational and professional activities. Limited vocabulary and loose usage are incompatible with these ends, so there is an enduring need for standard language which is widely recognised and understood and for vocabulary and syntax which permit maximum precision. Paucity of vocabulary and stylistic and grammatical laxity continue to indicate sloppiness of thought; imprecision may suit the popular press and broadcasting (even this is doubtful in an increasingly litigious age), but it compromises the accurate transmission of argument and information. The danger is that allowing looseness to become the educational norm, and leaving precision and nuance to the professions and those who need it, will exacerbate social divisions and further alienate ordinary people from the realms of debate and understanding which are essential to achieving informed political consensus.

The argument is complicated by the difficulty of specifying the relationship between language and thought. Whilst there is no simple correlation between vocabulary size or sentence construction and intellect, a restricted vocabulary and the limited use of certain verbal and subordinate clause forms would seem to be incompatible with highly abstract thought or intricate argument. However, caution is needed as it is equally clear that linguistic complexity does not equate to sophisticated thought and, conversely, that the most complex of arguments is sometimes expressed in the simplest language. For examples, consider the liar and the truth-sayer riddle, wherein a questioner is able to ask one question of one of two men, one of whom lies while the other tells the truth, in order to determine which is which, and Bertrand Russell's theory of types which asks the question: 'is a set a subset of all sets that are members of themselves?' Both problems require clear and logical thought but are stated in simple terms which contain neither linguistic nor conceptual complexity. Except where technical terminology is involved, there is no inherent need for language to be complex.

The unwillingness—or lack of political guts—to sustain independence of thought is a corrosive trend. It leads to the sanitising of language, which those who dumb down are prepared to see sacrificed to political whim, fashionable expediency, or weak logic. No longer can one discuss many ethical or political issues—e.g. those surrounding race, religion, abortion or elitism—in a dispassionate manner, despite the fact that the words involved have perfectly comprehensible, non-emotive meanings. Such issues are considered inappropriate merely because of their acquired overtones. Even many educated, influential people are seemingly unable to detach emotive connotations from the underlying concepts and therefore all references are considered pejorative and threatening.

The spread of dumbing down and the erosion of standard usage are significant components of the desire of governments to preside over inclusive societies. Inclusivity is regarded as beneficial, exclusion of any kind retrogressive. So, whilst the highly educated are still sneakingly respected, the unstated aim is to reduce as much public discourse as possible to the level of the lowest common denominator—an aim that is in danger of being all too easily achieved.

Another interesting aspect of the change in language is the proliferation of euphemism, jargon and techno-speak. Euphemism is a growing branch of the sentimentalist industry—using relatively neutral terms or expressions to replace others which have evaluative or emotional, and often pejorative connotations and thus to take the sting from the reality. Thus it is that people 'pass on' or 'leave us' rather than 'die', which is particularly mushy sentimentality, and no-one any longer travels second-class on British trains—but 'standard' class; in the air 'economy' has become 'coach' or 'world traveller'; abortions have become 'terminations' and countries are no longer poor but 'developing'. One American hospital apparently eschewed the word 'death' in favour of 'negative patient outcome'. Such absurdities make for easy humour, but it is the mentality that produces them rather than the individual examples that should give cause for concern. Diplomatic language is the ultimate refinement of euphemism: abuse, slanging and personal innuendo become 'frank' discussions, and the action of a country which kills your ambassador is 'unhelpful'. Concealing the real meaning with value-neutral language defuses confrontation and thus makes continued dialogue possible, which, on balance, is probably 'helpful'.

JARGON

Jargon concerns technical or quasi-technical terms which are either inherently inappropriate or else used in inappropriate contexts. In many cases this touches euphemism and may take several forms. Firstly, there are the new words or phrases which refer to everyday objects or situations. For example, as one commentator (William Lutz) has noted, in official American circles, farmers have 'grain-consuming animal units kept in single purpose agricultural structures', not pigs or sheep kept in pens or coops, and a plane crash is euphemistically described as 'a jet involuntarily converted by uncontrolled contact with the ground'. Jargon is rife in political circles seeking to endow their pronouncements and activities with mystique and complexity. Sir Ernest Gowers, who saw the damage that poor language usage can do and championed the use of 'Plain Words' and comprehensible language in official documents, is still fighting for his ground after some eighty years and several reprints.

Language is regularly employed to bolster status and self-image. This is widespread (and often silly). In working life, the designation of jobs by titles which change with rank has been hijacked to provide an unjustified aura of importance, particularly in America where everyone is a Vice-President for something or other, and high-sounding titles abound for relatively menial jobs. A lift operator becomes a 'member of the vertical transportation corps' and rat-catchers become 'rodent control officials'. This does no-one, least of all the employees concerned, any service — as the nature of their work is public knowledge — but perhaps bolsters weak self-esteem and certainly contributes to the culture of sentimentality that dislikes raw job descriptions.

Second, there is the deliberate use of over-long or technical language to obscure or confuse. For example, a recent European Union paper on 'Better Regulation' proposed to "improve the intrinsic quality of the impact assess-ment of EU legislation by ensuring on a case-by-case basis the ex ante valida-tion of external scientific experts of the methodology used for certain impact assessments". It was once remarked of a British EU Commissioner, renowned for his rambling verbosity that his problem, as a speaker, was that 'having no idea what he wanted to say, he had no way of knowing when he had finished saying it'. Verbosity is a tried and tested expedient which allows a speaker to rely on words to take the place of non-existent thoughts. Dissecting modern political utterances often reveals either a lack of substance, deliberate evasive-ness or muddled logic. Public figures are finely attuned to the art of non-communication, recognising well the value of not meaning what they say, whilst striving to avoid saying what they mean.

Thirdly, jargon is used to suggest expertise where the user is either not an expert in his subject but uses 'expert' language to deceive, or else the subject in question is not one to which the term expertise may properly be applied. As George Orwell succinctly put it, over half a century ago 'in our time, political speech and writing are largely the defence of the indefensible ... Political language has to consist largely of euphemism, question-begging and sheer cloudy vagueness ... [It] is designed to make lies sound truthful and murder respectable and to give an appearance of solidity to pure wind'. (*Politics and the English Language*, 1946). In all these instances, the aim is to give an impression of competence, knowledge or expertise where none exists.

Pretentiousness and obfuscation are close relatives of jargon. In much the same way that objects are judged on their appearance rather than on their utility or functionality, many people accept complex or obscure language as indicators of profundity. The usual markers for this kind of deceit are long, prolix sentences, often studded with obscure words. In many cases these are a foil for insincerity or imprecise thought, in others they are deliberate attempts to suggest that something important is being said when the reality is the opposite. Obscure language may create a favourable impression, but more often than not masks incompetence, vacuity or plain showing off. Where there is something genuinely useful to say, obscurity is usually the result of indolence rather than intellect; clear communication requires effort—and high-sounding jargon comes easily to those used to it as part of their working routine. As well as capitalising on peoples' willingness to equate obscurity with profundity, such language exploits the equally false equivalence of pretentious English with good English. Technicalities excepted, the expression of obscurity rarely requires obscurity of expression and even the most complex thoughts are usually capable of being set out in simple, comprehensible, language.

There is an element of the King's New Clothes in the use of obscure language or jargon. Many on the fringes of academia, even some within it, rely on it to disguise the fact either that their discipline is spurious or that they have little of value to say. Quasi-academic enterprises develop and perpetuate an insider jargon which they intend those on the outside to find obscure and therefore difficult to criticise. People are taken in, believing that the less one understands something the cleverer must be its creator. Few are bold enough to suggest that it might all be nonsense for fear of being shown up as ignorant. The proliferation of jargon can also be laid at the feet of management-speak, which uses high-sounding neologisms to indicate an expertise, much of which is suspect (see Chapter 11).

The 'insider' phenomenon is well-developed in the art world, where artists and critics have long been complicit in fooling the public. One only has to read descriptions of modern art to realise that there is much intellectual sleight of hand devoted to providing a veneer of respectability to indifferent work which has little but novelty to recommend it. It is not that the language of art has changed; rather that pretentiousness and obscurity are being used to mask a lack of profundity. Often, the description of a work is even more fraudulent than the work itself, particularly where it seeks to apply psychological jargon to endow an inherently ordinary artefact with unmerited importance.

The public are bemused rather than inspired, and generally wonder, wisely, whether the wool is being pulled over their eyes.

SENTIMENTALITY

The use of sentimentality to substitute Appearance for Reality is one of the most insidious misuses of language. We are invited to see the ordinary as the not so ordinary, and to put an emotive tinge on matters that do not justify it. In western cultures, especially America, euphemism and evasiveness are endemic; wrapping fact in cloying sentiment allows unpalatable realities to be side-stepped or avoided altogether. The preferred tool is language. It is now common practice for first names to be used, particularly in public or service industry environments, to foster an image of empathy and 'caring', despite being seen (and resented) by many recipients as over-familiar and disrespectful. It is difficult to see how a surgeon provides better care for his patient or a bank better service for their client by using their first name, and beyond belief to think that anyone might be so credulous as to think that it does. It should be obvious that the quality of care, in any circumstance, is primarily a function of how well a job is done, and to this end the use of social intimacy has no relevance whatever. (The fact that, over time, one may develop a deeper, personal relationship with one's doctor, bank-manager or attorney has no bearing on the issue.) This trend is in part the result of the appalling American habit of using first names on slight acquaintance, or no acquaintance at all. This destroys the conventions of social acquaintance and pre-empts an accepted signal of increased intimacy.

Insincerity devalues language. In the so-called 'customer-care' industry, recorded messages routinely apologise for poor service. However, someone left hanging on to the telephone listening to canned music for half an hour is unlikely to believe the computerised voice announcing every thirty seconds that 'your call is important to us'. Saying you care is not caring, and few are taken in. The irritation apart, this is counter-productive; both because it is blatantly false and also because it suggests that the initiator believes that their customers are stupid enough to believe it. Here, literal meaning and actual effect are directly opposed—the words convey one meaning which is vitiated by the context of their usage.

Sentimentality has spread beyond relatively harmless euphemism into such contentious areas as human rights. Until political correctness and international law got hold of them, rights were limited to those generally considered to be conferred on human beings either by existence—the right to life itself and possibly to liberty—or by the laws of the particular system under which they lived. The only universal rights were those considered as relating to human existence, *per se*. Whilst the US constitution regards these as conferred by God, their existence is by no means internationally accepted and in cases of infringement they are often difficult to assert. The unpalatable reality is that people, even in stable, civilised societies have few genuine rights. These, under the influence of courts, treaties and pressure groups have been supplemented by a variety of so-called 'rights' whilst others which were generally considered desirable have been watered down or removed. *Rights*, which are relatively rare, have become fused with *legal entitlements*. Do people really have the right to free accommodation, health care and education, or help with obtaining employment? The European Court of Human Rights appears to think so. Do animals and foetuses have rights? Many non-governmental-organisations appear to think so. If indeed they do, at what limits are these drawn and why are fruit and vegetables excluded? It might be thought that endowing animals with rights, which can be enforced, is a less sensible expedient to making their proper care and protection part of normal humane responsibility, which is less easily codified.

Whilst animals are gaining rights, elsewhere parents are losing them. In many countries they no longer have the right to use physical force in disciplining their children—even mild chastisement is outlawed—and children have successfully prosecuted their parents for doing so. This effectively negates the authority of parents and removes their status as superior moral beings. Putting adults on an equal level with children makes successful moral and social upbringing more difficult and introduces law into an area for which many feel it is wholly inappropriate.

It is clearly helpful to any self-interest group to be able to demonstrate that their rights are being infringed, so the greater the spectrum of rights the more likely is one or another to have been infringed in any given situation. Rights have come to mean generally desirable ends, which is fine for sentimental 'feel-good' and an image of social progress but is an unwarranted distortion of the word's proper meaning.

Politicians and political language have followed sentimentality in shaping images and defining policies. In the process they have caused much collateral damage to language and society. Political discourse now uses words primarily to sell policies, not to conduct arguments. Phraseology is chosen for its persuasive value rather than for its relevance. Punchy slogans and sound-bites are the currency, and if the choice of words does violence to language, so be it. Striving for comprehensibility does not always require simplification — clearer language will usually suffice. Too often, however, exegetical clarity is sacrificed to sloganising and forced simplification which not only emasculates thought but also to a great extent determines how we see things. Modern politics has more to do with advertising than with argument, and its language reflects that trend.

The preferred style of speech — one cannot call it debate — is stark and in presupposing the response invites neither reflection nor dissent: you are either 'with us or against us', 'in Europe but not ruled by Europe', accepting of the 'axis of evil' or an ally of terrorism, 'in favour of multiculturalism or against it'. This is the language of 'yes' or 'no' polling and mutual exclusivity. Such crude dichotomies, with their easy, implicit answers, pre-empt fuller discussion of the underlying issues, which are rarely so clear-cut. Where they are discussed, compromise solutions suggest that one can embrace both positions without contradiction: individual liberty can be preserved and enhanced without compromising social justice and responsibility; national loyalty and integrity are compatible with supra-national allegiances; multiculturalism can flourish in a truly integrated society, etc. Politicians can also do the impossible: increase spending on a deficit budget without increasing taxation; support free-trade and protect home industries; deliver better education without streaming or testing. In the European debate, genuine fears about erosion of sovereignty from the transfer of powers from national governments to Brussels have prompted some spectacular political linguistic conjuring tricks; for instance, the concepts of 'pooling' or 'sharing' sovereignty are routinely used to imply that sovereignty can be ceded to the EU whilst being retained by member states. This is complete nonsense — whoever has the final decision on a matter has *de facto* sovereignty over that matter. The words used are deliberately chosen to try and convince voters that sovereignty is therefore not being eroded. The usual addition of the phrase 'in the general interest' or something similar, gives the lie to the intended significance.

It is considered heretical to question the value of democracy, justice and freedom — at least when it comes to their imposition on countries which are not regarded as well governed. If they were ever truly in the race, benevolent dictatorships and alternative forms of law religion and social structures never leave the starting gate. This rigid political language invites the belief that problems and their solutions are reducible to simple, pithy alternatives, and that it is inappropriate to suggest otherwise.

Sentimentality is finely exemplified in language which is steeped in feeling and attitude but which is short on fact and relevance. In its desire to be 'caring' and 'sensitive' it rigorously avoids moral judgement, and in seeking to put feeling and sentiment at the heart of discourse claims to champion personal 'rights' and self-expression and to be the guardian of self-esteem. This makes dispassionate debate difficult, as to attack a position is immediately seen as an assault on the holder, a personal insult or violation of their right to self-expression. Absurdity, irrelevance and sheer nonsense share equal standing with well thought out opinion and sound reason. Sentimentality is corrosive of reason and decent debate, and occupies one end of a continuum at the other of which stands Political Correctness.

POLITICAL CORRECTNESS

One of the most dangerous products of modern life is Political Correctness. This comes as near to true Orwellian 'Newspeak' as one is likely to get in the real world. By 'black-listing' words, phrases or subjects which are considered inappropriate, the hope is that these will be erased from public discussion and, thereby, ultimately, from public and private consciousness. The impetus behind PC comes both from neo-liberal sentimentality which sanctifies self-esteem and decrees that no one should be stigmatised, and from a desire to avoid doing or saying anything which might conceivably cause distress—however slight the offence or over-sensitive the offended. This is not confined to matters of opinion but covers incontrovertible fact as well. A man may, as a matter of fact, be black, Muslim, imbecilic, old, fat or crippled, but one is discouraged from saying so, at least not in that precise language. (This can lead to absurdity, as in one case reported where someone was rebuked for using the word 'fat' to describe their assailant to the police.) Acceptable terms in which to convey such respective information might be: afro-Caribbean, a follower of Islam, intellectually impaired, senior citizen, clinically obese or disabled. Even this last is now the subject of revision, as witness the Assistant Secretary of the US Civil Rights Administration's request that people: "avoid using phrases such as 'the deaf', 'the mentally retarded' or 'the blind'. The only exception to this policy involves instances where the outdated phraseology is contained in a quote or a title, or in legislation or regulations; it is then necessary to use the citation verbatim".

The US National Federation for the Blind commendably took exception to such nonsense and passed a resolution to the effect that 'this euphemism concerning people or persons who are blind—when used in its recent trendy, politically correct form—does the exact opposite of what it purports to do since it is overly defensive, implies shame instead of true equality, and portrays the blind as touchy and belligerent; and WHEREAS, just as an intelligent person is willing to be so designated and does not insist upon being called a person who is intelligent and a group of bankers are happy to be called bankers and have no concern that they be referred to as persons who are in the banking business, so it is with the blind--the only difference being that some people (blind and sighted alike) continue to cling to the outmoded notion that blindness (along with everything associated with it) connotes inferiority and lack of status; now, therefore, BE IT RESOLVED by the National Federation of the Blind in convention assembled in the city of Dallas, Texas, this 9th day of July, 1993, that the following statement of policy be adopted: We believe that it is respectable to be blind, and although we have no particular pride in the fact of our blindness, neither do we have any shame in it. To the extent that euphemisms are used to convey any other concept or image, we deplore such use. We can make our own way in the world on equal terms with others, and we intend to do it' (US National Federation of the Blind, Resolution 93–01).

In this case twisting language to prop up sentimentality backfired. Those who are on the receiving end of such machinations (disabled, gay, black, poor, etc) often claim that standard language somehow removes their dignity. For example: "I'm never really seen as a full human being, with dignity and with a right to be who I am. People look at me and turn away or feel sad for me. I experience those discriminatory attitudes every day. Yet, I am proud of who I am and I wouldn't want to be any different." The real answer is that dignity comes from within, and those who are nervous about their position as a result of being visibly unusual are likely to be treated differently as long as they react abnormally. This is not to say that abuse and disadvantageous discrimination should not be the subject of regulation, but that reacting to every nuance of sensitivity by restrictive decree and linguistic contortion, rather than by education and gentle persuasion, fundamentally changes nothing and probably does more harm than good. People with two heads, or none at all, will continue to be stared at, however much correct politicians tinker with the linguistic niceties.

Deborah Cameron's notion that 'political correctness is largely an invention of its enemies' (*Verbal Hygiene*, quoted by John Humphrys, *Lost for Words*, 2004), is well wide of the mark. On the contrary, the reality is that those who finger and ridicule PC are not conjuring up an imaginary political movement—an aunt sally they can then knock down—but rather exposing the folly of dealing with sensitive issues in a maladroit manner. The British teacher who suggested, in all seriousness, that the term 'failure' be replaced by 'deferred success' might be protecting her pupils' sensitivities in the short term, but only at the expense of disillusionment and crushing reality later on. It also reinforces the point that those whom PC prescriptions are designed to protect are often disadvantaged and generally not helped by positive discrimination—to which the US Federation of the Blind's response is an admirable testament.

Those who champion the more extreme manifestations of political correctness not only discredit themselves but also damage social and political life. Riding roughshod over common sense for the majority to provide spurious protection for an allegedly offended or oppressed minority indicates massive collective insecurity and does no-one favours. It also exposes the crassness of the petty political mentality which supports such thinking and says more about the wretched state of a society than legions of underperforming schools or inadequate social services.

There is also an element of stupidity involved in the belief which underpins all this, that by manipulating language you also change attitudes. Confusing titles with descriptions turns 'Chairmen' into 'Chairs' or 'Chairpersons', and 'Spokesmen' into 'Spokespersons'—originals which should rightly offend no-one. The absurd becomes farcical and dangerous when a municipal functionary is dismissed as racist for stating that his department's budget is 'niggardly'.

The justification of much political correctness turns on sensitivity. What is at issue here is the extent to which it is reasonable to take offence at being called blind, black or a Chinaman. In America breaches of PC are often referred to sensitivity counsellors, whose job it is to re-programme the offender's behaviour to improve their sensitivity to whichever group they are supposed to have offended. An example from the USA illustrates this kind of PC: 'Cindi Laws said yesterday she plans to go through sensitivity training in light of recent remarks she made about Jews. After a sleepless night and waking up to newspaper accounts detailing her comments to labour leaders that Jewish property owners donated much of the anti-monorail money in last year's unsuccessful monorail-recall campaign, Laws called Rob Jacobs, regional director of the local Anti-Defamation League. Her call roused him from sleep. They talked about setting up some sort of anti-bias training for her and her campaign staff ... Laws made her comments about money from Jewish property owners ... after being asked to assess her election opponents. Laws' leading challenger for the board seat, Beth Goldberg, a county budget analyst and a monorail opponent, is Jewish. Laws said a Jewish candidate could "get that money more easily", according to notes taken by one of the union officials at the interview'. (www.seattletimes.nwsource.com—August 20th 2005). The sense of balance and reasonableness are what should be offended by the idea that the mere mention of Jews—in what appears to be a positive comment—should lead anyone to even consider 'anti-bias' training.

Sentimentality aims promote inclusiveness, and in pursuit of this has sustained Political Correctness, especially in cases where people show themselves apparently incapable of distinguishing religion from religious bigotry, or race from racism. This means that discussion of many social, racial or religious issues is hampered by the inadmissibility of much of the language in which it might be conducted. Minorities have seized on this to suppress debate and advance their cause. In Britain, constitutionally a Christian country, the drive for inclusivity has meant that Christianity is no longer the preferred religion of state education. As PC requires that all faiths are recognised and catered for on equal terms, what religion there is in public schools is reduced to 'but a pappy amalgam of neutral morality designed to include all faiths, however cracked and misguided; if the Almighty appears at all, he does so simply as a "good, democratic, guy"'. (George Walden, *The New Elites*, 2000).

Politically Correctness has a positive as well as a negative glossary. Making something 'user-friendly' or 'empowering' and being 'supportive', 'caring' or 'radical', is encouraged—indeed, you are almost as likely to hear such phrases from liberal modernists or 'with-it' ministers in Church pulpits, as from secular sources. Political language has readily cross-fertilised with business and military jargon, cliché and simile: 'thinking out of the box', being 'on message', 'taking concrete steps', 'drawing a line in the sand', 'having an 'agenda', 'moving forward or 'following a road map', is considered positive and progressive. Politicians like to use phrases which suggest positive qualities, peppering their speeches and writings with references to 'the many not the few', 'forward-looking thinking', 'transparency, openness, accessibility' and 'comprehensive frameworks'. Such dynamic language, once unpacked, generally amounts to little more than verbal froth. The reality is that impressive words are rarely followed by commensurately impressive actions, and the subsequent delivery failures result in reduced credibility and increased cynicism.

Language is further debased by changing the meaning of words or by using them in inappropriate circumstances. Political and business language is full of euphemisms, either to disguise the truth or to avoid saying anything significant whilst appearing to have done so. People who tell us that something (usually mundane) is 'awesome', rarely know the meaning of the word, and one should beware of politicians who tell us that an initiative is 'radical'—this sounds innovative and progressive but usually portends something likely to be unacceptable. The idea that identity cards should be 'universal' means simply that they should be compulsory. These examples illustrate how less than direct language can be used to take the sting out of unpalatable realities.

Those who deliberately select words to obscure or disguise the truth would doubtless like to spin themselves as merely modern exponents of the ancient art of rhetoric, rather than systematic practitioners of deceit. The two are, however, very different. Rhetoric works on the basis that words are chosen less for the sake of their meaning than for their impact. Sermons and political speeches often consist of little more than inspirational phrases tacked together—including plenty of positive buzz words—rather than concise arguments or expressions of clearly defined thought. The supreme masters of the art were the ancient Greeks who considered that rhetoric, which developed from the oral traditions of transmitted history and wisdom, should be judged by its effect on the audience rather than by its correspondence with the facts. In contrast, modern political spin, re-arranges facts to mask the truth or obscures it in woolly but fine-sounding verbiage. Spin may sometimes indeed be rhetoric, but, more often than not, borders on the dishonest. The two should not be confused. Spinning spin is at least an admission that the practice exists—but no less self-delusional than spinning, *tout court.*

Language is also a weapon in the drive towards inclusiveness, in that any expression or sentiment that might recognise elites or reinforce elitism is disfavoured. The principle of inclusiveness, it is felt, is incompatible with the existence of elites. In truth, they are entirely compatible. One can have elites without saying anything about birth or compromising inclusiveness; indeed, elites are remarkably robust and continue to flourish, whatever the rhetoric, even in aggressively egalitarian states. However, whilst elites are recognised and accepted, what is considered inappropriate is to admit it. The PC Image may trumpet a kind of superficial equality, but the Reality is that social systems can only function effectively on hierarchy and inequality.

Languages are not static. New words arrive to reflect new ideas and inventions, and usage evolves to reflect circumstances. This subtle mutability must not be seen as justification for infinite linguistic flexibility; the edges may be fluid, but the core should remain stable. The deliberately false use of language — where words used in one way are intended to be understood in another — both creates and sustains misunderstanding. Sloppiness relegates what should be the common currency of meaning to a hit-or-miss branch of personal language where words lose much of their relevance beyond the speaker's imagination. Excessive linguistic licence muddies argument and frustrates successful communication. Too often, effort is wasted arguing about words and concepts rather than using them to debate real issues. Using words is as much a moral action, with moral consequences, as any other action. Unfortunately, there is no law against language abuse, so those who deliberately misuse and distort it are unlikely to be brought to account for their mischief.

The trend against linguistic standards and conformity is driven by the erroneous belief that allowing people to express themselves in whatever way they choose encourages freedom and enriches life. On the contrary, the rules and conventions of language provide the framework within which complex discourse and inventive imagery can flourish. In this, paradoxical as it may seem, a tight linguistic discipline liberates rather than limits.

The power of language to promote superficiality and half-truth, and thereby to influence attitude and behaviour, is thus considerable. There is no doubt that it is a significant weapon in modern political and social life. It has not quite attained the state of liberal-authoritarianism where 'words mean what I choose', but in some instances it is not far off, and the trend is, if anything, accelerating.

Wittgenstein observed that 'the limits of my language are the limits of my world'. This is not entirely true, in that it discounts the possibility of non-linguistic thought. Nor, as it might initially seem, is he advocating linguistic laxity. Rather, this is a plea for diversity and the thrust of the aphorism remains broadly correct — by limiting a language you limit its descriptive potential and thus the richness of experience. What is clear is that the misuse and distor-tion which accompany linguistic freedom impoverish language and destroy its expressive value. In a mere couple of generations English usage has been transformed from a landscape of *matières nobles*—finely-crafted paragraphs and sentences embellished from a rich, expressive vocabulary—into a desert of staleness and imprecision. What Wittgenstein rightly sought was to preserve and extend this nobility.

CHAPTER 4

PERSONAL IMAGE AND PERSONALITY

'There are no other swindlers to the self swindlers and with such
pretences did I cheat myself'
Charles Dickens, Great Expectations

The need to belong is one of the most powerful human impulses, and rejection and the fear of rejection are strong primary drivers of attitudes and behaviour. Recent research into the phenomenon confirms that social exclusion damages more than self-esteem. It significantly reduces both the speed and accuracy of mental processes, such as intelligent thought and those involved in logic and IQ tests, and increases aggressive and self-defeating behaviour (Baumeister, R. F., Twenge, J. M., and Nuss, C. K. 'Effects of social exclusion on cognitive processes: Anticipated aloneness reduces intelligent thought'. *Journal of Personality and Social Psychology*, 83, (2002); also Twenge, J. M., Catanese, K. R., and Baumeister, R. F. (2003) 'Social exclusion and the deconstructed state: Time perception, meaninglessness, lethargy, lack of emotion, and self-awareness.' *Journal of Personality and Social Psychology*, 85)

Given the power of rejection, it is not surprising that people make considerable physical and psychological efforts to avoid it. Being sidelined by one's social peers is the converse of high-status and, of all the negative aspects of social life, among those of greatest and most durable impact. Rejection inflicts damage to personal image and self-esteem, the more so from someone we love or respect. The fact that it is often impersonal or based on false information makes little difference and whilst time tends to heal personal setbacks, social rejection is less easily overcome. Unfortunately, the advancement of meritocracy makes it a more frequent occurrence. If progress depends on merit, then those who fail to advance are deemed, by default, as it were, failures or losers. In older, traditional societies, where social status was largely determined by birth or occupation and the chance of advancement by one's own efforts was limited, being at the bottom of the social pile carried no sense of rejection. Indeed, there was both social and personal dignity attached to ordinariness and low rank, provided you did not fall further by laziness, drunkenness or disgrace. Whatever the level, everyone had both a place and the respect due to it. Now, with considerably greater opportunities for economic and social mobility, failure to improve yourself is seen as signifying that you have not made the requisite effort. Such implicit rejection has long-term consequences both for the individual and for society, although there are many who regard the generally accepted criteria for success—in particular the accumulation of wealth—as a distorted perspective on what should matter in our lives.

Avoiding rejection is but one end of a continuum which covers inclusion and status, and is one of many components with a role to play in determining social standing. The interface by which we are able to gauge and manipulate this is Image. This encompasses both our idea of ourselves (our status as we perceive it, together with self confidence and self-esteem), as well as the way we assess and interact with others. To some extent, our social image is a function of our personality and is increasingly seen as a barometer—a crude but ready measure of personal standing in the family or wider community. In more affluent societies, people spend considerable time and resources to achieve what they regard as the 'right' image and are image-conscious in a way in which those from less developed societies are by-and-large not. However, whereas personality is likely to have a significant inherited component, our image in society is not something that is gifted to us but is created as a reaction to social encounters. Unlike personality, it is thus not static but flexible, within limits, and subject to constant subtle adjustment.

It is only with the spread of affluence that Image management has really become a factor in wider social behaviour. Not only do we now have greater ability to express individuality through choices which were not available to most in the 1950s, let alone the 1850s, but also changes in social structures, particularly the erosion of rigid class distinctions and greater social mobility, mean more opportunities for personal progress. This contrasts with past generations: early photography recorded the lower and middle classes who were less trammelled by concerns of self-image and, of necessity, uniform, with similar living conditions and expectations that were unlikely to change much during the course of a lifetime. Now, people are more self-conscious and strike a pose, not only for the cameras, but for society in general. The external trappings of Image play a central creative role in the social sphere and we use them to considerable effect.

The real interest in the social aspects of Image is not so much for what they say about the way we view things, other people and events, but the information they divulge about society and ourselves. This chapter is concerned with the ways Image interacts with society—the way individuals use it to manipulate how they are seen or to further personal objectives, and how others interpret and deal with these self-images. It also observes the role of groups, which employ image-manipulation to heighten their appeal, and stereotypes which entrench what in essence amount to little more than irrational caricatures. The more images fail to reflect personalities, the more insecure their value as a means of evaluation. Where once upon a time what you saw was what you got, nowadays we need to be more aware of image-manipulation and to give much more careful scrutiny to what we are invited to accept or believe, whether it be as consumers, voters or simply as observers of our fellow citizens.

In general, our attitude to people is an amalgam of (a) our desires and expectations, (b) any formal role or status they may have (father, doctor, boss etc), and (c) their behaviour towards us. From these we infer such qualities as trust, honesty and reliability. From our earliest years, we learn to tailor our responses to the way others treat us and react in ways which reflect both conditioning and also our perceptions of the roles people play. We then factor this information into our character evaluation of those with whom we come into contact.

Initially, our reactions are more instinctive than learned—for example we react with fear to people who look frightening (e.g. men with long, grey beards or piercing stares)—but in time come to appreciate that outward appearances are not always a reliable guide to internal character. Frightening-looking people may in fact be gentle and approachable, whilst apparently kindly people may often act in ways which are malign and should engender fear.

As we develop and become more socially aware, the categories into which we pigeon-hole people and the way we react to social encounters become more complex and refined. Considerations of pure childish self-interest give way to more co-operative strategies and Image comes to have a moral component which it previously lacked. We also become aware of ourselves as part of society and thus, to a greater or lesser extent, sensitive to the needs and emotions of others and to how we are seen by those around us. Some children are markedly more self-conscious than others, and the sensitivity levels set then are likely to remain for the rest of their lives.

As our social awareness develops, we take increasing account of abstract qualities such as desires and motives. Whilst crude physical attributes and simple behaviour patterns are relatively easy to classify and interpret, when it comes to assessing moral or emotive qualities, the task becomes considerably harder. Easy categorisations — e.g. kind, unkind, generous, mean, loving, unloving — present no great problems, but more recondite second-order virtuous qualities — loyalty, honesty, trustworthiness, diligence, reliability — are not worn on the sleeve, but have to be inferred from experience. Unfortunately, such empirical data are notoriously unreliable — signals are easily misread or misunderstood and people may behave out of self-interest rather than the altruism they would have you believe, manipulating their persona to disguise their real character. There is also the problem of repeatability: today's signals, even if they are correctly interpreted, are not necessarily a guide to tomorrow's behaviour.

What many regard as acceptable mild deception to bolster image and social worth can easily transform itself into systematic deception — often for unworthy motives. Confidence tricksters and magicians throughout the ages have flourished on the willingness of people to accept at face value whatever is presented to them. The stock-in-trade of the confidence trickster relies on an ability to accumulate trust to the point at which it is then easily abused. In such cases, skilled impression-management works, the deception succeeds, and the Image becomes the Reality. Smooth-talking operators, whether salesmen or self-promoters, find easy pickings among the gullible. Cynics, pointing to litanies of undelivered promises, might say that such is the basis of much political activity.

Social Images are not neutral facts. Like the appearance of an object, for example, they can be distorted and manipulated in a variety of ways to conceal underlying realities. The role of Image in social and personal life is not confined to the simple interpretation of signals and responses or even to the interplay between self-images and our images of others. The web is infinitely more complex. In most developed social systems, the image you project is a determinant of your social standing, so an ability to develop and project what you consider to be an appropriate image may help or hinder your progress. For many people mutual acceptance is all, and they are prepared to work hard to achieve it.

The projection of self is complicated by constraints imposed by social convention. The difficulty, a genuine one for any supposedly civilised society, is to find ways of balancing the demands of reality and free speech with the need to respect feelings of others. In routine social interaction, convention dictates that, in the interests of maintaining civilised behaviour and social harmony some feelings are suppressed or else circumscribed by an elaborate code of manners (and mannerisms). Such social diplomacy is considered an acceptable limit on freedom of expression; it often requires the avoidance of saying what is patently true or sanitising facts and opinions to accommodate others' personal feelings or sensibilities. This can significantly restrict the scope for image-making; for example, matters surrounding sexual relationships are deliberately guarded and, in many societies, talking about one's wealth (but, curiously, not the lack of it) is considered inappropriate. This effectively closes two major avenues for personal image projection, leaving these matters to be handled inferentially rather than explicitly.

Personal Image has three main contributing strands:

1. The Image we have of ourselves—our self-Image.
2. The Image we wish to project—perhaps those qualities we hope might be attributed to us in an idealised funeral eulogy.
3. The Image we actually project (although it is a derivative use of the term, I call this the 'Reality').

The interplay between these is the province of social psychology, whose business is to unpick the detail of social interaction and the mechanisms which govern it. What matters here are the broad relationships between these strands and, in particular, the ways in which individuals manipulate their image. It is interesting to note, in passing, that although people want to be loved and admired for their inner selves, they spend a great deal of time and resources trying to perfect—or at least to improve—their outer form by whatever means is most congenial to them: workouts, make-up, dress, etc. We regard physical appearance as a major determinant of Image in general, and sexual attraction in particular, and the evidence supports our instinct: according to one expert, fifty-five per cent of the impression we get from someone comes through our body language, thirty-eight per cent is from the tone, speed and inflection of our voice, and a mere seven per cent is from what we're actually saying. (Tracey Cox, *Superflirt*, 2003).

The image we have of ourselves is a composite entity—a composite of our own assessment of ourselves as we are—our core qualities and attributes, in short 'character'—and of how we consider we are seen by others. The former, however honest, may be mistaken because it generally lacks valida-tion, while the latter is mainly derived from information fed back from our daily social intercourse. Both need constant monitoring and evaluation, and this will only happen to the extent to which we are interested in the results.

If we don't care what other people think of us, we are less likely to tune in to those signals. Even when we do care, there is obviously considerable scope for misinterpretation — either from failure to read the signals because we don't pick them up in the first place, or else, having picked them up, because we misread their import. In general, we are notoriously bad at assessing our own character, something which is not helped by the reluctance of others to put the record straight (unless of course, like psychiatrists, they are paid to do so). Most people consider themselves as possessors of a range of positive qualities and admit few negatives. In fact, it is not always the big-ticket items (e.g. generosity and being good company) which most influence our externally perceived character, but often the presence or absence of subtler qualities — e.g. 'being a good listener' or 'being interested in other people's problems'. These are not always significant components of our own evaluation and thus can let us down; indeed we may not even be aware of their significance.

The need for both positive and negative feedback is critical to refining our self-image. This information comes from others' attitudes and remarks, and their willingness to trust or not, and their readiness to approach or not. The more we ignore, or worse, disdain this information, whether we are thin or thick-skinned, the less the potential accuracy of our self-evaluation. In reality, we are often badly mistaken. This is in part because others regularly 'pull' undesirable messages to spare our blushes, so unless we have some friendly, independent, information source, we are never likely to know what people really think of us and our self-image will remain an approximation. People who are selfish or arrogant tend to ignore or dismiss negative signals, whilst the more receptive are genuinely shocked to be told that they are rude, short-tempered or otherwise insensitive, and work hard to change their behaviour. Some simply try too hard — for example, to be 'nice' — and end up appearing weak, obsequious and ingratiating.

Into this complex tangle are inserted social decorum and self-restraint. These serve to protect both ourselves and others and to maintain social harmony. They constitute a quasi-public version of Freud's reality principle, which exerts control over the unbridled fulfilment of the pleasure principle by striking a balance between selfishness and what one might call social frankness. There is a strong need for social frankness as a mode of free speech, provided, of course, that it does not amount to gratuitous abuse. At a personal level, we have to decide as individuals what it is reasonable to say and to whom. The outcome of that decision will affect our projected image as others react to our behaviour. Some people are able to 'get away with' what would generally be considered rudeness or unacceptable conduct, whilst 'the same' behaviour in others is condemned. Thus what others expect of us individually is in part a function of how they see our personality.

There are two further pertinent observations on this theme: firstly, that honesty, for its own sake, is not necessarily beneficial—what remains unsaid is often as important as what is said, and the fact that something remains unsaid and is discovered later (e.g. acts of philanthropy) can powerfully affect personal image. Secondly, social actions often have functional explanations—that is, they are accounted for in terms of their effects and results; in this respect, some widely held beliefs (e.g. in honesty and integrity) may be counterproductive. Being honest may damage self-interest, or keeping promises may damage others' interests. Behaviour is largely a matter of self-policing in the general interest, and this is broadly co-terminus with what is referred to as conscience. Assessing what is right, appropriate, reasonable, fair and honest demands the establishment of a credible balance between competing values and interests. The decisions we make in this regard form part of our view of ourselves and, equally, of how we are viewed by others.

The Image we wish to project is at the heart of our social activity. 'One of things people need to do in their interactions with others is present themselves as an acceptable person: one who is entitled to certain kinds of consideration, who has certain kinds of expertise, who is morally relatively unblemished, and so on'. (Hugh Miller, Paper presented at Embodied Knowledge and Virtual Space Conference, Goldsmiths' College, University of London, June 1995). Here the emphasis is on positive attributes such as being kind, a good friend, sociable, charitable, good company, generous, plus the greater virtues of loyalty, duty, honesty, reliability, tolerance, trustworthiness and diligence. Projecting qualities that are not in our core character is hazardous, requiring concentration and considerable acting skills. For this reason it is unlikely to succeed beyond a limited time-span. We drop our guard for a moment, and the truth is out. This is not always a matter of deliberate behaviour—unconscious traits of body language are often the give-aways. The way we dress, move, talk, sit and look all play a major part in transmitting true character, over and above whatever we consciously say or do. Characteristics may conflict: for instance, people who affect reasonableness are traduced by their short temper (this kind of intolerance is a strong measure of character) and a more sober demeanour shines through forced joviality. Speech gives useful clues to attitudes and feelings: when, how and how much we talk, together with voice tone, accent and language, all contribute to the composite impression.

An important further consideration is that in the sphere of image projection ends do not always square with means. I may wish to project a certain ideal but choose an inappropriate means of doing so. Expensive, designer clothes are generally a sign of wealth and 'chic', but worn inappropriately—by the wrong person or in the wrong circumstances—they can also convey poor taste; telling people to trust you is often interpreted (correctly, in many cases) as a sign of untrustworthiness; men wearing prominent gold jewellery and talking of little else but money often convey an impression of flash cash rather than that of substantial wealth. So the means has to be appropriate to the person and also to accord with the desired values. It is also the case that explicit transmission of personal qualities is likely to be counter-productive; if you have resort to telling people you are wealthy, well-connected, intelligent or powerful, the chances are you are unlikely to be believed. The Image we aim to project is also the key to revealing character—for example, it is not always cynical to ask whether people who show an inordinate desire to do good act from true altruism or from other, more self-serving, motives (e.g. to obtain social recognition or community advantage).

The third strand of social Image-making is that of the Image we actually project, as distinct from that we either wish to project or think we project. Psychologist Erving Goffman, who worked and wrote extensively on this subject in the late 1950s and 1960s, portrayed social behaviour as a performance whose mainspring was impression-management. As he and other researchers—notably, Michael Argyle—demonstrated, normal social behaviour is a complex amalgam of desires, motives, intentions and acting; interactions of subtle and not so subtle cues. By and large, people seek to present themselves in a positive light, both as to character and intentions, and also as deserving of the usual consideration from others. This is not always easy, and so we have an armoury of resources which can be deployed to achieve the desired results. In particular, Goffman cites 'backstage' preparation as an aid in projecting an effective 'front'. He considers the minimisation of embarrassment as a major determinant of social behaviour—both by those trying to project an Image and by those they target, equally anxious to avoid public awkwardness. This requires a high level of interpersonal co-operation, which is usually—but not invariably—forthcoming. Goffman suggests that social cohesion is often maintained by a tacit conspiracy between those involved, which works to detect and deflect trouble.

His work also highlights the fact that the ostensible business of self-presentation is as much the subject of involuntary as of voluntary communication. He elaborated the seminal distinction between the impression that we *give*, which is largely conscious, and the impression we *give off*, which is unconscious (E. Goffman, *The Presentation of Self in Everyday Life*, 1959). Face-to-face interaction is suffused with a great deal of communication that is involuntary and subconscious. Some channels of communication are susceptible to voluntary control—e.g. movements, speech, gestures; others less so—e.g. eye-contact, small muscle contractions. There are therefore two separate information channels to encounters—the primary track which is its focus or purpose, and the secondary track which allows information to be leaked out, as it were, unwittingly. It is not that we cannot, in principle, control these subtler movements and gestures, but that being unable to focus on more than a limited number of actions at any one time, we normally fix on those which seem to us to have greatest impact, and these tend to be the most obvious. The less apparent, subtler aspects of communication (eye-contact, foot and hand movement, facial signals) are not well recognised and so tend to be ignored. Once you become aware that when and where you look at someone is a powerful indicator of interest, you are likely to pay it greater attention and strive to bring it under conscious control.

Body language is particularly interesting—and revelatory. Involuntary gestures, posture and fine muscle movements are subtle yet powerful conveyors of information. Studying eye-contact by filming interactions and then analysing them frame-by-frame shows that eye-movements follow a discernible pattern: when we look, where we look and for how long convey a mass of information to those able to interpret it. For instance, men tend to make eye-contact more when listening, whereas women do so more when speaking. Observing general body language provides fascinating insights into the realms of non-verbal communication, especially as indicators of second-order qualities, such as honesty, affection and interest. Most people are barely aware of their body language, let alone its significance, which makes it a more reliable information source than more direct expressions of attitudes and feelings. Bodies often transmit messages that are at variance with what we are saying; where there is a conflict, non-verbal signals tend to be the better indicators. The results of analysing these behaviours have been a useful aid in training negotiators and refining interview techniques. The signals are often subtle and require sensitivity and instruction to detect and interpret correctly. The fact that they are largely beyond conscious control makes it hard to sustain a radically false image — one which is truly out of character. Subtle non-verbal signals regularly conflict with what is being said or done at a more obvious level and thus have the capacity to destroy the image being projected. There is, nonetheless, a tendency to continue with contrived self-projections well beyond the point at which they have ceased to be credible.

It is these subtle, quasi-subliminal signals which most often give us away. Since they are almost impossible to harness, underlying character invariably shows through. Covey refers to this as the real self—'The constant radiation of what man is, not what he pretends to be' (Steven Covey, *The 7 Habits of Highly Successful People*). In identifying and codifying these subliminal signals, researchers have provided us with a language that is both coherent and reliable and a prime source for determining real feelings and intentions and a means of stripping social information from contrived Images.

Our self image is in almost constant assessment and evaluation, fine-tuned by feedback from both internal and external sources. These enable us to re-appraise our image and to adapt our behaviour where necessary. The extent to which one succeeds in projecting one's ideal image is, in part, dependent both on the signals sent being reliably interpreted by the intended recipients and on the absence (or ignorance) of discrepancies between those signals and the desired interpretation. In short, signals must be both accurate and coherent and correctly transmitted and received. Discrepancies will only be noticed by someone tuned to correctly interpret the relevant signals, attending to what are often fleeting phenomena at precisely the right moment. It is also clear that certain signals override others; for instance, many people are impressed by designer clothes, whoever wears them, and by expensive cars, whoever drives them, so whatever else they might signal may be ignored.

Social Images are thus no more than overlays, which accords reading core character a central role in personality evaluation. A constantly changing 'theatre' of presentations and our ability to disguise or hide real character traits makes this a fascinating challenge.

Pragmatism has always been an appealing philosophy, to avoid having to look beyond semblance to the reality — and indeed, points up the difference between words (which are cheap) and deeds (which require effort). Alternatively, we may subscribe to the Biblical adage, 'By your works shall ye be known'—or as St. Ignatius preferred it, 'Let your works be your deposits, that ye may receive your assets due to you'. While this may serve in many cases, it fails to distinguish primary from secondary qualities. Someone who donates heavily and publicly to charity has secondary goodness (one can't dispute the giving), but may lack primary (fundamental) goodness (one can question the motives). Examples are legion: the media mogul Robert Maxwell supported several good causes in Britain whilst robbing his firm's pension fund to keep his business empire afloat. Like him, it eventually sank.

Distorted self-images are responsible for much of the shallow pursuit of materiality. The importance of establishing an appropriate self-image matters to most of us and is deep-seated. Even the wealthiest feel a need to set and preserve their social status just as much as those less well-off. Only the most secure—some hereditary Monarchs and religious Prelates—have no obviously compelling need to prove their position. This is not to say that they will not engage in image manipulation, rather that such signals are unnecessary for establishing or enhancing it in the first place. Lesser Monarchs and insecure rulers tend to exaggerate the display of their possessions and 'honours' way beyond their possible needs (and often their country's means).

Once established, the images we have of ourselves and others have of us are relatively inflexible. Whilst there will be subtle adjustments and refinements, there is strong resistance to major change however compelling the evidence. From the individual's perspective, we maintain a broad brush-stroke self-image which is then adapted to suit a spectrum of personal qualities and social situations. For example, the image we project in the office would probably be out of place at home, and vice versa. (An unusual experiment some years ago monitored a group of youngsters who were instructed to behave at home as if they were lodgers; not surprisingly, abandoning the expected social conventions produced significant changes in family dynamics). These internalised perceptions are amalgams of ideals and our (often much distorted) take on reality, and we cling to them like limpets. They are highly resilient and can withstand buffeting. This promotes stability but may give rise to problems when we are confronted with evidence that clearly contradicts our self-set evaluation. Unlike scientists, who progress by adapting working hypotheses in the face of adverse data, we prefer to retain the conclusion and either dispute or ignore the evidence. The preferred self-deception is to disregard the facts—either by dismissing them as irrelevant or by admitting them only as exceptions. In other cases, people simply don't pick up the signals which come their way, and so remain in ignorance—which, at least, has some personal survival-value as a defence mechanism. In general, the feedback we get from society is restricted and limited by social convention. If people dislike us or find unattractive qualities, the usual recourse is to avoid contact, rather than telling the truth. Trying to reform someone is the province of religious leaders and zealous lovers; most people choose the easy option and back off.

From the third-party perspective, images of others are equally subject to minor alteration, but major re-appraisal only occurs when there is incontrovertible evidence that we have got it wrong. Even then, there is strong resistance to revision. Reaction to the revelation that the kind neighbour is a multiple murderer, serial womaniser or a spy is usually disbelief. Even incontrovertible evidence may fail to dislodge the fixed impression; 'I still can't believe it' confirms the uneasy struggle to square proven fact with conflicting impression.

The categories we use to evaluate ourselves and others determine how we see things, and are subject to individual whim and mood. They cover a broad spectrum of attributes from moral values (loyal), aesthetic values (handsome, ugly), non-personal values (wealthy) to more abstract status values (important) and diffuse societal / class values (working class). This offers scope for misreading, both because we simply fail to put the signals into the appropriate category or, more often, because of an insufficiently developed category set. Rather as someone with a richer sensory vocabulary is better able to describe a wine and differentiate it from similar wines, so a more elaborate evaluative language enables people to respond more sensitively to subtle personal differences which would be missed by a less acute observer. It is important to note that having a more refined and diverse category bank doesn't actually change what one is categorising—experienced and inexperienced tasters taste the same wine. This emphasises the fundamental point that perception is as much what the perceiver brings to the party as what signals are there to be interpreted. For instance, the Japanese apparently have seven separate words for wind. This doesn't make wind in Japan any more complex than wind in Java, but merely refines perception.

Social Image and Reality are thus effectively floating concepts, without any fixed reference. We cannot handle all the signals presented to us and, in making the necessary selection, do so on the basis of past experience of what is likely to be reliable, trustworthy or useful and on the categories which we have assembled over time as best suited to our needs and circumstances.

The categories are not themselves neutral—but have a pecking order which varies from individual to individual. For some, wealth and social position matter above all things—in the cult of celebrity, for example—and moral failings, whilst noted, have no great impact. For others, virtue and moral probity matter most, and social status has less importance. For yet others, achievement is critical—and wealth, moral probity and social standing take second place. So men of notable achievement who happen to have what some regard as questionable personal morals (for example, Bertrand Russell or Bill Clinton) may stand in high esteem in spite of their failings.

Self-image has both a long and short-term component. The former is more durable, both in its resistance to change and in its time-span; the latter is more akin to mood, which is well known to be subject to a variety of psychological and metabolic influences. We are constantly being encouraged—particularly by those hoping to sell us something—to 'feel good about ourselves', as if this body cream or that car will make the critical difference. There is the suggestion that how we feel about ourselves has a greater effect on our self-image than external appearance—for instance, the reflection we see in the mirror. Low self-esteem is ranked along with low morals. This mistakes the nature of self-esteem: firstly, it is incorrectly taken to be part of self-image when it is largely a consequence of that image; secondly, it is regarded as something that we can directly influence—when, in fact, it is determined by how we are seen by others and how they behave towards us. Unlike dress or manners, one's self-esteem is not under personal direction and it is mistaken to regard it as such.

Self-image has strong external resonances—particularly in Body Image. This is particularly true for women, who are assailed by an endless procession of sleek models and celebrities which leaves many feeling flawed. Confessional television programmes confirm how intolerant women are of a poor body image and their willingness to suffer discomfort to correct visible signs of ageing. Even the slightest imperfections can play on their mind and taint their enjoyment of everyday life to the point at which they resort to cosmetic surgery. Most women believe that much of their value lies in their appearance and are relatively impervious to positive feedback from husbands or partners. Dealing with physical self-image problems by surgery without addressing the psychological causes is unlikely to work. As one magazine writer explained: 'Most women ignore positive feedback on appearance and focus on negatives. Evidence suggests that people will often transfer their low body image from one feature to another (skin, hair, nose) if the underlying psychological causes are not resolved. Which goes to show that changing your body shape without changing your negative thoughts doesn't work'. (*Body Talk*, Summer 2004). There is no doubt that women are still powerfully affected by images they see of beautiful actresses and models, and that many mistakenly feel that their lives will be changed if they look and act differently. This message is reinforced by fashion elites and style gurus who never cease to plug cosmetic image as the route to personal fulfilment. This ignores the fact that long-term contentment comes from 'inside-out', not from 'outside-in'.

Men are also encouraged to worry about their looks, and to some extent suffer from the same insecurities as women. They are increasingly being lured by fashion and commerce to uplift their appearance. In this blurring of gender differences more men are now reported as buying fashion brands and a significant minority say they wouldn't buy anything else: very few (around 10%) consider themselves as a "fashion disaster", rather more (around 20%) thought they were "very good looking" while a majority (nearly 70%) admitted to buying clothes to cheer themselves up. There seems, however, to be growing disillusion with the idea that using brands and artifice to enhance your external image will also alter your underlying personality. People are disenchanted when they realise that this doesn't work and are turning to spirituality to escape the superficial tread-mill of fashion. It is unclear whether this means that people now care less about impressing others or have simply tired of trying to keep up with senseless trends. In any event, 'the body beautiful' appears to be ceding place to 'the soul eternal'.

Body images are often extended by valued objects such as cars, jewellery or clothes. These powerfully reflect personality. Aggressive men prefer large, angular, noisy cars and may dress in mock battle fatigues to further signal 'power'. Threatening postures and identifiable walking styles reinforce the self-image. The influence of objects, though sometimes less obvious, is no less potent—even bizarre. A recent study of Italian men indicated that loss of their mobile phone 'ruined' their lives—evidenced by reduced sexual appetite, increased short temper and diminished ability to socialise.

Much of the development and management of external self-image (how we perceive others as seeing us) is driven by personal insecurity. People who are, as the French eloquently put it, '*bien dans leur peau*' (content in their skin) are more secure and thus less in need to foster an image, whereas those who underperform go to great lengths to protect their fragile status. This obviously begs the question whether their security flows from a self-image which distorts reality less, or whether it reflects a genuinely greater security and therefore lessens the need to present a false image. A self-image will be sustainable, and probably beautiful, if it is natural and comes 'hard wired' into one's own persona. Contrived glamour is ephemeral and takes continuous guile to maintain, as the reality has an inconvenient habit of breaking through.

Some people are constantly 'posing'—replacing natural behaviour by acting out a false image. This not only requires considerable skill and effort (it is tiring to be constantly living a lie) but also takes determination. Posing comes in degrees—from the acting out of a completely false identity to those who bully others to hide their own inadequacies. A particularly interesting social exhibit is the serial wit: someone who regards himself as excellent company and seeks to maintain that image by means of an unstoppable flow of amusement. In fact, this has nothing to do with wit—which is a rare manifestation of sharp intellect—and everything to do with humour—which is the province of those who have little wit. These jokesters are often deeply insecure—immature adolescents who have not developed beyond their school-days. As one British wit [Jeremy Clarkson] observed: 'Repeating what has been said by someone previously means you are a Parrot—not a wit'. The 'endless joke' tactic usually backfires as the amusement soon palls and others feel excluded. It should not be difficult to appreciate that conversation is not stand-up comedy but an interactive process whose participants are unlikely to be satisfied by an endless jokes or monopolistic chatter, however funny or interesting. What is also noteworthy about compulsive jokers as a social type is that they are generally accorded high popularity despite the fact that their behaviour is often resented. The dissonance between the Image and the Reality reflects an unwillingness to break ranks in case your opinion is not shared. It is also a good example of a tacit conspiracy maintained in the interests of social harmony.

The degradation of self-respect is one of the major causes of poor self-image. In cases where we ignore evidence about ourselves, self-image becomes prey to self-deception. Social conventions expect behaviour to consider the acceptability of its consequences; this is the province of self-respect of which lack of 'self-control' is but one aspect. Failure to control one's impulses and inclinations may be regarded as a serious or a minor defect, depending both on one's moral stance and the consequences—killing is serious, adultery (perhaps) less so. Self-respect is compromised when one bypasses one's own values and standards in the name of expediency. Components of self-image are both conscious and subconscious; for example, it is clear that guilt plays a major role in attitude and behaviour.

Since we all have sides to our nature that we prefer not to reveal, concealment is one of the essential arts of image projection. Maintaining an image which one knows to be false generally stems either from a desire to attain some specific end (e.g. getting a job or impressing someone) or to camouflage personal inadequacies. Where the falsity is a matter of fact or record, it can be checked and the lie nailed. More subtle deceptions are less easily exposed. People who fail to make their desired image statement by force of personality often seek to deliver it by other means, such as visible props or personal fabrication. As we have seen, props often convey the opposite message to that intended and signal inadequacy rather than success. Fabrication—for example, of one's background or qualifications—may work, but it requires good acting to deceive others. It also requires self-deception, otherwise the illusion disintegrates rapidly. Major Pollock in Terence Rattigan's *Separate Tables* played out such a role, until he was finally rumbled (and humbled), but his pathetic predicament elicits sympathy from those he dupes. Spies and confidence tricksters are generally not as fortunate. In some cases, years of living a lie results in internalising the image and the lie becomes the truth. In the current climate, blatant personal fabrication is often brushed off, at least where public figures are involved, but in closer relationships the response may not be so forgiving. In the end it is often not the short-term consequences of deceit which matter most but the long term fall out from damaged trust and credibility.

Insecurity is widespread and a major driver of self-Image. It comes from the almost universal need for social approval and from an equally strong wish to conceal personal inadequacies. The desire to manipulate one's image to counteract a perceived lack of popularity or to promote status is largely irrational. This is both because the perception is often faulty and because, even if it is correct, changing the externals is unlikely to have the desired effect. The belief that appropriate artifice can increase your popularity or status is firmly entrenched in people's psyches, so the fact that any such effort is probably wasted doesn't stop them making it. Often, the means selected are inappropriate: buying designer clothes or throwing lavish parties are more likely to result in envy or derision than increased popularity or status, and any change in personal standing is likely be transitory or disingenuous. Popularity comes from emotive responses to core personality and it is only by changing our inner selves that we can engineer durable changes in attitudes towards us. We may have difficulty in accurately assessing our own standing and worth, but we have an uncanny ability to spot a fake or poseur, which no amount of ostentatious display can disguise.

Personal insecurity often uses subtler signals than plain acting. Pretending to be something else is all-or-nothing with no halfway house, whereas insecurity is a continuum—some people are mildly insecure, others ragingly so. Extreme cases are relatively easy to spot: often evidenced by trappings such as large cigars, ostentatious cars, the need to shop incessantly or to acquire the latest fashion accessory, or by relentless name-dropping. As Dickens observed: 'In the great social exhibition, accessories are often accepted in lieu of the internal character' (*Little Dorrit*).

For many of society's insecure, the primary image prop is money—they need to be seen spending lavishly. The secondary props are the goods and services that money can buy. The ultra-wealthy are among some of the most insecure and, money apart, their principal prop is power—whether exercised directly by issuing orders which they expect to be obeyed, or indirectly through withholding or granting favours. In parts of the USA, in particular, where opulence and lavish spending are commonplace, the ultra-wealthy are driven to find means of differentiating themselves from the merely affluent; hence the thriving trade in rare, exotic pets, yachts and the like.

It is interesting to ask why, if money brings security, the wealthy are so often highly insecure. Their reliance on props to do what their personality cannot, or at least to bolster it, suggests a belief that these actually work which points up an answer to the apparent paradox. Part of being insecure is not being confident that the status you feel society owes you is in fact being delivered, so you look to reinforce the message with ostentation. Another part of the answer is that the self-confidence of insecure people diminishes when they are not the subject of attention and being unable to attract it outside their immediate circle of influence they resort to gratuitous show and spending as a talking point to replace their shortcomings. It is also pertinent to ask why, since wealth in itself so often fails to make it possessors fulfilled or contented, people devote so much of their energies to acquiring it. The equation is: money = all I want = contentment = security and freedom from worry. This has superficial plausibility but is based on a false understanding of happiness and a flawed perception of security. The false understanding is the idea that limitless material goods somehow bring happiness and the flawed perception is that inner security is obtainable by external means. These, as the hymnist portrayed them, in somewhat extreme terms, are 'spirits oppressed by pleasure, wealth and care'.

Security is to be distinguished from self-confidence. The line between them is fine, but in general people who are insecure do not necessarily lack self-confidence. Many of the most forthright, brash go-getters are highly self-confident, yet remain highly insecure. The difference lies in the effects of adversity. The insecure maintain their position by a fine balancing act which is easily upset; true self-confidence is far more resilient to reverses and more able to handle criticism. Insecure and apparently self-confident people dislike criticism and deploy considerable fire-power first to suppress it, and then to ignore or dismiss it if it comes too close. People who are truly secure are generally less concerned with their image than those who are not. Not that they don't care about how they behave — in fact they are often sensitive to a fault — but that they are content with their situation and see no need for artifice to enhance it. Their bicycle may not be high-tech but it works and is comfortable.

Having positional power, money or status helps but it is not the whole story, as one sees insecurity at all levels of society. It afflicts the high-status and super-rich as much as — if not more than — those struggling to make ends meet. Although fawning popularity comes readily to those at the top, having wealth or status does not mean that you are genuinely liked. So it is that even the wealthiest and most powerful feel themselves to be insecure — although they would not perhaps recognise or describe it in these terms — and are driven by ever stronger social ambition. One noted socialite, with access to almost limitless wealth yet remained dissatisfied; her desire to compete with the mega-rich of the USA became an obsession and she was reported as spending fortunes in pursuit of this goal — a $2,500 handbag, $53,000 holiday, private jets, butlers, chefs and several homes. She explained her status anxiety by a childhood embarrassment over a dress, but it is difficult to see in any such incident the seed which matured unchecked into a social ambition that was capable of powering such extremes of extravagance.

Business has long exploited personal insecurity. Directories of 'Important People' give the less secure the idea that they have been independently selected as people of note, and trade on the perception that inclusion makes them part of some kind of elite. The reality is a hard-nosed commercial enterprise in which inclusion has nothing to do with social status. Exclusivity is another means of overcoming personal inadequacy. Exclusivity based on money makes people feel good and even important but has no real bearing on status; ability to pay is not a determinant of social worth, and 'exclusive' hotels, 'clubs' and the like are nothing more than unsubtle cash filters. Indeed, ostentatious luxury raises question about the priorities of its consumers, who are often derided as having 'more money than sense' by those who may indeed be envious. Money, or more accurately, what money can by in terms of goods, patronage and privilege, undoubtedly confers influence, but this must be distinguished from personal qualities. Anything for which the sole requirement is cash has, *ipso facto*, only extrinsic value and no amount of the former will transform the coarse, boorish or dull into social swans. Wealth, by itself, has only a limited claim on society.

Image management, however skilful, is constrained by human frailty. In particular, it must co-exist with the reality that perception is imperfect — we cannot handle all the signals we receive, so we have to decide where best to concentrate our available processing capacity. This means that we often miss what is important or misinterpret what we see or hear. Even at a simple descriptive level, we are not reliable observers. Experiments in which a strikingly dressed actor walked through a university classroom showed that many of the intelligent students present were unable to answer straightforward questions about what he'd been wearing. If correctly describing simple colours and shapes presents perceptual / memory problems, it takes little to appreciate the scope for misinterpretation when subtler cues are involved. Failure to deliver the Image we intend and misreading the intentions of others are the cause of much social difficulty.

Properly directed attention is therefore critical to assessing social signals. As recipients, what we perceive is strongly influenced by our needs and interests, both in the sense that we naturally concentrate on the facets of someone else's image which particularly concern us and also because we use our cognitive faculties in an active role to filter out what we deem irrelevant or unpalatable. As transmitters, we aim to focus others' attention on the positive parts of the images we produce. We also tend to see what we want to in others and to evade what we dislike (we may see it and ignore it, or not see it at all): lovers are notoriously blind to each other's flaws, signals of dubiety are frequently ignored in personal or business negotiations, and consumers fall for the blandishments of salesmen into blotting out reasons 'why not' and buying products known to be unsuitable.

Deception is achieved as much by actions as through words. Lies are built into lives and relationships—and we even lie to ourselves to escape from the less pleasant realities of debt, friends, work, sex and much else. Thus, power dressing is intended to create an image of authority and status, while physical embellishments such wigs and false eyelashes disguise the more obvious depredations of age. The image industry exists to realise whichever impression we decide suits us—lies on credit. Deceit is often subtle, implicit rather than explicit, as when someone leaves an abstruse book in view to give the impression that they are reading it. Lies abound—even in architecture where *trompe l'oeil*, false beams and ceilings, and other pastiche fakery substitute illusion for reality.

Striving for a better image has led many into the hands of modern image consultants. This cluster of disciplines forms a surrogate branch of the social sciences, underpinned by some highly questionable theory. Armed with jargon and a veneer of academic respectability, these people will teach you how to flirt, dress, date, interview, and generally present yourself to maximum advantage. No doubt they are capable of refining gross social ineptitude but where personality transformation is concerned their client's real character is bound to surface eventually—shattering the illusion with reality. Image-transformation practitioners at least have the dubious comfort of knowing that their expertise is becoming ever more fashionable.

The desire to pursue personal image and social success beyond the comfort zone has been driven by a massive rise in consumerism that has formed many of the models which people strive to imitate. It has also brought more envy into the range of emotions self-image can be used to stimulate. As the business of self-advancement often ignores the rights and sensibilities of others, these trends have often been at the expense of respect and traditional values. People are too busy scrambling up the ladder of success to concern themselves with who they trample on the way. The idealised image of 'cool' does not encompass respect for third parties—it means doing and having what you want, when you want it. The aggressive, impatient society has diminished consideration for others, a trend reinforced by governments who seem increasingly obsessed with free-enterprise and moral liberalism, and consequently reluctant to enforce standards where individual behaviour conflicts with social obligation.

There is a wider social component of image: namely that related to groups and stereotypes. Societal groups acquire and disseminate their own images.

These depend, to a certain extent, upon the categories used to evaluate individuals and groups, and can become a source of tension and even conflict in many societies. Groups, like individuals, have social identities and in similar fashion seek to manipulate their image for collective social or political ends. They can be formal (political parties, religious denominations or airline pilots) or informal (single parents, retirees or old-age pensioners); they can be logical—for example, defined by profession (actors or police officers) or ad-hoc—for example defined by common interest (train spotters or model car collectors) or by loose allegiance (anti-abortionists or war protesters). Modern social arrangements encourage people to form groups to gain legal recognition, financial advantage or other privileges. This has a normative effect as social policy is increasingly made on the basis of the pressure that such groups can muster. If you are a single-mother and thus in receipt of special benefits in recognition of your supposed needs and status, then you are expected to conform to the group norms of single mothers, whether you agree with them or not. However, the fact of being a single mother does not necessarily mean that you share the social or political views of those who lobby for their special treatment. Those who do not to belong to any defined group, find their social needs less likely to be adequately met. In many cases, a group's identity is held together by no stronger glue than an amalgam of grievances.

The emergence of defined interest and lobby groups, and the public identities they have managed to forge for themselves, has shifted the focus of social reform from concern with the individual to concern with the group. Minorities with a suitably high-profile image are able to exert a disproportionate influence on social policy. Governments appear increasingly ready to bend to special pleading and to confer benefits on groups that can be identified with some collective need. This leads to expectations of assistance or recognition beyond what might generally be regarded as reasonable. For example, the demand from homosexuals for 'equality'—which was originally confined to eliminating job discrimination on grounds of sexual orientation—has been extended to include same-sex marriages, adoption rights, divorce, and parity of tax treatment with married heterosexuals. Redefining marriage to include the possibility of union between two men or two women turns the concept upside down and effectively reduces it to a matter of mere contract. This is rather like decreeing that henceforth all biscuits are cakes; perfectly feasible and arguably an administrative convenience, but essentially illogical. The spread of reverse discrimination to rebalance the presence of minority groups in employment or politics, for example, is a crude attempt to re-balance social inequalities on a basis of group identity rather than merit. Such artificial distortion is usually justified in terms of equality of opportunity or eliminating discrimination, when sense dictates that preferment should be a solely a matter of merit. This may help a political or group image, but puts undoubted pressure on individuals promoted above their capabilities and on organisations forced to live with their sub-standard performance.

Images also define stereotypes which, once acquired, are difficult to dislodge. National and occupational stereotypes abound: Jews are universally viewed as financially sharp and cliquish; used car salesman are seen as slick and not entirely honest; vegetarians are associated with woolly thinking, sentimentality and irrational environmental campaigns; Muslims tend to be guilty by association with international terrorism; Greeks and Italians are stereotypically friendly, lazy and incompetent and Italian men have an firm reputation as opportunist Casanovas. Jobs also have Image resonances—often identified with the tenor of their products: undertakers are generally portrayed as lugubrious, comedians as irrepressibly bright and breezy, doctors as enjoying perpetual good health, attorneys as prudent, and accountants as dull. These caricatures are generalisations and by-and-large false. They do, however, colour perceptions and provide a handy baseline for dealings of all sorts. It is unfortunate that national or group images are largely formed as the result of the behaviour or opinions of a high-profile minority (e.g. British football hooligans, Greek guides, or American tourists) and become too easily entrenched with repetition and, very often, through satire. The inductive inference from the minority to the majority is, of course, unjustified, but stereotypical images have reinforced our readiness to make it.

Societies themselves also have images, which transcend both individuals and groups. Most civilised societies like to present themselves as tolerant, humane, just, law-abiding, upholding of individual freedom and of civil liberties, and often multicultural. These images are often at variance with the truth. If you unpick, for example, multiculturalism—a currently fashionable, social, feel-good concept, you find that firstly that it rarely exists—in the sense of many genuinely different cultures cohabiting peacefully in one country; and secondly, that where it appears to exist—e.g. in Britain or the USA—it amounts to no more than ghettos of ethnic culture subsumed into a superficially tolerant, but otherwise awkward, social structure. This impression is strongly reinforced when one finds one group or another arguing for special treatment, either in terms of positive action to allow them privileged access to government or disproportionate air-time, or as the curtailment or removal of negative aspects of society which they find unacceptable. Some religious or social organisations make much of their support for free speech and their own right to criticise governments or others, but complain vociferously when they are on the receiving end. Those who question or criticise aspects of their creed may find themselves vilified; for example, many find Muslim doctrine on the education and role of women offensive, but to question it publicly is to invite condemnation as attacking the religion itself. Such irrationality means that much important political and social discussion, particularly in the areas of religion and race, is curtailed from sheer fear of reprisal from those who prefer summary justice to the rule of law. True toleration requires a reciprocity which is often noticeably absent.

The reality of tensions between different cultural groups is played down, for obvious reasons, but their existence becomes all to clear when loyalties or moral issues require public airing. How is a devout Muslim to square his allegiance to Allah with his allegiance to his non-Muslim country, when circumstances bring them into conflict? Having had an entirely different moral education to that of his host country, he is unable, honestly, to subscribe to its value system. More often than not, peer group pressures results in such conflicts being decided on the basis of religion. Encouraging ethnic minorities to retain their differences and celebrate their culture, makes many — especially youths — feel alienated from the mainstream. This is particularly true when the language of their religion differs from that of their country — so they are often limited in following religious instruction or debating issues within their cultural group. This identity and image tension creates profound individual stress and social difficulty. Alienation is another species of rejection which also leads to defensiveness and aggression.

The development of personal image clearly has an important social role. It is not just an interesting sideshow, whose phenomenology we observe with greater or less attention and whose micro minutiae are dissected by social psychologists. Image-making is one means whereby individuals and groups pursue social advantage in hierarchical societies where inequality is an essential element in their structure and functioning. It is to classes, elites and status that we turn in the next chapter.

CHAPTER 5

CLASS, ELITES AND STATUS

'Egotism is the anaesthetic that dulls the pain of stupidity'
Frank Leahy (Look, Jan. 10th, 1955)

'There is no merit in equality unless it be equality with the best'
John Lancaster Spalding (Quoted by John Honey, Language is Power)

'To consider our petty status-worries from the perspective of a thousand
years hence is to be granted a rare, tranquillizing glimpse of our own
insignificance'
Alain de Botton (Status Anxiety)

Class has a long and important social history. Within living memory, it was
accepted that the class you were born into was a strait-jacket from which
escape was virtually impossible. Now, although pockets of European aristocracy remain and there is still a sizeable manual labour force, the social
and economic dynamics of class have changed markedly. The post-war years
have seen the abolition of all but entrenched class distinctions and few now
hold humble origins against people. Social historians have dissected what
was seen as 'the class struggle' of working people against the bosses and
the more recent development of the meritocratic society. In parallel with
these changes, new money has replaced old money in the social stakes and
concern with class has been displaced by the scramble for status.

Old class bands (upper, middle, lower, working), were broadly functional;
that is, their usefulness was defined by the ends they served. These traditional
class distinctions helped maintain social order and community cohesion (you
'knew your place') and provided an element of stability and individual self-
confidence through shared values and opinions. Though these were blurred
by creeping egalitarianism and have now all but disappeared, the prospect of
upward social mobility has not. People still strive quietly to 'better' themselves,
as they see it, and though inflexible class-by-birth as a badge of intrinsic merit
and privilege is largely gone, 'the masses' still appreciate that a certain bearing,
manner and style of life marks those who are socially out of the ordinary.
Whilst personal aspirations may be limited to the second home or the new

three-piece suite of furniture, people know true class when they see it and often privately admire it, despite an avowed disdain.

Societies are now portrayed as egalitarian. This suggests, though doesn't strictly imply, a decreasing relevance of non-meritocratic social distinctions, including those of class. It is not intended to discuss here to what extent this has been achieved, but rather to show how, and how much, superficiality is integrated into social hierarchy, however this is described.

Whether or not classes exist as a matter of fact, they remain part of evaluative descriptions of society at many levels. Class talk has been superseded by the language of elites, where position in the hierarchy depends upon attributes such as power, influence, network and wealth rather than on bloodline or family connections. These are the new 'super-class' (Adonis and Pollard, *A Class Act*, 1997), and their influence, however disliked in some quarters, is beyond doubt.

It is against this background that one must consider the role of class as a factor in social behaviour. If any aspect of our social lives is affected by superficiality, it is that relating to our social status—often loosely referred to as class—and class mobility is a major component of social betterment. People talk less nowadays about moving 'up' or 'down' the social scale, but it is some such idea that lies behind efforts to 'get on in society'. It is therefore essential to understand class as it is now, as a prerequisite to understanding its relationship with personal image.

For social purposes, we find it convenient to pigeon-hole those with whom we have to deal in categories that reflect their perceived character and this within the social parameters that matter to us. We have a sharp eye for distinctions that allow us to behave and react to one another differently when we perceive there to be relevant differences of class or status. Whether with friends, close acquaintances or work colleagues, we need to fix their standing in our private world and in the wider social hierarchy, and to adapt our interactions accordingly. Equally, our desire to establish our own status in the social hierarchy leads us to note class differences and strive to emulate those traits we find desirable by whatever means we judge most likely to succeed. Thus we shape and crystallise our image of social status, and it becomes a more or less subconscious part of our persona.

Such categorisation is not always class-related, but provides an essential short-hand that enables us to predict others' behaviour and thus to fine-tune our own. Much of this is automatic—almost instinctive—and the process itself is continuously refined with experience. The particular ground on which we meet someone (socially, in the office, official function) automatically provides constraints which limit certain types of interaction. Once this is factored in, we use what we see and hear of their behaviour and demeanour to allocate them the appropriate class and predictive pigeon-hole. Such labels exert a strong influence on social behaviour, and especially on matters relating to status.

The social distinctions we make are affected by our own attitudes. For example, the belief that all farmers poison the land and are thereby anti-social, conditions our responses to farmers. Similarly, the impression that all members of Congress are important, high-status individuals will affect our demeanour should we come into contact with one, as might the more cynical view that 'politics and the fate of mankind are shaped by men without ideals and without greatness' (Albert Camus, *Notebooks*, 1935–1942). It is no accident that part of the durability of the traditional class system reflected the confidence that people were reliable — steadfast in their moral convictions and values, and honest and dependable in a way that is no longer the case. The 'free-for-all' of modern society has ushered in a distinct moral fluidity that has changed expectations. It is not surprising that the constant drip of prominent political, business and social malfeasance has diminished any belief in the integrity of high status and undermined respect for morality in general. Adonis and Pollards' 'super-class' 'have a self-Image of power, position and invincibility, which is not as widely shared as they might hope — they are regarded with suspicion, both as to their motives, which are seen to spring from self-interest above all, and to their morals, which are regarded as unacceptably flexible'. (Adonis and Pollard, op.cit.)

Class is more than the simple classification of individuals in society. The term — together with its close cognates 'elite' and 'status', are saturated with image-related overtones. We have our own perception, based on our private social classification, of where we stand in our own social circles and in society in general. To those who do not see class as an important factor in our lives, it becomes of relatively little interest. For many, however, class is of considerable concern — either because they need the prop of status to bolster their self-image, or else because they are looking to better their position and prospects and see upward social mobility as an expedient route.

Some are more sensitive than others to fine social distinctions and, indeed, to distinctions so fine that they over-specify reality. It is nonetheless clear that much of our normal social life is tinged with overtones that may cause image-related difficulties, not least because class distinctions are highly personal and our efforts to sustain our own self-determined status are liable to failure or discreditation.

Whether, and in what senses, classes exist is not the principal concern of this chapter. Nor is the purpose to debate whether societies are classless or not, although both issues will inevitably percolate into discussion about social superficiality. What matters is how the perception and language of class and status affects our self-image and how they impact on society in general. Because these perceptions, in the broadest sense, tend to be based on emotive rather than factual criteria, they carry a strong Image component.

Most evidently, our judgements about people are powerfully affected by context, at a barely conscious level. This is well illustrated by a simple, now classic experiment, in which researchers introduced two groups of subjects to other individuals and asked them to chat on a one-to-one basis, after which the subjects were interviewed about their perceptions. One group was briefed negatively on those they were to meet—they were primed with backgrounds of crime, irresponsibility, immorality, etc., whilst the other group was given positive profiles of these (same) people. Not surprisingly, the nature of the advance briefings materially affected how the subjects perceived those they talked to. If you are told that someone is a convicted murderer you are more likely to take a negative view of them than if you are led to believe that they spend their lives in altruistic charity work. These extreme examples illustrate the more general case that perception is deeply affected by both context and prior knowledge.

The general vulnerability of Image to contextual influence makes the issues surrounding class and status particularly fragile. With pre-established hierarchies—e.g. in the armed services, the law or a large corporation—there is no doubt as to someone's status and appropriate attitudes and behaviour are laid down for each level. For instance, you don't speak to senior officers, judges in court or royalty until they address you; this removes uncertainty and cements the hierarchy. In the wider world where hierarchies, if they exist at all, are less formalised, the relationship between positional status and actual status may differ. Thus, a manager may have status by virtue of his office or title, but if considered incompetent, he may lack it in personal terms. In the latter use, attributing status is a matter of judgement; in the former, it is not.

History has contributed to the classed society, which until relatively recently was virtually conterminous with social status. Over the centuries, ennoblement of those who aided Monarchs, and preferment for those who sustain the powerful in Church, Armed forces or the State, created *soi-disant* nobilities where there was often little natural nobility. Old European aristocracy, royalty, and American dynastic families continue to enjoy 'status plus' and to command limited respect, but the new elites have been tapping at their heels for decades, and well-publicised moral lapses have helped tarnish a hitherto unassailable image of native superiority. Earls and dukes are probably no less likely to get drunk, transgress sexually or otherwise disgrace themselves than they were in the past—or indeed than those without titles. The difference is now that the world knows about it in graphic detail the next morning, so peccadilloes are recorded and thus less easily shrugged off. (It is interesting to note that, while lapses by celebrities are usually tolerated, even lauded, rather than criticised, similar transgression by others of high status is often used to attack them). In recent times, preferment for purely political ends has weakened the class-by-birth component of social class. Nonetheless, the idea that class differences exist and that they matter is firmly entrenched and despite consistent and concerted attacks from many social reforming quarters, has deep roots that are not easily eradicated.

In Europe and to a lesser extent elsewhere, genuine aristocracy still exerts an indelible fascination. The public enjoys the history and mystery of great dynasties, great families and great wealth, the vicarious fantasy of lifestyles they can only dream of and the contact with history afforded by visiting the grand houses of the nobility and landed gentry. The fact that these people are as prone to moral failings and domestic upheaval as everybody else and that their misfortunes are paraded for public scrutiny adds spice to their appeal, and has undoubtedly removed an element of mystique. The old nobility may have been displaced by semi-literate celebrity, but the seemingly insatiable curiosity about them remains undiminished.

In general, popular class distinctions are derived from basic inequalities—whether of birth, wealth, health or education. These are sometimes based on fact—for example, people who live in grand houses in expensive neighbourhoods tend to be perceived and treated differently from those in less opulent circumstances—sometimes on subtler factors, often merely on whim. To the extent that class is in the eye of the classifier, social image and class are inextricably intertwined.

The concept of class as used by scientists to distinguish between social groups differs from the looser, more abstract idea of class employed by commentators and in general discourse. The former is derived from, and defined by, carefully prepared factual criteria and designed to aid understanding of how people behave, shop, vote, etc, and in this sense is designed to be value-neutral. Colloquial usage has no such factual underpinning and is capable of expressing strongly evaluative, often pejorative, sentiments.

Class also has residual political significance. In many countries politics and political movements have been persecuted on the basis of class-inspired policies. The French Revolution sought to eradicate the ruling aristocracy, and Marxism was entirely based on ideas about workers' rights and exploitation by the upper classes. In contrast, the social scientist rarely talks of 'the class war' or 'the classless society' and uses class measures merely as classificatory or heuristic instruments. The politico-social pundit, on the other hand, is full of rhetoric and opinion on 'the class struggle' and 'class distinctions'—the latter usually relating to the desirability of their eradication. The use of class language is employed to stigmatise or elevate people and is thus capable of causing considerable social tension. It is frequently intended to exploit tenuous, and often spurious, distinctions for social or other ends. Used as a political weapon, it is still capable of causing social division. Class is therefore both a socio-economic metric—a means of classifying and understanding societies in terms of certain value-neutral factual criteria—and, as loosely used in general conversation, a term that carries considerable moralistic and emotive baggage.

There are further distinctions to be made. First, there is that between class as a social entity and class as a possessive quality. 'Having class' says nothing about class membership—ordinary people can have class which nobility may lack. In this sense, class is tied to behaviour and style rather than to social position, and is dependent on individual judgement. Attempts to mimic class which fail, well illustrate the fragility of this aspect of class. Reproduction furniture rarely comes close to the indefinable authenticity of the genuine antique and people who affect upper-class attitudes and behaviour more often than not turn themselves into a laughing stock—something that the television sitcom industry has exploited most effectively.

Second, class must be distinguished from inequality, be it material, intellectual or physical. These are facts of life and should in theory carry no evaluative connotations, although it is often impossible to divorce the reality from its pejorative or approving overtones. To say of someone that they are a duke or a dustman, that they have a first-class University degree or that they are a brain surgeon, is to state a fact in each case, but facts which carry evaluative baggage and social corollaries. Such inequalities provide the raw data that sociologists use to describe and model society and are best considered as a limited framework for elaborating the conceptual terminology with which we interpret and discuss social behaviour. Facts, strictly speaking, are value-free.

In much of modern society, rigid class distinctions have been eroded to the point at which they are no longer socially significant. Societies manage perfectly well without the need for elaborate codes of dress, manner and behaviour that mark an individual's place in the hierarchy. Nowadays most who discuss class openly (sociologists apart) generally do so in pursuit of political ends. This is particularly true of the liberal agenda, which paints class distinctions as outmoded and strives for a classless society. Interestingly, the use of class labels is mainly confined to the left, who still see them as useful political battering rams. There remains a core of extremists from the old quasi-communist left who are unable to refer to workers without adding the epithet 'down-trodden' and still see the world in terms of 'the class struggle'. The collapse of communism has destroyed the appetite for this kind of agitprop, and these ageing radicals are largely talking to themselves.

Moderate argument about class revolves round three core questions: the first and second broadly factual the third evaluative.

1. To what extent, if any, do classes exist in any given society?
2. If so, does their existence have any discernible social impact (the extent of their harm being the usual sub-text)?
3. Are classes beneficial? Those who ask this generally see class as undesirable and turn the issue into a debate over what can be done to diminish or destroy its influence.

Being against class divisions is therefore both an argument about the existence of class and also about its abolition.

The vision of a classless society has considerable political force. It is also an emotive issue, being both judgemental and strongly moralistic. The goal of equality is often touted as the (desirable) basis for formulating (a classless) social policy. As we are all equal, the argument runs, there are no grounds for discrimination and everyone should therefore be treated equally. In one sense, human beings are indeed equal — in the nominal fact of partaking in the human race, or 'in the eyes of God' as left-wing, theist radicals tend to put it. However, this equality is trivial and an unsustainable basis for any broader theory of social equality. It is impractical, not to say irresponsible, to base social policy on foundations which conveniently ignore the manifest inequalities of talent, appearance, physical ability, living conditions, etc, that are so deeply unpalatable to those who, in pursuit of their political dogma, tout social engineering as the great leveller. The fiction of strict equality has led to a wealth of nonsense, notably in educational and employment policies.

The abstract nature of the concept of equality makes it an ideal vehicle for the pursuit of political ends. It has an honest, uncontroversial ring to it which gives it immediate popular appeal and its inherent looseness allows it to be fashioned to support any number of different objectives which may not necessarily be compatible. Egalitarians are usually eloquent and persuasive, and those taking a contrary view are easily represented as immoral — how could anyone possibly argue against equality? However, their passion is not always matched by intellectual clarity, in particular when it comes to setting out in precisely what respects equality is being sought. And it is on such details that the validity of the egalitarian case so often depends. There is no evident validity in the proposition which underlies much egalitarianism, that inequalities invariably result in adverse or undesirable consequences. Genuine equality is rare, in all but the most trivial sense, and to say that X is no different from Y in some respect or other cannot be taken as implying that they are equal. I may treat my cousin in the same way as my aunt, but this does not make them equal. When one delves deeper into what is being demanded, egalitarian propositions, however plausible, generally fail to pass closer scrutiny.

It is an easy extension of the doctrine of equality to the ideal of the classless society. This is an image which has Marxist roots and retains strong popular appeal. It is flawed, both because it flies in the face of reality and because it presupposes the existence of classes in the first place. The reality is that any society develops hierarchies of wealth, influence, intellect, talent and power which are not eradicable by even the most determined state apparatus. (A good historical illustration is that of Hitler's attempts to level classes by forming a classless youth movement, based on 'gleichschaltung' — bringing into line through ideological training. It failed. While you can forcibly remove the obvious trappings of class, impose uniform dress and confer status on merit, you do not thereby erase values and traditions which, at least in such a highly stratified society as 1930's Germany, are major determinants of class). The French Revolution sought to level class by decapitating aristocrats; while this worked at one level, it provided no durable solution. Although titles may no longer be recognised in its official circles, France's aristocratic families continue to enjoy high social status and many live in much the same manner as in pre-revolutionary times, if rather less ostentatiously.

Any discussion of society and class must recognise the ambiguities in the concept of classlessness, which make for unnecessary confusion and much emotion. It is essential, if apparently paradoxical, to realise that the notion of a classless society does not imply a society without classes. It merely demands that social class be determined by merit alone. Even the most rigorously communistic states had class systems which delivered benefits to the selected few — in many ways, not unlike today's western power elites.

Much of the fight against class is not so much a crusade to abolish social distinctions across the board (this, shorn of embellishments, is what the less sophisticated chattering egalitarians are really talking about) but a crude attempt to destroy the supports from those who are seen as unjustifiably privileged. In this instance, the criteria for what is, and is not, just are set by the crusaders. These people are seldom motivated by honest egalitarian considerations but, in most cases, by envy. This is apparent from the fact that, while they have no objection to rock stars and footballers earning and spending their huge fortunes on tasteless homes, flashy cars, overpriced hotels and vulgar parties, they take strong exception to those with much more modest means who opt for private health care or who choose to pay for better education for their children. Private schools and private health-care are presented as jumping the queue of state provision and thus put at the heart of the reformists' agenda. This conveniently ignores the fact that there are two different queues, and being in one has no impact on the length or speed of the other. If I elect to pay for a faster tram rather than for the slower bus, I do not thereby jump the bus queue or disadvantage anyone in it. This, the most influential version of the egalitarian argument, is a non-starter.

The intellectual mainsprings of the 'classless society' movement derive from two popular beliefs: first, that there is one law for the rich and another for the poor, and second, that ordinary people get a raw deal when it comes to dividing up national wealth. It is not to the present purpose to discuss whether these beliefs are well- or ill-founded, but to note that there is an unshakeable popular conviction in most westernised societies that the odds are unfairly stacked against the less well off.

Egalitarians generally gloss over whether the equality they seek is that of opportunity or of outcome. These are not the same. The latter is implausible, particularly in matters under governmental control—education, healthcare, etc; the former has greater credibility and is supported by those who see equality of opportunity, allied to technological progress, as destroyers of class and social levellers. In general, the demand for social equality is a positive agenda which goes beyond the mere absence of inequalities.

The image of class in society is confused and difficult. In any large community there are likely to be established social divisions that are used as the basis for privileges and other distinctions. It is these that are often implicit in class references. In closed societies these are known as 'castes' and are largely matters of birth or inheritance. In open societies the system is less rigid. Only to the extent that they have social or other devolved value are these distinctions of real importance.

The defining requirements for a classless society are first, that there should be mobility between one social level and another (put another way, that birth or position should not *ipso facto* impede or accelerate movement), and second, that merit should be the determining factor in attainment—a stipulation designed to eliminate, as far as possible, preferment based on non-meritocratic grounds. This appears to be entirely in order when it comes to the top end of the scale, but there seems to be no sense of the hypocrisy involved when skewing opportunity at the other end by distorting normal political or employment criteria, such as black empowerment or all-women candidate shortlists.

To the extent that disparities exist in wealth, intelligence, education, attitudes, birth, upbringing, social behaviour and values, then so (trivially) do classes. However, beyond the smattering of hereditary monarchs or titled nobility where class criteria are relatively clear, one cannot point to any single determinant of class. The most privileged are not necessarily the best educated (e.g. sports or entertainment celebrities), and the 'upper classes' are not necessarily the wealthiest. A barrow boy may have more income than a landed aristocrat and an impoverished clergyman may enjoy higher class status than a wealthier office worker. Class labels—working, middle, upper—are increasingly irrelevant as manual labour diminishes, as those involved in it enjoy middle-class lifestyles, and as the old aristocracy relinquishes its former political power to modern meritocrats.

Despite the realities of modern life, the ideal of a classless society remains highly attractive. However, its superficial plausibility crumbles under detailed scrutiny. If the motive of its proponents is the abolition of social division, they live in dreamland. If their prime focus is to eradicate inequalities of opportunity, the case has marginally more credibility. Generally, opportunity is defined in terms of access to social benefits — good schools, universities, healthcare, etc. But this is unlikely to achieve the grander aim of levelling. Intelligence is thought to have a genetic and thus hereditable component (although this is controversial) and the realisation of individual potential probably depends as much on attitudes, behaviour and environment as on genetics. Potential requires unlocking — and the keys are not necessarily all held by the state. The successful outcome of sending a potentially gifted child to a top school demands as much by way of parental support as it does of teachers. If the family environment is at odds with the ethos and values of the school, the key may remain half-turned in the lock. Appealing as the ideal of a classless society may be, the reality that it is largely unattainable.

Whilst every aspect of life is still subtly graded with class tags — where you live, your education, attitudes, accent, values — the more radical contemporary language of class, at least in Britain, relies heavily on extinct social stereotypes. Oxford is no longer home to a race of Sebastian Flytes living the life of ease and privilege at Christchurch 'high up in Meadow Buildings', with little work to disturb an endless stream of diversions. Nonetheless, his alter ego, the 'toff', continues to be satirised and derided as if he still exists, trotted out as a fantastic stereotype — a chinless, brainless, strangle-accented curiosity, living idly in luxury funded by inherited wealth, whose main activity is overseeing his estate when he is not debauching or gambling away his patrimony. Such caricatures travesty an era long gone but continue to tread the boards of social fantasy as useful props for the otherwise unsustainable case for yet further reforms to exterminate privilege and level the social playing field.

The reality, for those few with large inheritances, is unremitting hard work and the deployment of considerable skill to keep their houses and estates intact in the face of high capital and inheritance taxes and negligible government support. The image of an indolent and undeserving landed class, living off inherited wealth (let alone the backs of their workers) is kept alive by those intent on sustaining the notion of unfair class division and on drawing attention to the inequalities of the 'underprivileged' and doubtless 'highly deserving' proletariat. The British attitude is curiously schizophrenic, in that we affect to scorn the nobility, whilst visiting their stately homes in ever increasing numbers. It is implausible to explain such a gripping interest in something the very existence of which we claim to find inherently repellent, by mere curiosity.

The language of class envy still has potency. It is used by the far (and often, not so far) left to fuel popular resentment when in pursuit of policies which would be unacceptable without it; a topical example is the demand that British universities (especially Oxford and Cambridge) deliberately massage their admissions policies to bring in more students from working class backgrounds. These universities have long operated on the basis of academic merit (except for a few closed, privately endowed scholarships). Now they are being asked to abandon this policy because it results in greater intake from private schools, whose students perform better. Using class language to fire up opposition to what is a sound policy seems like cynical exploitation and a crude attempt to foment social division in pursuit of a socialist agenda.

Interestingly, once you have acquired your class badge, it is difficult to shed. Those who, through misfortune, struggle to maintain the trappings of class ('reduced circumstances' used to be the epithet) or whose situation propels them upwards, tend to retain their class despite the change. In many respects class is independent of lifestyle and dependent on personal qualities and values — on demeanour, attitude and bearing rather than on possessions. This means that, whilst upward mobility is theoretically possible, attempting it is largely futile without the requisite manners and social graces — or 'breeding' as it used to be called. Chancers are usually spotted at a considerable distance and rapidly seen off.

Extreme reforming agendas based on quasi-communist class-hatred have lost most of their force, as the class they purport to hate is largely extinct and its portrayal has long been seen to bear little relation to reality. Nonetheless, the existence and divisiveness of class provides too ready a platform for reformist zealots to be abandoned upon such a small inconvenience. Class and privilege are highly emotive, especially in today's consumer and image-driven societies, and emotions are the stuff from which valuable political capital may be extracted.

Whilst people occasionally talk of society in class terms, they do not, in general, *think* in these terms or even ascribe any particular class label to themselves despite the fact that surveys both in the USA and Britain regularly report that their citizens consider themselves part of highly unequal and class-ridden societies. Most who work describe themselves, if pressed, as 'working class', which is at odds with standard sociological criteria, which identify them as 'middle' class. Surveys also show that a large majority regards much of Western society as class-ridden and in the grip of a continuing class struggle.

In Western culture class (but not status) is based on an amalgam of money, behaviour, values and, to a lesser extent, inherited caste with the balance varying from country to country. How one handles class in its relationship to status varies from society to society. Where people see themselves as belonging to a class above that for which society confers them status, they may resort to classic status-enhancing moves to affirm their position. In Britain, members of the genuinely upper class (as opposed to the purely wealthy) eschew trappings to signal their status — and tend towards understatement, probably in the belief that true quality comes from within and that having class there is no further need to prove it. In America, a country with a relatively short history and thus no great tradition from which class stratification may be evolved, the reverse is true. There, it is not considered unseemly to discuss one's personal wealth, and conspicuous displays are common. If the image of high status is related to external trappings, then their absence causes problems. In some circles it is what you choose and buy that determines what class you are in. There is a distinction, however, between choices which simply indicate class and those which define it.

Class markers can be divided into primary and secondary. Primary markers are attributes such as title, family name, accent, education, housing, job, interests (sport, social, charitable). Secondary category comprises wealth, lifestyle (holidays, eating, drinking, shopping), comportment and dress. Final class attribution is, in legal terminology, defeasible — there are no hard and fast rules and in some cases the decision may be difficult. People who aspire to another class are often good mimics and their performances frequently carry conviction. Moving upwards from one's perceived class requires at least — but not at most — wealth, education and talent, and although it is entirely possible to acquire all the trappings of another class, this will not guarantee that you are perceived as belonging to it. Secondary markers pointing in one direction are easily vitiated by primary markers pointing in another. A duke will probably make a good job of pretending to be a dustman, but even if he tried, would have difficulty persuading people that he had shifted from one class to the other. On the other hand, a dustman would have the greatest difficulty even acting the duke. Aspirants with class ambitions, even given the requisite wealth and a superior lifestyle, are usually let down by lack of culture, poor education and bad taste. Belonging to such-and-such class, doesn't mean you have class. Class in this sense is more related to bearing and personal dignity — self-respect and values — and many upwardly mobile aspirations founder on these sharp, unforgiving rocks.

There is an element of mawkish sentimentality in class nomenclature. Why is it that people labelled 'working class' feel ashamed or inferior, and conversely why are the 'middle class' guilt-ridden about anyone labelled 'working class'? Any stigma attached to being working class or even, in some people's eyes, middle class, comes by association rather than from any intrinsic values, so reluctance to make class attributions may reflect a desire to shield others from realities that we, rather than they, find painful. One used to talk of the dignity of the working class, who — whilst they may have complained privately of their working conditions or caricatured their bosses — took pride in having a job and in doing it well (one only has to listen to almost any retired artisan, miner or railwayman to appreciate this). Now it seems politically incorrect to suggest that anyone might be below anyone else in the social pecking order — as if their job, income and surroundings were somehow their own fault and a justified cause for shame.

This change of attitude to class attribution has to do with the progress of egalitarianism and the rise in opportunity. As perceptions of a reliable connection between wealth — as merit — and social position solidify, and societies in which 'disadvantaged' meant 'disadvantaged for life' become fewer, there is an unspoken feeling that poverty is avoidable and that to be seen to be poor is a matter of deservedness rather than plain ill fortune. The argument runs: if you have opportunity to rise in the social scale, why have you not taken advantage of it? If you remain at the bottom of the heap, then you have only yourself to blame. This sits awkwardly with an increased willingness to lay personal misfortune onto the state, but none the less one can see why more fluid economic mobility has removed justification, and to a certain extent excuses, for those left behind. There is a stigma in poverty in developed economies which did not exist half a century ago.

The positive side of social levelling is that attributes which once were powerful class signals now matter less. For example, where once a 'proper' accent and manner of speech were reliable indicators of class, accent is now taken more as a mark of origin than of intellectual or social status (this is not so obviously true of syntax and grammar). In fact, a much broader latitude in speech and diction is compatible with being middle class than was the case a generation or so ago. Although a limited vocabulary, poor grammar and certain accents are still considered 'lower class', the attribution is neither infallible nor inevitable.

The obvious class markers have all but vanished. Indeed, so effective is the blurring of class boundaries that 'it is no longer clear which way is up, even if one wants to rise' (David Riesman, 'From morality to morals', *The Lonely Crowd*, 1950). The rapid spread of the *nouveaux riches* has demolished the exclusivity which once attached to grand houses, the best private schools, great hotels and restaurants and exotic holiday destinations. Hierarchy and status have largely supplanted class as social indicators. The subtler privileges of class have been eroded by consumerism. Although pockets of self-sustaining old class huddle together in the mutual comfort of exclusive clubs or residences, where you can go and what you can do now depends more on the size of your bank account than on your background. Money has brought much of the levelling that the 'class warfare' populists failed to achieve. Nowadays, 'common' is common but to say so is a social solecism and smacks of snobbery. In this era of anything goes, anyone also goes—anywhere. We must not be judgmental. One is left asking what, if origins, education, accent and lifestyle are no longer valid as class markers, is there about class worth discussing?

Whether or not in recognition of the futility of this debate, the anti-class movement has now shifted its attention to a more plausible target—the elites. Whilst it is *de rigeur* for political or social advancement in Britain or the USA to be seen as anti-elite, elites exist and are powerful. The anti-elitism of the elites themselves is not just the inverted snobbery of the upper echelons of the British medical profession, for example, which at consultant level drops the title 'Doctor' and reverts to plain 'Mister'. The game is much subtler than that.

Elites rise above life, rather like froth, and are largely self-made. Extending the simile, they are held up by nothing particularly substantial beyond a sort of self-sustaining gas. While sharing many of its attributes, they contrast with the permanence of class. This in two senses: first, that traditional class distinctions were solid and above other societal categorisations and upheavals, and second, that class was personal, and by and large independent of other attributions. In the traditional system, if you had a manual job you were probably working class; a clerical job meant middle class; a title and grand mansion, upper class; and so on through the finer sub-divisions. Even now, it is not unusual to hear of a well-paid manager exchanging his job for an artisan's lifestyle—but his values and social position do not thereby necessarily alter. The link between occupation and class is now much more elastic.

Whilst they may appear as 'froth' (an interesting conceptual contrast with 'scum' which also rises to the top), modern elites are entirely different, preferring anonymity and generally operating by stealth. To understand them, it is important to realise that a desire for power lies at their heart. Unlike the old upper class, they crave influence (although not necessarily formal power) at all costs. They prefer camouflage and low visibility to high profile, although this is sometimes hard to avoid, and see themselves as power brokers, operating behind the scenes of national life. As their political base is generally liberal or left wing, they have to square their influence with the prevailing egalitarianism, and this means appearing to be populist, whatever their feelings or self-image. In order to avoid charges of elitism, especially if they are public figures, the new elites take pains to emphasise their commonality with the masses. They dress down wherever possible, and talk down incessantly. This is intended to provide them with a veneer of ordinariness. Achieving this image, however, presents a dilemma: if you are a US Senator or a British Minister of the Crown, you are, whether it appeals or not, part of an elite. So, in order to be seen to repudiate the label, you have to make strenuous efforts to act on a level with the non-elite. This involves conscious condescension—in other words lowering yourself to the general level. The preferred means to this end is to dumb down—to become a populist. If you remain aloof, you risk censure for condescension.

In a world powered by business, media and the cult of celebrity, identifying yourself as one of the masses is the entry-card to social advancement. The true modern elites are those occupying positions of influence—politicians, media moguls and personalities, large company CEOs and the like. These people move effortlessly between the centres of power: you are just as likely to find a media mogul advising government on social policy, or a businessman chairing a political committee on broadcasting reform, as you are to find them in their offices running their corporations. Their defining characteristic, as George Walden has noted (*The New Elites*) are that they are, superficially, at least, strongly anti-elite. Whilst in private, these elites live a life of power and privilege, their public persona proclaims the common interest: 'I am really like you and share your values and aspirations'. This 'common touch' provides the base from which they draw their authority. They are an unresolved contradiction: common, but uncommon. They know the lives and aspirations of the masses and feign to share them—so what they say and do has, as it were, the populist imprimatur. The appropriate image is what matters, however much it may conflict with reality. This public stance contrasts with a private despising of the masses to which they so convincingly claim to belong. In this, they rely on building and sustaining a populist image and on massive self-deceit.

People have always aspired to rise in the social scale—pulling upwards, as they see it. What today's social elites see themselves as catapulting into reflects the widespread perception of the existence and importance of social class—the reality against which one must contrast the populist ideal of a classless society. These elitist inverts openly reject elitism, whilst cultivating their one-of-the-masses image for use as a populist tool; privately, they enjoy as much of the high-life as they can lay their hands on, punch-drunk with the gewgaws of office, expense-account wealth, VIP travel and status and the headiness of power.

Modern elitism spouts the politically correct mantras of a classless, inclusive society. These are practically and theoretically meaningless, but populist and therefore fashionable and effective in creating the desired image. The language of inclusiveness and egalitarianism carries the implication that elites of any sort are incompatible with the new view of society (unless they are sportsmen, film-stars, captains of industry or military top brass). Celebrity is acceptable as long as it conforms to anti-elitist norms, in particular that no-one should be considered better or superior. You may have risen to the top of your tree, but you are really on an equal footing with everyone else. (For celebrities with minimal talent, this is probably the only brush with reality in an otherwise Image-driven existence). In this social order, intellectual elites are frowned upon. The cult of celebrity is conveniently egalitarian in that it is open to all and does not rely on demonstrable talent; indeed, much of celebrity is either illiterate or merely decorative, often both—based on who's 'hot', who's 'in', which restaurant you eat at and where you holiday. This is another kind of self-supporting elite also sustained by froth and very little else. Unlike the clergymen, doctors and professional men of the nineteenth and early twentieth centuries, whose class was at least related to a modicum of competence, there is no such requirement for modern celebrity.

The opposite of elitism is inclusiveness, which has a subtly different emphasis from egalitarianism. The egalitarian stresses our essential equality and strives for equal treatment irrespective of circumstances (the absurdity of this hardly needs spelling out). Where possible, class markers are studiously obliterated. Those who seek inclusiveness are prepared to admit some inequalities, but seek a society where no one is excluded or stigmatised, which, in practical terms, requires levelling down to accommodate the baseline of attainment and values. It is this kind of extreme social engineering that has devalued much higher education (everyone who wants a degree must have one) and sought to close private clubs (e.g. golf and social clubs) which confer membership by election, especially if they exclude women. Interestingly, some of the most powerful elites — for example, the US MBA and business school programmes — exact strict social and stylistic conformity. 'They dress and speak in the same way, are fascinated by euro-fashions and have fixations with materialistic symbols (ties, cars, personal-computer planners). They talk in obscure and grotesque jargon, e.g. "Yeah, she really adds value" which means "she's good company"' (Simon Sebag-Montefiore, UK Observer newspaper article, October 2001).

In its refusal to recognise any other criteria of preferment than merit, meritocracy is sometimes presented as the ultimate anti-elitism. For meritocrats, advancement and status are a direct and simple function of merit alone. Merit, however, is about how you progress, and is neutral as to what you are once you have arrived. Even the most egalitarian of meritocrats cannot guarantee that those at the top of the meritocratic pile are not elite. Meritocracy may arrange things at the input end so that progress does not depend on birth, wealth or connections — though even this is hard to arrange in societies where connections count — but is unable to give similar guarantees at the output end. Elites have a habit of forming and surviving even the most populist social theorising and, once formed, tend to favour and recycle their own. This is a form of group protection, because even merit has its image problems. As La Rochefoucauld suggested: 'The world often rewards signs of merit more than merit itself' (*Maxims*).

The anti-elite movement attacks on many fronts. Where the arts are concerned, it makes determined efforts to marginalise the high-brow, transforming it progressively into low-brow and no-brow. The criteria of artistic merit are generally functional (i.e. what most appeals or makes most money — which often equates to least subsidised). Opera and the more recondite visual arts are the main battlefields here. Opera in particular attracts contumely. It is seen as offensively elitist on the grounds that it is expensive to stage and therefore, despite public subsidy, to attend, and as having no discernible practical value. This image has resonance, to some extent, in Britain, but says more about the philistinism of British society than the value of the arts. In Europe and parts of the USA, the many major cities and provinces have well-funded civic orchestras and opera houses with varied repertoires, supported by a wide cross-section of society and of which the community is justifiably proud. A minority interest, certainly — elitist, certainly not. In Britain, while eradicating opera altogether is not a realistic goal, the reformers' compromise is to direct subsidies to houses which are prepared to stage the most popular works. This is in line with the 'easy way' agenda — nothing too demanding or esoteric and a perspective which closely allies 'investment' in the arts with popular culture and perceived returns. If the public don't attend a play or exhibition then, the argument goes, it is obviously not worthy of public funding. This essentially puts the interests of the audience before those of artistic and aesthetic integrity. Judging artistic endeavour in terms of commerce is entirely consonant with the populist agenda. The British National Lottery has somewhat muddied the picture, as it provides substantial additional income for minority artistic interests (including opera), which is represented by some as mischievous, topsy-turvy re-distribution — not, as with Robin Hood, from the rich to the poor, but the other way round.

Despite the public anti-elite image, the reality is that elitism is thriving across the globe. The New Elites so trenchantly described by George Walden (op.cit.) work the platform that 'no-one, however unsuitable, should be excluded from anything ... women, blacks, etc'. These people show an overt distaste for intellectuals — the image of populism is anti-intellectual — who are regarded as an undesirable elite. 'Like the most fatuous of snobs, they are mesmerised by status and interested in nothing but social tone'. Their policies have achieved a spectacular levelling down which is itself socially divisive. As Walden pithily concludes, 'who better to exalt the mediocre than an elite of mediocrities?'

Does this matter? Despite the continued efforts of the anti-class, anti-elite lobbies there are still well recognised social strata in most civilised countries. The reality is that although these exist, their social significance is limited. The exploitation and poor working and housing conditions of the 19th century are no longer present, the lowest level of society now being supported by a network of organisations and agencies that provide help for the worst off. The privileges once bought by money are now within the reach of many — so other indicators must be used to signal social divisions. Apart from the grosser disparities in wealth, housing and education, the social divide is more accurately marked by differences in values and culture as compared with half a century ago when there was greater social cohesion and values were more widely shared and less class dependent. There is a strong sense of irrational guilt in expressing differences in class terms; 'working class' was an attribution to be proud of in the 1950s, now it has become a term of opprobrium. Even 'middle class' has mildly pejorative overtones and 'upper class' is, if anything, even worse. Where people do perceive class divisions, they often see these as a significant contributory factor to inequality rather than as its result. That this should be so is largely due to the irrelevant and poisonous language of 'class warfare'. It is this, more than any actual inequality that fuels the largely spurious class debate today. Class is probably more accurately viewed as the interplay of social forces, rather than any immutable aspect of social order.

Classes and Elites converge on the territory of status, where the argument shifts from distinctions based on privilege to those based on merit. Status is a major component of self-image, and hence very capable of reinforcing or deflating it. Having decided upon the status to which we consider ourselves entitled, we work to achieve and maintain it. This involves monitoring (a) external signals that inform us of our status and (b) whether or not our image matches that of those with whom we have to deal. We frequently miss cues, or else over-interpret or misinterpret them, which may cause us to take remedial action unnecessarily when the status accorded fails to match that to which we deem appropriate.

Individuals, societies, nations, corporations, neighbourhoods and clubs all have status. As for individuals, status can vary with environment—the boss of the large corporation often loses his unquestioned authority when he walks through his own front door, and perceived influence is often at variance with actual influence. Status is a distinctly fragile commodity, of which people are particularly conscious. It is context dependent in a way that class is not, to an extent that exercises in self-promotion employ stratagems of varying degrees of subtlety to enhance or publicise it.

Achieving what we see as an appropriate status is driven by the powerful need for recognition, respect and love from those around us. We use various means to realise that end, principally the pursuit of influence, fame and money. The difficulty is that there is considerable uncertainty in obtaining an accurate take on our status, which is, after all, in part a function of how others see us. It varies from one social group to another and may alter, even within a given situation. Our sense of our own social identity is fluid and fragile, and we often find it difficult to ascertain what others think of us. As this is a major determinant of what we think of ourselves—unless we are exceptionally egocentric, narcissistic or thick-skinned—the task of arriving at a balanced assessment of self-worth is akin to crystallising a constantly moving target. Even if we accurately assess our status, there is no guarantee that society will agree with us, and even if it does, will act to deliver it. It is perfectly possible to imagine situations in which claims to status fail because of other factors such as personality problems or simply ignorance. Many ordinary people achieve extraordinary things, but do so quietly, without fuss or notice, and their status remains uncredited with their achievements.

Status is complicated by the fact that it has no fixed value, in that it varies with those bestowing it. A person may, for example, have high status in his family and low status among his work colleagues. Status divergence is often acute when it is derived from only one source—a waiter (low status) may in fact be a high-flying engineer or a doctor (both high status)—so it is inappropriate to assess status on limited information. Nor to do so where a single variable colours judgement: for example, many people reactively stigmatise those who are black, or have a certain accent or a speech defect, and thus have difficulty when someone has incontrovertibly high status by other criteria. Such misconceptions and prejudices put status decisions, to a certain extent, out of our hands. People concerned about the accuracy of their self-image or social status must seek feedback from an audience with accurate and complete information.

The precariousness of high status makes it a less than ideal goal for personal aspiration—yet its pursuit seems an indelible part of our psyche. Devoting time—often a life-time—to the pursuit of something that is uncertain, high-maintenance, often unsatisfying and that can be demolished in an instant seems misguided, so why do we do it? Part of the answer is that we crave security and see status as providing it. This craving comes from fragility; we need constant reinforcement of our worth and value, and to the extent that it is not forthcoming, feel insecure. Interestingly, there is an element of fear in this insecurity in that we feel vulnerable to society's scorn. That such fear exists is evident from the exaggerated performances of the ultra-insecure. These people prop up their own insecurity by making others feel inferior and this leads them to disdainful, spiteful or snobbish behaviour. Name-droppers and those who constantly discuss their wealth are among the cruder examples of the genre, which often includes the super-rich. Many have little need to reinforce their position in this way, but do so because their own security is fragile and prey to the slightest hint of vulnerability. One can tell as much about someone from how they cope with proven failure as how they handle success. Highly insecure people need constant external reinforcement of their self-image and are highly sensitive to even the mildest criticism. They tend to be overbearing and often shelter beneath the security they see as coming from the control to be had through patronage or by monopolising conversation and social interaction.

Status is also used as a prop for incompetence, and the status you grant yourself is not necessarily that which others are prepared to accept — legions are the managers who are the laughing-stock of their subordinates. It is a sad but important fact of life that social perceptions are often reactions to inappropriate cues. In academia, status — and thereby research funding — too often depends more on the quantity rather than the quality of material published; thus it is that a great deal of second-rate work finds its way into so-called 'learned' journals. In group decisions, it is all too often the most bombastic or persistent member whose opinions determine the outcome, while less vociferous quality is overlooked.

People have difficulty in assessing others by their real qualities, which frequently remain hidden. To the extent that status is correlated with physical trappings, it provides an easier, less challenging route to determining a person's position and worth. The outward signs have to be highly visible otherwise they are not seen as adequate markers: a plusher more spacious office, a larger car, better housing quarter, prestigious social or sports club membership, etc. Within communities, the signals are usually more subtle but no less important: executive wash-rooms, lunch rooms, hotel rooms, business class travel all mark out the arriviste as surely as a lapel badge proclaiming his position. In business, the conspiracy of status has been nurtured to extreme levels, often by those with a vested interest in its continuance. 'You are where you eat' is not just a clarion to senior management to frequent the 'in' restaurants but a call to those establishments to participate in the game. This becomes absurd when 'certain tables at high-tone restaurants are as much a part of the pay package of a top job (in the USA) as the company car and the key to the executive loo. In many cities the ability to stake out tables at key restaurants defines your professional status with taxonomic precision' (Rory Ross, 'You are Where You Eat', UK Sunday Times, 27/10/01). The restaurants cater for a particular clientele—some for politicians, others for wannabe film stars, other for TV heavies for instance. There is even role reversal: 'The Maitre d' is a critical ingredient. A great Maitre d' knows his customers, the deals they're cutting, the films they're making, the people they're sleeping with. He has the power to bestow the table that will land you the deal of your life' (ibid.). The servant thus becomes the master. Moreover, the arrival of the 'power table' and the realisation that the harder a booking is to get the more people covet it, has spawned a breed of arrogant, imperious functionaries who turn on its head the rule that the customer is king. Not only is it a privilege to dine at these establishments, it is one that is frequently paid for. This is a finely-honed example of elitism, snobbery and raging class distinction rolled into one—a meticulously choreographed social pantomime!

Physical props play an important, if subsidiary, role in establishing and maintaining status. Where these are concerned, sociologists distinguish between non-positional material goods (which are theoretically in unlimited supply) and positional goods (which are not). Most luxury goods fall into the former category, while Old Master paintings, rare orchids, exotic animals and 17th century country mansions fall into the latter. Positional goods are traded in a zero-sum market as availability is finite and generally confer higher status than non-positional goods. Quasi-physical props that are not obtainable merely by wealth—trophy blondes or membership of exclusive clubs for example, fall somewhere in between.

Naturally, the status-value of any given prop is maintained only as long as it remains affordable to only a few. Once supply increases or incomes rise and it becomes more widely distributed, it loses its positional status and the search is on for the next status-rarity. The image factor is important here—as possession must be visible or obvious for its status-value to be unlocked. Owning a rare object will not enhance status if it lies unseen in a bank vault. In today's consumerist society, income (as distinct from wealth per se) has become the highest status prop, and income and status tend to be correlated. However, whilst high income may confer status within an organisation, it may not necessarily do so in wider society. Thus, a bond trader earning a telephone-number salary may be rated by outsiders as a sub-species of bookmaker or barrow-boy and accorded commensurately low status. This status image is confirmed by inappropriate spending choices (ostentatious clothes, cars, watches), by dissonant behaviour (loud, vulgar parties, drunkenness, insider share dealing, or tacky companions) or by plain boorishness. It is also worth noting that because people fawn over someone or defer to them doesn't mean that they necessarily regard them as high status. In many cases deference reflects expediency rather than any consideration of status.

The attainment of status is often motivated by social ambition. There are people who see themselves as in some way special or important, and regard being like everybody else as some kind of calamity. They are just like the rest of us, but either feel strongly that they are not or should not be, and this drives their unquenchable ambition. This relationship is not straightforward, as it seems that social ambition rises with status — the higher (as you see it) your status, the further you seek to climb and the greater your need for recognition and deference. For some, there comes a time when obsessive social ambition and an excessive sense of self-importance detach them from reality. At this point, they act as if their wealth or celebrity has somehow excepted them from the norms and expectations of society. The attitude this can create is scarcely credible. Leonora Hemsley famously opined that "taxes are for the little man"; another prominent socialite declared that she would never go to public movies again: "never again — all those smelly people". She also declared that "Jewels are a defining attitude rather like your intelligence. It's one thing to make the wrong choice from Prada, but quite another to buy the wrong piece from Graff or SJ Phillips". The raging snobbery apart, such a remark exemplifies the blinkered stupidity of someone who sees society as defined by and conforming to her own distorted values.

This is nothing new. Adam Smith commented on the phenomenon in 1776 deriding those who consume their lives chasing 'baubles and trinkets' (*The Wealth of Nations*). He added that such people, pathetic as they are, contribute massively to civilisation and social welfare through their uninhibited spending and an unbridled desire to accumulate wealth and display its ornaments. (cf. A. de Botton, *Status Anxiety*). None of this is to undervalue the pleasure to be had from good living or to decry the aspirations most people have for a better life; nor is it to suggest that we should all be self-effacing. It does however highlight the fragility of exaggerated self-esteem, aggressive status aspiration, deification of wealth, and the savage disdain for the lives and values of others that frequently accompany them. It also demonstrates a failure to recognise that there are equally valid alternative conceptions of what constitutes a worthy and satisfying life.

In considering status, it is important to recognise its links with expectation. One consequence of more or less full employment, welfare provision and the increased purchasing power of average incomes has been a significant rise in individual expectations — of what we want and what is attainable. It has also levelled society in expanding the old middle-class. The result is that there are more people one can look in the eye as social equals — if not in status, then at least in moral terms. (This, incidentally, does not validate radical egalitarianism which pedals the fiction that individual differences merely reflect a mistaken reconstruction of social reality. Those whose ideology is based on the premise of absolute equality also maintain a derivative fiction; namely, that while I may not, in fact, be equal to you I'm at least as good as you.) None of this can mask the fact that the fulfilment of expectations does not erase them; others merely arrive to take their place. There is thus an ever-present gap between desire and fulfilment which creates dissatisfaction (and anxiety) as long as it remains. The situation is not improved by others whose material and social circumstances appear better than one's own. The greater their number the more obvious the disparity.

There are various ways of diffusing the stress without trying to compete. One can limit one's expectations and reject the link between greater ornament and higher status — after all, the higher the expectations, the greater the potential disappointment. Alternatively, one can diminishing the status anxiety by confining one's society to those who most closely mirror one's own circumstances. To Rousseau, who rejected the implied definition of wealth as possessions and regarded riches as satisfaction irrespective of what we own, the sole route to greater riches was therefore to fulfil aspirations either by increasing financial means or by restraining desires.

The links between class and status are complex — complexities which are increased by the emergence of powerful social, economic and political elites. Image drives the pursuit of status and is a product both of the view we have of our personal worth and the extent to which we see that to be both validated and shared by our own circle and by wider society. In general, society is not always a reliable conveyor of status information; people are often surprised to discover in how much (or how little) esteem they are held. This may, of course, reflect poor assessment of good information rather than any lack of it. Gross disparities between self-evaluation and external evaluation offer the alternatives of re-aligning the former or changing the latter to close the gap.

Much depends on the weight we place on external indicators, both in the sense of their reliability and in the sense of the extent to which we take notice of them. We may consider them to be more or less reliable — that is, whether they accurately reflect the feelings of society or the group—or more or less reasonable—that is, irrespective of whether or not they reflect those feelings, the extent to which they correspond with the underlying realities. It is not just a matter of listening intelligently to criticism of oneself but also of assessing its quality; what matters is not just what others think but whether they are right to think it. Public opinion has often been called the worst of all opinions, so making judgements on the basis that it is either reliable or reasonable may be bad strategy. The philosopher Schopenhauer was no fan of either individual or collective capabilities and suggested that most people are either evil or dull (neither makes them unwise or incorrect), and castigated the 'superficial and futile nature of other people's thoughts, the narrowness of their views, the paltriness of their sentiments, the perversity of their opinions ... the number of their errors'. Whether or not such pessimism is justified, what Schopenhauer ignores is that people have little option but to take the prevailing arrangements as they find them, and therefore, anyone intending to live in society of any sort (rather than becoming a hermit), must evolve adaptive ways of dealing with its quirks and deficiencies.

The final piece in this jigsaw is respect—that we have for ourselves and for others, and that we receive. To a large extent, respect stands apart from other social evaluations in that it is logically independent of them; that is, to say something about class or status is to say nothing necessarily about respect. This is often expressed in terms of human dignity—and is the true recognition that, unless we deliberately forfeit it, we have a mutual right to expect a minimum level of respect. In this sense respect refers to our very existence and status as moral agents, rather than to any notion of deference. In a different but related connotation, respect is not automatic but is judgemental and must be earned. Respect is worked out in behaviour and attitude. It is in this sense that, for example, a wealthy landlord respects his workmen, and those who comprise the social and power elites can be said to have high respect for themselves and low respect for the rest of society. (As to the latter, the feeling is often mutual.)

Self-respect is subtly different from self-esteem in that it is entirely possible to have high self-respect and low self-esteem or vice versa. Self-esteem is, as we have seen, an amalgam of internal and external factors. Self-respect, on the other hand, is entirely self determined and has little to do with status or position in society. Others can impugn one's self respect, but cannot directly affect it, because it depends on an integrity of behaviour and values. You lose self-respect when you fail to act in accordance with your values—however perverse these may be. People who obtain wealth or advantage by dubious means may have low self-respect but high self-esteem without contradiction. Someone who says of another that they 'have no self-respect' is making a judgement both about behaviour and values.

It is a matter of sociological fact that much modern youth operates on respect from others, which they regard as the yardstick of self-worth. This, in turn, is measured by how much you contribute to the group—not the family group but your peer group, which in many cases is likely to be a street gang. This accounts for the prevalence of violence, which is a convenient response to almost everything, both because it works and also because it generates respect—both in its extreme form as fear from your foes, and as approbation from your peers. In general, the broad focus of society contrasts sharply with that of earlier generations where the parameters of respect were set by community and family.

The determinants of status, class and self-image and their inter-relationships are thus complex. Much attribution of status rests upon celebrity and while people who are wealthy, pushy or simply loud may command more attention, this is no durable yardstick of value. Those who are least secure in their own perceptions are often those most in need of constant reinforcement of their own position. It is such insecurity which drives much of the anxiety surrounding social status and self-esteem. Finding ways to increase security would lessen these concerns and the importance we attach to them.

Many pursue wealth and power in the belief that these automatically produce high esteem and respect. Indeed, among those who share the same values and aspirations they may do so. However, the bases of respect and value are not universal, and the fragility of status and social esteem make pursuit of goals based on wealth and power vulnerable to lapses in behaviour and changes in fortune, not always within personal control. In these endeavours, failure and success are not entirely reciprocal. While success tends to be slow and cumulative, failure is often instant and punished harshly. In such a context, humility makes more sense than arrogant and aggressive self-promotion.

We also need to put ourselves into perspective: concern with status rapidly evaporates when we are faced with more pressing challenges—serious illness or death—which tend to highlight the vacuity of the pursuit of advantage or influence. Taking an even wider view, experience suggests that those who make the most durable and positive social contribution are not politicians, power brokers, media moguls or the wealthy, most of whom are soon forgotten, but the great creative geniuses — writers, artists, musicians and actors, whose work endures and delights long beyond their lifetime. Nowadays, the egalitarian agenda has put traditional social hierarchies out of fashion. Nonetheless, these evolve in societies, without regard to ideology or prescription. It is clear that some form of class system, whether formal or informal, is an indispensable part of most social life, which in developed economies tend to be meritocracies. This is entirely reasonable. However the quest for personal status *per se* , rather than the status that follows achievement, is fraught with difficulty, not least because it comes with pressures and anxieties that make for dissatisfaction and disappointment. To this extent that it is impermanent, it also makes us vulnerable.

CHAPTER 6

LIFESTYLE, ART AND FASHION

'Fashion is gentility running away from vulgarity and afraid of being
overtaken'
William Hazlitt, The Conversations of James Northcote, (1830)

Sir Thomas More castigated those who 'count themselves nobler for the
smaller or finer thread of wool in their coats' (Jacob Bronowski, *The Western
Intellectual Tradition*). Had he lived several centuries years later, he would
doubtless have added 'or for the flashiness of their car, the length of their
cigar or the trophiness of their blonde companion'. The range and availability of goods has accelerated remarkably in the last half century and with
it their use as social tools. The spread of disposable income and credit across
the social spectrum in western societies means that most people can aspire
to own all but the rarest of articles, and this has led to the widespread use of
material objects both as wealth-indicators and as an indirect means of conveying social standing. Today, buying decisions are often influenced as much
by image considerations as by intrinsic worth or utility. We buy for impact
or to make a social statement.

Changing social structures are a seminal factor in this trend. Before the
modern consumer revolution, people lived in close communities where they
knew their place—defined mainly by occupation—and tacitly accepted the
norms and values those societies imposed. Sanctions for transgression were
swift and sure: disgrace, to a greater or lesser degree, was highly effective
punishment. The relationship was reciprocal: the community also knew the
value and place of its members and the scope for exaggerating one's status
was therefore circumscribed. Whilst one might reasonably have saved to buy
expensive domestic items—a car or washing machine—acquisitiveness
outside the generally accepted essentials was more likely to be met with mild
derision than with admiration or envy.

Many societies have largely abandoned the notion that social cohesion
depends upon social or religious conformity. The normative force of social
convention has progressively weakened as patterns of social interaction have
altered. One hears little talk of disgrace nowadays, and even egregious sins

(if any still remain) are sighed over for a while and then forgotten. The dog of social disapprobation has lost its teeth, and lasting stigma is a thing of the past. Now that social structures are looser and homes have become places to stay and work and less part of tight-knit communities, social cohesion and community sanctions have been replaced by other imperatives. The focus of the moral economy of reward and punishment has shifted. People now see themselves as citizens of a wider world and less as 'reporting' to their immediate community or subject to its strictures. The circumstantial fact of living in a community no longer exacts automatic allegiance or implies shared ethos.

The change is significant, because it signals a shift in responsibility for enforcing moral and social values from the community to the individual. This removes one layer of independent scrutiny and thus weakens social cohesion. Increased physical mobility has made communities more fluid and less settled, and the communications revolution has rendered the traditional structures difficult to sustain. Hitherto one's physical community was also one's social community; the immediate neighbourhood — village, district or suburb — which provided the majority of friends and acquaintances and social life. Here were the people who were most likely to be influenced by changes in one's circumstances and to whose good opinion behaviour was directed; they also meted out any sanctions that were deemed necessary. While this remains broadly the case in rural villages and remote settlements, it is no longer true for densely populated urban environments.

To the extent that friendship and community develop and are reinforced by shared experience, these are dependent not just on physical proximity but on a network of communication. Interest groups now cover a wide geographical spread and it is therefore reasonable to extend the definition of 'community' to reflect this reality. While the immediate social environment will always continue to influence, and be influenced by, behaviour, the more individuals regard easier communications and increased mobility as removing their social and emotional focus outside this circumscribed arena, it is this wider community which will increasingly set and monitor norms and values.

Other factors support this broader perspective: first, because people are now physically present in their immediate community for shorter periods, the scope for sending and receiving behavioural signals is reduced; second, because as we no longer see the immediate community as our principal focus we take less notice of what it has to say; and third, because even when we are in our domicile communities, altered physical and social structures mean that we interact less; more time is spent watching television or surfing the net, and the spread of urban high-rise housing means less opportunity for chat across the garden fence. From the community point of view this loosening of ties greatly reduces its normative force and the relaxing of internal bonds and values means that the will to exert community pressure is also diminished. Weaker community ties lead people to look elsewhere for platforms upon which to demonstrate their social standing and recast their personal Image.

This is not to say, however, that deviant or out-of-character behaviour in a close-knit and sharp-eyed community will not be punished. If you act in ways that are at variance either with your personality or with your accepted social status, such sanctions are still available and likely to be applied to enforce conformity. What is true is that their force has been diminished, especially by the shift in social emphasis from the community to the individual. In close communities, people have therefore to be realistic about their self-perceptions and to avoid setting up unsustainable images; intellectual pretension, unwarranted 'airs and graces', and most other forms of humbug are invariably spotted and duly punished. In contrast, the progressive disintegration of community structures has left the field open for more subtle image-related deception.

These social changes also reflect shifts in income distribution and the way people work. No longer are we plugged into the job-for-life mentality and there is a significant sector working from home, either as employees or as sole traders. High wage rates for self-employment mean that within a physical community income distribution can vary widely. You may not be able to afford to move to a grander neighbourhood, but may choose to signal your (superior) wealth with an infinite variety of expensive, more portable consumer goods and these, rather than work status, have become the visible manifestations of much social commerce. This is particularly true when housing is uniform and status distinctions must be made by other means.

As Sir Thomas More deprecatingly noted, visible and expensive goods have long been used as badges of wealth or status. The rarer an item, the more desirable it becomes and thus the more potent the signal it sends. (This is discussed in greater depth in Chapter 5). The relevant point here is that much possessiveness aims to impress others, and we are easily convinced into believing that the right trappings indicate influence, wealth or status. There is, of course, no guarantee that those who are impressed by your display are those who you intend to impress; or that those who you intend to impress will not see through the deception and so render the gesture futile. In general, your everyday choices often speak louder than those deliberately used to engineer an effect, and where there is any doubt it is the former which carry most weight.

In social life, image has always been driven by money. Historically, this was 'old', aristocratic money. Now it is 'new' money which is more often than not flashy, vulgar and lacking in taste. The change was succinctly encapsulated by the late Duchess of Windsor, who ventured the opinion (which might well be regarded as a mission statement for modern consumerism), "You can't be too rich or too thin".

Wealth is generally only perceived in monetary terms—and then, as wholly beneficial. In fact, beyond a certain point, increased wealth has negative effects: it breeds distrust—both in the possessor and in their immediate social circle. The more money someone has the less secure they feel in whom they can rely on for disinterested advice or true friendship. There is also a belief that significant wealth makes people more fickle and less dependable. There is another, secondary, sense to wealth, in which it is seen as residing in personal qualities and circumstances beyond money, as a dividend of a balanced attitude and inner contentment. This is a stock metaphor of much religious teaching. A derivative of this model uses the concept of individual or social capital in discussion of sociological phenomena: people or organisations accumulate 'capital' as a function of their personal and societal contributions, which then becomes a determinant of status. Positive social involvement accumulates credit; inappropriate behaviour is accounted a withdrawal—and so on. Those whose personal qualities make them less able to contribute may try to top up their account, and thus enhance their social position, in other ways—most commonly through high-status contacts or displays of visible wealth.

The links between wealth, social status and personal goals are both interesting and complex. While it undoubtedly commands a measure of respect and confers some powers which are independent of personal qualities, social status is not obviously a direct function of wealth. The connection is strong, but circumstantial rather than causal. Where someone's wealth is demonstrably greater than the community average, other things being equal, status will be enhanced. The 'equality' rider is important: beyond love and sex, what people strive for are power/influence, status, respect and admiration, but the latter may be compromised by adverse personal character. Great wealth is no guarantee of a pleasant disposition and many of the world's wealthiest people have repulsive personalities, retaining power by virtue of their position, but often heartily disliked. In some circumstances, therefore, perceived character may be a more significant determinant of image and status than perceived wealth. This is particularly so in high net worth communities, where wealth *per se* is taken for granted and thus of less significance than it might have elsewhere.

For the majority, increasing wealth is seen as a means of improving social status, and its pursuit often figures large in their lives. The development of certain social behaviours, which many take as defining marks of higher civilisation, has been notable for a strong acquisitive trend rather than for any significant increase in spiritual refinement. A better life is seen as one measured in terms of physical circumstances (possessions, standard of living) rather than in terms of mental or spiritual development, although one could argue that beyond minimum physical needs, quality of life depends at least as much on spiritual as on material factors. In an age in of declining moral values and behaviour there is good reason to suggest that rampant consumerism has, in general, been detrimental to happiness and personal development rather than the reverse.

The attraction of wealth is greatly enhanced by the feeling that it is a route to personal happiness — in part the dividend of the added status. This perception is particularly true in the USA where the pleasure principle rules unopposed, pumped daily into people's homes by television output that glamorises the material lifestyle. The selling pitch here is: more equals better — reinforced by public slogans that makes the USA the home of the 'buy-one-get-one-free' and 'all you can eat' culture. The idea is facile for most consumer durables — are you really better off with three cars than with two or one? — and patent nonsense for steak or shrimp. The pursuit of this false nirvana has led directly to misery, not the least manifestation of which is obesity, and indirectly to much pain and stress.

Nonetheless, the impression that wealth does increase happiness is entrenched, particularly in developed societies, and its implications for behaviour are significant. 'We could all use more money' is probably a truism, but wealth-enhancement is more than this. People seek wealth both as an end in itself and as a means to material acquisition which is, in turn, viewed as a lever to enhance social status or as a distraction from more pressing emotional and personal problems. Whilst is easy to ridicule the shop-till-you-drop mentality as vacuous and unenriching, many people are driven by an acquisitive urge;

an increasing number are obsessive. (One might call this 'need' but that is the language of marketing and debases the term).

There are deeper forces at work here than simple acquisitiveness: to function effectively, the built-in obsolescence, consumer society requires that the stimulus (e.g. 'I want — or better still, 'I need' — X') is swiftly followed by the reward (X). No longer prepared to wait for what we want, we have replaced deferred gratification with immediate payout and thereby signal the abandonment of the traditional virtues of thrift and restraint. Older people know that it is often ultimately more rewarding to have something you have planned and saved for rather than getting it as soon as the idea enters your head. The adage that you value something more if you have earned it includes waiting and garnering your resources as part and parcel of the transaction. Certainly, things that come easily, or freely, tend to be less regarded or valued. It may indeed be that the 'get it now' mentality in part reflects the reality that many of today's desirables are soon obsolete (though this is not universally true) and that the purchasing power of savings are easily eroded by inflation — a phenomenon largely unknown a few generations ago. Nonetheless, it is plausible to construe instant gratification as part of modern impatience along with instant messaging, instant food, instant gardens, on-demand entertainment and instant credit.

These considerations merely serve to reinforce the fundamental point that the western (and increasingly the eastern) mindset has shifted in an important way and that self-restraint is now generally anathema. We are encouraged to satisfy our wants immediately and easily persuaded that spending what we do not have is prudent, when in fact it is nothing more than self-indulgence. The marketing mantra is 'Go on treat yourself — you know you deserve it'. The implication that waiting is stressful and that we must 'feel comfortable with ourselves' allows self-gratification to be portrayed as a sensible, even noble, undertaking. It is not simply that slick marketing and the ready availability of credit have rendered self-restraint unnecessary, but that it offends the modern egalitarian because of its strong resonance of old-fashioned values. The 'save and thrift' mentality cut across the social spectrum — for the upper classes it was a virtue, for the working classes, a necessity. Unrestrained spending liberates everyone from both.

Serial acquisitiveness often springs more from the psychological need to be distracted from psychological problems than from social motives, and is not always actuated by the desire to use what we buy to impress others. Although possessions increase our comfort to a limited extent, it is more often than not their perceived ability to transcend well-being and deliver happiness and fulfilment which drives the acquisitive urge. The difficulty with this line of thinking is to demonstrate its application beyond the basic level of necessity; the converse of eliminating negatives is not necessarily to deliver positives. As with wealth itself, what evidence there is suggests that the relationship is far from clear-cut: more possessions, particularly if they are of high value or bought on credit, often bring stress and envy, which can sour lives and relationships. The conclusion from the available research indicates that greater material prosperity does not produce greater happiness, and may indeed even lead to discontent—a finding which has remained firm over several decades of monitoring. The obviously adverse impact that the acquisitive mentality has on so many individuals and societies—not least in distortion of values and production of stress—is hard to overstate.

The determinants of happiness, and its relationship to wealth, have been widely researched. Whilst there is no consensus, some of the findings throw interesting light on the likely factors involved. The fine details are overlaid by our inherent capacity to enjoy life and prosper, which, as multitudes of commentators have noted, is not primarily a function of external circumstances but of attitude and perspective. Reviewing the scientific evidence to date, Oliver James suggests that 'it is the care we receive in the first six years, not our genes, that primarily determines our capacity to enjoy our unprecedented affluence in adulthood'. (Oliver James, 2003) Our early experiences, especially parental neglect, abuse or maternal depression, affect brain chemistry in general and in particular levels of cortisol (the fight-flight hormone) and the volume of the emotion-controlling hippocampal region of the brain. This effectively sets an 'emotional thermostat', as it were, which establishes the basic template through which we interpret the world.

This individual factor sits alongside the well-established fact that happiness comes from within us, not from externalities. The latter can be limiting factors, but only in extremes of poverty and even of wealth. Happiness, prosperity and quality of relationships come from the quality of our habitual thoughts and attitudes. An ability to react positively to adversity, for example, is a potent source of equanimity in dealing with life's problems. Some people have a happy disposition, whilst others seem perpetually miserable, whatever their circumstances; it is those who radiate happiness who have fuller social and personal lives and, indeed, who are less likely to suffer from stress-related illness such as digestive complaints and psychosomatic disorders.

As for wealth — which many see as a prerequisite, if not a prime determinant, of happiness — what evidence there is, is both complex and equivocal. This is not the place to dissect the relationship, but the available data suggests that while the rich are generally happier than the poor, happiness is not correlated with wealth in any straightforward way. For example, the massive increasing in material prosperity between the 1960s and the 1990s in Japan, where incomes rose to the highest *per capita* levels in the industrialised world, was not matched by any measurable change in reported happiness. Even in wealthy nations, happiness does not rise with income over time. One study found that 37% of a sample of 49 super-rich people in the USA was less happy than the national average and another that there was no difference between the happiness level of twenty-two lottery winners and comparison samples of average people or paraplegics. A recent re-evaluation of international surveys of happiness found that there is no consistent correlation between a nation's GDP and its happiness level. Respondents from Forbes's annual list of the 400 richest Americans score 5.8 on the (seven point maximum) happiness scale. But so do the Inuit of northern Greenland and the hut-dwelling Masai of Kenya. Slum dwellers in Calcutta score 4.6, admittedly better than the homeless of that city, who score 2.9.

While it would be unjustified to interpret such findings as demonstrating a negative correlation between wealth and happiness, it is not, as many appear to believe, self-evident that they are positively correlated. In other words, from information about wealth nothing can reliably be deduced about happiness. Two additional factors should be borne in mind: first, that one person's happiness is not interchangeable with another's — putting a Forbes 400 leaguer in a Calcutta slum would certainly alter his rating; second, the 'money = happiness' equation discounts the fact that wealthy nations are democratic societies with relatively efficient government, fair legal systems and respect for human rights, all of which must be considered in any personal evaluation. If these are factored in, the significance of wealth or income on happiness becomes negligible.

This is paradoxical and invites the obvious question: if increased wealth demonstrably fails to produce greater happiness, why do people make such efforts to accumulate it, given the certain increase in stress and the other pressures involved? In a cogently argued book, Robert H. Frank claims that the ability of higher income or greater wealth to increase happiness depends on how it is deployed. Spending merely on what he calls 'conspicuous consumptions goods' (e.g. larger houses, cars and so on) is unproductive, whilst spending on inconspicuous goods — things that make our lives easier and directly relieve pressures (alleviating long commutes to work, making more free time for family and friends; more sleep and exercise) can indeed augment happiness. He also discusses the phenomenon of human adaptation, which allows paraplegics, for example, to adjust to their circumstances and report themselves as content, despite adversity. This also explains adaptation to gains as well as losses and why absolute living standards appear to matter less beyond the level of abject poverty. Frank concludes that 'additional spending in these categories appears to have the greatest capacity to produce significant improvements in well-being'. (Robert H. Frank, *How Not to Buy Happiness*)

Despite these research findings, a strong impression persists that acquiring material goods brings a sustained increase in happiness and fulfilment. Surprisingly little thought is devoted to what there is in multiplying possessions which intrinsically makes for either a better person or greater contentment. The unshakeable conviction that it does reflects both a fundamental misunderstanding of the nature of happiness and the belief that this is a realistic undertaking.

There is no doubt that the act of acquisition gives a pleasure buzz. But this is short-lived and is not to be confused with the happiness that most people claim they are seeking, which might more accurately be described as 'inner contentment'. Part of this popular misconception comes from the false equation of pleasure with happiness. Pleasure is superficial and transient whereas happiness is deeper and more durable and has little or nothing to do with either the act or the fact of possessing. Pleasure can be achieved in a variety of ways, many indeed linked to money and possessions. Happiness, by contrast, is rather the consequence of many other less obvious events and attitudes and less easily attained.

Improving one's surroundings and personal circumstances will improve quality of life up to a point and, in consequence, increase happiness. But this baseline is low, and reached when you have somewhere dry and warm to live, reasonably sound health, and enough food and water. Removal of deprivation is a lukewarm definition of happiness. Beyond such minima, needs and expectations increase as do the means of satisfying them. Proliferation of choice is seen nowadays as an unmitigated benefit; in reality, multiplying options merely adds to the complexity of the selection process and thus to the opportunity cost of every decision. It has also led to a profusion of decision-aids which further increase decision time as cost, value, quality, benefits and the rest are factored in to the process.

The mistake is to see happiness as a direct result of external influences when it is actually a by-product — possibly, but not necessarily, in response to outside events. Happiness is better characterised by reference to emotional rather than material goals, although these are not always independent of each other. It essentially requires an appropriate attitude or disposition, and in this respect is unlike pleasure which is generally a specific response to an identifiable stimulus. This does not, however, make pleasure a causal relationship as the cause does not always produce the effect. Those who seek happiness in itself start from the wrong place and commit what Gilbert Ryle termed a category-mistake; rather like someone who, having seen all Oxford's Colleges individually then asks to see the University.

Contentment (which is not quite the same as happiness, although often equated with it), also comes from within, not from without and is something that comes upon us, rather than the result of any deliberate act, especially not shopping. It is compromised by regret, unhappiness or displeasure, so is perhaps better defined negatively, in terms of their absence. The differences between pleasure and happiness and happiness and contentment are more sharply defined by the circumstances of their opposites: displeasure is not the same as unhappiness — being more impersonal — and unhappiness does not always imply discontent for much the same reason. It is also worth noting that 'being pleased' is not entirely the same as raw 'pleasure', which is altogether a more personal expression of feeling. These inter-relationships are complex and confusing; a lack of understanding of their true nature leads to much unnecessary heartache from the pursuit of happiness through an artificial consumerist dream.

This heartache may be literal as well as figurative. In many developed countries obesity is increasing as a health problem (it affects around one third of Americans), fuelled in part by indisciplined displacement eating as a reaction to stress. This contrasts with a world in which one fifth of the population are either chronically hungry or dying of starvation and the richest fifth consume some 80% of the world's resources and control most of its money. The wealth ethic tends to increase inequalities and entrenches extremes. For example, the combined economies of the forty-eight poorest countries are significantly lower than the assets of the three richest people in the world, and one-fifth of the world's population exist on less than a dollar a day.

It is not far from the image of plenty to the reality of excess. Nowhere is this more evident than in the USA, where waste is an integral part of the culture. You are encouraged to consume more than you want (or need) and then to discard the excess. Instead of buying a single doughnut for, say $2, you buy 5 for $8; the choice is then whether to eat the lot and court obesity or to throw away food which would help feed the hungry. Buy one for $1, buy 5 for $4 or perhaps you can be tempted to buy 20 for $13; 'Eat one of our twenty-ounce steaks and we'll give you another one free'. Self-restraint is not part of the good-life script nor does it seem within the wit of the average American to see through the proposition that 'more' equals 'better'. They also appear oblivious to the inference from junk pricing to junk quality. The ironical result of this boundless self-indulgence is that, having ingested mountains of mass-produced food, millions of Americans are now clinically obese and at heightened risk from obesity-related illness. However, far from blaming themselves for their plight, some now seek to hold food companies legally liable for their self-inflicted problems.

Unfortunately, the culture of cheap food, fuel and much else is endemic in America, and the government lacks the will to change the public mentality or to restrain the aggressive multi-nationals who stoke the consumerism that drives the US economy and upon which it increasingly depends. The depressing fact is that, despite its obvious shortcomings, this culture is more likely to spread intact than to mutate into something more benign as conspicuous consumption is presented to the world as an enviable way of life—the American Dream.

The ability to acquire great riches speedily, combined with the fact that many of those who do are *ipso facto* not imbued with the upbringing or tradition of money, puts the power of wealth into hands which are unaccustomed to it. Spending is easy enough, but coping with the personal and social consequences of wealth is more problematical. Being instantly catapulted from a modest income to riches tests the boundaries of friendship and tears families and lives apart, as many sporting stars, pop celebrities and lottery winners have discovered. Wealth, like any other tool, can work to your advantage but only if you know how to use it.

Wealth has no obvious relationship to education or taste, and the newly rich are often perceptibly lacking in both. To help them overcome these deficiencies, there has emerged the style guru. Such 'experts', or something like them, have existed for centuries in various guises—restoration comedies and 18th century operas abound with wise and scheming servants—and trade profitably on wealthy ignorance and the enduring but mistaken belief that money can buy taste, style or class. Then, as now, the servant is often in effect the master—the butler telling his employer how to behave, and the personal shopper advising her client what to wear. Unfortunately, whilst clients may pay lip-service to the 'taste' they are buying, they often impose their own and so end up with the very tastelessness they wish to avoid.

The cult of celebrity is a potent player on the stage that is personal image. Saturation displays of luxury living invite us to believe that people with celebrity lifestyles have worthwhile, abundantly fulfilled lives. These people are presented as contented, stress-free, and powered by permanent good fortune. Problems, if they have them, are confined to high-profile extra-marital affairs and how to spend their extraordinary incomes. If the celebrity culture has spawned imitation, this is probably because in recognising the influence and status attached to celebrity, we take the material trappings surrounding it as an integral part of the image-package. Without these trappings, so the thinking goes, celebrities would not be celebrities. Such logic, whilst compelling, is suspect.

This constant diet of vicarious luxury tends to breed dissatisfaction and inspires imitation, in the hope that some of the magic dust will rub off and improve our own lives. This ignores the fact that much so-called celebrity is talentless and transient and that we are only shown the desirable side of the picture. It is also fragile: celebrities, for all their status, are not superhuman and have just as much, if not more, stress and personal misery as anyone. The popular press thrives on exposing the flaws, shame, misery and dysfunction behind celebrity glamour, but the world is seduced by the image and finds it hard to see how people with apparently limitless wealth, grand homes full of desirable things—exotic cars, beautiful wives or icon husbands—could possibly be unhappy or unfulfilled.

The lack of an intrinsic relationship between wealth and contentment is unable to shake the entrenched conviction that there is. This breaks down into two separate ideas (both false): first, that increased material prosperity somehow frees you from life's problems; second, that acquiring accessories and using them skilfully can increase one's importance and social standing. The justification for imitation comes from the premise that material trappings are somehow identifiable with success; in other words, you can't be successful and not have them; conversely, if you have them, then success will inexorably follow. Put thus, the argument is seen to be shaky.

There is also the problem that as well as buying the image you have to live up to it which is akin to acting out another personality. But, as already discussed, struggling to sustain a deceit is more likely to generate unproductive stress than benefit. When it fails to deliver, people who try to live out a dream, often at the risk of their own and their family's lives, are deeply disillusioned. One particularly disastrous response is to strive for even higher profile props rather than recognising the futility of the entire enterprise. It should be obvious that changing one's external circumstances (the Image) does not change one's internal attitudes and values (the Reality). Although the trappings of the high life may briefly distract from one's problems, no amount of luxury will produce permanent escape from one's self, one's circumstances or one's inadequacies.

The logic of imitation founders on several mistaken assumptions: first, that the reality behind the image you are copying is better than your own; second, that imitation will automatically produce that reality; third, that mimicking a more attractive image will, by some unspecified alchemy, change your own fundamental character or circumstances. It also falls foul of the generally unremarked difference between imitation and emulation: emulation requires hard work and the effort to build something from scratch (neither is popular in today's 'have it now' culture) and is potentially productive; imitation is seen as a convenient short cut and is usually unproductive.

The desire for material wealth has been fuelled by relentless exposure to the Hollywood celebrity lifestyle. This is the apotheosis of the American Dream — a powerful stimulus derived from an uncompromising, image-driven, market-oriented culture. It is perhaps unfortunate that in its unremitting pursuit of self-improvement for itself and the world in general, and despite an explosion of home-grown religious sects and evangelical proselytising, America seems to have collective difficulty distinguishing material from the spiritual. There is nothing in having six homes and two hundred pairs of shoes which obviously makes you happier or superior in any important respect to someone with one home and five pairs of shoes.

In the western world, there is much media output designed to reinforce the idea that material success is the single most significant source of contentment. Television, in particular, is a powerful role model in suggesting that this or that is the proper way to conduct one's life—the way you should dress, behave or think. 'We are offered a continuously reinforced vision of people whose social and material status seems to bring them unadulterated joy ... [and] ... are trapped in this distorted system to the extent that people seem to think—not only that wearing this perfume or driving that car will itself bring success, but that reaching some goal (e.g. being made a partner or director) will somehow instantly transform your life. "When it (*promotion*) finally happened, I felt a brief stab of euphoria, but after that my life continued pretty much as before. Somehow, I assumed that I would be transformed into a different person—cleverer, more desirable, happier. In fact, I felt empty". There seems little realisation that the things which seem to define someone as successful—job, money, status—are impermanent and thus that basing one's self image and life on externals, you are likely to be disappointed. The shock of this realisation forces many people to redefine their values and to think about what really drives their life and gives it meaning.' (Kathryn Hughes, *Redefining Success,* Options 1993)

Much pleasure-seeking is simply a means of avoiding personal problems. How we identify and confront life's realities differs from person to person, as does the outcome of the process. The essential insight is to recognise and focus on what is capable of control, rather than seeking to change aspects of our lives that we are less able to influence. Some are closely personal and alterable (e.g. health, stress, and spiritual values); others are less tractable (e.g. careers, how others see us, social status). It is often said that the most content, and indeed the most successful people are those who are mostly closely in touch with their inner selves—their own attitudes, motives and needs. Concentrating on these puts external influences into perspective, which is often the catalyst for rebalancing one's values.

Many personal problems are based on distorted images, and as such are more readily dealt with by straightening the mirror rather than trying to re-fashion the image—in other words, they are more readily dissolved than solved. They often stem from inappropriate, self-inflicted responses to others who we feel threaten us, either by their status or by their achievements. Such threats are generally illusory and are best met not by confrontation but by establishing what makes you content. There are gender differences in the way we deal with such perceived problems; some observers have noted that men tend to work by competition, women by consensus. This is not to deny the genuineness of the pleasure of health spas, shopping, good food or fine wine, but rather to point up the need to realise that they are non-essential. The extent that we cannot live without them tells us much about ourselves. Some of the most fulfilled people are those who enjoy relatively simple things. In allowing ourselves to be unduly influenced by events, people and general circumstances we render ourselves vulnerable. Living too much from the outside-in impedes the search for inner security which would recommend the reverse.

The cult of celebrity also reflects the powerful human wish for popularity, and fame is seen as an ideal route to this end. There is no set route or set of rules to achieving fame. "Talent doesn't even really come into being famous any more ... it is just about being seen with the right people and then knowing how to capitalise on it." (Max Clifford, PR agent) Most of us want to be recognised, popular, and to stand proud of the pack. Unfettered libertarianism, freed of most moral and social constraints, now makes it possible for anyone to be famous, however minimal your talent or banal your ideas. As long as you can get yourself noticed, you may succeed, if only briefly. 'If you're hot, you scoop the lot' is today's golden rule. Genuine celebrity has a strong seductive force. However, modelling ourselves on someone else compromises our own identity and when it falters, as is inevitable, it results in greater, not less, insecurity. Seeking an anchor outside our control makes us vulnerable to that anchor being weighed.

Paradoxically, much of the modern celebrity people admire and ape is itself insecure. The realisation that celebrity is transitory and may last no longer than the time you remain at the top is its own driver of values and behaviour. This includes the recognition that wealth alone is of limited social value unless you have some of the style and taste that it supposed to accompany it, and in this respect old aristocracy has been helpful. One finds modern celebrities buying large country estates and adopting old aristocratic ways: hunting, shooting and fishing as pastimes, butlers and servants in attendance, and traditional social gatherings, polo and race meetings—whether they enjoy them or not. Not only is there tacit recognition of the value and durability of genuine nobility; the *nouveaux riches* like to cement the connection and their social position by hobnobbing with old aristocracy. Unfortunately, all too often they turn themselves into parodies of the landed gentry. Fame is a thin veneer which cracks easily; the image is all too often compromised by drink or drugs and *parvenus* frequently squander whatever credibility they have when they misbehave and return to type. Such false society tends to be sustained by a tacit, mutually reinforcing conspiracy. Everyone is aware of the reality, but fiction is not fact and deception rarely convinces beyond these artificial confines.

As personal insecurity increases, we are becoming ever more mesmerised by celebrity. A British newspaper set out to find someone on earth who did not know who David Beckham was — and finally found someone in the Saharan city of Timbuktu. There are over 100,000 web sites dedicated to Madonna. (Focus article, *UK Sunday Times*, c 2002). There are documented instances of people whose interest in celebrity amounts to clinical obsession and research suggests that many are socially dysfunctional as a result, with symptoms bordering on the pathological. If you must copy someone, it makes sense to copy a winner; indeed, who you choose to idolise says much about your personality, attitudes and ambitions. The trouble is that people copy only the externalities they can see, which is an unsound route to self-improvement.

Fashion is part of the imitative syndrome — you dress and behave like your favourite celebrity — and integral to the pursuit of image. There are some people who have little better to do with their lives than follow fashion, irrespective of its suitability or where it leads them — this is particularly true of trends in diets and body-image products. If an A-list celebrity wraps herself in treacle, then so will thousands of others, even though some may have misgivings about the wisdom of doing so. It is fickle fashion that spurs the herd instinct and leads people to spend time and money in what are, arguably, some of the worst places on earth — if not before the fashionable invasion then certainly afterwards. Celebrity and style are uneasy bedfellows! Fashion, in that it recreates itself periodically, is also novelty; and since those with shallow lives need something undemanding to do, they follow fashion. It stretches the wallet, but not the brain. The Kinks song "Dedicated follower of fashion" no doubt had such people in mind.

Why has celebrity such a strong grip on people's lives? After all, it is no more than a superficial compound of insecurity, vanity and cash, sustained by more or less talent and a large dollop of exhibitionism. It lacks both durability and intrinsic worth, and has little significance beyond its own image. Yet, celebrities are idolised, and not just by the masses. They are a convenient foil for the subtler, more insidious, pretensions of elites who use the icon's idealised image to project a reality they know to be false. As George Walden notes, elites derive considerable advantage in passing off Image for Reality; 'Idealisation is a great way to do people down. They can never live up to the image you project of them, and the more you patronise them … the more you emphasise the gap between you and them'. (*The New Elites*)

The image-culture is inextricably linked with fashion and in particular with brands. The more expensive branded goods scream on their owners' behalf. "I'm wealthy! I've bought the best! I have style and taste!" The ostentatious use brands extensively to prop up their image and the suppliers eagerly oblige—this season's 'must-have'. For some reason this particularly applies to women's fashions although men are increasingly becoming brand marketing targets. Fashion brands are particularly clever in that they send positive messages both to the users and, through them, to their acquaintance. Brands also help consumers who are often unable to distinguish good from mediocre and provide those who can't tell a well-cut suit or finely-crafted handbag from a mass-produced version some guarantee of quality and that their money has been well spent, and a measure of comfort that they will not suffer social disgrace. In turn, their circle of influence receives the value-added signal that the suit or handbag is expensive, which they hope will broadcast a positive message about their taste and wealth.

In the early days, fashion ranges started off with brand names prominently emblazoned on the products, so that their wearers would leave no one in doubt of their affluence or chic. Then the branding became subtler and took an identifiable, patentable, style or logo to replace the crude lettering. Now an even subtler styling—e.g. Gucci stripes or Burberry checks—replaces the ostentatious branding. Unfortunately, excellent fakes abound and imitation jewellery, watches and clothes are virtually indistinguishable from the authentic article—even, in some cases by experts. This has compromised the image potential of many luxury brands to the point at which the prominently-lettered cardboard carrier-bag has taken over from the article itself. Self-deception has thus replaced other-deception in the Image stakes.

The culture of fakes has many manifestations. In the daily market-place, much of what is on offer is mediocrity skilfully presented. The knock-on effects of a powerful mass market on production techniques and on the environment are well documented; products with the appropriate appearance sell well, so that is what comes to market. For example, food colour and flavour are enhanced, often to the detriment of taste, to endow indifferent quality with broad market appeal. The demand for ever cheaper products is well met by intensive mass production—cheap raw materials fashioned by cheap labour into cheap articles. Its success relies on the fact that consumers in general have a limited appreciation of quality despite attempts to educate them into becoming more discerning. (If they are dissuaded from buying mass-produced food, it is more likely because the have discovered how it is reared or culti-vated, rather than because it is tasteless.) This is fertile ground for the peddlers of mediocrity—provided, of course, the price is right. Such manipulation is not confined to the mass market. Mediocre quality is often presented as top-level with a price tag to match. The ubiquity of indifferent food served in pretentious surroundings, poor wine put into fine glasses, and fawning servility exemplify such deceits. Gullibility is not just the prerogative of low socio-economic groups.

Naïve consumers are fertile ground for product marketing which thrives in markets which have poor understanding of quality. People expect beef to be vibrant cochineal red rather than its natural greyish colour and fish to be bright pink rather than neutral or pinkish because that is how they believe it should be. Store buyers have become equally obsessed with cosmetic standards and demand of their suppliers that everything looks perfect. This makes sense for clothes or wheelbarrows, where any damage is a defect, but not for food, where perfect appearance has little to do with perfect taste. A misshapen tomato often has a far more flavour intensity than one that is ovoid or beautifully spherical, but the consumer is seduced by appear-ance and knows no better, so misshapes don't sell. Thus tasteless over-cropped hydroponic produce is what is offered. The requirement for uniformity leads to massive waste. Farmers are obliged to dispose of tons of edible, nutri-tious food simply because it fails to meet cosmetic norms. Much of what is rejected is unsaleable—ridiculous in a price-conscious market, even more so in a world full of starving people. American food stores have perfected this cosmetic culture—everything appears splendid and enticing but is all too often completely devoid of flavour. Consumers evidently prefer to sacrifice flavour to appearance, and presumably believe that you can somehow taste the shape! Education is the key to changing this state of affairs but, despite the valiant efforts of consumer organisations in many countries, appears to have limited impact. This is a predictable dividend of the way industry now views consumers—not as one end of the supply/demand relationship, but (as the late J. K. Galbraith noted) as the final leg in the production cycle to be managed to need whatever maximises corporate profit. In a world capable of producing affordable quality, this state of affairs is deplorable.

Fashion is fast moving. In an age of image-loving people, with high disposable income and constantly in search of novelty, designers have skilfully exploited the potential. This often means 'quick response' design and manu-facturing, enabling the market to react rapidly to consumer whims and fancies. These are often created, sometimes unwittingly, by celebrities, as much as by designers themselves. Celebrity both drives fashion and follows it. The finest details of celebrities' lives—what they do, where and how they live, how they dress, behave and what they buy—constitute part of their image for those who follow them. What pop or sporting stars wear has enormous influence on style and trends. Fashion is often created unwittingly when something worn or done is seized upon by the fan club and rapidly becomes the 'in thing'. When a casual dress item in a video or film captures imagination and defines the New Look, the market is quick to respond. Designers also define 'cool' and are adept at telling people what they should be wearing while fashion consumers are acutely perceptive, demanding the latest fashion item almost before it has appeared.

Elsewhere, fashions change more slowly—wearily and without apparent logic. In *Adventures of a Suburban Boy* (set in 1960s Los Angeles), John Boorman commented: 'Over the years, I have watched the fashion change as movie people went from bourbon to martinis, from martinis to Scotch and from Scotch to red wine; then from red wine to white wine, from white wine to Perrier and finally, from Perrier to Evian'.

Fashion has percolated through to the nursery as parents extend their own image through their children by exhibiting them as expensively dressed. This does not always deliver the desired message in that dress says nothing automatic about either good upbringing or proper care. It merely signifies parental ostentation. The children themselves have taken up the thread, pres-sured by peers into wearing this designer shoe or that T-shirt. While grown-ups covet Hermes or Gucci, kids demand Kickers. Idol-worship now demands that children be seen in this or that baseball or football stripe or sporting the latest electronic toy or media gadget. Image-consciousness now comes early, imposing stress on parents who struggle financially to keep up, and on children who feel 'deprived', socially outcast, even 'stressed out', if they cannot keep pace with their schoolmates.

In many areas utility has been replaced by fashion. For a product or idea to succeed in today's competitive market-place, it is not sufficient, or even neces-sary, to be well-made or useful; it merely has to be fashionable. The converse, however, does not apply. Being fashionable does not entail being either well-made or useful. Indeed much of what is fashionable at any given time is of low worth in absolute terms. Marketing is now less directed at pushing products as products, more at pushing them as fashion items. Soap is sold as a beauty product or for its quasi-medical benefits — it moisturises, exfoliates, protects, oils and generally does us good — not for its cleansing properties.

The superficial pursuit of a fashionable image has infected, and damaged, the arts. The boundaries of what is and is not art have been eroded to the point of invisibility. In many departments, the arts seem to have lost any sense of value and direction. The rise of celebrity and popular culture has also blurred the distinction between elite art and mass art. There is a sense in which the art and art forms enjoyed, for example, by the old aristocracy of Europe, in their search for, and patronage of, talent defined art and set standards within it. These were fluid, but operated within an accepted, albeit elastic, framework. Now what is considered good is more or less equated with what is 'hot' or 'funky' and what has mass appeal. Artistic elites, even post-aristocracy, are considered as a branch-line of eccentricity and dismissed as out of touch with popular sentiment. 'Some collectors are noble, philanthropic and educated; others are swindling bores who would still think Parmigianino is a kind of cheese if they didn't have the boys at Christie's to set them straight'. (Robert Hughes, *A Culture of Complaint, The Fraying of America*). There is still a strong interest in the Old Masters, classical sculpture, poetry and literature from, for example, the very people who patronise the funkier end of the popular music scene. They are keen to appreciate the finer manifestations of artistic tradition alongside the less refined offerings of modern music. Too often, there is a feeling of a progressive deterioration of taste and that we are presently wallowing in a morass of mindless artistic triviality, much of it vulgar and driven by money. The fact that television costume dramas attract massive audiences on a regular basis, suggests that we have not entirely abandoned our souls to artistic nihilism. Nonetheless, from such conflicting evidence, it is difficult to develop any sense of a progressive cultural evolution.

The state of modern art, if it can be considered a unity, is due in large part to the divorce of mainstream art from its traditions. Modern art has made determined efforts to discard its cultural heritage and to obliterate the links between art and beauty. Indeed, if the trendy apologists are to be believed, the search for beauty in art is not only futile, but also misguided. Today, art is no longer seen as a development in a sustained progression, another discernible stage in an evolving culture, but rather as a deliberate rejection of tradition and an overwhelming desire to discard what is regarded as old-fashioned and dull.

In this, the modernists mistakenly paint the espousal of traditional ideas and forms as putting them in some kind of thrall to the past, rather than as drawing on the accumulated wisdom embodied in tradition as a source of artistic and cultural inspiration. Dada and Surrealism also broke with the past, but their exponents at least recognised rather than repudiated their heritage, and were excellent executive artists to boot.

In Victorian times, determined efforts were made to bring art to a wider audience and to cultivate in ordinary people a sense of beauty and artistic worth, whether through the visual arts, music, literature or architecture. In general, modern art shows little respect for, or recognition of, its cultural heritage. It is difficult not to sympathise with the suggestion that it corrupts our 'sensibility towards tradition and nature' in that 'the culture it touches is Utopian, evolved in the recesses of abundance and ennui. It is devoid of human understanding and has little interest. Art has become divorced from national cultural expression.' (Athena S Leoussi, Appreciating the Arts, in *The War on Wisdom*)

The core skills of traditional art schools comprised the disciplines of drawing, perspective and composition. These skills have no place in the modern milieu which considers them outmoded and indeed unnecessary for the expression of abstract ideas. (It is difficult to find any obvious artistic or imaginative skill in many modern artists, for example, the much lauded works of Warhol or Rothko). So, they are either actively discouraged, or else—to the limited extent that they are required—belittled ('if you can see, you can draw'). This reflects an unbridled artistic liberalism—the artistic interpretation of 'anything goes'—that exemplifies the wider desire to break with the past. One gets the impression that the mainstream western artistic tradition is seen as an unwarranted imposition and as evidence of the power and control vested in an artistic elite.

Modernism is by and large nihilistic. It makes no attempt to elevate the spirit or gladden the soul. If it recognises the imaginative and uplifting, it prefers not to mention it, and generally refuses to make evaluative distinctions between what is beautiful and ugly, sacred and profane and, ultimately, good and evil. It encourages and vaunts self-expression and in doing so disparages or ignores its audience. It also rejects the idea that artistic creativity should provide a comprehensible experience. The artist is there to express himself, and it is seen as no part of his role to explain himself or his work to the public. Art in these hands is knowing, stultifying, impoverished and, above all, condescending. In as much as it pitches taste and discrimination out of the window, it is also depressing.

Some have equated what is seen as the malaise in contemporary art with changes in contemporary culture. The parallels are compelling. The shallow, concept-dominated ideas of modern art—and its attendant 'expertise'—are evident in many aspects of life. The abandonment of tradition in favour of unfettered individual expression is a recognisable social theme, and the search for the eye-catching and the shocking regardless of intrinsic merit, have obvious parallels in broadcast and print media. The *raison d'etre* of the entire artistic enterprise has been diluted by personal, social and commercial considerations. 'Good art' is redefined as that which sells or attracts large audiences.

These trends mark a caesura from the traditions of western art. Much of the visual and media arts are in the firm grip of sensationalism, where artistic fashion, and even what is considered meritorious, effectively coincides with novelty. As public funding dries up, the need to attract audiences increases, and often overrides, the need to create interesting or inspiring work. Instead the artistic elites have gone for the sensational, the shocking, the subversive, the amusing—whatever is freakish or wacky. In order to square their choices with the reality of what is generally regarded as art, they simply broaden the definition of art to encompass an ever more bizarre range of expression. It is therefore not surprising that the boundaries between art and non-art have been progressively smudged or, as some would argue, obliterated entirely.

The undercurrent of political revolution in modern western art, evident since the early 20th century, seems to have taken a more urgent tone. Artists increasingly see themselves as at the forefront of society—a social or political *avant-garde*—although society does not always share their assessment. While artists can no longer be bothered to interpret their works, they are all too willing to proclaim their anti-establishment credentials. Art has become even more than in the past a political weapon, either as an activist route to 'addressing issues' or as a statement of disaffection. One only has to look at what is valued in contemporary art—popular music in particular—to see that works with social or political themes, particularly if they are radical or subversive, attract undue praise and attention. It is more often than not their political stance, rather than any technical or artistic merit, that defines an artist's public image.

The instant appeal of much modern music and art relies on a tacit agreement between producer and consumer to gloss over deficient quality in favour of an image of thrusting, razor-sharp modernity. In many instances the reality is of untalented artists purveying sub-mediocre work to an audience incapable of distinguishing the good from the worthless. In this it is no more than a conspiracy between superficiality and gullibility to legitimise work produced for mass appeal. In short, artistic mashed banana. Whilst the public has always enjoyed great art, there has never been mass appetite for the intellectual effort necessary to understand and appreciate it, and people are happy to defer to experts over what is worthy and to suspend their own (limited) artistic judgement. As Sir Thomas Beecham remarked of British musical appreciation: the public knows nothing about music but thoroughly enjoys the noise it makes. However, the public tends not to suspend its instincts and, where the greatest excesses are concerned, those tell it that it is being hoodwinked. Confounding public ignorance with public stupidity is likely to inflict incalculably greater long-term damage to art than any amount of worthless artistic output.

In vain one looks for beauty in the bleak displays of intellectual, conceptual, esoteric modern art. Not only is much of what is highly valued in this precious, self-conscious milieu not beautiful, it is uncompromisingly ugly. In the twisted logic of these things, this may be part of the appeal. "You've seen the beautiful; why not try the ugly, tasteless, vulgar and obscene? Roll-up for The Modern Novelty!"

Classical abstract art opposes representational art, but is nonetheless tied to standards and a clear stage in art's evolutionary progression. The new 'abstract' is not of this lineage, lacking the emotive and evocative markers which characterise the abstract movement. Modern abstract art, takes the 'anything goes' rule of unregulated self-expression to its extreme and, in this, follows an ideology which does not recognise absolutes. Removing standards in this way devalues the currency; if everything is art, then nothing is. There is a strong whiff of nonsense in the pronouncements and postures of modern art; sometimes brilliant, often attractive, but nonsense nonetheless.

The traditional guardians of artistic value—museum curators and art critics—seem to have thrown in the towel as the market increasingly dictates on matters of taste and aesthetics. The new elites of the art world have been duped into accepting as art much work which is devoid of conceptual or artistic skill. To maintain their self-esteem, faced with a public bemused and privately derisive of prevailing artistic values, they cultivate an attitude of loftiness and contempt. A public that does not understand is simply ignorant. The main supporting constituency of modern art appears to consist of a narrow caucus of artistic elites—artists, art critics, selection committees and dealers—propped up by the *nouveaux riches* who like to see themselves, and to be seen, as discerning and perspicacious—as having cachet as well as cash. There is, as Dickens remarked, no deceit to equal self-deceit.

In much modern art, the normal flow of communication and the metaphor of art as a supremely aesthetic language has been turned upside-down. Traditionally, the artist communicated his meaning through the skilful use of his medium (colour, perspective, composition, etc) in much the same way as speakers or writers use language. This was apparent to the viewer, listener or reader and, to the extent that it was not, the communication failed. Where the great Old Master works can be appreciated on several planes and admired by the least tutored of novices, now the art world talks in garbled, incomprehensible language (if language it is at all), using a variety of idioms, for which the viewer (consumer, in modern terminology) is expected to supply the interpretation. The stripping of meaning from painting in particular has been paralleled by a shift in the onus of defining the artistic significance of a work from the artist to the 'consumer'. So-called conceptual art is not to be understood by its subject matter or its relation to ideas and relies entirely on a third party to supply a commentary. Hitherto, this was the province of the artist. No longer: the artist may create, but he is not to be prevailed upon to explain. That role now devolves on the viewer who is expected to take personal responsibility for interpreting what he sees (or buys). The circle of comprehension is incomplete until the end-user arrives to supply the final link. Making the interpretation of a work subjective in this way conveniently neutralises the charge that it might be meaningless. If you, the viewer, fail to discern its meaning then either it has none or your antennae are bent. In no case is the artist to blame for producing nonsense. To this arrogance is added the conceit that you are effectively only paying for half the work (or possibly less)—though the artist will probably tell you that you are in fact getting more than you are paying for in being granted the chance to complete the work to your own sense and satisfaction.

What the elites of the artistic establishment lose sight of is the difference between embracing or reacting to popular culture and being subservient to it. It is entirely compatible with sensitivity to public taste and changing fashion to make the public want what you give them; but not, at least openly, to give them whatever they happen to want—as appears to have happened in the broadcast media. Art should lead and shape taste, not be led by it. Public figures in arts administration generally defend the artistically trivial and incomprehensible, afraid that to attack it would be to be seen as old-fashioned and out of tune with the modern spirit. It would seem that the emperor's new clothes are indeed bright and well-ironed, at least in the higher echelons of the artistic community.

To the extent that artists themselves are prepared to play this game, they are party to the fraud. Thus it is that much artistic talent is wasted on puerile superficiality and political activism. On a more general level, the artistic canvas is wide and wide open to a sentimentalist, populist programme which influences everything from minimalism in furniture and interior design to trendiness in the kitchen. Minimalist furniture exemplifies a thoroughly silly fashion, deliberately designed for the image it creates rather than for comfort or utility. In the minimalist, less-is-better, school of design, beds are cupboards, tables are skeletal and chairs uncomfortable. The clinical, hospital look is favoured, with sharp, clean lines in brilliant white or metal and awkward formal settings. Minimalist home interiors resemble hotels—possibly to remind people of their (increasingly frequent) foreign holidays. This is not to suggest that functionalism be the defining element of interior design, but that designing essentially functional objects with little regard to their intended purpose is perverse. People who buy into this trend are making a fashion judgement first, and furnishing their homes second. Their choices also make a strong statement about their aesthetic values and personalities.

The minimalist trend spread to the kitchen where *nouvelle cuisine*—surely one of the more ridiculous modern-day infections—was hailed as a breakthrough by countless gastronomic sophisticates. Chefs presented ever smaller dishes to their hungry and increasingly disillusioned clientele who became angered both by not being fed properly and by the apparently inverse relationship between quantity and price. This triumph of presentation over substance (literally—there was rarely enough on the plate) made no sense either in weight-control or nutritional terms and the fashion thankfully passed. The fine dining public expects to be well fed, but the more theatrical aspects of food presentation linger on as publicity-hungry, media-aware culinary luminaries try to cram ever more diverse, often outrageous, combinations of flavours onto one plate as a means of adding value. This does not always make for appetising eating. Meanwhile celebrity chefs deluge us with 'how to' cooking 'shows', often crudely dressed up as competitions or travelogues. We reverentially buy their cook books but don't seem to cook much better, and are becoming steadily more obese as convenience foods provide a nil-effort short cut. Modern gastronomy is now devoted as much to fashion as to feeding.

Architecture is not immune to the modernist trend. Throughout history, those commissioned to design buildings have always had an eye to their own reputation, as well as to satisfying their clients. As with minimalist interior designers, many modern architects have sought to make a personal style statement, putting self-aggrandisement above the need to produce a fine or functionally satisfactory building. Much municipal post-war work has, or will soon be, demolished—ugly, poorly-conceived buildings which follow no discernible trend or tradition; stand-alone 'carbuncles' of little aesthetic or architectural merit. Elsewhere, the fashion for putting the guts of buildings on the outside, making them look like chemical works or oil refineries, is also, after a rather lengthy period in vogue, now happily on the wane. As in so many spheres, the relationship of (pay)-master dictating his requirements to his servant (however talented) has been turned on its head. Chefs, architects, artists, interior-designers are now celebrities who see their clients as privileged to have access to their services. Patrons may pay, but what they dispense is no longer patronage.

In the Opera house, avant-garde producers and designers have imposed their radical interpretations on old and much-loved work. Not content to tell us something new and inspiring, or to re-interpret work within its context, they resort to shaking up the cherished and familiar to the point that, were the music not there, audiences would no longer recognise it. An eighteenth century Italian palazzo becomes a 20th century brothel, a cosy hotel supplants Wagner's stark mountains and halls, and a petrol station replaces an intimate artist's loft. The changes disturb and shock without intellectual justification or purpose, whilst the perpetrators depart with substantial fees and over-inflated egos. They perhaps forget that to be clever is not always to be wise.

What has happened to common sense and perspective in all this? Where is the good sense and wise counsel of art critic, theatre critic, restaurant critic and film critic? Many appear to have abrogated their independence of judgement because of a general desire to be seen as fashionable and open-minded; 'go with the flow' is their motto and a sort of artistic political correctness stifles their judgement (or is it cowardice?). Those who pontificated on the vision and conceptual boldness of 'paintings' which turned out to have been created by elephants, exposed the fragility of this 'expert' world. Without sound, reliable insight and guidance, it is less easy for a receptive but untutored public to settle its opinions on what is and what is not art and to decide what is worth their time and attention. Although we might have strong opinions on dirty, unmade, beds, stuffed sheep, elephant dung, and disorderly piles of bricks, we will always welcome the reassurance and interpretative guidance of an impartial expert, especially in areas which might be unfamiliar. We need a pilot to navigate us through what Salvador Dali dubbed 'this grandiose tragedy that we call modern art'.

The trends covered in this chapter fall loosely under the heading of Lifestyle. It is worth asking whether this term is not itself a product of the image culture — merely a neologism for how we live — a modern packaging around age old ideas. Lifestyles, in the literal sense, vary widely, and have always done so. What is debatable is whether there is anything with sufficient separate identity to be termed 'lifestyle'? Alternatives presented as 'lifestyle' usually signify that they affect our lives in some radical way. This suggests that we do have meaningful choices of this sort and that it makes sense to talk about something which corresponds to lifestyle, above and beyond the way we live.

Until recently, lifestyles were considered to be broadly dictated by circumstances — choice was limited by availability, money and ancillary factors, such as physical ability. It was only when personal wealth and the variety of things to spend it on increased that it became meaningful to talk of lifestyle decisions, in this secondary sense. Now, it is perfectly possible for people to decide on a given lifestyle and act it out, although for most of us, this option remains more dream than reality.

The concept of lifestyle is derivative coinage of marketing. Relating something to lifestyle seems to endow it with an extra cachet which it would not otherwise deserve. Indeed, such is the shibboleth of 'inclusivity' in modern society that bankruptcy is now considered a 'lifestyle choice', on equal footing with retirement and dropping out. The social stigma that used to attach to feckless spending and inability to manage one's financial affairs no longer exists, so building up debt and then going bust is seen as an entirely acceptable option.

Much of the lifestyle prescription industry is no more than slick image management, which solves little and is, at worst, fraudulent. For example, there is nothing wrong with losing weight to bolster self-confidence, but those who sell vibrating armchairs as a substitute for genuine exercise are peddling delusion. Those who fail to look after themselves now find that being fat has become a valid 'lifestyle choice', on equal terms with those of fitness and health. An alliance between political correctness and the equal rights lobby has effectively suppressed the opprobrium once levelled at obesity, stifled (at least in the USA) by campaigns to encourage people to be proud that they are fat and to promote the so-called 'rights' of the overweight 'community'. This makes it difficult to change public perceptions or to restore any shame associated with loss of self-control, which might be seen as a sensible way to deal with what is admitted to be a serious public health problem. (Hopefully, attitudes themselves have not altered, which might allow a more sensible approach when the social climate changes).

The superficial idioms of lifestyle and fashion play a seminal part in many lives—in the way we see ourselves, in the way we assess society as seeing us, and in our attempts to manipulate either or both for personal ends. To the extent that reality is distorted in pursuit of image creates difficulties for us and others; it also undermines personal integrity and thereby the likelihood of happiness.

The greed creed is not entirely selfish, in that it comes with a wide recognition of the need for charity, generosity and fairness. Nonetheless, the unrestrained pursuit of material wealth solves few problems (except self-inflicted financial problems), distorts values and destroys spirituality. Those whose warped sense of perspective about themselves and their place in society leads them to spend their time worrying about whether or not they are fashionable or following fashion for social advancement, generally waste their lives.

This, and the foregoing chapters, point to the futility of chasing image, and the benefits of living within the realities of our personalities, qualities and capabilities: life is best focused inwards, not around the transient values of money, power or status. Inner peace and balance and the ultimate prize of happiness, do not come from the external stimuli of success, cash or approbation (pleasurable as these may be). The belief that they do points to the need for a major reappraisal of what really matters to society in a world which is increasingly cash-rich but value-poor.

CHAPTER 7

ACCOUNTABILITY, TRUST AND PERSONAL RESPONSIBILITY

'Man must cease attributing his problems to his environment, and learn again to exercise his personal responsibility in the realm of faith and morals.'
Albert Schweitzer

'Hypocrisy is the homage vice pays to virtue'
Francois de la Rochefoucauld

The evolution of civilisation is generally characterised as a development of social structures. It has, in an equally if not more important sense, been a process of refinement of behaviour. An essential feature of any fully developed society that maintains order through a process of law is moral agency—the requirement that individuals are held responsible for the consequences of their actions. As choices have become more varied and education more widespread, one might have expected this accountability to have strengthened.

In fact, the scope of moral agency has narrowed significantly over recent decades as the emergence of a substantial ill-socialised underclass has forced societies to extend collective responsibility over a wider area of individual behaviour. It has also been circumscribed by a willingness to blame someone other than the agent for deviance and perceived misfortunes and by the reclassification of much abnormal behaviour as illness which is seen as removing it from the ambit of personal responsibility. Not only do individuals no longer regard themselves as fully responsible agents but increasingly see themselves as victims, an attitude encouraged by governments, society, well-meaning special interest groups (victim support agencies, charities, stress counsellors, etc) and by the less scrupulous opportunists who seek direct profit from the compensation culture. This is moral engineering, pioneered, developed and refined in the USA.

There are two strands to this culture. First, many of the needs which were once met by family or community are now expected to be met by society (the state, the government or local agencies). Where these are issues of welfare, assistance that was once assessed on the basis of need has now become an entitlement. This represents a significant transfer of responsibility away from the individual to the state. As long as rights alone dictate benefit, individuals have no incentive to behave responsibly, safe in the knowledge that society will bale them out if they get into difficulty. Divorcing welfare from need is part of the image of the universal caring society. One result is that people no longer rely upon their own resources — neither physical resources such as savings, nor spiritual resources such as resilience — or are inclined to accumulate reserves against adversity. In general, societies are weakened by these so-called 'enlightened' policies.

A second, more sinister aspect of this phenomenon has been the incorporation of a moral dimension into what has been called the 'victim culture'. It is an easy step from abrogating responsibility for the social or financial consequences of an act to divesting oneself of responsibility for the act itself. The prevailing default attitude is 'someone else is responsible'. People now entertain not only the idea that they can evade their responsibilities and should do so wherever possible, but also that they are entirely justified in doing so. Societies, egged on by progressive sociologists and educationalists, have wilfully played up to this. It is one thing to look to others for help when you are out of work or ill, quite another to slough off responsibility for criminality or anti-social behaviour. Both strands are, in the main, dividends of the de-moralisation of society. How has this come about?

The first thing to note is the shift from the inviolability of the rule of law to the inviolability of the individual. Until the latter part of the 20th century, laws were generally seen as superordinate to individual desires or determinations and commanded commensurate respect and obedience. As affluence expanded and choice and opportunity widened for many in western societies, supremacy of the law gave way to the desire for individual freedom. The tensions between these were increased by the extension of state powers over the individual well beyond what is necessary to maintain basic law and order. New generations saw families and society in general as unduly restrictive and repressive and sought personal freedom — which they characterised as moral (particularly sexual) liberation. Dispositions which carried normative force — notably society, law and religion — were seen as antithetical to that aim and rejected. In the case of law, the move backfired, as one notable result of this shift in attitude was that much of the behaviour once effectively regulated by the province of manners soon became the subject of formal legal regulation.

The pursuit of individual freedom as a counterweight to rules and *mores* that were seen as unnecessarily oppressive became a desire for unfettered self-expression. This easily transmuted into the idea that 'anything goes', which came to justify a creeping disregard for other people's rights and sensibilities. A corollary of this was that artificial restrictions on behaviour were considered inimical to true self-expression and thus no longer acceptable. So manners, dress codes, and the rest of the unwritten apparatus which had evolved to sustain social cohesion, were deemed inappropriate and progressively overturned.

As money transferred from the very wealthy few of the early- and mid-20th centuries to a broader celebrity- and technology-led base in the decades that followed, people saw riches as a means of liberation. Being told what to do and how to behave by parents, society or the state was not part of the deal, as anti-authoritarians envisaged it, so money talked and manners reluctantly listened. Those who were prepared to compete in the wealth stakes sought also to re-write (or more often, scrap) the social *mores* they regarded as unnecessary and outmoded, with the result that manners and much of the institutionalised traditions and customs that accompany them are now ridiculed and held in contempt. Trivialising social standards—'what does it matter how I dress / talk / behave?'—became the creed. Money no longer marched with social background and education, and the aggression displayed by the *nouveaux-riches* in acquiring it conveyed a powerful message to society to 'get lost'. They were the new wealthy and from their view-point money not only talked, it also dictated the terms of trade, including social trade. These people and groups could not see beyond manners, in the broadest sense, as behaviour that they considered incompatible with their new freedom-driven lifestyle, to the wider social implications of breaking the chain in a centuries old evolution. This signalled the triumph of impulse over intellect as the demands for freedom triumphed over those of social cohesion.

The most recent phase in the evolution of the individual in democratic society, now that personal liberty is by-and-large a *fait accompli*, is the pursuit of equality. This is a diffuse concept, beyond the scope of this book to dissect, but its proponents see its principal features as encompassing the abolition of elites and class distinctions and the eradication of prejudice and oppression. In its most common sense, equality means egality—we are all equal. This is not, however, co-terminus with the other main contender—equity—as there are other principles of equity that are not necessarily egalitarian.

The abstract nature of equality causes difficulty in respect of practical implementation. Where equality simply facilitates — e.g. freedom of speech or worship — it is relatively straightforward. It is far less so where requirements make it necessary to treat individuals having regard to their personal qualities and dispositions, rather than as impersonal 'units'. Education, for example, has notably suffered from muddled ideas about what constitutes equal opportunity whilst recognising the need to accommodate the diversity of potential, personal skills and motivation. Marked differences in personalities and capacities make practical implementation of the principle of absolute equality problematic. Indeed, in view of the fact that individuals with similar levels of natural intelligence often follow entirely different courses of intellectual development, it might even be said to be undesirable, given the undoubted contribution inequalities of talent, intelligence and temperament have made to western civilisation across the centuries.

Equality, on any definition, dislikes elites. In the modern egalitarian world, some individuals (particularly sporting and other celebrities) escape the anti-elite opprobrium — an instructive indication of the values that determine the modern social pecking order. The reality is that equality, as it is propounded and practised in many quarters, is no more than crude social engineering and unlikely to achieve much other than creating new oligarchies of the kind its advocates seem concerned to abolish. The difficulty in trying to destroy any social order with something that is itself based on bad logic and prejudice is compounded several-fold if the protagonists are less civilised than those they wish to replace. The battles for relaxation in manners and personal responsibility have only been won by sheer force of numbers, helped by the popularity of a superficially persuasive, but flawed, liberal ideology. In both cases the arguments for change are generally weak and based upon a warped view of the nature and function of society. In particular, the reformers fail to recognise that it is precisely the structures they ridicule and seek to destroy that uphold, not constrain, personal liberty. In itself, unrestricted liberty is not particularly liberating — as any true universal liberty cannot escape from countervailing responsibilities, without which it is compromised, and it is precisely these responsibilities that are seen as anti-libertarian.

There is a strong air of paradox about a policy which has as its consequence that the greater our freedom of choice — whether as producers, consumers or simply as citizens — the more limited is our circle of personal responsibility. This social change mirrors decline in community cohesion and personal morality and is in part their outcome. In particular, it reflects an unwillingness of societies to restrict the scope of assistance for those in difficulty to the genuinely needy. This is driven by an amalgam of political correctness and sentimentality, which dislikes means testing and is squeamish about stigmatising people as needy or indigent, with the result that aid is extended indiscriminately, irrespective of genuine need or capacity for self help. There are therefore few attempts to identify the poor, and policies are based on blanket coverage — universal provision — rather than the recognition that, in many cases, poverty is an impermanent state rather than a chronic condition.

The failure of people to look to their immediate community or their own resources means that the state becomes provider of first, rather than last, resort. To reverse individual dependence upon the state is not just to admit the reality that public arrangements are often inadequate and slow, or to advocate returning to the shameful conditions of Victorian poverty provision. It is rather to recognise that social attitudes and conditions would improve immeasurably if people were expected, as default, to rely on their own mental, physical and material resources and to look elsewhere only when these were exhausted, and to advocate that provision should be tailored accordingly. Self-reliance is a tested virtue which strengthens society and has benefits which transcend mere independence.

Apart from its inherent absurdity, dogmatic reluctance to separate the needy from those able to provide financial and moral support for themselves also fails to distinguish between responsibility and eligibility for assistance. It is entirely consistent with helping someone following a misfortune to hold them responsible for it, and equally inconsistent to equate the provision of any such assistance with absolving them of responsibility. Responsibility for an action should entail responsibility for consequences that could reasonably have been foreseen. However, the attribution of strict (moral) responsibility for an action is neutral as to who should accept (social and financial) responsibility for dealing with its consequences.

The reluctance to identify genuine need exemplifies the sentimentality which has infected much public policy making, both in Britain and the USA. Indiscriminate welfare makes little economic sense and even less psychological sense, in that people become dependent and unwilling to make their own provision. This leads to a moral mindset that erodes belief in their own status as responsible moral agents. Sentimentality is not, as some would suggest, the kinder alternative to being hard-nosed, but rather a willingness to act in ways that it is felt will please and appease people. This, as with much else, is designed to create an image of caring, which is the opposite of what is achieved in practice.

The main defect of the sentimentalist approach is that it sees personal and social difficulties as evidence of defective systems rather than failings of attitude and behaviour. Making faults systemic implies that the situation can only be changed by altering structures rather than by re-educating people in their responsibilities. This turns reality on its head. The social environment may be imperfect, but personal difficulties are more likely to arise from inappropriate or ill-considered responses to circumstances than from institutional flaws. Striking an appropriate balance between what is expected of an individual and what an individual can reasonably expect from society is a problem which has as much a moral dimension as a socio-economic one. In general, where causes are personal rather than systemic, it makes sense to expect people to manage for themselves, especially where the solutions are well within individual or family capabilities. Morality is not sidelined or diluted by revising social policies.

The exposing of sentimentality would not be so important were its reach not so pervasive. It is driven by a genuine desire to help, but by a warped perception of what effective help consists of. There is no doubt that resources can make a difference, but indiscriminate provision erodes both self-respect and moral independence and, crucially, gives little incentive to develop personal resources for the future. This is particularly true of aid policies for the third world where developing societies would be much more effective were more effort to be directed towards delivering skills to the poor rather than giving help in kind. The reality is that sentimentality too often assuages the emotional needs of providers—to make them feel good themselves—instead of addressing the deeper needs of those on whom their sentimentality devolves. This is reflected in a tendency to throw resources at poverty. Some disasters obviously warrant this approach, but it has doubtful justification for long-term deprivation. People become more self-reliant, self-confident and self-respecting when they are able to make efforts in their own behalf and sentimentalising their needs does little to advance their causes. Prime the pump, by all means, but don't deluge everyone with water.

Personal responsibility arises from collective social consciousness and is made possible by recognition of a common morality. These, in turn, rely on the perceived importance of social cohesion. If people see that it is in their interests to have an orderly society they will accept rules and strictures which make this happen. The moral concepts that underpin these rules entail propositions which in turn set out the limits of acceptable behaviour, with appropriate sanctions to deal with transgression. For offences considered important enough to interest society itself, the sanctions are legal and public; for those of more limited or domestic interest, the sanctions are social or private. In an orderly society, the process of individual socialisation moulds and inculcates these concepts and defines the differences between good and bad behaviour. At maturity, they are then taken as understanding the social framework and thenceforth held responsible to themselves and to society for their actions. The hope is that the child's experience of restraint, discipline and required work will in time become the adult's internalised self-control, self-discipline and self-induced motivation. Unfortunately, in many societies, the failure to deliver adequate early discipline has meant that for too many, developmental progress to full moral agency has broken down.

In the less formal milieu of domestic and community life, normal behaviour was historically regulated by a more or less elaborate system of manners—codes of decency for language, dress and behaviour. This is still the case in many communities where rules exist and are strictly enforced (e.g. sporting or social clubs). These provide a framework of predictability and, to use an unfashionable concept, decency. However, in wider society, manners no longer hold the sway they used to. Their observance and force have gradually eroded and, with no other local sanctions available, the law has increasingly stepped in to deal with errant behaviour.

There are good reasons for believing that the legal approach is not viable.

1. Laws governing social behaviour (nuisance, public order, trespass, bad language, racial abuse and so on) are difficult to police and, as most of the behaviour they cover is widely seen as minor offending, are not at the top of enforcement priorities.

2. Legal sanctions are barely deterrent, as many offenders see themselves as heroes to their peers, content to kick over the traces of what they regard as a restrictive and stuffy society.

3. Using the law as the prime enforcer of behaviour and standards is inconvenient, slow and costly. It lacks both main well-documented attributes of condign punishment: immediacy and appropriateness. Its mainly

retributive focus means that there is little likelihood of reform and a strong prospect of re-offending.

Unfortunately, the swiftest, most effective sanction—social disgrace—no longer operates or, if it does, has greatly reduced bite. Communities have disintegrated, families lack the social cohesion they once had and undue permissiveness has eroded parental authority at much the same rate as the morals and manners it tries to instil.

Into this moral vacuum stepped the 'victim culture' as a convenient means of dealing with social aberration or personal misfortune without directly invoking criminality and the law or, more importantly, ascribing blame. It is a simple step from deciding that individuals are no longer responsible for their behaviour or its consequences to the idea that they are victims of whoever is responsible—be this society in general, the state or its agencies, or simply 'the system'. People are increasingly labelled 'victims' by government, and individual misfortunes landed squarely upon those who are identified as having failed to provide the necessary conditions to prevent them from happening.

Detaching personal responsibility in this way is considered liberating. In one sense, it is, but in removing one burden it imposed another—that of dealing with an increasingly disorderly society. Divorcing personal responsibility from its consequences contrasts strongly with the traditional—and in fact, truly liberating—belief that your destiny is in your own hands. The semblance of greater freedom as a concomitant of diminishing responsibility confronts the reality that it is greater responsibility which is the genuine liberator. The less responsibility you accept, the more morally cramped you become.

The abdication of personal responsibility has been helped by the more general feeling that our fate, and that of the world around us, is beyond our personal control. This depressing prospect is reinforced by a sense that society itself is conniving at this sleight of hand. Among those who are prepared to take responsibility for their lives this impression is compounded by the knowledge that the less socialised among us are becoming wilfully inconsiderate and morally self-indulgent in consequence of rarely being held to account for their behaviour. This is a major causal factor in the accelerating erosion of self-discipline.

In discussing the decline in personal responsibility, it is important to mark the difference between disillusion—exemplified by the attitude:"I can't make a difference", and laziness: "Why bother—someone else will sort it out". The one denies influence over what the other accepts. For those concerned, the attitudes coalesce in "I don't care". While all these sentiments abrogate responsibility they are subtly different. "I don't care" and "why should I bother?" evince a strongly selfish individualism. "I can't make a difference", suggests a more desperate feeling of impotence. The underlying thought has changed from recognising moral agency but ignoring it because someone else will pick up the pieces, to the quite different thought that, although you may have done wrong, you are not in fact responsible because of your circumstances (housing conditions, poor education, deprivation etc). This both removes moral agency and breeds dependency. People are more demanding of society now—the less they know, care or are capable, the more they expect someone else to provide, and are angry and often aggressive when they don't. Societies have tacitly connived at this and in failing to recognise and reward personal effort have allowed responsibility to be replaced by entitlement.

People now tend to believe that:

1. That the world is run by the few people in power.
2. That individual influence in social and world order is very limited.
3. That success comes from luck rather than from hard work.

This mindset and its attendant attitudes have a profound effect on social, political and personal life. Feeling that our sphere of responsibility is severely circumscribed and that we are virtually powerless to change what many see as defective societies and political systems has a deep influence on our behaviour and the way we view the world. It increases selfishness and leads to disillusion. Where individuals regard themselves as essentially powerless or marginalised in their communities which they regard as having no significance or compassion for them, it is hardly surprising that they despair of society and for themselves. As a result, they cease to care and turn to crime and/or drugs. The more you remove responsibility the more you encourage irresponsibility.

Turning people into victims has negative consequences for them as well as for society. If you feel that you are a victim, you soon learn to rationalise laziness, self-indulgence, indiscipline and irresponsibility. Why, for example, should you bother to eat sensibly, behave respectfully or keep out of debt, if society is there to ensure that you are no worse off than if you had taken the prudent route? Increasing social wealth has given societies greater scope for interference and made social agencies more aggressive and intrusive into what was once considered private space. The paradox is that while we now have theoretically greater control over many aspects of our lives than ever, and are thereby better able to limit chance and surprise, we readily accept ourselves as hapless victims. Given the prevailing climate, the arrival of generation "WHATEVER" should have surprised no-one.

Part of this perspective shift is that alternative explanations of individual responsibility have become well-understood and socially respectable; for example, psychotherapeutic attribution of much deviance to roots in childhood, which might have been derided fifty years ago, is now taken seriously for a widening menu of anti-social behaviour, often with designer medication to match. It is easier to medicate away everything from deviance to depression than to deal with them as personal failings. It is by no means clear that the existence of anti-depressant drugs puts depression (or 'bipolar syndrome', to use fashionable terminology) beyond self-help, any more than the increased sophistication of car safety devices absolves us from reckless driving, or the super-abundance of fattening food from the need to eat sensibly. Appetite-suppressants may curb the desire to eat, but over-eating does not thereby become an illness.

Once inappropriate behaviour ceases to be a matter of individual responsibility — whether by admitting strict liability and then ascribing it to psychological failing or by re-classifying it as the fault of society — the sting is taken out of dealing with people as social deviants and law-breakers and the problem thrown back on the society which allegedly created it. On this view, a great deal of crime is no longer the result of defective morals, inadequate socialisation or wilful self-interest, rather the product of mental illness and social deprivation. Anti-social behaviour is passed down a ladder of causality which ends in low educational attainment, inadequate housing or poor diet, none of which has a direct moral dimension. This is the front-line of societal de-moralisation.

There are thus two separate issues: first, the idea that someone else is to be blamed for misfortunes and second, the notion that those directly involved are victims. As to the former, it simply distorts the concept of blame. As to the latter, when society sees people as victims and reacts accordingly, they see themselves as victims and react accordingly. Society's reaction consists of providing compensation, counselling etc, and, in serious cases (e.g. school massacres) of reviewing the relevant systems and passing laws or regulations which it considers will prevent similar occurrences. The 'victim's' reaction is to place increasing reliance on government and its systems to sort out their lives—even though they may be perfectly capable, intellectually and financially, of handling their own affairs.

The Victim Culture has engendered a 'no fault' mindset. This has serious negative consequences for individuals and society as people have become skilled at working the system, using a variety of stratagems to deflect personal blame—onto our genes, our upbringing, parents, even our birth sign ... in other words, anything but accept responsibility for our actions or personal circumstances. It might be argued that if we made half the effort at behaving responsibly that we do dodging our responsibilities, social environments would be considerably improved.

It is not surprising that we don't. We find superficial comfort in the belief that responsibility does not lie with us; and, even if we are technically responsible for our misfortunes, we are delighted to learn that these are attributable to stress or to some other newly-coined syndrome (repetitive strain injury, post-traumatic stress disorder etc). Reassurance is further sweetened by the prospect of compensation if the problem relates to employment or public service, or can be visited on the failings of some other identifiable external agency.

At the extreme, this leads to absurdity. Bankrupts blame their banks for lending them too much money, businesses and shareholders seek to make auditors scapegoats for poor business decisions, intemperate shoppers blame stores for enticing them with irresistible displays, and the obese try to shift responsibility for their condition onto food companies.

This perspective is counter-intuitive, as most people, however ill-educated, recognise what is right and what is wrong, and are well aware when they have failed either morally or in their social or parental duty. The tension between that knowledge and peoples' image of themselves as victims leads to widespread disillusion, alienation, self-loathing, cynicism and apathy. Disillusion because the better educated see all too clearly the absurdities of Political Correctness and that society is irreversibly deteriorating under the impossible weight of its self-inflicted responsibilities. Alienation, because people feel they are no longer part of a secure, cohesive or worthwhile society. Self-loathing because it is demeaning to be told that you are no longer responsible and thus are deprived of moral agency—an essential component of individual liberty and self-respect. Cynicism, because people understand the impossibility of sustaining the victim project indefinitely and cannot comprehend why governments continue to support it—this merely adds to disillusion with politics. Apathy, because the implication of the new order is that there is no need to bother about smoking, obesity or being unfit or unemployed because society will provide for you, whatever your difficulties, whether self-inflicted or not.

Even if personal misgivings manage to reach the surface they are likely to be stifled by the realisation that it is expedient not to argue, especially when compensation depends on toeing the official line. For instance, tripping over a misaligned paving slab must be the fault of the department that laid it and in no circumstances attributable to someone not looking where they were going. This culture has led to the need for a mass of regulatory legislation to define limits and responsibilities—for example, how far a paving slab must protrude for its victims to be eligible for compensation—and to an explosion of contingency fee lawyers on both sides of the Atlantic chasing potential claimants and unearthing a gold mine of medical misdeeds and other lucrative 'paving slabs'. Victim vultures find nothing wrong with lifting pavements to support false claims. In this situation, fraud is (unsurprisingly) rife.

The American-style victim culture has been supported by governments passing into law measures that allow people to sue companies and providers of all sorts for virtually anything to which the use of goods or services might lead. Successful claims range from the frivolous (burns as a result of spilling hot coffee) to the mildly amusing (fat people claiming damage to their self-esteem when offered two aircraft seats because they cannot safely occupy one) to the medical consequences of persistent cigarette smoking. The abrogation of personal responsibility has reached the point where a plaintiff's negligence or a requirement for people to act sensibly or make reasonable assumptions (e.g. about hot coffee, heavy smoking or eating large amounts of junk food) appear to be incapable of defeating compensation claims or mitigating the disproportionate damages awarded. The prospect of massive rewards only fuels the fire. This litigious culture spread rapidly from its birthplace in the USA, to the delight of lawyers and the dismay of those who see the longer-term damage being done to society.

It would be wrong to suggest that the victim mentality and compensation culture is confined to the indigent. Whilst there are indeed those who cannot, for one reason or another, be expected to take personal responsibility for aspects of their lives, there are many who can but are dissuaded from doing so. Even those prepared to accept their responsibilities and well able to look after their liabilities are dragged into 'victim hood' and thus help perpetuate the culture. Apart from the satisfaction to be derived from knowing that someone else is responsible for your problem (analogous, perhaps, to the comfort people feel from the knowledge that their medical symptoms have a name), the prospect of compensation is a powerful spur to deciding that it really wasn't your fault, after all. In such circumstances, any lingering moral doubts are easily rationalised.

The erosion of individual responsibility, and with it the notions of virtue and blame, have replaced moral judgement with causal explanation. We now live in a relativistic world where everyone sees such matters from a highly personal perspective rather than in terms of set values and fixed principles. What were once moral absolutes are now matters of choice. Behaviour that was once clearly right or wrong is now thrown back into the melting-pot for debate. Bereft of accepted standards, people see themselves as free to act in whatever way suits their personal style. Self-interest, often driven by irrational impulse, now takes precedence over social obligation.

The image of behaviour as the terminus of a causal chain is reinforced by a legion of disciplines and experts, to whom officials and families can turn for advice. The idea that if you have a problem—real or contrived—you are *ipso facto* in need of professional help is the logical extension of the victim mentality. A massive counselling industry has emerged to bridge the divide between the victim and the oppressor and to put lives straight when they go wrong. Where people once fell back on their own mental resources or on family and community support, they are now assigned advisors who will help them deal with anything from grieving to being gay, from sexual abuse to stress. There seems virtually no circumstance in the modern world for which professional counselling is not apparently beneficial. Much of this is suspect—not only for its value in purely pragmatic terms but also for its intellectual underpinnings. With roots in social science and a veneer of academic jargon for respectability it remains of doubtful worth to those who pass through its hands. Indeed, there is little hard evidence to suggest that counselling is of any real long-term benefit. (This recalls a classic study in which a group of patients presenting similar symptoms which indicated psychotherapy as a treatment were randomly assigned to therapy or sent home. When they were reassessed at the end of the evaluation / treatment period, no statistically significant difference between the groups in terms of improvement was found.) At a descriptive level, counselling is little more than paid conversation, which, at a psychotherapeutic level, justifies itself with the claim that 'talking through' ones problems will bring the subject to an appreciation of their aetiology. The implication of psychotherapy that every problem in life has a cure, is at least questionable, at worse false

Demonstrating a negative is, however, not equivalent to proving a positive. Even if the efficacy of psychotherapy could be proved — which it can't — there is no obvious relationship between appreciating the cause of something and removing the symptoms. Take school bullying, for example. Causes are often external — rooted in the inadequacies of the bully rather than motivated by anything particular in the behaviour of the victim; so talking through the problem with the victim is unlikely to result in identification of causes in a way which would alleviate the problem. Even if the victim accepts that his tormentor's problems are the real cause of his misfortunes, he is no better off. The only effective method for dealing with most bullying — as legions of parents and children can testify — is to ignore it, and that prescription is best dispensed in the family.

Talking through one's problems, whilst comforting, is hardly a sound intellectual basis for an entire therapeutic industry. Indeed, it is more likely that those who have a close personal interest in your problems can help you solve them, rather than a dispassionate paid professional, despite their making a virtue of that detachment. To the extent that counselling encourages people to think more constructively about their problems, it is arguably beneficial, but perhaps no more so than talking to an intelligent friend. When it encourages dependency or distracts people from developing and relying on their own inner resource and support networks, it may even be counter-productive. This is not to be trivialised by examples of acute hardship, injury or oppression — where sympathetic advice and help are clearly beneficial.

There is also a need to consider the impact of counselling on other relationships. The increasing readiness — especially in the USA — of people to build psychotherapy into their everyday lives cannot but impoverish relationships with family, friends and colleagues. Bonds are established and enriched by the sharing of experience, and are weakened to the extent that this is attenuated. Simply put, if you take your most serious personal problems and confidences to paid help, then the intensity and value of normal interaction is commensurately reduced.

Stress is arguably the most widespread, and incontestably the most lucrative, of the victim syndromes. It casts a wide net as a catch-all designation

covering the consequences of everything from minor travel delays to acri-
monious business and marital difficulties. In fact, stress itself is often not the
issue—but how we prevent or cope with it. The reality is that the problems
and pressures have probably not altered greatly either in type or intensity over
the decades, just the image we are invited to have of them. To an older generation, stress is part of life and to be dealt with as such; now, we are obsessed
with it as a quasi-medical condition. Today's youth is apparently in a perpetual
state of being 'stressed out', notably from peer pressure, relationship difficulties
and examinations, and stress counselling is presented as a desirable response.
It is unfortunately politically incorrect to suggest that the best expedient for
dealing with avoidable stress is to neutralise the cause rather than treat the
'victim'.

Nonetheless, the stress industry is in full spate—with stress counselling
widely available at public expense and stress counsellors dug in as part of
any organisation whose employees might conceivably be affected. With true
Gilbertian absurdity, stress counsellors themselves apparently sometimes suffer
to the extent that they require stress counselling. The modern preoccupation
with stress reeks of sentimentality and self-indulgence.

Once anti-social or deviant behaviour is reclassified as falling into this
or that category of misdemeanour, suitable treatment is then prescribed. The
implication is that attributing it to a cause somehow crystallises the agent's
absolution from any personal responsibility and neutralises him from blame.
If—so the typical argument runs—car stealing is the result of social deprivation and poor education, blame properly falls on the society which allowed
this to happen, not the thief. For individuals, the implication is clear: we are
absolved from responsibility and what needs changing is our environment.
Whilst the 'victim' is being treated by the experts, society must interest itself
in reforming the systems which gave rise to the adverse conditions which
lead to car theft.

It is not difficult to pick holes in this logic. While it is often the case that
social deprivation of one sort or another contributes to criminality or anti-
social behaviour, it is only in a derivative, secondary sense that it can be properly regarded as a cause. The classic causal paradigm is of the form: If A caused
B, then in all similar instances of A happening, B will follow. Philosophers have
argued about causality in modern terms ever since David Hume's assertion
that we have no right to assert anything more than 'instances of A are generally followed by instances of B', as all we have to go on is our own experience,

and this is insufficient to permit us to make the leap from 'All instances of A in the past have been followed by instances of B' to the law that 'A is always followed by B'—since it is logically possible, though unlikely, that the future may not follow the past and that one day the sun may not rise, or oil will be found to mix with water.

For the social scientist, the difficulty is to decide whether it is justified to allow the notion of cause which repudiates blame to be extended to general social circumstances. In several societies—notably Britain and the USA—that decision has already been taken and in many areas individual guilt has quietly been replaced with collective responsibility. This is no more than a convenient sleight of hand. To put the distinction I am making in concrete terms, consider the notion of a 'dangerous road', a phrase often used to explain an unusually high incidence of accidents in a particular place. If the road is truly the cause of accidents, it is indeed appropriate to seek a solution in improving the road itself with better signage, lighting or highway markings. A truly dangerous road would, for example, be one onto which large rocks regularly descended and even then it might better be said that the surrounding environment not the road itself was the real danger. If, more credibly, roads are not themselves intrinsically dangerous and therefore not properly construed as the cause of anything, the appropriate solution is to address the driving habits of those who use them. If one extends this thinking to social situations, it is easy to see that whilst, for example, poor education or substandard housing may indeed contribute to social misdemeanour, it is only in a derivative sense that they can be said to be its causes. It is, incidentally, similarly misattributed causality which talks of marriage failure: the reality is that it is people, not marriages that fail; the marital problems simply highlight the individual shortcomings. It is such illogicality that facilitates the transfer of problems from individuals onto institutions.

The desire to shift blame in this way has been escalated into the magnificent idea that because circumstances are particular to each case it is unreasonable to hold people to account for anything. This is an extreme version of the argument that no two instances are identical, and falls apart on closer scrutiny—the flaw comes in glossing over the requirement that to negate moral equivalence, cases must differ 'in morally relevant respects' rather than just differ *per se*. However, its superficial plausibility provides a convenient cover for moral relativism and those who see misbehaviour as attributable to wider social factors rather than to individual failings.

The removal of responsibility from individuals has come about partly because of a failure of moral education and the weakening of social standards. It would have been unthinkable a few decades ago, even in the free-thinking 1960s, to sue tobacco companies for smoking-related diseases or food companies for obesity. It is a powerful commentary on the change in social and political attitudes and particularly on the easy transfer of moral responsibilities that such suits are now both unexceptional and successful.

It is important to appreciate current thinking in order to understand its contribution to the victim culture and in particular that element of it which demands that every event or circumstance must have an explanation. It is not that one cannot find someone to blame for everything (this is the causal model again), but the false equation of cause with blame which does most violence to personal responsibility. Mistakes happen and produce unfortunate consequences, but whereas in the recent past one would have put these down to 'tough luck' or 'the rub of the green' and accepted them as facts of life, now such 'chance' is not countenanced and society routinely requires some individual or organisation be held to account. The disappearance of the 'blameless event' has kick-started the compensation culture; if every event has an identifiable cause, then there is someone to blame who must therefore take responsibility (which usually means paying compensation). On this logic, genuine misfortunes and accidents no longer happen.

Whilst society has connived at this moral relativism, individuals have conditioned themselves to accept what in any credible moral system would count as opportunism and sophistry. Ready to ascribe blame when things go wrong, they are equally content to take credit when they turn out well. In psychological jargon this attitude is an example of 'cognitive dissonance' which, as Ken Fisher suggests 'encapsulates the human tendency to take pride in our achievements and to distance ourselves from any responsibility for failings; it can also be described as "shunning regret" and "accumulating pride". Accumulating pride is like this: "I bought it, it went up, I'm smart". Shunning regret is like this: 'I bought it, it imploded, my broker misled me". The former associates success with skill and repeatability. The latter associates failure with victimisation or bad luck. Doing both maximises our motivation to keep trying. This kind of thinking goes back to the Stone Age … ' (*Forbes Magazine*, 28/11/03).

The struggle — not an overstatement — between individual freedom and social responsibility continues; not as a single pitched battle, but as a series of individual skirmishes: in parliaments, courts, towns, villages, offices, families, marriages — in fact wherever there is a social element to life. The image we are invited to accept is that freedom is compromised by responsibility. In consequence, any restrictions are retrogressive and moreover, a choker on individual enterprise and creativity.

This notion is particularly strong in the world of art, which is now taken to encompass everything from advertising to graffiti. By subsuming as wide as possible a spectrum of ideas, 'art' seeks to gain dominance beyond its traditional realms. However, it is by no means reasonable to say that because something or other involves an artistic medium, it is art. There is no doubt an art to casting a fly over a river or to using a spray-can to paint a wall, but this alone does not turn fly-fishing or graffiti artistic enterprises.

This reckless twist of common sense is bolstered by the claim that it is wrong to prevent the public from being given what they want. This seems innocuous enough, until one considers the consequences of indulging people's fancies, however immoral or misguided. In this, the libertarian lobby turns on its head the long-held belief that the public should, as far as possible, be protected from desires that are inappropriate or downright immoral. It is a false extension of the 'people as consumers' metaphor to say that we should be offered everything anyone can dream up, and then signal our wishes by selecting what to see, hear or read. The filters of taste and decency are the ground upon which the battle to maintain a minimum element of social morality is currently being fought.

There may indeed be some truth in the view that traditional artistic disciplines are sometimes stifled by regulation, but against this must be put the need for safeguards against the unscrupulous, who, given half a chance, would deluge the vulnerable with corrupting material under the protecting canopy of 'art' and 'what the public wants', with no other motive but profit. Freedom to invent and to create must factor in the responsibility not to offend or corrupt — and it is on such considerations that the desirability of unrestricted artistic freedom fails.

The need for limitations in the interest of social cohesion is recognised by all but the truly anarchical and vacuously dim. However, there is a need to strike a balance between social loyalty and self-interest — the collective interest versus the individual interest. In modern pluralistic societies this is becoming increasingly difficult, as religious and other group demands compete with those of society. It is arguable that what recent decades have seen is not so much an acceleration in the evolution of societies but a revolution, as elements essential to social cohesion have been removed rather than redefined. In much the same way that Karl Lashley excised progressively more of a monkey's cortex to determine how little the animal needs to function 'normally' (he found that it needed remarkably little) one can argue about the point at which a social structure progressively deprived of key safeguards becomes critically impaired. It may be that apparently functionally equivalent systems conceal deeper structural impairment and it is likely to be the quality rather than the quantity of what has been destroyed that is the determining factor, the more so if the changes are irreversible. What is clear is that the competing demands of self-interest and self-restraint have created much social tension.

Individual responsibility transcends the more obvious requirements to act sensibly and not trample on other's rights or sensibilities. It also imposes on individuals a minimum duty of care which implies the need for general vigilance in belief and action. We cannot function effectively in society unless we are able to assess the demands made on us by others and to establish a personal basis for evaluating information, people and organisations. The superficially tempting image of people living in a freedom-rich personal world, shorn of accountability to society at large is unsustainable and barely survives initial scrutiny. Throwing over the traces may provide the young with a means of asserting their independence but is not a long-term recipe for civilised living. Societies and individuals need a measure of certainty and predictability and this is only possible where there is reciprocal trust. (This is not to pre-empt the entirely separate question of where the lines should be drawn.)

Society itself is the real victim of the false image created by governments, egged on by the freedom lobby, of the role of the state in personal lives. The transfer of responsibility from individual to collective has made society and its ills the focus of attention. Re-investing responsibility in the individual requires a shift away from the culture of victimisation, which in turn will only happen when legal frameworks cease to reward individuals for defalcations in their perceptions or actions. It should be no excuse to plead that the coffee I spilt was hot and therefore the restaurant is to blame for my burns, or that the ladder I used to burgle the house was rotten and therefore the householder is liable for my injuries. People who are deliberately deceived and the victims of provable negligence deserve sympathy; the careless, the wilful and the gullible do not.

The path to redressing the perceived imbalance between individuals and the state is therefore to return responsibility for decision-making and behaviour regulation to individuals and to adapt social systems to this new reality. The 'responsibility' element is critical and for this to succeed there must be, first, a general recognition in both law and society that the responsibilities have fully transferred and second, an improvement in moral education, to the point at which people accept restrictions on conduct and the social (not legal) sanctions which follow transgression. Societies have gone too far down the road of removing responsibility from citizens to believe that it can be returned swiftly and the political will to make the necessary changes is presently lacking. Unless there is a change of mindset in favour of a social environment which recognises and expects individual responsibility and is armed with a suitably robust response-mechanism to disarm the claim and compensation culture, the dependency virus will spread even further; regulating conduct by law and decree will become the rule rather than the exception.

Just as unfettered freedom of behaviour does not amount to true liberty, so infinite variety does not amount to true freedom of choice. This reality has not dawned on many governments who still pretend that people are free to decide on a wide range of social issues — education, health, policing, etc. — when in fact many are scarcely capable of making informed decisions or, if they are lack the requisite information to do so. Politicians like to talk of 'empowerment', and to point to targets, charters and suchlike as evidence of this. However, people are only empowered to the extent that they are genuinely able to choose. Where choice is not practicable, empowerment is illusory. While individual empowerment is seen as a desirable political goal, it is often compromised by legislation that intrudes deep into people's lives and behaviour.

Politicians continue to believe that one route to public empowerment is to increase access to information — the more information you have, it is argued, the better will be your choices. 'Openness', 'Transparency' and 'Accountability' are the fashionable concepts here, but the argument is flawed. Whilst it is clear that withholding relevant information may compromise decisions and is undesirable, the converse does not apply in that access to unlimited information does not necessarily improve decision-making. The missing links are trust and accountability.

Trust is an essential prerequisite for social, political and commercial life. For society to function we have to trust one another, at least to the point of reasonable expectation. Where image-manipulation is deliberately used to distort reality, trust is compromised. We trust on a variety of bases: that information we are given is accurate, that a person has the necessary skills to do what is being asked (competence), that they will in fact do what they say (reliability), and that the outcome will be as stated (performance). Failure at any of these levels reduces trust, and serious failure may destroy it altogether. Trust is compromised for a variety of reasons: people may have the requisite skills and may try their best to perform, but through no fault of their own fail to deliver. At the other extreme are cases where skills are deliberately misrepresented or the agent has no intention of performing—this is the province of the con-man and the political despot. In between are moral lapses which challenge personal relationships, and the degree to which these destroy trust is often an individual matter. In some marriages, an extra-marital affair is fatal to the relationship, in others it is regarded as an acceptable, or at least pardonable, part of the marital arrangements. In such situations, public and private feelings often diverge. 'It doesn't matter' often means just the opposite.

The perception of trustworthiness—as distinct from actual acts of trusting—is compromised by unclear language; the greater the linguistic opacity, the greater the feeling that something is being hidden. People talk and write obscurely both because they wish to conceal the truth about the facts, their intentions or their feelings, or else because they simply do not understand the issues and want to disguise their inability to argue a credible case. Language, as Chapter 3 suggests, is a powerful tool and detecting its wilful misuse needs constant vigilance. Politics, most notably, suffers from deep public mistrust, some of which is attributable to inappropriate use of language. For example, western politicians are prone to use placatory language when talking about terrorists or those who intimidate or flout international conventions if their economic or other national interests are involved. We must reject 'the politically correct vocabulary in which crimes are renamed and perpetrators accorded respectability … we can stop using euphemisms to placate those who threaten or do injustice; we can refuse to dignify community intimidators by speaking of them as community leaders … (and) stop using vocabularies of community protection and freedom fighting to dignify crimes … trust is destroyed by deception; destroying deception builds trust' (Onora O'Neill, *A Question of Trust*, 2002, p. 37).

Trust is eroded ('corroded' perhaps better emphasises the long-term damage) by language which suggests one sentiment, when the reality is the opposite. This is the world of political spin where noises of acquiescence and understanding, and promises of change, turn out to be nothing more than 'business as usual'. In the view of 19th century British Prime Minister W.E. Gladstone, politics depends entirely on the 'good sense and good faith of those who work in it'. Now, the unwritten rules have largely been torn up by spinners who seem unable to appreciate the difference between putting the best gloss on the facts and turning the truth upside down, and see no shame in proclaiming policies which have popular 'feel good' appeal but which they know to be undeliverable. It is such machinations that have severely damaged trust.

How is trust verified? How is it falsified? Many people work to present an image of trustworthiness but fail to deliver, so they have to go into deeper deceit to spin away their incompetence. The problem with trust in public life is that, generally, the public are ill-equipped to verify claims of competence or performance, and thus to estimate reliability. However, the widespread feeling that politics is more about self-advancement, retaining power and covering up incompetence, rather than by the application of serious intellect to delivering good government, means that cynicism and systematic mistrust are now the default responses to political pronouncements. This makes the problem of independent, reliable, verification even more pressing.

This is not helped by governments claiming to take over verification on our behalf, by deluging us with information designed to substantiate political claims and thereby to reassure their electorates. It is not difficult to see why detaching responsibility from individuals makes failures of trust more likely: there is more blind trust about. This gives greater scope for failure and then we complain, as we are encouraged to do, when things go wrong. The situation is exacerbated by media which tend to play up minor breaches of trust. This gives an impression of generalised incompetence and, where the failings are moral, a feeling that corruption is institutionalised; a sentiment well expressed by one disillusioned investigator: 'I expected to discover bad apples, but not to find that the barrel itself was rotten' (Ian Hay-Davison, *Lloyds: A View from the Room*, 1987).

There are matters where trust has to be blind and verification is impossible — not because we don't have the necessary abilities or resources but because verification itself is a theoretical impossibility. Many of the tenets of religion are unverifiable in this way. 'God is good' is taken by some to be a tautologous truth as goodness is seen as part of God's nature. Others say that it is demonstrably false, as no credible definition of goodness could be stated which covered the evils of a world for which God is said to be responsible, a claim which believers reject as an erroneous understanding of the workings of God's goodness. In many cases, the very need to verify implies that trust itself is at least uncertain, or at worst, insecure. Having to resort to a contract to secure performance is generally a sign that either trust is in doubt or else the stakes are too high to rely on it alone. Such arrangements are now evident in a wide range of social and personal dealings.

The image we are invited to accept is that civilised societies are well managed, responsible and transparent, and that public bodies and corporations are increasingly held to account for their decisions and their actions. At a personal level, we are encouraged to believe both that government is being taken off our backs and also that we can trust what it tells us. This platform is bolstered by laws purporting to guarantee freedom of information and to assign responsibility where it is perceived to be due. In many cases, genuine accountability is limited or unachievable and the reality is that as regulation and centrist, *dirigiste*, government increase, so do the constraints on personal freedom. It is paradoxical that passing ever more laws to protect individual rights and freedoms actually diminishes them. Freedom — as a feeling rather than a political, legalistic fact — was arguably much greater in times of fewer laws and a strong ethos of individual and community responsibility. Having more comprehensive legal redress for grievance does not necessarily equate to greater freedom.

Accountability is seen as the ultimate stamp of verification. If people and organisations have to account for their actions, spending, social priorities, etc., then the scope for deception is commensurately reduced and the basis upon which decisions are made commensurately strengthened. More information equals progress all round.

While in some respect this is true, there are serious caveats. There is no doubt that undue secrecy restricts freedom and makes for suspicion and distrust. However, there is no reciprocal rule that turns unrestricted access to information into a social benefit. In the first place, information has to be provided by some agency or other, and is invariably subject to filtering. So there is no way of knowing the extent to which what is offered is complete. Second, information itself is value-neutral, in the sense that it says nothing as to what is useful, important or relevant. Third, information is broadly restricted to what can be measured or accurately described. This limits its scope and, to the extent that the validity of any measures is not apparent from the information itself, its accuracy. There is therefore no guarantee that what is presented is either accurate or comprehensive. Information can be withheld, deliberately incomplete (remember 'economical with the truth'?), embellished or distorted (misinformation / disinformation), and without independent verification there is no means of evaluating what is being offered. This requires trust—in particular, that information from a source is complete, relevant and reliable. All information comes with a background and even if it meets these criteria it still has to be assessed and interpreted before it is of value to decision-makers.

Where information itself is restricted to what can be measured (and within this framework, what is most readily measured) it does not always provide a guide either to achievement or to quality. For example, the principal functions of schools and hospitals are poorly assessed by measuring examination results or university places gained, or by counting operating rates, waiting times and deaths. The fact that school X has higher examination grades than school Y or that a higher proportion of people die at hospital A than at hospital B may merely signify disparities in intakes which are then reflected in outcomes. Much of importance intervenes between input and output which comes under the heading of 'quality' and as 'quality' has no obvious metric, statistical or other simple targets are inevitably unreliable and arbitrary. The rush to determine appropriate measures and then to publish results in the form of league tables puts strains on personnel and resources whilst providing information of questionable relevance to parents, patients or customers.

Accountability seeks to transpose the notion of 'audit' from its financial base into non-financial systems. Despite good intentions, in many public services the idea has not been properly thought through and the use of such measures as a social tool does not appear to be working. Educational standards continue to deteriorate, recidivism has not declined, and public healthcare (at least in the UK) has not noticeably changed for the better. The perception that greater accountability and more comparative data will spur improvement and inform choice belies the reality. At the political level, the explosion of micro-management of government-funded organisations, which are supposed both to provide the raw data for public accountability and also the means to fine-tune performance has led to a explosion in bureaucracy which diverts resources from those who need them without delivering much by way of compensating benefits. The debate simply shifts from apportionment of blame and moral mudslinging to argument about statistics—what the figures mean, what they measure (if anything), and whether they are comprehensive, correct or relevant. Accusations of incompetence soon become charges of statistical chicanery.

Greater accountability is seen as a means to restoring trust. Here again, the idea has superficial plausibility but disintegrates on closer inspection.

Trust, as Onora O'Neill points out, is not based on full disclosure but on lack of deception. Transparency may destroy secrecy but it has little impact on deception, and it is deception, not secrecy, that erodes trust. Indeed, there are many circumstances where we bestow trust with no expectation of full disclosure. In reality, genuine transparency and freedom of information are myths. Governments and corporations only disclose what they feel is appropriate and routinely withhold information for a variety of reasons. Citizens no longer trust organisations for full or even accurate disclosure and feel they are only fed information on a 'need to know' basis. Indeed, despite the legal provision of 'freedom of information', trust continues to decline.

Liberty is only possible to the extent that individuals and organisations play an active rather than a passive role in society and use their intelligence, status and influence to hold other individuals and organisations to account. The regulation that is really needed is not that designed to force people to think and behave in certain approved ways but that which imposes truly enforceable obligations on governments and organisations to become properly accountable to their citizens, their electorates and society in general. This requires a massive change of culture, including taking responsibility for the consequences of their policies, especially for breaches of trust. Such accountability is probably only to be guaranteed at a supra-national level. It is definitely not guaranteed by courts designed to uphold contentious individual and collective rights or, indeed, to determine what these should be.

The theoretical delivery of individual liberty and social equality is a false reflection of reality. There needs to be wider recognition that social and political problems and behaviour have a strong moral component. In many secular or multi-ethnic societies, where religious influence has declined, morality remains the only viable social cement. The corollary is that if moral responsibility and the personal accountability that should accompany it are eroded or compromised then we cannot escape the consequential decline in social quality. To avoid this requires a reduction in the culture of 'rights' and recognition that moral transgressions demand punishment, not compassion.

All this points to an urgent need to reinvigorate personal moral agency. In order for individuals to regain control over their lives they must be supplied the appropriate tools, and this means better education and recognition that rights and entitlements come with countervailing responsibilities. For this to happen, governments must dismantle the apparatus of micro-management and regulation, and signal a phasing out of the victim and compensation cultures.

This will require a seismic shift in moral mindset from individual and families and throughout education systems. It will also require — and this is much more difficult — the re-establishment of trust and accountability. Deluging people with information is no answer — it is merely paying lip-service to public accountability. People and organisations have to accept (and internalise) the need to change their behaviour to conform with public expectations, not just to deploy a synthetically more rigorous apparatus for handling failure. It is the eradication of failure that engenders trust, not the knowledge that there are sanctions in place to deal with defaulters.

CHAPTER 8

INFORMATION, NEWS AND THE MEDIA

'Television was not intended to make human beings vacuous, but it is an
emanation of their vacuity'
(Malcolm Muggeridge, I like Dwight, 1966)

'When distant and unfamiliar things are communicated to great masses
of people, the truth suffers a considerable and often radical distortion.
The complex is made over into the simple, the hypothetical into the
dogmatic and the relative into the absolute'
(Walter Lippmann, The Public Philosophy, 1955)

'Whoever controls the media — the images — controls the culture'
(Allen Ginsberg)

The ubiquity and influence of the mass media have never been stronger. Not
only are there now more ways of receiving output (internet, email, mobile
telephones) than via traditional television, radio and print media, but also
more channels, magazine titles and websites to choose from. With non-stop
media transmission over television, radio and the internet, this amounts to a
massive increase in scope and coverage. There is now greater accessibility to
more, and more diverse, output for longer periods. As a result, we live in an
information-saturated world, bombarded with an almost inescapable barrage
of news, advertising, propaganda, opinion and general entertainment.

We seem to relish this constant stimulation. Broadcast media are no longer
an occasional adjunct to our lives as we are now, more often than not, volun-
tarily tuned in to some kind of output and therefore available to influence.
Media sources have increasingly reflected this sociological change and transformed themselves, from relatively straightforward news and entertainment
providers into finely-honed manipulative tools, designed to shape our opinions and lifestyles.

These changes have not been forced on a reluctant public but are generally embraced as desirable elements of progress. In general, people enjoy not
having to think for themselves, and accept undemanding entertainment as
a substitute for creative activity, reading or other more effortful recreation.

Viewing and listening have replaced much active intellectual participation and few are without 'passive' opinions on the issues and topics of the day.

The broadcasting media proclaim a largely non-interventionist platform, seeing themselves as dispassionate providers of news and entertainment. They view their role as reflecting public demand in their output and are aggressively dismissive of charges of dumbing down and of pandering to the appetites of the lowest common denominator in audience intellect. Vigorous in boasting impartiality and independence from political influence, they admit to no role beyond informing and entertaining. There must be doubt as to whether they genuinely believe either. If they do, they deceive themselves. If not they deceive everyone else. This chapter discusses how the media contributes to the culture of superficiality and some effects of the way news is structured and disseminated. As usual, the image does not entirely square with the reality.

The information explosion has profoundly changed social and community dynamics. Family life is fragmented as people watch, listen or log-on for hours on end, and time once devoted to discussion or small-talk is diminished as meals are eaten in front of the television or at the computer. In an impatient, time-poor environment there is less opportunity for general conversation and inconsequential chat. Many public venues now offer sports broadcasts and other distractions, so the same is true in wider society. As communication patterns are a major determinant of social structures, to the extent that inter-action is altered by media habits, these are also changed.

This 'tsunami' of media output has had an equally profound affect on our intellectual lives. In particular, it strongly influences the way we think and behave, how we see the world around us, and the content and conduct of public debate. Our perceptions of ourselves, our environment and our aspirations are shaped by a constant drip-feed of glossy images conveying messages of affluence and hedonism. A neo-liberal broadcasting ethic has echoed the political sentimentalisation of many aspects of public life.

In as much as it affects the way we perceive and react to events, media output also bears upon public policy, social attitudes and the conduct of politics in most developed countries. Its influence is pervasive, often insidious, and not always benign. Invariably, those responsible tend to play down this influence and to defend the social value of their choices. Yet the power of the media remains considerable and its ramifications far reaching.

People widely regard the media as their main source of information and see little need to look elsewhere to deepen or refine their own opinions. Reliance on the convenience of instant judgement from the broadcast media tends to blunt the appetite for independent thought. Despite welcome pockets of journalistic excellence, this makes for public opinion which is both facile and volatile. Superficial input tends to produce superficial output.

We are invited to accept that where the media are concerned, 'more' equates with 'better'. The argument is that ever more television and radio channels putting out a vast array of programmes for longer, together with a multiplicity of general and specialist magazines and newspapers and the internet, means higher quality information and thus better informed public opinion. Although more information has the ability to improve knowledge — especially that provided by the specialist press — there are good reasons for thinking that this is not, in general, the way things actually happen.

1. Quantity of information is not to be equated with quality — the media explosion and the consequent increase of airtime that requires filling has led to much indifferent output. Reportage frequently confounds opinion with fact, and argument, where it exists at all, is often superficial and inconsequential. In general journalism, 'greater depth' usually means 'greater length'. One might expect that the proliferation of channels for disseminating opinion and our apparent insatiable hunger for news would have led to more profound argument and better discussion. To a limited extent, this has happened. However, profusion of choice and immediacy of transmission have produced a culture of sound-bite, clip and short-take. Broadcast interviews are rarely long enough to enable the development of extended argument and important issues tend to be treated by slogan and catchphrase rather than by serious debate.

2. One of the more destructive dividends of modern news broadcasting is the culture of instant judgement. The delay between an event and it being reported has shrunk to nil, largely thanks to mobile telephony, so breaking news is flashed across the globe in milliseconds. This requires journalists and other opinion formers to react instantly to events with little time to formulate ideas or research comments: instant news, instant reactions.

3. The high-intensity, high-impact message, so finely tuned by the advertising industry, has spread to newsrooms, where the aim has become to put over the information in as short a time as possible. Whether this reflects short audience attention spans or diminished time available for

listening, compression has become the norm for broadcast news. Such constraints inevitably impact on content — relevance, balance, reliability and completeness are sacrificed as news is delivered in short, assimilable packets to suit instant, hurried lifestyles. The impression of an absolute necessity for brevity is reinforced by the behaviour of 24 hour news channels which fill their time with endless repetition rather than encouraging extended argument.

Immediacy and brevity promote distortion. Reacting on the basis of incomplete information is an unsound basis for decision or opinion and, in many cases initial impressions turn out to be invalidated by subsequent events. Information that is compressed is necessarily incomplete. On the credit side, the greater availability of live footage makes it more difficult to misinterpret or spin after the event. In pre-telephone times, letters were despatched and long intervals perforce elapsed between events and responses to them, time in which further events occurred or other relevant facts came to light which might influence the overall picture.

The present state of affairs is unlikely to change. Not only are public figures expected to make policy 'on the hoof', in response to events as they occur but there is the general impression that this is how public servants should be held to account and how public affairs should be conducted. This encourages poor policy-making (e.g. a mass school shooting invariably brings immediate calls for new gun control laws which are difficult to resist in the face of rows of children's coffins) and preferment for those with the loudest voices rather than the soundest arguments.

4. The ready availability of mass media — especially television and radio — has bred a reluctance to look beyond broad superficialities. First, people take the 'facts' broadcast as the limit of what is needed to make informed judgements. Second, the constant, repetitive barrage of news and 'information' — has displaced dispassionate reflection. Third, the opinions expressed by reporters are frequently regarded as definitive. More profound thinking is the exception, with extended discussion on political, social and economic issues largely confined to the specialist press read only by a small section of the better-educated. The wider public has neither the appetite nor the intellectual capacity required to make properly informed decisions and is content, on most matters, to subcontract this to the political executive. Unfortunately, in many developed countries, politicians are not generally trusted, so the result is

profound public scepticism. As with any institution, government is only as good as the general intelligence which holds it to account.

5. There is also the matter of how news and opinion are presented. In general we are fed information in small, digestible chunks — brief snippets of information and soundbites — the chicken nuggets of the information age. This dovetails well with the culture of mental dilettantism which believes that knowledge can be had without serious study by casual grazing. We like the idea of knowledge but dislike the effort needed to acquire it. This is less a reflection of constraints on media time and space than of diminished attention spans and a general requirement for constant stimulation and distraction (the causal direction is indeterminate).

The stimulation overload has led to a general impression, in both private and public lives, that silence is unproductive and needs filling. Nowadays, it is virtually impossible to find an enclosed public space devoid of background music or other competing stimulus. It would seem that our inner lives are in need of constant external stimulation — a single source of input is never sufficient. We are apparently even incapable of eating or shopping without musical assistance, although it seems more likely that muzak is there for the benefit of staff with boring, repetitive jobs, than to please the clientele. Try asking diners in an upscale restaurant! (One might add that if what is offered as background is great music, it is an insult to the composer; if poor music, an insult to the clientele.)

Important issues are usually complex, involving detailed, often convoluted, argument which demands sustained attention to absorb. In a stimulus-hungry world, both are rarities. The ethos works through to media producers, fearful of damaging circulation or ratings, and thus advertising revenue, if output is clogged up with argument. This means that they cater for the lowest common denominator of audience intellect and are satisfied to inform without resorting to undue detail. Since such detail differentiates good argument from bad, the quality of debate inevitably suffers and much superficial thinking passes unchallenged. There is no justification for expecting what may have taken time and deep reflection to develop to be capable of full or accurate presentation within the compass of a short interview or news report. Yet that is what modern media increasingly requires.

There is also the matter of what we expect from news. Cravings for sensation have led to innuendo and embellishment displacing sound, old-fashioned reporting. The mass appetite prefers gossip, rumour — something sensational — rather than fact, which is often humdrum and dull. This invites a narrow perception of events and issues and circumscribes our understanding of the world. In these circumstances, it is not surprising that fact is doctored or distorted to put across a plausible argument in less than adequate conditions. Important issues go unexplored and often become liable to destruction by talking out, or worse, derision.

6. It is clear that the focus on human interest and the superficial in news and other reporting at the expense of more demanding issues influences and distorts priorities and how people react to events. The culture of celebrity plays a significant role in a media circus relentlessly driven by ratings and the need for advertising revenue.

7. News media compete for our attention. In a market dominated by appearance, this means making their offerings as attractive as possible. In many cases this leads to undue sensationalism, often achieved at the expense of truthfulness. In many quarters, sensationalism and the need for immediacy have replaced intelligent, self-critical, journalism.

This overall situation is compounded by poor educational standards in general and a lack of thinking and reasoning skills in particular (certainly in the UK and USA, but less so in parts of continental Europe). The mental capabilities of the 'average' listener, viewer or reader, now drives the mainstream mass media which adapt output to make it more palatable to an audience preferring simplicity, cliché and simple information to fit into its rudimentary pigeon-holes. If the media dumb down, the inevitable result is public debate conducted at a commensurately undemanding level. This is evident to anyone listening to phone-ins, 'vox pop' interviews, or reading the letter pages of tabloid newspapers where one finds facile argument devoid of intellectual depth or rigour, and opinions based on the most superficial of perspectives. Facts are relegated to the margins of such debate as there is, which is frequently more concerned with personalities and sentimentality. Political utterances are often little better: trite and evasive, determined more by expediency or self-interest than by genuine concern for clarity.

It is also interesting to note the various ways in which the media, desperate to retain audience share, has adapted to the reality of reduced attention spans. News channels now use a two- or even three-handed approach to news casting, with each presenter delivering a sentence at a time, so no one will get bored and switch off. Serious programming is gilded with irritating distractions—unnecessary background music, repetitious and often irrelevant film footage and pulsating graphics which add little to the content and are simply designed to retain attention. This is the disc-jockey approach to broadcasting—a *pot pourri* of cheap, noisy, multimedia ingredients, pulped into an attention-grabbing intellectual equivalent of fast-food.

Documentary programmes now present information in a condescending, populist manner, often resorting to an exaggeratedly modulated diction (sometimes even hectoring). Speech is deliberately stripped of recondite vocabulary, abstruse concepts or convoluted argument. The quiet, impressive, scholarship of genuine authority which appeals to a certain level of intellect has been replaced by high-impact instant 'expertise' designed for mass appeal. Looks and manner are of greater moment than content to the extent that a presenter's credibility is determined by their persona rather than by their opinions.

There is no doubt that the need to entertain drives the visual media and, to a lesser extent, the print media. Newsreaders, and even weather-forecasters, must now be personable and glamorous. Informality reigns—with presenters either perched on the front of a desk, their decorative legs very visible, or else wandering round the studio pointing at giant screens which mirror their words in text. The modern news format requires that spoken words be reinforced with written ones and large, simple, graphics. Where once a kind of studied blandness promoted concentration, this, as it is meant to be, is highly distracting, intended to keep audiences constantly stimulated and to avoid any possibility of their becoming bored or—perish the thought—switching channel.

This approach to news delivery is matched with a changed perception of the constitution of news itself. There are two competing theories: one sees news as a reflection of the world, the other as an artificial construct. In reality, the totality of news is not a mirror of the world but rather a selection of events chosen by programme makers for their emotional impact and local interest value. Emotional impact is essential to retain audience share, so this takes precedence. The daily round is, in the main, dull. The news cannot afford to be, so massaging and selection are essential. News selection also favours parochialism with local matters supplanting regional or national stories—especially in the USA, where international affairs are poorly reflected by broadcast and print media. This is reflected in the average American's ignorance of much beyond their immediate state borders.

News, as much else, has succumbed to the dictates of image, and style usually takes precedence over substance. Melodramatic language infects the reporting of relatively ordinary events, turning the mundane into a serviceable story, sometimes even a 'sensation'. The workaday disagreements and disputes of public and private life are presented in mock-epic terms as battles, struggles and confrontations—the journalism of hyperbole and dramatic over-statement. The routine of war (even war has its routine) becomes the stuff of heroics and the parochial business of small communities is sensationalised for the local front page. Far from news reflecting the world, it is increasingly hard not to view the world as a mirror of the news, and even more difficult to separate what is irrelevant or contrived from what matters. Presenting news in the modern way greatly increases the difficulty of forming a clear, balanced view of world events.

The heightened image-consciousness of the broadcast media raises the question of whether they should reflect or lead their host nation and to what extent, if any, they should seek to become arbiters of taste or fashion. As purveyors of entertainment they have no particular obligations in either direction unlike stations with a public service element in their remit. In its early decades, the British Broadcasting Corporation was seen, and indeed saw itself, as standard bearer, setting guidelines for taste, as a guardian of pronunciation and language usage and as an upholder of morality and decorum. In this it both reflected and monitored the national culture and, to a great extent, influenced and defined it. Changes in taste and behaviour were noted, but adaptation was slow and lagged behind social trends. Whilst it provided unashamedly popular programming, catering for mass taste, its core output consisted of serious, middle-to-highbrow programmes, designed to educate, entertain and improve—a project that was largely successful and drew international respect for standards, as did its news coverage for reliability and impartiality. The appearance of pop and the disappearance of the censor around the 1960s, together with increasing competition from pirate radio and commercial television, changed the corporation's emphasis from 'educate first, entertain second' to a ratings-driven broadcaster competing in the wider market. Now, in the spirit of the age, it is more reflective of national diversity at many levels: vocabulary, accents, dress, habits, customs, religions, minorities and values. The BBC now aims to hold up a mirror to British society rather than standing aloof from social trends, and a more or less monocultural output has been superseded by programmes aimed at specific social groups. One result of this compartmentalisation is that people tend to tune in to whatever reflects their social culture and personal interests which works against cross-fertilisation. What may appear as desirable diversity may in fact be entrenching social divisions.

The manner and content of news presentation strongly affects the way we look at the world and our perspective on its realities. Our own priorities are shaped by those of news programmes — which items are given prime time and most space. This in turn reflects the market-reality that to succeed in today's attention-poor culture the need for news to correspond in some way to some the external world has been superseded by the need to grow audience share. Celebrity items and minor political scandal displace international events, and popular celebrities are interpolated into serious discussion output, not for the perspicacity of any contribution they might make, but as audience-bait. Television and radio news outputs are no longer 'programmes' but 'shows'—stuffed with as much glamour, background film footage (if TV), interview material and soundbites (if radio), as possible. An item's newsworthiness is more likely to be judged on its entertainment value as on its intrinsic importance. News has become 'infotainment', with the emphasis firmly on entertainment. This is generally justified as 'reaching out to our audience' and 'increasing accessibility', which has a superficial ring of worthiness about it, but not much else.

The media are thus deeply involved in business-image creation and management. They may extol their function is as disseminators of public information, but the greater reality is that they are primarily entertainers, political campaigners and opinion formers. In all this, the provision of balanced, reliable news often comes a poor second. The new media elites are there to make money and wield influence, which they construe as being directly correlated with circulation or viewing figures.

The entertainment mentality has spread beyond news dissemination to politics. Spurred by the shape and focus of the media, politicians quickly learned to play the populist game. Public figures are trained in media techniques and polish the skills that enable them to ignore or deflect awkward subjects and inconvenient questions and to steer an interview to their preferred agenda, while media consultants help their clients obtain greater exposure. Politicians now (wisely, from their point of view) regard their job as promoting brand awareness—the brand being their party, their policies or, more often than not, themselves. A publicity-hungry political class see interviews primarily as PR opportunities and, with that in mind, communicate in assimilable chunks, starting with the slogan or soundbite and then working backwards through however much they can fit in to the time allotted. Interview questions are merely triggers for extended, repetitious propaganda statements which often bear no relation to what is being asked. Serious political debate is relegated to the niche print media and to graveyard slots on late night TV or radio.

This shift from informing to entertaining has irretrievably blurred the distinction between fact and fiction. One of the worst effects of media intrusion is that we tend to evaluate and perceive real events with a fictional eye. Few happenings now genuinely shock us and those which should are all too readily absorbed as yet another disaster movie. Wars become episodes of Reality TV, which we turn on and off at our discretion. We expect a regular injection of drama (battle, death, scandal, romance) and have little interest in mundane realities, however important. Thus the American Presidency and British Monarchy are seen as family soaps, providing periodic 'juicy bits' to excite and retain our interest. The press is content to concentrate on romantic events, lurid gossip and revelation, moral failings, and peripheral matters, such as presidential sexual intrigue or Queen Elizabeth's personal wealth. This is not to say that the lurid revelations are false, merely that to emphasise them to the exclusion of everything else, is unbalanced *reportage*. Once again a superficial image overplays the profounder reality.

This has two noticeable effects. First, in the same way that soap producers need to keep an ever changing storyline in their output, so news producers have to vary the pace and content of their programmes. Second, familiarity has inured people to the reality behind disturbing images to the point where, if the shock element remains, it is strongly attenuated. The result is that news is now regarded as a variety of soapy fiction as viewers switch between live events (invariably shorn of the shocking images which only reality is capable of generating) and their regular soap opera diet almost as if there were no distinction. Many are anaesthetised to the point where they can barely see 'reality' behind the images, any more than there is reality behind the soap characters—or at least, their reality status has coalesced. Much as readers write to fictional detectives for help with their real life problems (for example, Sherlock Holmes receives thousands of letters at his fictional Baker Street address each year), some people seem unable to register the emotional difference between fact and fiction on their TV screens and therefore prefer the mentally soft option of regarding everything they see and hear as fictional, even though they are well aware of that war (for example) is real. This de-sensitising enables them to cope with the more unpleasant side of life and takes the sting out of realities which might otherwise be distressing. Constant repetition of images, however unpleasant, neutralises their emotive force, so we browse from one source to another to find something that interests us: "What shall we watch — *Everybody loves Raymond*, or the Iraq war?" — is, unfortunately, an all too credible scenario. Keeping abreast of the news is no longer considered a part of civilised living; it is merely one entertainment option among many.

The Image that the media has of itself as a responsible, broadly politically neutral and impartial purveyor of information and informed comment, acting in the public interest, is thus increasingly at variance with the reality. Its relationship with its consumers has also changed in ways that blunt its impact. In particular, the media now dictates the terms of trade. Those who remember when interviews with senior public figures were rare and highly prized will readily mark the difference. Today, in contrast, most scramble over each other to get on air or contribute a newspaper column. The emphasis has shifted from organisations that collect and disseminate news to the world to a world which itself now effectively performs for the media. Where possible, major public events are planned and scripted to fit in with media scheduling and to maximise their publicity value. In short, today's news dances to the media's tune.

In this image-dominated universe, the print media are at a disadvantage to the broadcast media — which now includes the internet. To retain market share in the face of intense competition and to preserve what they regard as their individuality, sections of the daily print media have responded by increased sensationalism. As reporting and commenting on routine news events is no longer sufficient to keep circulation alive, so ordinary 'stories' are amplified beyond what the facts can justify, often in lurid detail, and gilded to appeal to the jaded audience appetites. They have also boarded the 'lifestyle' bandwagon, filling page after page with advice and recommendation, much of it superficial and ill-researched, and with features which, though nominally editorial, appear to be driven by advertising.

The question of the extent to which the media actively constructs, rather than reflects, what is happening in the world has come into focus with a notable rise in sentimentality as a force in journalism. Sentimentality here is broadly opposed to factual argument, and this dovetails conveniently with journalism which generally has an agenda beyond what it prints or broadcasts. The victim culture (cf. Chapter 7) exemplifies the triumph of sentimentality over reason by removing blame from individuals and transferring it to society or 'the system'. Journalism follows this trend and, where possible, seeks cause and effect in society, where blame can be used as a campaigning weapon. And, where blame can be ascribed, calls for 'action' are swift to follow. This adds to the crusading, socially responsible, self-image of journalists, and gives them a sense of power that their contributions seldom merit. The rewards for scoops or sensations are disproportionate to the sanctions for inaccuracy or misleading reporting, and those responsible walk away with relative impunity, whereas the damage done to their subjects is often significant and long lasting. Apologies for inaccuracies are slow and retractions grudging, couched in tones usually far removed from the forceful language of the original piece. The broader reality is usually that there is right and wrong on both sides, but this reduces the impact of a story, so a judgemental standpoint is preferred.

With good journalism there should be no blurring of fact with interpretation, deliberate construction or evaluation. Much of what is now broadcast as news is heavy on opinion and irrelevant padding, making it sometimes difficult to disentangle hard fact from speculation. News is delivered as 'stories', which are packages of related events and facts glued together with comment. Editorial selection imposes a filter on what is and what is not considered newsworthy. Journalists need an 'angle' on each story, and it is through this filter that information is most often compromised in interpretation. In many cases, news is selected for its emotional impact rather than for its strict relevance or wider significance. Pieces about the misdemeanours of minor celebrities regularly grab the headlines from more significant but emotionally less appealing events, and news gaps are easily filled with reworked old material or speculation on the future turn of current news threads. As with soap-opera, news must not be dull, so it is worked and massaged to suit.

There is also the question of what constitutes truth and how this relates to the news media. Truth, as seen by most journalists is neither more nor less than information, and information is neither more nor less that facts, which they equate with statements or images. This rather linear vision of the world is an oversimplification and there are good reasons for repudiating both equations. Some truths may indeed transmissible in simple statements—e.g. 'The King is Dead'—but much of what news organisations report is infinitely more complex and not reducible to a series of bald propositions. What journalists experience has to be conveyed by means of words and images to their audience, and this very fact interposes elements of selection and interpretation between the reality they seek to communicate and the image they actually convey. Words are not themselves events—they are at one remove away. This is not a facile, academic point, but an observation that between facts or events and *reportage* there is a gap to be spanned, and this gap reflects the reality that there is no simple correspondence between the two, as journalists would have us believe.

This is also the case with visual images, which many see as the true raw material of news. Cameramen and producers face a similar requirement of selection, partly because they can't show everything and partly because much of what is relevant is often off-limits to the media, either because it is inaccessible or because it is unsuitable for broadcast. So what finally appears reflects someone's interpretation of what is newsworthy and of the permissible images which most aptly illustrate that interpretation. This makes it difficult for the viewer to judge whether or not it what has been chosen is either important or representative, and whether the images have driven comment or vice versa. To these considerations must be added the fact that the emotional force of a single well-chosen picture can colour perception of the wider issue to the point that it conditions opinion irrespective of subsequent events.

News does not, in general, arrive fully formed on an editor's desk. It is created out of fact and circumstance and tailored to fill the requirement for so many column inches or broadcast hours. In the very selection and presentation, stories reflect political preference and editorial bias. What is reported—or indeed is not reported—as much as the terms in which reports are couched, is an integral part of editorial news control. News is made 'in the edit'.

Reporting is rarely neutral but designed to support a particular agenda or to appeal to a target audience. It takes little to turn the sense of a comment on its head, to the point at which interviewees complain that their words have been taken out of context. All too often the reality is that the context itself has been changed whilst the words remain as spoken. In the worst cases, journalism works backwards from a desired conclusion to finding or manufacturing evidence to support it. Anyone with expert knowledge of a subject will have sometimes winced at its superficial, sensationalised, journalistic treatment.

There is no doubt that the way news is packaged and presented powerfully affects our perception of the world in particular and our view of reality in general. Media presents us with an endless repetitive stream of heavily frag-mented and highly selective detail, in the context of hourly, daily and weekly output. There is no attempt to balance stories of misery and distress, which are considered newsworthy, with those of good deeds and noble actions, which, by and large, are not. Clearly, things that go wrong have greater urgency and drama than those that go right, so they naturally attract more attention. This makes for a strong pre-disposition to report the world in general as lawless and evil.

Understandably, news tends to treat 'stories' in isolation or on a short-term perspective. There is no doubt that the best judgements about current events, their causes and consequences, come from gradual refinement in the light of subsequent events and better evidence. Proper understanding of most national and international affairs requires contextual background which sets imme-diate happenings into a broader temporal and physical perspective. Explana-tions may be radically altered by facts and events which do not emerge until many years later. Dealing with news in the scientific and non-crisis political fields, requires less immediacy and a more dispassionate approach for a deeper, more secure, understanding. The underlying logic of scientific progress — the progressive refinement of hypotheses — is not reflected in mainstream news, which reports 'discoveries' as 'breakthroughs' which, in the majority of instances, they are not. The judgements of the news media do not come with a stamp of reliability, yet they influence perceptions of reality — perceptions which, once formed, soon crystallise and assume a factual life of their own.

What is broadcast or published as news also reflects the tension between the search for the unusual, which is newsworthy, and the need for news events to have a core of normality as a basis for extracting wider social implications. Constant emphasis on the negative — and thus more newsworthy — inevi-tably instils the impression that this is normality. Worse still, it suggests that public policy should be made around that 'normality'. The normative force of what is reported is an important element of news journalism, which it is not slow to exploit.

As well as reporting, the media also campaigns. In this, it sees itself as a power in the land and, in so far as it reflects public opinion, an agent for change. It has undoubted influence which it mobilises for political and social reform. It is therefore not surprising that it is constantly searching for those to praise and blame, and in doing so relies on the false idea that there is invariably a straightforward causal relationship between an act and its consequences. Those who consider events from an historical perspective take a different view. The public record often shows that what appeared at the time as explicable in simple cause-effect terms was in fact the outcome of a range of factors — personalities, circumstances, situations — which do not readily fit into this tight, deterministic mould. Events taken out of their broader context often seem odd, yet are more easily understood when seen in the light of the circumstances, emotions and personalities, which gave rise to them. Rarely does an event have a single cause. It is usually the result of a network of circumstances and is generally not a case of lighting the fuse and setting off the rocket. Correlations and probabilities do not constitute a chain of causality, a fact too often forgotten by media hungry for instant explanations. Journalists like the cause-and-effect model as it enables them to determine guilt and apportion blame, then to moralise on social issues and campaign for reform.

The journalist's quest for truth means that the attribution of blame has become an integral part of his work. In consequence, social reform is firmly on the media agenda. Investigative journalism exists to identify the guilty or imperfect and to proclaim (usually in banner headlines) the need for urgent action. Life, as many journalists see it, is an amalgam of man-made events which exemplifies a broader causal picture. This tight-knit view of the human universe, which leaves little room for chance or accident, invites us to view the world in terms of strict cause and effect and to re-shape it to take account of effects which turn out to be undesirable, or to remedy the causal end of a link which is corrupt or defective. As causes are rarely as definable or easily pinpointed as this perspective might suggest, the entire enterprise is suspect.

The model of cause and effect that sustains much journalism assumes a link which is at best questionable, at worst false. It is tempting to draw two inferences from the idea that A caused B. First, that by removing the circumstances which gave rise to A one can avoid events of the type B. Second that one can diminish the likelihood of undesirable consequences by reforming the circumstances which give rise to them. To take a concrete example: a motorist on a wet road skis and collides with the vehicle in front. The motorist is blamed for the damage (this model admits no possibility of accident) and, as a result of media campaigning, legislation is introduced to regulate tyre tread, raise the minimum standards of road surfacing and require anti-lock brakes to be fitted to all new cars. Removing the possibility of interpreting such events as an accident, insisting upon a cause-effect chain and then applying strict blame is to take a deterministic view of the world which is unjustified and limiting.

In addition to the (understandable) desire to fit events into convenient pigeon-holes, journalism reinforces the approach by resorting to over-simplified categorisation. It is much easier to discuss issues, mount campaigns or draw conclusions if people and situations are presented in terms of a definable series of groups (for example, war veterans, baseball supporters, binge-drinkers, single-parent families). In subsuming people and events into simple classifications journalists invite us to identify the attributes of one individual with that of the group. As group labels carry emotive attributes beyond the identities of their members such inferences are unlikely to be accurate; family resemblance is not the same as shared identity. In terms of journalistic convenience, this is relatively unobjectionable once it is recognised for what it is and its limitations understood. However, the step from crude descriptive classifications to the conclusion that these groups exist and can therefore be considered as sociological entities is a false reconstruction of social reality. They have no identity beyond that of the individuals who comprise them, and it is a profound mistake to think that they do. This is especially damaging when such factitious grouping is used as a lever to engineer social change or to influence public policy — e.g. in the provision of care or in eradicating discrimination. Media editors find this a convenient campaigning tool, tacitly inviting us to identify ourselves with one group or another and to respond accordingly, particularly if that group is seen as disadvantaged. If you are unfortunate enough not to fit into a defined group, then you tend to fall through the cracks in the journalistic floorboards, as least in respect of your prospects of figuring in public policy or attracting media support.

Despite protestations that their role is merely to report events and to entertain, the media are also instrumental in influencing community ethos and broader moral values. There is an underlying tension in journalism between a desire for the 'truth' and the consequent attribution of praise or blame, and the spirit of tolerance which is preached by governments of developed countries and has become a cornerstone of the new morality.

The desire of journalists to draw wider implications from news and to use these in pursuit of social and political reform entrenches a particular — and, many contend, misguided — model of the state and its role in people's affairs. This model is bureaucratic and authoritarian. It portrays the state as deciding what is acceptable or not, and then making policy to enforce its ideals. This quasi-communistic style of government leaves little room for citizens to shape their own moralities and suppresses individuality and broader creativity. As the previous chapter shows, this undermines individual moral behaviour and effectively de-moralises society, as well as making the elementary mistake of endowing what the majority do with normative force. Policy made on the basis of such a distorted view of what is acceptable is likely to be of questionable value.

In their quest for truth, journalists have become modern moral crusaders. Their demands for political action to correct the wrongdoing they strive to bring to the public's attention forces government onto the back foot. Not to act is easily presented as unsympathetic and ineffectual. Acting — i.e. changing policy and laws — in response to public and media pressure, entrenches an action / reaction model of policy-making, which effectively puts government in the hands of the press and public opinion. This also reinforces the tendency to blame the system rather than individuals. Subsuming individual acts into a wider circle of responsibility takes pressure off everyone — if the system is at fault, then less blame (or even none) attaches to anyone else.

Constant tinkering with morality in this way stems from a worthy, but misguided, desire to explain behaviour in causal terms and thereby to open the way for endless corrective action (gun laws for gun crimes, dog laws for savage dogs, motoring laws for reckless or angry motorists). It shifts the focus from the wrong-doer onto society at large and suggests that the only way of dealing with misbehaviour is by further regulation. The modern philosophy is that when regulation fails it is usually because we do not have enough of it. This is inappropriate and inevitably weakens people's sense of personal responsibility. 'The striving to perfect the world by stopping evil is what makes journalists tick, and it leads to a ceaseless reforming activism which destroys morality by either not giving it time to work, or by stepping in to demand political action to help those who suffer the consequences of their own bad acts' (Kenneth Minogue, *The Silencing of Society*).

The rush for ratings and commercial success has led to a strong decline in morality of the media itself, particularly in television. This, in two senses: first, that there has been a noticeable loosening of what is considered permissible in any circumstances — language, violence, sexual explicitness — and second, that producers and editors are now prepared to do almost anything to succeed commercially. Until recently, there were widely recognised boundaries of decency which it was unacceptable to transgress. However, the pressure to innovate in the name of entertainment has eroded these until almost nothing remains. 'Giving the public what they want', is a thinly disguised euphemism for satisfying a consumer demand fuelled by prurience and the desire to be shocked. It is not enough for plotlines to hint at sex or violence in the way that writers and film producers achieved in such a masterly fashion in the early and mid-20th century. They now have to be seen and heard at length and in as realistic a manner as possible. This is yet another fallout from the 'anything goes' hedonism of the 1960s and 1970s. Bedroom and other walls took time to fall, by slow attrition, but fallen they have and more spectacularly, perhaps, than those early libertarian campaigners could have imagined. It is not part of this book to ask why we need head-on explicitness and uncut realism, but the question (for sociologists and social psychologists) is pertinent and the answer would undoubtedly add insight to our understanding of modern 'civilised' society. What is evident is that there is no place in the modern mainstream media for subtlety or understatement.

The endless search for novelty now permits programmes to deal with hitherto taboo subjects such as cannibalism, incest, death rituals, post-mortems, senility etc. These are probably truly shocking to many but are justified as 'brave' or 'cutting edge', which somehow sanitises them and makes them acceptable. Freed from self-restraint, people are naturally curious and flock to view.

Publishers, editors and producers routinely seek to justify licentious, deliberately shocking, personally invasive or potentially libellous material as 'in the public interest'. In doing so they fail to distinguish (or deliberately confound) 'what interests the public'—which has little to do with what should be allowed—from 'what is in the public interest', which does.

The liberalisation movement has gone yet a further step from explicit sex, violence and bad language. Not content with maximum shock, we are now invited into the largely unscripted world of Reality TV. This derives its consumer appeal from the unexpected, titillated by the possibility of confrontation, unexpurgated sex or even disaster, with plenty of raw, unedited emotion thrown in to keep interest alive. The formula has obvious attraction for programme-makers: low production costs, massive audiences (equals high advertising revenues) and long runs, plus the bonus of edited updates which cost virtually nothing to splice together.

In the USA Reality TV programming is extended to include children, put on television in the hope that they will become stars. 'This can be seen as a show where caring parents who want to see their kids get on are giving them encouragement. It can also be viewed as a forum where disturbed nutcases who need social work, family support and personal therapy vent their spleen. The result is probably the most nauseating repeat case of child abuse possible on television. It is so crass and unbearable. Cheap, hollow, enjoyment from somebody else's humiliation and embarrassment' (Irvine Welsh).

Reality TV started by confining a dozen or so carefully mismatched volunteers together in a house and spicing the mix with competitive tasks for rewards and public voting to exclude participants one-by-one (about as far from Reality as one can imagine, so the genre started as a distortion by even mis-describing itself). It now extends to the less dramatic format of putting experts to work to change some aspect of an individual or family that is seen to be inadequate—uncontrollable children, obesity, bad dress sense, dull homes, jungular gardens, irremediable untidiness, deficient social and dating skills, and so on. The image here is of well-intentioned experts trying to improve people's lives by showing them how to behave, dress or interact socially in a more appropriate manner. The reality is that behind the slender (highly repetitive) output of useful information, the entertainment value consists in taking ordinary people and systematically humiliating them. Helping people quietly, out of the public gaze, is laudable. Putting them in a studio where experts shame them and denigrate their attitudes or behaviour bears all the hallmarks of exploitation.

On occasion, the presentation itself is suspect—one programme started with the presenters interrupting a church service to inform the congregation that their Minister had been secretly filmed and was to be the subject of a dress makeover. Here was a conjunction of disrespect for the subject's office and, in treating a religious service as no more than a social event, unbelievably bad taste.

More recent offerings lack even the superficial justification of personal improvement. Couples or wives are taken from one social milieu and put into another, as far removed from their own as possible; working-class pitched into a middle-class environment and vice versa, solely for the purpose of generating maximum discomfiture, confrontation and embarrassment. The residual educational value is minimal and the reality is that, shorn of their humiliating content, such contrived situations would leave little to attract an audience.

One has to ask how, commercial considerations apart, such broadcast dumbing down can be justified. Fly-on-the-wall output, operates on the basis that audiences will stay tuned in the hope of being shocked by disaster, sex, rage, outright violence or extreme emotional distress. It can have no other purpose. This, as one commentator put it, is nothing more than opportunistic surveillance. The public is complicit in the success of Reality TV, queuing up to take part, presumably believing that exposure of any sort, however demeaning or tasteless, confers some kind of distinction. "There are absolutely no limits to what people are prepared to do nowadays if they think it will achieve their dreams of fame."

This genre of programmes illustrates the worst of media populism. Such levelling down invites abandonment of traditional values of broadcasting, both in terms of minimum quality standards and of its role as an informing and educational medium, in favour of what is merely voyeurism. The phenomenal worldwide success of these programmes proves beyond doubt that people want to watch them but one can reasonably ask whether this should be the standard by which the suitability of programmes is judged. In particular, it begs the question of how far public taste should be indulged. Pushing the limits may well bring us weekly executions, autopsies and floggings. The media elites and their dumbed-down audiences respond indignantly with 'Why not?', or 'If people want to watch X why shouldn't they, it's a free world'. Such a facile response only reinforces the impression that self-control has been abandoned at every level in a mass market which seems content to ignore the wider interests of society to indulge low-grade appetites in pursuit of its own brand of aggressive selfishness. It also conveniently sidesteps the question of whether media output should be subject to the same restraints as society routinely imposes on its members. Most people refrain, as a matter of courtesy, from telling others that they are obese, unattractive, poorly socialised or ill-dressed. So why should broadcast media be encouraged to do so in the name of entertainment? It is indeed curious that societies which frame their laws to avoid giving offence, however slight, to any individual or minority, revel in programmes which rely for their audience appeal on doing just that.

In any case, the world, as presented by Reality TV has little to do with reality. What viewers appear to want is life in the raw, as exaggerated and pumped up as possible. In this, they fail to distinguish reality from realism. The reality of policing, for example, is a mass of dull, humdrum work, occasionally enlivened by violent crime or disaster. It is not this workaday routine but the unexpurgated realism of the corrupt policeman, freak accident or violent crime that people want presented to them, whether in documentary or drama.

The new media barons are as complicit as their audiences in the vulgarisation of taste. To sanitise their connection with their down-market output, they have crafted an image which bears almost no relation to reality. They portray themselves—and in some cases actually see themselves—as ordinary people who happen to have influence, and so champion a public oppressed by an over-bearing, uncaring, mechanistic state. Their privileged lifestyles belie this characterisation. The programmes and print works from which they derive their (often considerable) fortunes are justified on the grounds of entertainment, pure and simple—which they well understand as output devoid of intellectually demanding content. In public, they paint their audiences as intelligent, civilised people who would not dream of watching or reading rubbish. In private, they are sharply aware of the socio-economic profile of their target market and have scant respect for it. Having thus cleansed their consciences, they then dish up precisely what they claim they would not countenance—witless, vulgar trash. This is the reality behind the new media elites. Their convenient fiction, which they may well, through endless repetition, come to believe, is on a credibility par with politicians' frequent appeals to 'the good sense and intelligence of the electorate'. This, in reality, is no more than 'taking the moral high ground, whilst descending into the gutter' (George Walden, *The New Elites*).

For such mass market suppliers, the notion that a programme might be both entertaining and intellectually stimulating is not even contemplated. If you can make good money out of low-cost, undemanding ephemera, why waste time on anything else? The ubiquitous dumbing down of media is matched by the refusal of producers to admit, even to themselves, that they are doing this at all. This is self-delusion on a grand scale.

Whilst it makes sense in commercial terms to target the largest audience, the argument is self-justifying: the average market intelligence is low and will not buy above that level, so only offer low-grade, and low grade is (perforce) what sells. There is ample support for the view that more challenging material does well, if sensitively presented—but this falls foul of the 'why bother?' argument, so there is little on offer. On the occasions when serious topics are broached, the tendency is to treat them in a casual, non-intellectual fashion. It is easy to forget that much that has memorably caught the public imagination—in the arts as well as the broadcast media—has been serious and high-brow and there is considerable evidence to suggest that people want to be inspired as well as entertained. The commissioning barons either ignore this aspiration or else confuse it with diminished intellectual content. It is patronising to assume that all the masses want is low intellect pulp; even if they cannot afford fine wine or fine art, it is arrogance to assume that they don't want to know about the best.

There is much evidence to suggest that they do. The great British television epics (for example, *The Forsyte Saga*, *The Barchester Chronicles*, *Civilisation*) which attracted a vast worldwide audiences across a broad social spectrum, presented classic literature with fine sensibility and great art through expert eyes. The remarkable exhibitions of painting, Egyptology and artefacts that travel the world to sell-out audiences and the apparently insatiable desire to visit the magnificent houses of great and noble families reinforce the view that beyond the ignorant, brain-dead masses, there is a significant market for serious programming. The public service element of broadcasting is under threat from the new media elites and can only be rescued by a deliberate re-balancing of commercial and non-commercial interests.

One further dividend of the dumbed down mass-market approach is that many programmes originally designed to inform have been handed over to the entertainment camp. It is not that these aims are incompatible, rather that the requirements of entertainment have stripped out much of the informative, educational content. The balance has shifted from 'gilding the philosophic pill' to removing content to the point at which only the sugar coating remains. It is no longer enough for cooks to demonstrate how to prepare food—they have to be entertainers first and cooks second. Frying an egg on the top of a jeep in the Gobi desert, surrounded by a group of bemused natives, has nothing whatever to do with cooking, nor is it of the slightest relevance to ordinary people desirous of improving their culinary skills; it is entertainment which happens to involve cooking. Travel programmes no longer offer the individual passion and questing intellect of an informed traveller; the modern version is low on information and high on decorative, mind-numbingly unintelligent presenters, fronting a series of predictable locations and unimaginative situations. Amusing—perhaps; but of negligible value to prospective travellers. This is highly lucrative, platinum-plated, surround-sound, Technicolour prole-feed.

The rise of populist, sentimentalist programming is paralleled by the rise of the cult of celebrity. Whilst genuine skill and talent have always been appreciated and admired, many modern 'celebs' have neither. The principal qualifications for media stardom appear to be based on extremes of one kind or another, once all the routine, normal manifestations have been worked through. This means either physical attractiveness—of the eye-catching, surgically-enhanced, libidinous variety—or deep repulsiveness—offensive, provocatively insulting and foul-mouthed (much modern so-called 'comedy' relies for its effect on bad language or explicit insult). Failing that, you can be thoroughly ordinary, studiously eccentric (e.g. a cross-dresser or ragingly camp) or have an unusual job. Merit has ceased to matter; what does matter is that whoever you are, you are 'hot'—the sensation of the moment. Once discovered, celebrities are spun round the programme circuit in an incestuous vortex; producers preferring the relative certainty of the known to the effort involved in scouring the rich public vein of expertise and talent in search of a new face or interesting idea.

This mentality has seeped into much of the arts and media world. An illiterate celebrity writes a trivial book (or, more likely, employs a ghost writer) and is guaranteed sales whatever the worth of the content, by virtue of celebrity. Publishing houses scramble to pay ever higher advances for these titles whilst the genuinely worthwhile gets left behind, because it is not celebrity-tagged and therefore carries a higher publishing risk. Understandable, perhaps, but hardly a recipe for intellectual diversity. This extends to high-intellect celebrities who achieve vast sales for books that are incomprehensible to all but a fraction of those who buy them—if they overcome the mental struggle to get beyond the opening pages.

The terminus of the fame-at-all-costs-irrespective-of-talent trend, which we rapidly appear to be reaching, and with no undue concern, is the eradication of value. 'If there is no good outside celebrity, money and marketing ... everything becomes the same in the end ... a uniformity in which everything has its price but nothing has value. In such a condition, we will have plenty, but though we shall know what plenty costs, we shall not know what it is for' (Brian Appleyard, *UK Sunday Times* 27 October 2001). This aptly makes the point that modern celebrity is not determined by any consideration of merit, and that we are rapidly losing the yardstick of value by which to judge what we see, hear, read, eat, drink and, in the wider sense, consume. This highlights the gap between the image of the media as an improving influence, and the reality that it is eroding discrimination and sensitivity. The parallel tragedy is a stubborn reluctance to admit that any of this rampant superficiality, dumbing down, patronising and vulgarity, is happening at all. The question, if raised, is either rejected out-of-hand as nonsense or else dismissed in a shallow riposte about delivering 'what audiences want' and 'freedom of expression'. Those who seek to criticise are branded intellectual snobs. In fact, tastelessness is not opposed by snobbery but by dignity, and it is this element of media output that its purveyors steadfastly fail to address.

In addition to their core news output, the main media have become increasingly involved in the way people live and conduct their lives. The new makeover programmes referred to above exemplify the direct form of this influence, whilst the flow of celebrity reportage and glamorous lifestyle series serve as constant reminders that there are better things out there for the taking. Whilst TV series may highlight the personality defects and conflicts of glamorous characters, they do so in a way which presents even these challenges and difficulties in the context of an idealised, highly desirable, lifestyle. Luxurious settings create a subconscious desire for the trappings of affluence, which remains as a powerful motivator long after the personal strife comprising the story-line has been forgotten. The inference we are invited to draw is clear: better material circumstances equals a better life. Not only is this false, but in appealing to the emotions rather than to the intellect it also strongly sentimentalises reality.

This vein of sentimentality has extended to the growing number of courses in Media Studies. Apart from dedicated vocational modules which teach practical technical skills, students may be invited to dissect particular plot lines and characters to determine the psychology behind them and how they achieve their popularity and influence. One University prospectus offers a focus 'on the textual and contextual study of television's key fiction and entertainment genres — soap operas, sitcoms and other styles of comedy, game shows, lifestyle television, daytime television, and music television among others ... [Exploring] the defining generic characteristics of those televisual categories, their representational strategies, their ideological implications, their particular pleasures and their relationship with audiences.' One book, devoted to the Simpsons, apparently shows 'how The Simpsons has been able to talk back to three of television's key genres — the sitcom, adverts and the news — and on how it holds the potential to short-circuit these genre's meanings, power, and effects by provoking reinterpretations and offering more media literate recontextualizations. Examining television and media studies theory, the text of The Simpsons, and the show's audience ... attempts to fully situate the show's parody and humour within the lived realities of its audiences.' Whilst it is all to tempting to take the unwarranted leap from the frivolity of the subject matter to concluding that the research behind it must also be super-ficial, the value of this kind of sociology as worthwhile education remains questionable. There are undoubtedly serious and valuable veins of research and academic excellence in Media Studies departments, which are too often held up to ridicule. However, it is not difficult to see how such courses as those described perpetuate a cheap and sentimentalist media philosophy dedicated to an uncritical mass audience.

The greatest social fault-line is not that dividing rich and poor, upper class and lower class, or indeed any other factitious class distinction, but that separating the educated from the uneducated—those able to look beyond the superficial and to make genuinely self-improving choices and those who are not. This gives the media an important social role, which it seems increasingly reluctant to accept. In its never-ending emphasis on what is shallow it lures people away from serious intellectual endeavour towards the easily digestible and the trivial. This facilitates bad output and drives out good.

The main obstacle to reversing this trend is the denial that it is happening. The media barons, who exercise control over a significant share of what is available, dispute the imputation of general cultural decline and regard them-selves as blameless. Understandable expediency—why kill the golden goose? It may be that limiting exposure to media output, either by restricting supply or by restraining demand, is a lost cause and that it is pointless to try and create artificial defences against the hegemony of those who push the limits of taste and decency. Public battles to reclaim tastefulness from the tasteless-ness, dignity from vulgarity and intellect from sentimentality will doubtless continue. In the meantime, we must rely on self-policing to keep out the worst excesses.

This is not a manifesto against entertainment, rather a plea for improved baseline quality and a recognition that it does not have to be tasteless. Whilst there is clearly an overriding need for the development of a more critical attitude which is less tolerant of excess, there is an even more pressing need for producers, publishers and broadcasters to temper financial considerations with a greater awareness of the broader moral and social effects of their output. That is the modern media's most urgent challenge.

CHAPTER 9
THE FAILURE OF EDUCATION

'The price of excellence is discipline. The cost of mediocrity is
disappointment'
(William Arthur Ward)

'Difficulty is a coin which the learned conjure with so as not to reveal
the vanity of their studies, and which human stupidity is keen to accept
in payment'
(Alain de Botton, Consolations of Philosophy)

It could be argued that the most damaging divisions in modern societies, both developing and developed, are not the relativities of wealth versus poverty but the disparities related to education and competence. Lack of money and basic resources, though important, are essentially remediable, whilst inadequate education and consequent skills-deprivation are generally lifelong handicaps. This is as true for nations as it is for individuals: education not only equips for the continuing learning which is life and facilitates dealing with personal, social, moral and financial problems, it also supplies and sustains a nation's skills base. It is the most dependable route to financial security and welfare independence, and those with education deficit are at a significant disadvantage. Deficient education, both in quality of provision and level of attainment, imposes heavy direct and indirect costs on society.

A critical restraint on the progress of education is the negative attitude resulting from the tendency of popular western culture to trumpet the lifestyle and material success of 'celebrity'—the high-living, 'flash' wealth of mass media 'royalty', with little of substance beyond looks and attitude. Children rapidly learn that play is more interesting than work, and realise, through images of wealth and preferment that the pop, media and business worlds continually pump out, that there are routes to success which bypass the discipline and graft of formal education. This leads to the search for short cuts to eliminate the intervening steps; visions, as it were, of economic prosperity without the exigencies of learning. Fame encapsulates this quick wealth mentality and drives the aspirations of younger generations, who regard qualifications as having little relevance to 'real life', as they see it.

Education — or the lack of it — also shapes society, particularly in its values and moral base. Therefore, any tinkering with an education system for political or social ends that risks undermining the aim of fitting children for adulthood as qualified, intelligent, responsible citizens is to be deplored. A nation needs the best-trained minds to lead its efforts in business, intellectual life, science, the arts, industry and government, and this requires a refined system of streaming and testing to identify the more from the less able, and thus to nurture the intellectual capital at its disposal.

While the third world struggles to provide even a basic learning, education policy in much of the developed world is driven by concerns which have less to do with these core goals and more with political expediency. As a result of a widespread adoption of progressive philosophies and a distorted vision of what constitutes sound schooling, education systems have not delivered in many high GDP/ income-per-capita countries. The continuing debate about teaching methods, the proper aims of learning, the value of examinations, and the practical steps necessary to prevent education becoming indoctrination, provides a convenient smokescreen for the appalling learning deficits apparent in many developed countries, most notably Britain and the USA, and delays urgently needed reforms of the systems that have produced them.

The inadequacies of publicly funded education are well documented. The report of the US National Commission on Excellence in Education (1984) reports that 'Some 23 million American adults (10% of the total population) are functionally illiterate by the simplest tests of everyday reading, writing, and comprehension', and that 'functional illiteracy among minority youth may run as high as 40 percent'. It also records lower standards among high school students than 26 years ago, declining achievement levels for college graduates and a 'dramatic decline' in both the number and proportion of students demonstrating superior achievement in Scholastic Aptitude Tests. In *To Renew America* (1995), Newt Gingrich records the failure of US public education and in particular what he describes as a crisis in higher education: 'academics want to deliver less education for more money, enlightened leaders want to deliver more education (e.g. via internet) for less money to more people'. Campuses are frequently run for the benefit of the (tenured) faculty, not for the students, and many have courses which reflect the worst in Political Correctness. One faculty refused to teach Western Civilisation: 'instead there were seminars about radical history, labour history, gay history, lesbian history, multi-cultural history, and all the other pet obsessions of contemporary academia'. (Gingrich, ibid.) American children also suffer because they are not taught proper history and are consequently ignorant of their national cultural heritage. They 'are being cheated; they have a legacy that comes from they know not where, paid for by men whose names they scarcely know, at a price they cannot comprehend'. Gingrich concludes that 'money is being used to subsidise bizarre and destructive visions of reality. People are paying to have their children mis-educated.' In the USA, the educational pyramid is being sliced off at the top and is sagging at the bottom. During a period when successive US administrations have vaunted the achievements of the public education system, it would appear that educational attainment has regressed rather than improved.

The picture is no less disturbing in Britain, where despite considerable year-on-year increases in real terms in government funding, the public education system continues to deliver falling attainment, high drop-out rates and at its worst, an ill-educated, semi-literate citizenry which, in many cases, verges on the moronic. Minimum curriculum standards are not being met, there is a lack of individual competitiveness, and many schools find it difficult to maintain even a semblance of order in oversized classes. Discipline is particularly problematic where intake comes from low socio-economic catchments with unsupportive homes which fail to reinforce the most basic of standards and values. Deprived of the ultimate sanction of expulsion, teachers and schools are facing an impossible task even to reach minimum academic levels, let alone to inculcate any spiritual values or artistic appreciation. In 2004 over 200,000 exclusions averaging 3.8 days were recorded—evidence of disruption and indiscipline which allows unruly pupils to damage their own and other children's learning. Apart from the long-term social and national implications of legions of poorly educated adults, unfulfilled intelligence is undoubtedly a source of individual frustration and unhappiness.

Thus it is that Britain and America, two of the world's richest countries, are failing a significant proportion of their children. Despite paying lip-service to education as a top priority, successive administrations on both sides of the Atlantic have failed to reverse this trend. Indeed, in some cities, it would amount to dereliction of parental responsibility to send a child to the local state school.

Yet politicians continue to assert that, contrary to the evidence, standards are rising and all is well. They promulgate an image of improved facilities and are disinclined to admit that the funds devoted to education are not delivering any improvement in scholastic achievement. This undoubtedly reflects the prevailing political conventional wisdom that 'more' automatically equals 'better'. Many would argue that smaller school units, where pupils knew each other and were able to form productive personal relationships with colleagues and teachers would be a better environment for learning and personal development than large, impersonal schools. There are many factors which change when the size of a community is arbitrarily increased and economists are not obviously correct to assume that other things will remain unaffected when they simply multiply 'independent' elements (money, teachers etc). In a large school a child is likely to feel anonymous, and the maintenance of discipline becomes impersonal and regimented rather than being handled on a more intimate and individual basis.

Professionals attribute the problems to a potent mix of chronic underfunding (notwithstanding the increases), varied teaching standards, constrained or diluted curricula, and lax discipline. The problems are not confined to the lowest achievers: research reports point to a *cycle of failings* leading to an *acute skills shortage*. There could be no starker dissonance between the image and the reality. Something is clearly wrong. This chapter examines some of the false ideology and imagery which have infected educational practice and contributed to the continuing failings.

Imagery first: the usual political response to poor school and college results is to spin away substandard teaching and low pupil attainment. Manipulating the statistics to prove that standards have not in fact fallen is the usual first line of defence. Thereafter, the argument shifts from provable, and therefore uncomfortably verifiable, facts to woolly generalities, expressed in a variety of ways: education is more than passing tests; examination results do not really matter and are not, in any case, a valid yardstick of educational achievement; formal testing only shows up one sort of ability; there are other means of measuring achievement and success; tests are too circumscribed; rote learning and absorbing facts are only one part of the education process — and so on. If education is not to be measured in traditional ways, then one may not reasonably use such measures as evidence of decline — nor indeed may one use them as measures of improvement.

Whatever the excuses, the decline in standards is not so easily finessed. Nor is the obvious contradiction between the facts and the 'explanations'. Whilst there is undoubtedly excellence at the top level, there can equally be little doubt that systems are not working as they should for the less able. Employers (at least those who are educated themselves) continue to comment on the low level of basic education of many who apply to them for jobs — barely literate, barely numerate, lazy, fickle, poorly socialised and in many cases weakly motivated — and resent the resources they have then to deploy to remedy these deficiencies. It is the job of the education system, not employers to teach these skills, and on that single, simple measure it is failing. Unfortunately, basic levels of numeracy and literacy are too often the goal rather than the starting point of educational attainment. At an anecdotal level, one only has to listen to the standard of public debate on topical issues to be aware of the low degree of articulacy and general intellect. The voters whom politicians never fail to flatter as 'well-informed' and 'intelligent' are, in the main, neither. The entire political culture would be transformed if they were.

It is difficult to ignore the problems in the face of the evidence and of persistent, well-informed criticisms. However, it is unreasonable to conclude that problems *of* education are necessarily problems *in* education. Low achievement is likely to have social and economic, as well as scholastic, components. Education, like other disciplines, adapts to needs and evolves with technological and theoretical advances. Valuable debate continues on such issues as the frequency and value of formal examinations, the balance to be struck in curriculum construction between knowledge and critical thinking, and how (and what) values are to be taught in multi-ethnic societies but these should not be allowed to obscure the reality. While it may be naive to conclude that recorded deficiencies in educational output, measured solely by exam results, invariably signify poor education, or that they can be ascribed to a few simple factors, it is nonetheless possible to identify an overarching ideological trend. This derived from the tenets of 'progressive' education, developed by John Dewey in the USA from 1896 onwards and highly influential there ever since. These have cost at least one post-war generation dear. Now, like *nouvelle cuisine*, the *nouvelle vague* in education appears to be on the wane, but it still attracts powerful adherents and a corrosive residuum lingers stubbornly on.

If spin and imagery are political stratagems for dealing with education failure, it is these influential educational theories which have caused the continuing damage in the first place. The principal ideological battle has been that between traditionalists and progressives, and this is best illustrated by setting out the main differences between them. In broad terms, traditionalists emphasise subject-centered, knowledge-based curricula, facts and rationality, objective testing, selective streaming and competitiveness, underpinned with a clearly defined morality based on old-fashioned virtues and recognition of right and wrong. Progressives, on the other hand, recommend child-centered, skills-based, curricula that promote understanding and individual experimentation and emphasise feelings and creativity over factual learning; they prefer continuous, subjective assessment and co-operative projects, and stress the importance of the process over the product.

These alternative philosophies are not merely cosmetically different but reflect a fundamental divergence of belief in the purpose of education. Progressives prefer subjects which have greater cultural importance and often make use of this emphasis to inculcate attitudes and further the aim of constructing a politically correct socialist society. This philosophy dominated teacher-training and the teaching environment for several decades and effectively ensured the hegemony of progressiveness. The traditionalists were stigmatised as old-fashioned and reactionary on the false reasoning that long-held beliefs are old-fashioned and therefore *ipso facto* at least outmoded, at worst wrong. If 'old-fashioned' is defined to include 'long-held', the premise is tautologically true, but the conclusion false. If 'old-fashioned' is meant in its descriptive sense of 'traditional', then nothing of importance follows from such attribution. Despite the deficiencies of the progressive system, it enjoyed strong mass appeal and gained ground with an influential breed of liberal educationalists.

Why was traditional teacher-led, factually-based education, backed by shared morality, which worked well and evolved over the centuries, discarded so readily in favour of an untried system? Part of the answer is that those who were drawn to it intended it as a component of a broader movement to further a socialist, egalitarian agenda. This required that individual differences be glossed over, or preferably eliminated altogether, and as objective testing points up such differences (and also failings in teaching and learning) progressives sought to change tack to privilege individual preferences and child-centered activity. Their ideology crystallised round a number of misconceived ideas about the nature and purpose of education.

1. Wisdom and moral development and that of cognitive skills were taken to mutually exclusive and ceased to be a focus for education among many experts. In fact, they are complementary and entirely compatible. This mistaken belief led to them being sidelined in both schools and universities in favour of knowledge, learning and skills development. Whilst the acquisition of knowledge and skills are essential in an increasingly technological world, there is no justification for pursuing them at

the expense of wisdom or the inculcation of moral conduct. This shift of emphasis is of major significance; so much so that it has been suggested that 'examination papers measuring wisdom rather than learning would probably result in an immediate re-alignment of the hierarchy of intelligence, and a surprising new elite' (de Botton, *The Consolations of Philosophy* p. 136).

The problem has deepened as, for quite separate reasons, the teaching of moral values has all but been abandoned in state-funded schools in the USA and Britain.

(i) Because it is seen as politically incorrect to favour any one morality over another in so-called multicultural societies.

(ii) Because the traditional requirement to censure transgression invites parental and authority intervention (unwise in an increasingly litigious society).

(iii) Because it is almost impossible to agree on what principles are correct.

(iv) Because whatever schools do teach is unlikely to be reinforced by home backgrounds—especially in deprived urban areas where, unfortunately, moral behaviour is less considered. Christian religious schools which continue to teach traditional Christian morality are in some difficulty handling the demands of the egalitarian multiculturalists, but turn out children with at least a grounding of sound morality.

This is particularly unfortunate when not only is there a pressing requirement for an agreed value system—even if this only extends to a minimum core—but also a need to ensure that, as far as possible, the system is understood and accepted by the wider community. Moral precepts will only be internalised if they are reinforced both in and outside school. Even this limited development has been hindered by the suggestion that you should not impose what are seen as middle-class values on children. On the contrary, such moral values are classless, and failing to instil them effectively deprives children of their moral status. The recurrent phrase 'middle-class values' suggests a political agenda behind the educational theory. Even egalitarians resort to socially loaded language when it suits their case.

Progressives believe that values are learned *in vivo*, as it were, as a reaction to example, by some process akin to osmosis. Whilst it is undoubtedly true that children are strongly influenced by example, they are unlikely, unaided, to always choose good from bad, particularly where the issues involved require subtle judgement. Nor is it evident how they are supposed to learn one value system rather than another. Moral precepts are culture dependent and thus need to be taught as much as do mathematics or geography. The difficulty with the progressive, pluralistic approach, which champions inclusivity as the supreme goal, is that it allows considerable moral flexibility and regards censure on behavioural matters as unacceptably judgemental. This is a strong platform for multiculturalists, who justify abandonment of cultural and moral absolutes as a necessary prerequisite to accommodating a diversity of creeds and cultures. Christian morality has thus been left stranded, stigmatised as inflexible and discriminatory. If, as the current tendency has it, all values are to be accorded equal weight, there remains no means of distinguishing between competing systems in terms of moral goodness. If such judgements are impossible, the clear implication is that, where morality is concerned, 'anything goes'. This dangerous doctrine derives in part from the desire, for motives of social inclusivity, to incorporate all religious or secular moralities on equal terms. Where this conflicts with, say, Christianity in hitherto Christian countries, there is no mechanism for resolution other than by dictat. *Lex Talionis*—'An eye for an eye'—is a perfectly coherent, if extreme, system of punishment, but one which happens to conflict both morally and legally with Anglo-Saxon law and Christianity. It is on such issues that true multiculturalism is seen to be unworkable.

Clarity in the discussion of values in education is compromised by an imperfect understanding of what constitutes a value. Too often one sees 'excellence', 'innovation' or 'diversity' cited as values, when in fact that they are nothing of the kind. Values, properly defined, are standards or principles of behaviour, and excellence and the rest, whilst certainly desirable aspirations which may indeed have value, are not in any morally relevant sense values. Excellence, for example, is relative to individuals; one person's concept of excellence (say musical or academic attainment) bears no relation to, for example, an athlete's conception of excellence for which academic proficiency is an irrelevance. The pursuit of excellence, innovation, or diversity is an attitude which has no universal application

THE FAILURE OF EDUCATION

and indeed would be detrimental or impossible to many students. Citing such feel-good concepts avoids the real debate about values, which are best described as equivalent to the old fashioned virtues. Teaching these is a difficult task demanding cross-cultural consensus and discipline, and often requiring moral judgements about individuals which many both inside and outside education go to great lengths to condemn.

The emergence of widespread anti-social behaviour across a couple of generations is one dividend of the failure to identify, teach and enforce clear values. Inculcating an effective moral code is considered too restrictive of personal freedoms for modern libertarians who have, thus far, offered no effective solution for squaring this awkward circle.

2. Political Correctness, in the form of the doctrine of Equality has seeped into the direction of many educational systems. Equality, especially of opportunity in education, is one of the most powerful contemporary shibboleths and its value and justification are widely regarded as self-evident. However, when it comes to defining its meaning and practical implementation, the case is far less clear cut.

There are three separate platforms for equality. The most basic — Equality of Endowment — ignores what scientific evidence there is and, moreover, is based on shaky logic. Science suggests that human brains are not identical because of prenatal hormonal differences which appear to influence the type of brain we have. We know that some children are naturally stronger at certain skills (e.g. verbal reasoning) while some excel at others (e.g. spatial judgement). The shaky logic is to assume that even if we are all born with physiologically similar brains, one can extrapolate to the conclusion that we all are capable of becoming first-class minds. This absurdity is on a par with the supposition that physical similarity makes everyone potential Olympic athletes. There is no ground whatever, scientific or logical, for concluding that morphological similarity implies functional equality.

It is particularly dishonest to assume equality of endowment or to use it as the basis for an education system, yet this has underpinned much post-war theory in Britain and the USA. Politicians generally dodge the direct question because of the awkward consequences of answering it either way. However, since one's position on this is fundamental to developing any coherent schools policy, governments owe it to their citizens to make clear their stance on the issue. Education needs a base of sound fundamental assumptions and should not be founded on unresolved science. Prudent policy-making should recognise the balance of probabilities and accept the inequality of individual endowment, however politically unpalatable that may be. While no obvious foreseeable harm flows from doing so, much does from failing to do so.

Faced with the unsustainability of the equality-of-endowment argument, progressives fall back on that of Equality of Opportunity. The considerable populist appeal of this idea has led to its being given weight it cannot bear. A particular difficulty comes in defining what is to be equalised in order to deliver equal opportunity. Accepting inequalities in intellectual capacity may be controversial (despite strong evidence that they exist from an early age), but there can be little doubt as to the existence of significant differences in educability, motivation and aptitude — let alone in personal attitudes and dispositions which bear on the entire education process. These can no more be equalised than can differences in personal circumstances — home environment, parental support and a host of other variables which significantly affect the chances that innate potential will be realised. This is particularly true of cultural development where children from homes with a history of cultural interests have a clear advantage. This is not simply a matter of money — in fact, often the reverse; parents with recently acquired wealth have often not themselves had the time or disposition to develop their own cultural education, so these supportive resources are not available to their children. The Equality of Opportunity platform is therefore in difficulty from the start.

Glossing over the fact of considerable disparities in circumstances and pretending that all backgrounds provide the same chance of success or of surviving intellectually in a high achieving stream, whatever the provision in terms of teaching and the school environment, is the only way out of the impasse. Levelling up social conditions is a very desirable aim but until it is achieved the assumption that inequalities do not exist or are unimportant is nothing more than unrefined deceit. Equality of opportunity in this sense can only be achieved in a Utopian society where homes are equal in wealth, intellectual attainment and moral outlook. It flies in the face of reason as well as of science to continue to pursue this particular egalitarian chimera on the basis on which it is generally advocated.

Realistic equality of opportunity is a limited licence, confined to the requirements that no-one who is suitable, or appropriately qualified, is excluded from competing, and that competition is conducted on merit alone. It is worth restating unambiguously what equality of opportunity is often taken as meaning, but does not:

(i) That everyone starts with the same capability or circumstances.
(ii) That everyone is *ipso facto* eligible to compete.
(iii) The appropriate end is equality of outcome — e.g. that everyone gets a particular qualification or school / college place.

The waters have become further muddied by the introduction of 'entitlement' into the debate. The implication here is that equal opportunity confers entitlement on all. This has a feel-good liberal ring about it and, in its pursuit politicians continue to maintain that intellect and talent are more or less evenly distributed throughout the population. The problem, as they see it, is that entitlement is not being delivered as it should be. Unpick this with reference to education and you find, beneath the egalitarian image, a rather more pedestrian reality. The public perception of entitlement parcels out as a somewhat ill-defined (and equally populist) mantra of 'excellence for all'. However, given the impossibility of equalising endowment and personal circumstances, all that can realistically be achieved is parity in the resource aspects of schooling — teaching, class sizes, facilities, etc. Even this cannot be guaranteed to deliver much by way of benefit unless an effective means can be found of excluding disruptive pupils and weeding out non-inspirational teachers. Excellence at the teaching level is as important to delivering educational equality as curriculum construction, consistent and valid testing, and striking a sensible balance between course work and formal teaching. Failure to admit inequality of scholastic endowment or to allow for inequality of motivation reduces the practice of equal opportunity to the simple provision of adequate schooling for all — and this is far from happening even in the developed world.

The third strand of equality is that of Equality of Outcome. This is the final refuge for egalitarians, who seek to rationalise their untenable position by substituting 'outcome' for 'opportunity'. Downward convergence makes it possible for all eligible children and undergraduates to receive cosmetically similar qualifications and thus to engineer an image of equality — of an inferior sort. The fact that this requires simplified examinations tailored to the lowest level of attainment, curriculum dilution and massaged pass rates is seen as an acceptable price for political dogma. The reality—that equality of opportunity, in this sense, is only achievable by levelling down rather than up and by the abolition of targeted streaming of brighter pupils—is regarded as a necessary expedient, irrespective of its detrimental effect on the broader educational canvas.

Some spin the practice of selective streaming and classroom competitiveness as condemning some children to the scrap heap even before they have started school. On the contrary, recognising the reality of individual differences in potential is entirely compatible with constructing an education system to bring out the best in every child at every level of ability—indeed, it promotes that end. Unfortunately, in the politically sensitive milieu of modern education it would be almost certain suicide to admit that ability and talent are not distributed evenly across the population. True liberals, in pursuit of the elimination of elites, demand equality of everything that is measurable but conveniently forget that equality is invariably compromised by differences elsewhere. This is a depressing dividend of dogmatic thought.

Only by lowering standards or worse, deliberately scaling them downwards to accommodate the baseline of achievement, can a kind of cosmetic equality be achieved, though this is manipulative and without value. Allegations of declining attainment—whether measured in terms of fewer exam passes, easier exam papers or less rigorous curriculum requirements—continue to surface in countries as politically and economically diverse as South Africa, the USA and Britain. Governments are understandably unwilling to admit to realities that conflict with their desired image and drum out a repetitious line about increased resources as if these alone might improve matters without accompanying policy changes.

3. Discipline, or the lack of it, also divides progressives from traditionalists. An unspoken but nonetheless central tenet of much modern education theory (famously propounded by the philosopher Rousseau in the 18th century) is the belief that children are born innocent and good, only to be progressively corrupted by society. The notion of innate goodness is one that earlier generations would have rejected roundly, yet the modern rebellion against manners and social custom could be said to have begun with Rousseau. However hard it may be, faced with a group

of 'innocent' happy children, to believe that some will turn into thugs, criminals and misfits, this is slender justification for an assumption of universal natal purity or for the generalisation that this is subverted by social forces, let alone a rational basis for designing educational or social policy.

Progressive ideology contrasts with traditional philosophy—deep-rooted in generations of parents and nannies—which sees children as tyrannical and in need of civilising. Casual observation of unruly children in public places, unchecked by doting parents, suggests that this is not far from the mark. It is a well-remarked paradox that the parents of unruly children are more often than not top tier career achievers. However, whatever child-rearing instincts they possessed seem to have deserted them and they resort to experts and books for appropriate advice. One only has to watch these highly-educated, materially successful people struggling—or more often than not, not even trying—to deal with their children's bad behaviour to see the extent of the problem. The justifying creed is, 'If it feels good, do it'—another social dividend of modern liberalism. Except in the rare cases where they simply can't be bothered to attempt discipline (which is not the same as not noticing), their attitude amounts to self-deceit and selfishness on a grand scale.

The deluge of 'expert' advice has resulted in unbelievably badly social-ised children, particularly in the USA, where much of this child psychology originated and where, to even the casual observer, are to be found some of the most over-indulged, repellent, self-centered and ill-mannered children in the 'civilised' world.

Sociologists will no doubt determine whether unsocialised children are more likely or not to be the product of unsocialised parents, but it is remarkable that many parents seem totally oblivious of their children's failings; 'just high spirits' and 'boys will be boys' are typical excuses, if any are offered. This may be either because they genuinely believe that their children have no behavioural problems or because they think that wilful behaviour somehow doesn't matter. A more credible explanation is that parents are disinclined to confront and discipline their children for fear of alienation. Here sentimentality acts as a convenient cover for distasteful reality, blotting out what parents and teachers are reluctant to face. This is a kind of tacit conspiracy to avoid trouble and pretend that all is well. Such unrestrained altruism, in education as elsewhere (e.g. in health, welfare, foreign affairs) leads to poor-policy making. 'Tough love' is not an oxymoron and 'firm but fair' disciplinary regimes have proved, time and again, well suited to children at school and at home — even to those who are otherwise disadvantaged. Such a regimen is critical in developing respect, both for ones self and for others — a disposition singularly lacking in much of so-called civilised society.

Both images — 'natal purity' and 'natal tyranny' — are powerful, and each has its adherents. As always, there is someone willing to fill the gap between the extremes. In this case, it is those who reject both these views of human nature in favour of the idea that human beings are 'socially constructed'. According to this idea, differences between us are the products of artificial social structures. These structures, themselves products of society, are characterised as both paternalistic and unnecessarily oppressive, whilst traditional education, which emphasises teacher-directed learning, is seen as numbing the critical faculties of students and, more worryingly, 'preserving the oppressor class'. The more extreme called for a change of both method and content: 'Teachers should present new content that would celebrate the culture of the oppressed, and they should also instruct in new methods that would encourage intellectual resistance.' (Quoted by E D Hirsch, *Why Traditional Education is More Progressive*) This philosophy clearly links teaching with a revolutionary political agenda, and political revolution with progressive education. Others disagree, suggesting that traditional, rather than progressive, education is more likely to improve the social, political and economic power, especially of the disadvantaged.

The next stage in the process which seeks to avoid formal discipline sees the move from *laissez-faire* in the name of 'love' to attributing anti-social behaviour to external causes. The continued sentimentalising of child-rearing and education means that 'just where moral discretion should begin, however, when boys and girls are old enough to sustain serious blame for their misdeeds, they are made the objects of determinist understandings of their condition and the sense of their human agency is profoundly weakened' (Cooper and O'Keefe, op.cit.).

In many British and American schools, especially those in urban areas, indiscipline is rife. Indeed it is a constant subject of complaint from both teachers and parents. Too often significant lesson time is wasted restoring order to the point at which teaching can begin at all. In such situations, teachers are driven to compound with pupils to ignore past transgressions in return for nominal obedience and a semblance of work. Not so long ago, schools were permitted to mete out discipline (including smacking) to badly behaved children and were supported by parents for doing so. It worked, even if it was rough justice. Now, mindful of teachers with sadistic streaks, childrens' rights, parents' rights, and everyone else's rights, not to mention the pecuniary liabilities attaching to anyone found transgressing them, governments have inserted the law between the child and society. Children sue teachers, and even their parents, for exercising authority and are considered their moral equals.

Into this disorderly mêlée wade the 'experts', advising teachers and parents how to bring up and socialise their children. Discipline has been replaced with 'negotiate contracts with children, ignore inappropriate behaviour, and reinforce positive behaviour: Avoid anything that might damage a child's self-esteem or repress creativity. The result has been disastrous. Schools and day-care centres are still faced with unruly children, now free to tyrannize everyone'. (John & Karen Danford, *Raising Children'* in *The War on Wisdom* ed. Digby Anderson, 2003).

The need to deal with ill-socialised children has led to increasingly desperate remedies. One US state suggests that parents file a court complaint against their child so that 'the child can receive counselling, testing for learning disabilities, a psychological evaluation or community service'. (Cuyahoga County Juvenile Court). Doctors and drugs now play an increasing role as parents seek to medicate away the results of their failed upbringing. In the UK in 2005 some 362,000 children were prescribed Ritalin—the 'good behaviour' drug. This is no more than discipline in pill form and delivers parents the convenient fiction that there is nothing fundamentally the matter with their child (or their parenting skills) beyond a temporary medical problem. It also helps meet the requirement for conformity in schools and thus enhances the chance of decent academic results.

It would seem that despite unprecedented material prosperity children are not thriving in the modern environment. The conversion of sin in general and anti-social behaviour in particular into forms of disease allows parents and society to transfer responsibility away from themselves onto psychiatrists and others. There is little evidence that either the medical or psychiatric approach works, in the sense of producing fundamental change. This is not surprising when one considers that these treatments are symptomatological and that the causes remain intact to re-emerge once the short-term palliatives have worn off.

Modern science and technology sees itself as *in loco parentis* and as the proper resource for regulating many social and non-social aspects of children's lives. Expertise bids fair to take over from parents who are regarded as insufficiently equipped to handle the task of upbringing. The model is that of a deterministic system which requires specific inputs and constant monitoring to produce optimal function. As to handling children, indiscipline and deviance are explained by the idea that if we are fully aware of all the circumstances we can better understand the behaviour. It is but a short step from here to sympathy and unbridled sentimentality.

One notable dividend of the progressive agenda has been an increased emphasis on 'caring' at the expense of discipline and academic rigour. This focuses on the child and his supposed emotional welfare. The general idea is that you should do nothing to interfere with, or taint, what is seen as unspoilt young nature. One way of guaranteeing this is to make sure that children are not forced to involuntary participation in any activity or to learn anything they find distasteful. This mushy sentimentality, often dressed up as promoting 'individuality', is both disastrous for the child and intellectually suspect; disastrous because it encourages idleness and sustains deficient education; intellectually suspect because it stems from the mistaken belief—from child psychology—that discipline invariably entrains mental or physical harm.

'In both America and Britain, education has set aside discipline and obedience, and replaced them with false love and slackness. This is the defining error of our educational practice … Sentimentalising childhood means you do not have to deal with real children, with their idleness, selfishness and potential for violence. Instead you talk cant about unspoilt young natures' (*Sweetness and Light in Schools*, Bruce S Cooper and Dennis O'Keefe, in *Faking It*, 1998, ed. Digby Anderson and Peter Mullen). Many high-profile progressive schools operate on deliberately non-disciplinarian lines, which they justify in terms of maximising self-expression and care for their children. On the contrary, children both benefit from and respect disciplinary limits, as long as they are reasonable and impartially enforced, and those who suggest that a light disciplinary touch and self-discovery morality amount to loving care are profoundly mistaken. Inequalities, in the form of authority, hierarchy, privilege and status and their disciplinary corollaries, are essential components of all social structures and experiencing them is an important part of human social development which should not be diluted or avoided.

Parents and schools enforcing a firm but fair disciplinary regime do so precisely because they love children and consider this part of good upbringing. Unfortunately, many parents fail to emulate this and end up with unruly, poorly socialised children with little motivation to learn. Experts in 'parenting skills' suggest that parents—especially in those households where both work—should try to become their children's best friends, and many who follow them see the maintenance of discipline as antithetical to that end. They believe that the limited time they have to spend with their children must be 'quality time', often interpreted as time when they indulge their children morally as well as materially, and that keeping order is incompatible with that. Indeed, it is often those parents unprepared to enforce discipline themselves who expect schools to do the job for them. This is an unrealistic demand, especially when those values are not reinforced at home. It is also true that in the contemporary moral climate, the exercise of authority is all too readily represented as authoritarian which is regarded both as judgemental and an unacceptable interference with pupils' rights. This misrepresents the status of pupils during their moral development, when they are in greatest need of guidance. It is the dangerous (and false) assumption that children have identical rights to adults in respect of discipline and authority which has allowed this pernicious egalitarianism to take hold.

4. The spread of sentimentality through educational philosophy has significantly hindered progress. It comes principally from those who, for one reason or another, do not wish to admit the realities of intellectual inequality and prefer the illusion that every child is capable of high achievement provided that (a) enough resources are poured in to the system to unlock the potential and (b) competitive elements are eradicated from it. Allied to this is the modern mantra that everyone, lazy or not, must feel good. The unwillingness to admit the unequal distribution of talent comes in part from the feeling that to do so would inflict lasting psychological harm on the less able and also from a determination to enforce equality at all costs. The sentimentalists both disadvantage children and deceive themselves.

The dogmatic pursuit of equality and a fear of damaging 'frail psyches' have made common cause with sentimentality to campaign against rigorous testing and identifying failure. In consequence, less effort is now required to reach a given standard, homework is light, and formal testing is being replaced, as the emphasis shifts from classroom learning to course work or projects (the value of which is being sabotaged by the availability of ready-made material on the internet). While excellence remains concentrated in the best private schools and universities, academic life in the public sector is widely seen as increasingly undemanding at all levels.

This sentimental attitude to testing twists and turns to eliminate demonstrable failure. Among the educational establishments of both Britain and the USA there has been a strong resistance to the imposition of rigorous testing to separate the able from the less able and to monitor standards across the educational system. This 'Assault on Categories' (*Education, Equality and Society*, ed. B.R. Wilson), is a prominent feature of current educational debate and an important tool in the realisation of equality. Its thesis, that 'to categorise is to stigmatise' is designed to destroy 'the whole social apparatus of order, gradation, status, distinction and categorisation … Fine discriminations and interpersonal differences which had been steadily elaborated and which had been employed in the attempt to make more appropriate the treatment and facilities for individuals were now to be eliminated in favour of mass provision' (ibid. Introduction). While the desire to avoid failing any child at least recognises some non-manipulable differences in individual ability, it remains a prime example of misguided sentimentality. Setting credible predetermined targets is an entirely reasonable part of education and whilst occasionally failing a test may cause transient pain, it should do no lasting damage to any well-adjusted student. Yet, liberal educationalists prefer to water down curricula and abolish competition rather than to set suitably high standards of attainment and expectation. This egalitarian zeal is also regarded as sufficient justification for decreeing that because all cannot succeed then no-one should. This determination to protect the less able is a deceit which achieves nothing positive and does great harm. Failure is part of life and we have to learn how to deal with it, preferably productively. Those who seek to eliminate it from the teaching lexicon also confuse failure in this limited sense, with the more generalised notion of 'being a failure', which is either wilful mischievousness or else remarkable naïveté.

Levelling down has spawned a flourishing breed of third-rate universities. The cash value of the degrees conferred by the bottom tier of higher education is sharply borne in on graduates when they have to compete in the skills marketplace. Having a degree bolsters their self-esteem until they discover the reality of their employment prospects and realise that a non-academic, vocational training would probably have served them better as a passport to secure and fulfilling employment. Pupils are thus being cheated both by the system into over-valuing their worth and, to the extent that some plagiarise to obtain a better grade, by themselves. Nations lose out as their skills base is undermined by poor-quality graduates, while lower-grade universities debase the currency of academia in general. In the USA, as in Britain, many students graduate with high self-esteem but poor skills, relatively little knowledge and even less wisdom. How this benefits them or the societies they live in is far from evident.

Falling higher education standards are a predictable product of the egalitarian creed which, in the UK at least, was interpreted as the policy requirement that some predetermined proportion of the school leaving population has the right to higher education. Some years ago, a higher education target figure was set at 50%, which the government declared as 'an economic imperative'. Once you accept that even 50% of those of suitable age have *the right* to a university education, the only possible way of accommodating such a wide spectrum of ability is either to level down standards or to eliminate testing so no-one can be stigmatised for not attaining goals. The aim of universal higher education has undoubted, if superficial, appeal; however the belief that half the eligible population, irrespective of intellect, educability or motivation, has top-level educational potential is no more credible than the notion that they would all make good violinists.

There are distinct signs of increasing public anger at the erosion of standards. It is not the degree or certificate but its extrinsic value that ultimately counts and students with low-grade qualifications, and their parents, soon realise the deficiencies and are resentful that the education system has failed them. Efforts to identify the weakest establishments led to the introduction of school league tables in the UK, a move much criticised by educationalists and welcomed, despite the imperfections, by almost everyone else. Parents and pupils now have access to information, 'outing' poor schools and substandard education and so value an independent yardstick that many are prepared to relocate to be in the catchment area of a good school. Publishing regular comparative data has put additional pressure both on underperforming schools—particularly in areas where parents have a real choice—and on government to impose remedial measures.

5. Another important element in the 'progressive' influence on education is the intervention of psychologists. Their main contribution is the proclamation that self-esteem is fragile and one must not, at any cost, make children feel inferior by making them aware that they have failed. Stigmatising a child or adolescent as a failure is damaging and therefore to be avoided, even if it entails abandoning most meaningful tests of competence. So, 'no one is stretched, no one fails, no one points a finger, no one feels badly about his or her efforts and no one is identified as a winner or loser.' (Cooper and O'Keefe, op. cit.)

The idea that children should not be exposed to competitive pressures for fear of psychological damage has led to a preference for continuous assessment over rigorous and more searching formal examinations. This is sometimes disguised by the call for 'less dogmatic' and 'more imaginative' testing, with a resulting shift in emphasis from classroom learning to course-work or projects. The stress of examinations is regarded in some quarters as unnecessary and even counter-productive—which is curious, to say the least, at a time when workplace stress is increasing and performing under pressure is a normal part of everyday life.

It has also led to absurdities. A well-publicised case in the UK concerned a primary school teacher who decided to cancel her school's sports day to avoid negative consequences of competitiveness. Another school abandoned the parents' sports races altogether, as parents were training for the events and becoming increasingly competitive. In the USA, schools are apparently not allowed to formally grade children for grades 1–5, and one serious (British) proposal was that the word 'failure' be removed from education and replaced by 'deferred success'.

The notion of self-esteem is critical to this debate and merits further consideration. In particular, it is reasonable to ask whether self-esteem is something to which you have a right, irrespective of the effort you invest, or whether it is only to be earned by hard work. The pursuit of self-esteem through the dilution of grading would suggest the former, as you can only damage something that is there in the first place. So the proposition then becomes: everyone has the right to (high) self-esteem. What possible justification is there for this? It seems perverse to argue that children (or indeed adults) who put in minimum or no effort and consequently fail are entitled to expect, let alone to receive, a high sense of self-worth; or worse, that the entire education system should be designed round the need to protect their apparently fragile sensibilities. The counter-proposal is that students should be told what is expected of them, with grading criteria tailored to individually attainable levels, and then pushed to reach those clearly defined goals.

The squeamishness about grading—whether by streaming pupils at the start of their studies or by assessment at the end of them—is driven by the effete idea that lasting psychological damage is inflicted by allowing less intelligent children to become aware of their own position among their peers in the intellectual hierarchy. Life affords us no cushion against those sort of knocks, so it seems adaptive to accustom youngsters to having and coping with them early on. Falsely inflating self-esteem by massaging grades, or seeking to protect it by avoiding streaming and testing alto-gether, probably does more, and more lasting, psychological harm than any testing or competitive peer pressure. Sooner or later reality kicks in with the realisation that competence matters more than artificially inflated self-esteem. Learning that self-esteem has to be earned and that personal value accrues from hard work are good lessons, and it makes no sense to shield anyone from them, least of all children. It is hard to give credibility to the fashionable notion of the inviolability of the individual psyche.

Egalitarians see streaming itself as divisive, so mixed ability classes have become the norm. It may well be that exceptionally intelligent (political correctness requires the term 'gifted') pupils will somehow inspire the less able to excel, but the more likely result is that teaching will be geared to the slowest and the top tier will be held back. This is supported by recent British research which suggests that bright children need to study with other bright children to fully develop their potential; if not, they under-perform. Indeed, it is hard to see how a wide spectrum of intellect can be both satisfied and stretched in a group. Diversity delivers benefits which are not always given due weight in the dogmatic pursuit of equality.

6. Another seminal tenet of progressive educational ideology is that children should be allowed to discover things for themselves. This replaces formal teaching with 'directed' play and self exploration. It is argued that by restricting natural exploratory tendencies we are 'stealing' children's childhood. It is easy to see the appeal of systems that, by promoting exploration and free-expression, direct the spotlight away from academic results. There may indeed be certain lessons that are best learned through direct experience (a child only puts his hand in the fire once), but the randomness of child exploratory behaviour provides no certainty of acquiring basic knowledge or skills, let alone moral values, for which there is no effective substitute for formal instruction.

Whilst it may possibly be true that discoveries made personally are more likely to stick, it is unrealistic to suppose that, left to themselves, children will discover what are generally considered the educational basics in spoken language, mathematics, reading and writing, let alone technology, geography, science and the arts. John Honey, noting a change in the 1960s from explicit teaching of language skills to 'the assumption that these basic skills would develop by a process of osmosis', quotes an American educationist describing the results of a similar shift in his country and characterising English teaching there as 'an amalgam of journalism, play-production, business letters, research techniques, use of the library, career counselling, use of the telephone and advice on dating'. Honey comments that whilst 'many British pupils did not even receive all those arguably useful elements … the school subject "English" had come to be regarded by many teachers as a "free-wheeling vehicle for the child's emotional and social development" rather than a rigorous academic discipline to be learned'. (John Honey, *Language is Power*, 1997)

This self-discovery creed derives from the contrived concept of 'ownership' of knowledge which decrees that true knowledge is only possible if children discover factual and moral truths for themselves. This is reinforced by the idea that by allowing children to roam at will through the intellectual and physical universe you are giving them something they would not otherwise obtain. This is often referred to as 'empowerment'—a much overused term that has been adopted by social reformers and presented as a desirable ideal in many spheres of personal and social activity. You empower someone either by giving them authority or by giving them skills. Giving authority without the necessary skills or skills without the authority or ability to use them is deceit, not empowerment.

Apart from the matter of what it means to 'own' knowledge, or to 'negotiate cognitive moral issues', unregulated children, as most teachers and parents would doubtless confirm, will soon lapse into an unbalanced routine of computer games, television viewing and other marginally educational activities and consequently learn very little.

Making the idea that children must take responsibility for their own learning a central plank of education ignores the inspirational value of good teaching and, moreover, is irresponsible. What does make sense is to give children the intellectual tools to explore fruitfully and evaluate what they find; then treat them as adults, as individuals with respect and worth, without patronising or dominating them, unless they overstep the mark and misbehave. This is not the same as a *laissez-faire*, self-discovery regime, which achieves little in either educational or social terms.

The discovery theory of learning paints pictures of bored pupils subjected to dull lessons and questions the desirability of written work and examinations on the grounds that these destroy the sense of excitement and discovery that motivate learning. This happens, but is not a systemic failing. Traditional education recognises set basics as an inescapable requirement, and also the need for intellectual stimulation, but differs from progressive theory in suggesting that its proper source is an attractive curriculum and inspirational teaching, not child-centered exploration.

7. Progressive ideology came with a call for 'higher-level thinking', a concept used as a justification for an assault on memorisation and rote learning. As one US report parodied the difference: 'to learn the Periodic Table of Elements is mere rote, but to square-dance while imagining oneself to be an electron orbiting around a nucleus — that is higher-level thinking. A child who can recite the Gettysburg Address is exhibiting mere knowledge, but one who wrote "teecher stincks" is exhibiting judgement'. (Jerry Jesness, *The Legacy of Progressive Education*, 2000).

It is important to this general discussion to distinguish Education from Learning. In its broadest sense, education transcends factual knowledge. That does not mean that it should not teach and test it at the most demanding level. However, the emphasis on ticking the correct boxes in pursuit of standardisation rather than standards means that even such testing is limiting. It should matter little if a student is a year adrift on the date of an important historical event, but more that he should be aware of the circumstances that brought it about and its repercussions. Testing pure knowledge must be part of a balanced educational diet rather than the sole dish on offer. Facts matter, but so (if not more) do the principles behind them.

There are two competing images of the education process: one, sees teachers delivering their knowledge into the largely empty Lockean *tabula rasa* minds of children; the other, posits a more dynamic process of children seeking, by whatever means, knowledge through direct experience, which is not necessarily school-based. In the former, what is learned is the teacher's responsibility; in the latter, it is the pupil's. For some, these are incompatible; indeed, they regard as failures systems which seek education rather than learning.

To a certain extent, it is unnecessary to decide between learner-focussed and teacher-focussed systems. It is evident that without the requisite intellectual tools—which must be acquired somehow—the student is in a poor position to capitalise on opportunities whatever the learning environment. Progressives view learning as a lifetime activity and contrast this with the old-style segmented or modular system which places emphasis on the teacher as the formal repository of knowledge to be transferred piecemeal to the pupil. These are far from being incompatible. Indeed, it is entirely reasonable to take the view that learning is multifaceted—*what* is learned should be directed by the teacher, whilst *how and when* may well be left to the pupils, provided they are properly equipped and monitored. However the individual balance is met, it is important that non-specific skills which train the mind remain at the heart of any education system.

8. The impact of the Elitist versus Democratic debate on educational thinking and policy revolves round the revulsion that many socialists and liberals have towards anything that is seen as exclusive or elitist. As with radical egalitarians, such people find it anathema to countenance any system which streams the brightest from the less able and elite standards, whether within or between schools or colleges, are seen as inherently divisive.

There is nothing wrong with elitism in education, as long as this is confined to the pursuit of excellence free from extraneous social or other influence. This will not do for the anti-elites who, through decades of innuendo — often with political support — have sustained a vigorous campaign against the best in education where it depends upon grading, streaming or parental income. Many state schools in Britain and USA have failed, yet those who choose to spend money on private education are privately, and often publicly, reviled. Educational excellence has long been bedevilled by hostility to fee-paying schools and universities. The high quality work done by the best of these establishments (which continue to thrive, especially in times of economic hardship) is constantly undermined by unsubstantiated charges of elitism and privilege. In some countries their existence is under more or less constant threat from egalitarian politicians, many of whom send their own children to these places, as long as they exist. These people find it abhorrent that excellence in education can be bought and is thus denied to those who cannot, or choose not to, afford it. They do not disclose whether their greater dislike is of well-rounded children or of the schools that nurture them.

This attitude is difficult to construe in any terms other than envy. Those who speak so vehemently of class divisions, elitism and privilege appear to have no emotional difficulty with excellence in sport or lavish personal spending on holidays, homes, yachts and cars, yet it irritates them intensely when people choose to save — often at considerable personal sacrifice — to ensure that their children are properly taught. They recognise that a first-class education confers an advantage in life and that private schools deliver it, but believe that this should be open to all. This Utopian ideal ignores the fact that there is not the capacity in the private sector to accommodate the numbers involved and falls foul of the deeply unpalatable reality that many children would be ill-suited to a system of education that puts strong emphasis on personal responsibility, self-reliance, traditional virtues and tough discipline.

The generation reared in faulty education systems are now parents themselves, and their children would flounder in a scholastic ethos which insisted on values and disciplines not reinforced by their home environments. All too often, it is such people who suggest that those who choose to educate their children privately are somehow depriving others of a good education. Such ridiculous cant has enduring appeal to an unthinking liberal public but has no moral justification whatever. In the first place, removing children from the state system allows more resources for those who remain, so private education is an unqualified benefit for the public sector; second, the nature of the alleged deprivation is not explained — buying a place in a private school or college deprives no one of anything; third, the unspoken creed behind the suggestion — namely, 'if everyone can't have it, no one should', is nothing more than envy; fourth, a fact which has been re-stated *ad nauseam*, if state provision were to match the private sector in quality the latter would wither and become redundant. All this is lost on people who have no scruples about seeking the abolition of excellence in pursuit of political dogma.

The ideological battle is bitter. In the UK, the tax regime allowing fees to be offset against pre-tax income has long been repealed, and threats are regularly made by socialist governments of ending the charitable status of independent schools that confers certain tax exemptions. There is also financial inequity in that no allowance is made for the savings to the public purse from those who elect to pay fees because the state resolutely refuses to recognise that contribution, either by any direct grant towards fees or in the taxation of personal income. In Britain and the USA an entrenched hostility extends to any financial measures that might promote private education whereas common sense would dictate that a failing system should encourage migration to another that is demonstrably more successful.

9. If there is any doubt as to the anti-elite, democratic agenda in education, it should be dispelled by the progressives' approach to standards. Tradition has it that testing both separates the bright from the less able and raises overall standards through competitive pressure. This may be difficult and even painful for those involved, but those who seek excellence as the ultimate aim of education believe that competition between pupils, and high achievement targets, are essential. The educational democrats claim the opposite: that intellectual competition is the enemy of the sound and equitable education that is the right of every child. Their desire is for equal opportunitie,s by which they mean getting everybody up to a satisfactory level. (It is interesting to note that, in general, talk of standards is usually in terms of the minimum which says much about the state of public education). In practice, this can only be delivered by

reducing standards to the lowest common achievable, which further encourages the anti-testing tendency.

The belief that it is wrong for any student to be seen to excel because this makes others feel inadequate is contemptible and patronising. This sentimentality is driven by the idea that all pupils have merit and should be encouraged to feel good about themselves. For the anti-elitists, achievement is a personal matter, not something to be defined and measured by public competition. In this they align themselves with the progressives, preferring project work and continuous course assessment to formal examination. This dovetails well with progressive ideology that dislikes the traditional notion of transmitted cultural values and wisdom and substitutes this with exploration and self-directed learning. The primary aim of having happy children requires that play replaces work and that the 'fun' curriculum takes over from serious study and measured intellectual development.

The progressive programme puts heavy emphasis on finding something at which every child can be shown to excel. This is unobjectionable in itself, but as a central plank of educational policy it fits ill with society's requirement for a common core of attainment. The elitists, in contrast, target demonstrable excellence and believe that it is streaming and the pressures of public examination that produce the highest level of attainment and benefit, both for individuals and society.

The fallout from the anti-elitist attitude to standards and testing has spread well beyond vilification of the private sector. In particular, it has led to a failure to identify and fast-track the most intelligent children and to the dumbing-down of school curricula — spun as 'increasing their relevance to modern society'. Many schools and colleges have sidelined the classics of literature, the basic disciplines of language and the experience of history, replacing them with popular authors, colloquial non-grammatical language and history options expanded to embrace popular culture. Meanwhile, their university colleagues have abandoned the pretence of providing an all-round education, instead offering courses in 'soap opera', 'traffic management' and the like; intellectually undemanding fare tailored to less able students. In this egalitarian milieu, media studies marches on an equal footing with mathematics and philosophy. The Humanities course at one well-known university announces itself as 'designed for all students who are interested in man, his history and his cultural achievements'.

As one commentator remarked: 'This is an ominous preface to a course which seems to try hard to find the most appealing combination of triviality and fragmentation—a nibble at Vasare, a chunk of Descartes, a bite at St Mark's Gospel' (Ian Robinson, *The Survival of English*). Environmental and community studies now enjoy equal (or even greater) status with learning something of your country's literature and history or how to speak and write correctly.

The *summum bonum* of the anti-elitist prospectus is 'Excellence for All'. As has been seen, achieving this superficially attractive and highly populist ideal in any worthwhile sense is impossible. The idea becomes particularly absurd when it is interpreted as meaning that educational achievement should no longer be a matter of IQ. This is an extension of the idea that achievement is a fundamental right of citizenship, and making it near universal is seen as the task of social democrats in the 21st Century. Unable to realise even the limited goal of parity of facilities, the British socialist Prime Minister chose to attack the very concept: 'There is a reactionary right-wing which believes that more means worse, that exclusivity in education is positively good to preserve social elitism, that success is only valuable if it co-exists with widespread failure … It is the conventional wisdom … that there should be a cap on aspiration, with only a fixed percentage getting good qualifications as a matter of principle'. This is ideological nonsense. The essential truth is that recognising that intellectual ability is unevenly distributed makes the achievement of 'Excellence for All' only possible, and only then in a thoroughly degenerate sense, if you destroy what is truly excellent at the top level and inflate achievements at the bottom level. As one respected education commentator put it: 'The purpose of exclusivity in education is to preserve not social elitism, but intellectual distinction. Equality of opportunity is an admirable goal; equality of outcome is pernicious nonsense. When everyone gets an upper second, no-one gets an upper second worth having. Similarly, when educational achievement is divorced from IQ, "excellence for all" is excellence for no one'. (John Clare, 'Excellence for All': *Daily Telegraph*, 21 July 2004).

There can be little doubt that the failures of much post-1945 education can be ascribed to policies driven by an inflexible, irrational ideology based on misconceived sentimentality. In its desire to be egalitarian, non-divisive and anti-elitist, education has not delivered even at the fundamental level of turning out children with minimum skills. These policies have reduced education to the lowest common denominator of intellect, motivation, aptitude, zeal and eventually attainment. What was once prized and worked for has now become the 'right' of all, with entirely predictable consequences.

These failures have been compounded by the twin drives towards inclusiveness, which embraces all cultures and ideas as of equal validity, and political correctness, which eschews teaching anything that might give offence to any group or religion. The emphasis on caring for the child, rather than on academic discipline and rigour, has further undermined the foundations of sound education, and a continuing failure to insist on and inculcate acceptable standards of behaviour has contributed to a culture of non-conformity and to an erosion of obedience and respect. A generation — possibly two — of poorly educated and socialised parents has left today's schools and colleges bereft of the parental backing they need to staunch near-anarchy in many classrooms. A teaching environment of indisciplined, disruptive pupils is not one in which learning is likely to thrive.

In pursuit of the appropriate image, society and its educational institutions seem to have entirely lost sight of the basic purposes of education, and of the work, discipline and dedication required to attain them. Listening to some educational theorists, one might well conclude that schools and colleges are institutes of social therapy designed for the preservation of students' self-esteem rather than seats of learning.

Children no longer appear to value education, either for itself or for what it offers them for the future. 'Today's students are more materialistic, more interested in power and status, less altruistic and less inclined to be concerned about social issues and problems' (Gingrich, *A Nation at Risk*). One might add that many have no idea why they need to be educated at all and see wealthy celebrity as their preferred route in life. Despite living in an extraordinarily culture-rich age, many young people are feckless, easily bored, disruptive and truant, and prefer to spend their time playing computer games, painting graffiti or engaged in other wasteful or delinquent pursuits rather than occupying themselves with something intellectually stimulating or enriching. This contrasts starkly with developing countries where schooling is far from universal and any form of learning is at a premium. There, despite desperately poor family circumstances, children value any opportunity to learn sitting on the floor, in crowded, primitive, ill-equipped classrooms, often with minimum facilities, thrilled to be there and lapping up everything they see and hear.

Parodies of the extreme manifestations of progressiveness are facile and do little to further the aims of better education and it would be wrong to blame the undoubted failings of much western education entirely on progressive ideologies. Where it is most misguided is in shifting the emphasis from curriculum / factual / teacher-based education to creativity and child-centered learning. In this, it evinces a strong anti-academic, anti-intellectual, anti-elite bias. It also falsely accuses traditional education of irrelevance and of failing to adapt teaching to individual abilities. That system of education, which has delivered with conspicuous success for at least a century, is perfectly compatible with progressivism provided one takes a moderate, rather than an extreme, fundamentalist position.

Any worthwhile system of education will recognise that the time spent outside the classroom confronts students with personal, social and moral situations they must learn to handle — not just as one-off problems, but as an essential accumulator of experience to develop sociability, standards and values. These are not instinctual. Without sound guidelines and sensitive help raw experience is unlikely to provide a dependable base for later life. It is the absence of such solid guiding foundations which makes personal decisions difficult and life unnecessarily stressful. By avoiding addressing these issues in early education, the progressive system exacerbates the problems.

In its emphasis on individualism progressive ideology has found a sympathetic audience among parents, teachers and educational theorists. It needs little acquaintance with western political thought to realise how entrenched and widespread these philosophies have become. Their branches are highly visible and their roots tenacious, particularly in the USA. However, after decades of experimentation, it is abundantly clear that the progressives' tenets are not super-empirical beliefs incapable of verification but principles that have been tried and found wanting. People know perfectly well that hard work and intellectual discipline are indispensable to success and those who try to explain away poor educational achievement by reference to social condition generally ignore the fact that intellectual excellence is entirely compatible with material deprivation. Nor is it reasonable to blame children alone for the shortcomings. Instead, one must look to the prevailing spirit which prefers to accommodate rather than acknowledge failure; to a reluctance to admit and adapt to individual inequalities, to a blinkered zeal to achieve educational parity at whatever cost, to decades of misguided sentimentality in child-rearing and education, and to a welter of pernicious talk about fragile self-esteem and ownership of knowledge.

Ultimately, the choice depends upon what society expects of education: well-rounded, independent-minded, critical, knowledgeable people, who use their skills for their own and society's benefit and are capable of learning; or a tool for social and political engineering.

That public education is failing both children and nations is not in doubt; the facts are a matter of record. Notwithstanding the overwhelming evidence, governments continue to spin failure as achievement and to sidestep the reality that education based on progressive principles, spurious sentimentality and unsustainable notions of equality does not work. It is hardly surprising that, faced with the very evident shortcomings and the self-righteous attitude of fervid egalitarians and progressives — let alone the stupidity and sheer illogicality of much of their ideology — impatience and anger are rife.

CHAPTER 10

BUSINESS MANIPULATION

'Men in general judge more from appearances than from reality. All men
have eyes, but few have the gift of penetration.'
Machiavelli

Business has been at the forefront of the image industry for decades, both as
manipulator of product image to underpin marketing, and latterly, as a consumer of image manipulation, as large firms tailor their corporate profile to
reflect changing values and to keep in tune with what is currently considered
socially and politically acceptable. The influence of image in corporate affairs
is, if anything, increasing, with greater sophistication in PR and marketing,
the growing importance of corporate political lobbying and with intensifying
competition. Firms which can convince the world that they are well-behaved,
acceptably transparent, eco-friendly, charitable and non-exploitative have a
business (and marketing) advantage over those that cannot.

Image is now of seminal importance to business, not just to lever commercial benefit but to avoid stigma, as shareholder and other pressure group activism
become more aggressive. Scrutiny of business ethics, employment policies,
manufacturing standards, accounting policies, executive remuneration and
attitudes to shareholders, suppliers and customers has never been more intense.
Spectacular corporate failures, many the direct results of fraud or corruption
rather than incompetence, have focused attention on business practices and
reinforced demands for tighter regulation. Managers increasingly appreciate
that a company's image depends not only on the quality of its products or
services but also on sound and transparent ethical and accounting standards
and management integrity. However, there are still those who continue to
work on the assumption that having the appropriate image is sufficient rather
than just necessary for success. Their hope is that if you appear clean what goes
on beneath the surface is less likely to be questioned or dissected.

At the public level, there is an element of schizophrenia. On the one
hand, even in an age of rampant consumerism, there is a general inability to
distinguish good quality from mediocre: 'If it looks good, it must be good'
is the prevailing attitude. Presented with a superficially appropriate appear-

ance, people readily suspend common sense and sound judgement and are prepared to trust a brand they recognise rather than make the effort to scrutinise more closely what they are being offered. On the other hand, a growing breed of vigilante consumer is critical of indifferent service, poor quality or what it considers to be inappropriate production methods. A trusting, brand-loyal consumer base contrasts with a vociferous militant minority who see themselves as guardians of responsible business practice. Any adverse publicity tarnishes images, so businesses take notice.

At the corporate level, we have become accustomed to larger-than-life high-profile CEOs exuding self-confidence. Many see themselves as inviolable, above the law and normal social constraints and beyond the influence of market forces. Such arrogance is deeply unattractive and justifiably fuels demands for greater accountability. Corporate celebrities, driven by inflated self-esteem, often wield disproportionate political influence and, like their media counterparts, have become part of society's powerful new elites.

This chapter considers the impact of some particularly important influences on business image — corporate social responsibility, corporate culture, management training and customer care. In these, as in much else, the superficially appealing disguises superficial thinking.

CORPORATE SOCIAL RESPONSIBILITY (CSR)

In recent times, businesses and managers have come under particular pressure from two increasingly influential sources: first, shareholders and stockmarkets seeking to maximise profits and shareholder value, and second, social and political groups demanding that an ever increasing proportion of those profits be allocated to advancing social projects and ethical policies outside the main line of corporate activity. The expectation is that socially responsible capitalism must satisfy both these lobbies, and this has led to major changes in the ways in which companies view their aims and how they structure and conduct themselves.

The CSR ethos has as a subtext the notion that the unfettered pursuit of profit is socially and environmentally damaging and therefore unethical. Companies are invited to accept and implement responsibilities that go well beyond considerations of profitability. As their mission statements and annual reports attest, those who agree consider themselves especially virtuous and see their CSR credentials as a valuable marketing tool. They accept an obligation to give greater consideration to non-core aspects of their businesses and thereby to rebalance the relative weighting of shareholders' and society's needs to reflect what they see as their financial, environmental and social responsibilities.

This new perception has been brought about by pressure from groups opposed to globalisation or to business activities that they regard as irresponsible, and thus represents a significant threat to corporate profitability. Under the banner of promoting CSR, this lobby derives momentum from public support that does not care to examine the arguments too closely. The CSR image appeals to an environmentally active, anti-business constituency and is highly populist. However, this image does not reflect the underlying business realities. Adam Smith argued self-seeking interest serves, rather than hinders, the public good, and it is self-evident that increased business profitability creates and retains jobs, sustaining local communities through direct and indirect spending and national finances through higher tax takes, and enhances investor confidence through increased dividends and share price growth.

Undoubtedly, some companies behave badly—they pollute, destroy and exploit—and are, rightly, taken to task. Some unedifyingly attempt to duck their responsibilities, especially where compensation or restitution claims are high or involve an unacceptably long-term commitment (e.g. marine or nuclear pollution). But these transgressions justify neither the general image nor the requirement that companies should spend the sums expected of them by advocates of CSR. The demand that businesses adopt a more humane face is entirely different from requiring them to undertake activities fundamentally alien to their core objectives.

CSR concerns cover both acts of commission—doing the unacceptable—and those of omission—not doing enough of the acceptable. Among the most important areas are:

1. Environmental: *pollution control*: limiting emissions contributing to damage to the ozone layer and to global warming; *conservation*: not exploiting or destroying eco-systems; proper re-instatement—e.g. after mining; *recycling policies*: appropriate waste management (e.g. not sinking unwanted oil rigs or dumping spent nuclear fuels rods in the ocean); *sustainable development*: non-destructive agriculture.
2. Market: avoiding anti-competitive activities—e.g. by limiting ownership of news media to a given level or outlawing aggressive pricing designed to drive out competitors.

3. Employment:non-exploitative employment and work conditions—suitable pay levels etc; conformity with local laws and practices; health and safety issues.

4. Charitable works: support for local communities and projects—often unconnected with the firm's activities.

5. Customer welfare: product quality control, service levels in call centres, after-sales service.

6. Financial issues: accounting transparency, 'reasonable' executive remuneration packages; performance-linked bonuses etc.

7. Promotional activities: not promoting undesirable habits, especially at sporting events—e.g. smoking at motor-racing circuits; maintaining ethical advertising standards.

8. Responsible approach to broader community: workers, customers, communities, in addition to shareholders.

9. Protection of life: animal testing / embryo research / abortion; limited to essential minimum (much argument as to what constitutes this) or outlawed completely.

10. Maintaining human rights and rights of minorities and indigenous peoples.

11. Business practices: ethical dealings with customers and suppliers.

12. International responsibilities: trade agreements, sensitivity to political issues.

13. Ethical issues: e.g. arms dealing, bribes, setting up explosives factories in high density communities etc.

Making demands, however popular, does not mean that they are well-founded. Lobby groups have become considerably more aggressive in recent years, putting companies under virtually permanent scrutiny and forcing them onto the back foot to deal with accusations that are not always justified. Their efforts are often supported by specialist experts, consultants and institutes (mainly unelected and non-governmental) who dictate policies and monitor compliance. The concentration of major-company stockholdings in institutional hands and the emergence of shareholder pressure groups have facilitated such activism. The image promulgated by all these groups is that of ordinary, concerned, socially responsible people, outside government, struggling to persuade large firms, bloated with profits, to behave—as they see it—more responsibly, or, in cases of extreme disapproval, to close them down altogether. The less demanding version has it that capitalism is acceptable but prone to misbehave and therefore incapable of effective self-regulation; the stronger statement is that it is socially and ethically unjust and needs to be made subject to the laws of distributive justice (usually, as interpreted by Marx).

It is not clear—probably deliberately so—precisely what the CSR lobby is asking business to accept. Its most basic statement confounds two propositions. First, that adopting so-called socially responsible corporate policies will sustain, or reinforce profitability—in other words CSR makes sense in business terms. Second, that business should forsake delivering profits and shareholder value as their main objectives and admit CSR policies as an integral part of corporate activity—in other words, that CSR is justified by wider social and political considerations. Otherwise put, the former contributes to your business, the latter to broader society. The first is unlikely to be true in any but the most diluted sense and the second has no moral justification. Except in cases of gross abuse, it is the business of government and society in general to determine and fund policies for social welfare and the environment not that of ad hoc, unelected pressure groups.

Those who advocate these propositions present themselves as being driven by specific goals rather than representing any particular social interest. Their focus extends to products as well as processes and their activist constituency is wide—from animal rights groups seeking to cripple research laboratories and anti-abortion groups wanting to close down clinics, to local lobbies trying to re-site a superstore or re-route a road to avoid disturbing wildlife habitat or preventing a landowner chopping down an ancient forest or a developer from spoiling the view.

Whilst the language used is usually populist, strongly emotive and deliberately designed to persuade, the arguments advanced in support of CSR propositions are, in many cases, shallow and logically suspect, and based upon a naïve idea of how businesses actually work. They also exhibit a strong ethical aversion to capitalism.

Constant negative lobbying, together with occasional mass protest (e.g. at G8 meetings) has resulted in 'globalisation' and 'capitalism' being tainted with profound suspicion. Capitalism is seen as greedy, exploitative and inimical to the environment, and its global spread is seen as disadvantageous, particularly to the economies of developing countries. Companies' defence of their activities is not helped by being often weak and craven in tone, further deepening public cynicism about corporate motives and transparency.

Such suspicions are not wholly without justification. Large corporations are not invariably blameless of the charges levelled at them, are well versed in the use of image manipulation and prone to employing PR expertise to refocus attention from unpalatable aspects of their activities towards those that are socially acceptable, charitable and positive. In the best cases, firms want to ensure that governments and their customers are aware of their high standards and moral credentials. In the worst cases, they use image-gloss to mask practices they know to be unacceptable. Oil or agro-chemical companies that pollute, or market products that generate escalating resistance to the organisms they eradicate, make strenuous efforts to spread a 'caring about the environment' message for the good work they do in one corner of the globe, thus deflecting public gaze from the wider reality. Tobacco companies sponsor sport — a healthy lifestyle choice — whilst profiting massively from sales of products generally considered harmful. Here they benefit twice — from their endorsement of the healthy lifestyle, and from the increased sales that such sponsorship brings. They routinely deny, or at least evade, the negative aspects of their products and the associated social responsibilities many believe these should entrain.

CSR glosses over the marked moral difference between exposing cover-ups of bad practice and forcing companies to undertake programmes and assume responsibilities that are, in many cases, contentious. The record of free enterprise may not be perfectly clean, but the Corporate Social Responsibility band-wagon has rolled too far, too fast. Many businesses have taken on board the concept, investing significant cash, personnel and management resources in its implementation. Top managers undoubtedly enjoy the ego-trip associated with charitable giving and pepper their annual reports with uplifting words designed to put the corporation in the spotlight for its enlightened social and environmental credentials. However, much of this is window-dressing rather than deep-seated commitment, and many CEOs may reasonably ask themselves what their company, or indeed society at large, really gets out of their generosity.

CSR advocates rarely discuss or appear concerned about the costs involved, which are often considerable. Some are incurred in compliance itself, others from the need to measure, monitor and audit compliance, often against targets and in areas which are barely reducible to numbers. These erode both competitiveness and profit margins.

The fundamental principles behind the CSR movement have been trenchantly dissected by academics (notably David Henderson in *Misguided Virtue*, 2001, Wilfred Beckerman in *A Poverty of Reason* 2003 and Elaine Sternberg, *Just Business*, 1994 / 2000). How do they stand up to closer examination?

It is important to distinguish standards and requirements that are mandatory from those that are merely desirable. All that is actually required of companies is that they obey the law. Anything else is discretionary. Nonetheless, the demands of CSR are couched in terms that appear to carry the force of law, and companies, fearing bad publicity or — worse — sanctions, often comply. It is often the activists, not governments that set standards — e.g. on pollution control — and demand that companies meet them, whether or not they are either feasible or realistic. In many instances the expense of compliance is disproportionate: for example, the marginal cost of reducing sulphur emissions beyond a certain point far outweighs any possible benefit to companies or the environment.

CSR is closely allied with groups supporting 'ethical investment'. Individuals and trusts seek to change policy either by investing in companies with good CSR credentials, or through enabling shareholder activism by taking small stakes in companies they disapprove of. They target products and processes alike — pollution and arms sales, media ownership and insecticides. There are grey areas where practices may be questionable (and indeed profitable) but are not outside the law. For example, bribery is legal in many countries, but it is widely considered unethical — or at least, anti-competitive. The same is true of predatory pricing, hard-selling, and monopolistic activities which aim to squeeze out competition. To the extent that the limits of commerce are not defined by limits of legality, they are proper subjects for ethical debate; but this should not mask the principal purpose of business which is to maximise shareholder value.

It may be prudent or desirable for companies to devote some of their profits to improving working conditions, reducing pollution, promoting local community welfare or other philanthropic works, but beyond what the law requires these are not obligations. As Elaine Sternberg has argued, the key purpose of business is 'to deliver long-term owner value', and people or organisations that deflect companies from this aim 'are guilty not of socialism, but of theft' (Elaine Sternberg, *Just Business,* 2nd edition, 2000).

The CSR Image relies heavily on public support. In doing so, it makes three assumptions. These, as Henderson puts them, are that what it is advocating (i) 'mirrors society's expectations'; (ii) 'is both well articulated and legitimate', and (iii) 'the extent to which a company meets these expectations will now determine its profitability'. The first assumption is unlikely to be true, the second is certainly false and the third probably false. When it comes to profits, the CSR movement espouses what are, on the face of it, contradictory views. On the one hand, it suggests that adopting CSR policies will enhance company profits; on the other, the side of CSR which disparages the profit motive reveals two further implied assumptions: first, that profit has nothing to do with public good; second, that the pursuit of profit requires companies to place unacceptably heavy burdens on the environment and on society. The first assumption further breaks down into a weaker and a stronger version, respectively: (i) the search for profit serves no public interest, and (ii) the search for profit actually works against the public interest. These two main propositions are ill-founded in most instances, and rarely questioned by advocates of CSR. A third proposition — that profits made by companies are a useful guide to the value they create for society — is well-founded but dismissed by not being admitted into discussion.

A central component of the CSR philosophy is that economic growth, of itself, is environmentally and socially damaging. More economic activity, the argument runs, consumes more natural resources, creates more pollution, etc. Indeed, but it is the step from here to the conclusion which is defective. And that step relies on the further premises that natural resources are finite and that pollution is invariably harmful. The facts are that most natural resources are renewable at greater rates than either current or projected consumption. In the case of oil, which seems to provoke particular panic, reserves in 1999 are calculated at twice the level of 1970 and more extractable oil is routinely being discovered — enough at any rate to meet reasonable requirements for the foreseeable future. (Wilfred Beckerman has argued this cogently, both in *Small is Stupid* (1995) and *A Poverty of Reason*). As for pollution, the problem would appear to be control rather than creation. Much of the global expansion to which CSR groups object is zero, or only marginally, polluting, and that which does pollute significantly — e.g. China's rapidly expanding heavy industry — is effectively beyond international control.

If 'Misguided Virtue' describes the moral stance of CSR, 'A Poverty of Reason', characterises its underlying logic. This is well illustrated by the concept of 'sustainable development' which the CSR movement has stated as one of its principal aims. Companies are frequently taken to task for actions which are seen as incompatible with this end.

'Sustainable development' has become highly fashionable. It is widely accepted as a universal good and its reference in practical terms is considered self-evident. When one asks people what it actually means, responses are generally less than impressive. Wilfred Beckerman dissects the concept and makes a strong case for concluding that it is not definable in a way which makes it logically coherent. In particular, its fundamental assumptions are unjustified: for example, resources are not being depleted to the extent that sustainable development policies are required to prevent further damage; there is no sound argument for rationing resource use to conserve known reserves, and there is a credible case to be made for the view that global warming (if it is indeed a genuine, demonstrable phenomenon, which is far from proven) may be more beneficial than harmful. The ethics of sustainable development are equally shaky in that they rely on the contentious idea that future generations have similar rights to current generations in terms of welfare and resources. This ignores the likelihood that future generations will have discovered alternative sources of food, energy etc and alternative, non-polluting means of manufacture. There is also no case for attributing 'special status to certain aesthetic environmental assets that give them "trumping" power over innumerable other claims on resources'. Nor is there 'any ethical justification for public bodies to have a bias in favour of the private preferences of some citizens for certain environmental assets, such as beautiful scenery, as against the private preferences of other citizens for other assets, such as decent housing, schools, health and education services'. In short, 'minority tastes must not be excluded, but this point ought not to be confused with an ethical case for their being given special priority.' (W. Beckerman, *A Poverty of Reason*). The popularity of the concepts of 'sustainable development' and that of conserving 'finite natural resources' is such that it is considered heresy to doubt them, which makes dispassionate argument all but impossible. Their positive image is based more on feel-good sentiment than logic and there are serious ethical issues that need resolving in advance of policy. That governments have generally swallowed the hype greatly decreases the likelihood of this happening.

On the periphery of CSR, concerns for the Third World and a vociferous animal rights lobby have made many firms jittery about the acceptability of their own means of production — fair trade (for cosmetics, coffee, tea etc), no animal testing and the like. Consumers are highly susceptible to these influences and prepared to sideline the fact that because something has been produced in an environmentally sensitive way or without sweat-shop labour, whilst laudable, this says nothing about the quality or value of the product. The extreme wing of the animal rights lobby continues to ignore overwhelming professional scientific opinion that, for certain medical and associated products, animal testing is an indispensable development step — not least to ensure safety and avoid human disaster — and has consistently failed to suggest credible alternatives. Much of its platform is based on according equal rights to animals and humans; a nonsensical argument one sees mirrored by those who equate the moral status of children with that of adults.

The CSR movement has shifted from highlighting the negative aspects of corporate activity — the 'do not do' — to a position that makes heavy demands in terms of 'you should do', Much of this exceeds minimum legal requirements and, in some cases produces the opposite effect to that intended. For example, not content with requiring companies manufacturing in third-world countries to meet local wage and employment conditions, some lobbyists now demand that they meet first-world conditions. To do so would, in most cases, destroy the competitive edge which led these companies overseas to source product in the first place, and, indeed, make economic life very difficult for other companies operating in the same country. If they are forced to withdraw, then the target economy loses in several ways: prestige, jobs both in the company itself and in the local business community (shops, restaurants) and among those who provide the first-world services that companies cannot leave home without (health-care, secure transport, etc.)

It generally makes good sense to temper dogma with pragmatics. For instance, recycling is nowadays unquestioningly regarded as a universal benefit. However, market pricing reflects scarcity, so automatic sorting and reprocessing of waste is justified only where the savings outweigh the costs, and this is not always the case. Recycling comprises two entirely different processes. One enables an item to be reused in its original form. The other enables the material to be reprocessed either in its original form or put to another use. The costs of the former are often high, which makes the economics unviable.

There is every reason why sound environmental policies, backed by local and international law to bring transgressors to book, should be part of any company's normal operating philosophy. It is probably in this latter area that some strengthening and tightening is required. In circumstances where governments are complicit in undesirable practices, even laws will fail to deal with miscreants. But CSR goes further than simple compliance in suggesting that businesses should re-orient their thinking to make CSR an integral part of their business plan, rather than a desirable, but optional, adjunct. It is worth noting that much of the world's environmental damage is done, not by large corporations, but by smaller firms or groups. Tribes cutting down virgin forest to obtain plantable land on which to grow crops necessary for survival can hardly be blamed for the environmental harm they cause if governments offer them no alternative.

The majority of firms at whom CSR directs its fire are socially and environmentally responsible. The few who flagrantly breach regulations and disregard local and national sensibilities are usually punished by the markets long before CSR lobby groups get to them. Those who operate on the policy that 'if it isn't specifically outlawed, then it's legal' as a yardstick for their decision-making in contentious areas, deserve all the opprobrium levelled at them. A few are never held properly to account. But this is not the aim of the CSR troops, who pressure companies not just to abide by minimum standards, but to conform to their own more stringent and costly agenda. And this, as has been argued, is riddled with falsehoods and distortions. By focusing on the relatively small number who are not compliant, and on trying to force businesses to accept uncompetitive conditions, these groups do significant damage, both to the individual firms and to the economies of their target countries. CSR is rightly seen in some quarters as 'serious surgery to fix what doesn't need fixing' (Economist, January 2005). Its arguments may be flawed but they have the marketing advantage of considerable popular appeal.

The CSR lobby has another major string to its bow, in that it has been vociferous in promoting the idea of communities and consumers as 'stakeholders' in companies, and by this association, as groups with a legitimate interest in their activities. The theme has been enthusiastically taken up by business schools, no doubt wishing to add a high value module to their seminar curriculum, e.g. 'What's a CEO to Do? Integrating Corporate Citizenship with your business strategy will enhance your firm's competitiveness' (Seminar advertisement from a Toronto management school). Socially agreeable as this 'joint stakeholder' image may seem, it is false. Whilst those who work for a company or depend on its existence in other ways, indeed have an interest in its continued and responsible operation, they are not to be equated with the interests of the company's owners—its shareholders. It is to this group, and none other, that the company owes its primary duty and it is to this group, and none other, that it is uniquely accountable.

Most companies are acutely aware of the wider social implications of their activities, and incorporate this awareness into their policy-making. Any responsible CEO is mindful of other interests and the damage that negative perceptions from ignoring them may do to profits, corporate image, and the share price. A company may have to answer to local or national government for covering the urban surroundings of a factory with soot or a sulphurous cloud, for which it may be convicted and fined. But it is to shareholders that it must answer for the general conduct of the business and their interests take precedence over all others. Obviously, poor environmental or employment policies damage a company's public image and probably lose sales, so policy in such areas must be accounted for to shareholders in the annual reckoning. In so far as those cause damage, sensible management will take steps to reverse or reform them. However, a company's directors can only answer to one set of masters, and this—providing they keep within the laws of the countries in which they operate—must be their shareholders. This clear, well-established chain of responsibility has been severely muddied by the CSR lobby, which has sought to interpose between management and shareholders a layer of other interested parties to whom the company should also consider itself responsible. The shareholders are not just one of many 'stakeholders' in a company, they *are* the company. In suggesting that it is wrong to run a business in the interests of just one set of people—the shareholders—CSR advocates deliberately confound the notion of 'taking account of' with 'accountable to'. While companies *may,* and are often prudent to, take account of outside interest groups and their concerns, they are 'accountable' only to their shareholders.

There is also the matter of enforcement. For companies, as for people, control by education and consensus is more likely to be effective—and cost-effective—than control by regulation. Yet CSR protagonists seek change by law—further tightening the noose round the corporate neck—and see achievements in this regard as tangible proof of their success: the more law, the better the image of CSR. However, a prerequisite for codifying responsibilities in law is agreement on standards, which is problematic in many areas, particularly the environment. It also removes the flexibility to tailor requirements to specific companies and circumstances. In judging any behaviour, context, sensitivity and discretion play a role which the passage from code of conduct to law tends to eliminate.

The CSR culture has also derived strength from the anti-globalisation lobby, which paints an even blacker picture of business and profits than CSR. It portrays large corporations as unstoppable economic juggernauts, wielding more power than politicians in many smaller countries, stifling competition, creating product and distribution monopolies, sucking profits from poor economies, further impoverishing these countries and their citizens, whilst fattening shareholders. The traffic is seen as entirely one-way: win for the corporations, lose for everyone else. This image plays well with an ideologically dogmatic, left-inclined constituency and with those who have come off worse in dealings with such firms. As one might expect, the reality is rather different.

The general thesis is that the continuation of global business expansion is producing massive material wealth for the few at the expense of poverty—social, economic and environmental—for the many. To deal with these problems, anti-globalisation promoters seek to establish a set of global corporate norms and standards. Much of the popular appeal of the movement is based on a sense of alarm at the possibility of permanent environmental change (climate, depletion of resources, etc.) and pessimism at the general state of things—all usually painted in extreme terms. These are largely unfounded. As Henderson puts it, 'past and present widely accepted visions of environmental deterioration and disaster, also of a generally worsening human condition, have little or no basis in fact. There is a strong and consistent bias towards pessimism, drama and overstatement. Businesses subscribing to CSR have both tolerated and encouraged this'. (*Misguided Virtue*). The fact is that the available evidence suggests that increased global economic activity raises living standards and general prosperity. In many countries where there is chronic poverty and low economic activity their circumstances are generally the result of identifiable internal influences such as war, famine, disease, despotic government or political instability, and are rarely attributable to global corporations. In contrast, countries that have emerged from an impoverished state have generally done so because of strong inward investment, much from large international companies.

The anti-global movement is, in reality, little more than a branch of the wider anti-capitalist movement. It employs much the same emotive language to describe the supposed effects of what it dislikes—exclusion, marginalisation, disadvantage—which has a sound liberal / socialist ring to it but is an inaccurate reflection of the facts. Countries and societies that encourage investment and create stable conditions for it to flourish generally benefit, as do the companies making it. Those that make life difficult for business, either by over-priced services, high taxation, excessive regulation or by greedy employ-ment and social costs — as in much of Europe — disadvantage themselves.

There is also the matter of the role that business pressure groups allot to society: they cleverly ally it to their philosophy by claiming that it has 'expec-tations' which companies must meet. They then bestows a 'licence to operate' with associated rights and permissions, on those who adopt socially and envi-ronmentally responsible policies. If anything, the converse is the case: socie-ties may have loosely framed expectations, but they do not bestow licences, nor is their approval required for companies to operate in normal areas of activity and in normal circumstances. Society's role is to discipline companies infringing its laws or acting in ways that damage it. Putting responsibility for CSR onto society deflects attention from the fact that its arguments fail to stand up to scrutiny and disguises motives that derive more from a dislike of capitalism and the desire to promote what is termed 'social justice' than from any genuine wish to protect or improve society. Much of the appeal of CSR is based on feel-good superficialities that have little basis in reality but carry strong popular resonances.

The credentials of the CSR lobby itself are thus questionable and the image that CSR seeks to promote in need of re-appraisal. Their troops comprise an intelligent, often politically left-wing constituency, driven as much by uncon-scious jealousy and conscious motives of 'justice' for the masses as by genuine concerns for social and environmental welfare. Their aims are largely Utopian and unrealistic and their activities impose significant costs on companies without benefits to them or to wider society. To the extent that they seek to compromise the status of shareholders, their activities are also pernicious.

It behoves companies themselves and the general public to look more closely at the arguments before caving in to 'trendy, but unethical demands for social responsibility in business.' (Elaine Sternberg, *Just Business*) Businesses, particularly in areas which impact on the environment or society, have come under unremitting pressure from CSR activism. Most of their demands should be resisted and strategies based rather on maximising long-term shareholder value, within 'the principles of distributive justice and ordinary decency' (Elaine Sternberg, op.cit.). As Sternberg also points out, there is no *a priori* incompatibility between ethical actions and those that benefit business; nor is purity of motive a necessary requirement for an ethical action. 'The moral quality of an act is not determined by the motive that inspired it.'(op. cit)

In practice, however, it is often difficult to ignore an idea or movement with such strong popular support. Dealing with mischief-making and nuisance can be just as costly as dealing with genuine complaints. So businesses must ask themselves whether they are embracing CSR to forestall criticism, to improve their performance or out of concern for general social conditions. Good business policies will be socially responsible, but not everything that CSR suggests as socially responsible is necessarily good business. There should be no doubt that business focus should be on business, and ethical conduct within it, not on incoherent ideas of social justice or social responsibility put about by pressure groups in furtherance of other agendas. This is not a demand for a change in business practice, rather for straight thinking. Business interests and others might find a more credible standpoint in the idea that the general public welfare is a natural by-product of good business practice and that proselytising for it as an end in itself is unlikely to be either productive or cost-effective.

CORPORATE CULTURE

As well as looking to their external obligations, companies have made radical changes to their internal arrangements. To produce product volume, at a consistent quality level (often low), in tough, competitive markets, demanded a re-thinking of how people fitted into organisations. This has been an evolving process. At the start of the industrial revolution the focus was the individual worker and the maximising of his skill and efficiency as part of the production process. The idea was that optimising the constituent parts would improve the efficiency of the whole. This was a kind of mechanistic solipsism, in that the individual was expected to perform at maximum efficiency and not required to consider anything beyond the achievement of that limited goal. In a system requiring simple skills this worked, but it did not address the question of what was required to improve the system itself. The development of automation shifted business thinking from skills-based to knowledge-based and the problem changed from improving individual skills and efficiency to creating and managing systems for maximum corporate profitability. Individuals still had an important role to play in this process but were essentially subservient to it. So, whilst corporations continued to strive for the best image for their products they also worked to promote the corporation itself and its values to their employees. Thus was born the corporate culture. Whilst businesses have embraced and refined this, governments and public institutions have largely remained stuck with a model which sees the individual as a cog, and one who is not encouraged to question either the design or the workings of the wheel of which he is part.

Any self-respecting medium- or large-sized company nowadays is brimful with mission-statements, team-building, management training and bonding exercises. Its employees are encouraged to consider themselves part of the corporate family—with, in many cases, the implication that your own comes second. It is not enough to work for a company, you must love it. This means embracing the corporate image, living its values, and being prepared to sacrifice leisure time to the corporate need. To achieve this, a company's image has to be implanted into its staff as well as spread abroad. The individual no longer works in isolation but as part of a team, and it is felt essential to inculcate the team's values and attitudes and to reinforce these periodically with refreshers.

The image of the corporation started to change in post-war Japan, where employees were encouraged to see themselves as equals, an impression reinforced by uniformity, open plan offices, obliteration of hierarchy markers and daily singing and fitness sessions. This rigorous corporatism also played a significant part in the restructuring of post-war Germany and its subsequent industrial success. The ethos spread to the USA and, with less enthusiastic uptake, trickled through to a more traditional Europe, often on the back of Japanese-managed firms opening up overseas.

Yet there is no credible rationale for the assumption that a uniform corporate culture works, or that the model is valid beyond large-scale industrial production. Modern corporatism has a strong moral flavour, and those who preach its gospel see it as salvation for out-dated economies with scope extending well beyond its industrial base. The downside of turning employees into team players is that it stifles both individuality and reasoned dissent. In a milieu where it is counter-productive and often career damaging to question the corporate culture, the best strategy for keeping your job, pension, status or company car is to toe the company line—in corporate parlance, to remain 'on-message'. Too often, the 'positive contributions' and 'frank discussion' from brain-storming sessions result in managers being told what they want to hear, which is not surprising in an environment where rigidity and conformity reign. Better a genuine, open debate than a 'fudged, woolly, consensus' (S. Williams, *A Balloon Waiting to Burst*, 1996). This consensus culture ignores the fact that the best thinking comes from individuals, left to reflect without external 'political' pressures. Innovation—'eureka'-type thinking—is more likely to come from constant questioning, doubting and off-beam thinking, from intelligent and reflective individuals rather than from highly structured brainstorming sessions which are often hijacked by self-promoters, who say much but contribute little and where what is missed may be as important as what gets noticed.

In the modern company, the appropriate jargon often displaces any consideration of its meaning. For example: 'structures' are central to control and output; having the right ones is deemed an integral part of the corporate self-image. Unfortunately, structures themselves don't produce anything, but, as the jargon has it, 'frameworks' are 'enabling' so structures there must be. It is all too easy to regard the mere provision of 'systems', 'structures' and 'targets' as indices of progress.

Whilst a plethora of 'appropriate structures' conveys an image of efficiency, it is possible for them to have the opposite effect. People are able to hide behind procedures to delay or unnecessarily complicate the decision-making process. The compliance culture, which makes demands in the name of accountability and probity, is particularly fruitful for diverting attention from functional inadequacy or substandard performance. There are facets of every business that prevent it from running efficiently and people in every business who contrive, whether unwittingly or purposely, to clog up the works. Few of us have not encountered organisations riddled with unproductive meetings, pointless committees, and personnel who would "like to help, but I can't"; systems crippled by their own constraints which nobody seems able to loosen. This kind of corporate treacle was admirably satirised by Dickens in *Little Dorritt* as the Circumlocution Office. This portrays a working environment hobbled by structures circulating applications and paperwork round and round; a magnificent example of 'how not to do it' that many firms, NGOs and government departments worldwide have emulated with conspicuous success.

This systems- and structure-driven corporate culture has spawned an entire industry to develop and nurture it. The departure point is the 'mission statement'—the encapsulation of corporate aims, ideals and values. A brief statement of a firm's guiding philosophy has a place to remind those involved what it is about. Nowadays, however, mission statements have become the company washing line upon which is hung meaningless moralistic verbiage designed to inspire the laggards within and impress customers without; bill-boards for corporate moral credentials.

Indeed, it is an irony that much of the slack in many firms can be traced to those whose job it is to ensure that employees are kept up to the mission statement mark: 'human resources'—HR to those on the inside, personnel departments in the old world. For them, mission statements and the corporate culture have been a boon, and reinvigorated their *raison d'etre*. Once employed to make sure the company had the right people doing the right jobs, they are now seen as the guardians of the mission statement and enforcers of the corporate culture. Armed with management goodwill, devolved responsibility and well-padded budgets, they arrange team-building exercises, management training courses and seminars, designed both to keep the mission firmly in view and to promote corporate cohesion and thereby, it is argued, to stimulate productivity and sales. The modern 'corporate family' ideal must embrace everyone involved, from the Chairman to the storeman and, ideally, their wives and dependants as well.

The end-product of all this expensive activity is seen as a more fulfilled, more content and more productive workforce. It also inculcates the idea that corporate life should extend beyond the workplace and take primacy over home life and other interests. This is nothing sinister beyond the desire that a worker's principal loyalty should be towards the company. The threat, of course, is that if this is not acceptable, there is always another who will play the game—so your job probably depends on your attitude. Thus is achieved the subtle transition from the idea that you work in order to play and pursue your own interests, to the idea that play is something which you are allowed to do when there is nothing pressing at the office. It is this shift, and the ultimate job sanction that underscores it, that keeps American workers, at every level, prepared to work late into the evening and at weekends, in defiance of every study that correlates reduced efficiency and productivity with diminishing leisure time.

The corporate culture image is not confined to business but has—with plenty of political support—spread across the broad operations of government to such diverse organisations as the armed services, the Church, and local and national bodies established to dispense welfare. It is far from obvious that this language and corporate ethos are applicable here, yet governments increasingly choose to describe their citizens and operations in corporate terms. One cannot escape the jargon—indeed, it is difficult to discuss public policy without being weighed down with 'vision', 'empathy', 'delivering objectives', 'excellence in the sector', 'fulfilment of expectations going forward', 'adaptive strategies' etc. Hospital patients, university students, service personnel, even prisoners have become 'customers' of government departments and agencies. No longer are they primarily people who require healthcare, teaching, fighting skills or correctional disciplines. They are transformed into so many units of consumption, services and resources—data objects in a complex system of 'targets', 'outcomes' and cost-effectiveness.

The adoption of corporate jargon is not just an administrative convenience—it is doubtful whether it is even that—but also a means of justifying expenditure or this or that reform. In this, it relies on an ideology which characterises all organisations as commercial enterprises, with a common corporate structure and the consequent need for mission statements, brand images, plans and strategies—in fact, all the paraphernalia of corporate life.

In pursuit of uniformity, the corporate mentality views all hierarchies in managerial terms and thus anyone in authority as, functionally, a manager. All organisations are considered to be both democracies and commercial enterprises, whether they sell anything or not and, as such, deemed to require a shared corporate structure and culture. Certainly, disbursement of resources is best done according to some plan or other, and the results of various types of expenditure require monitoring, but this is insufficient reason for making universal managers, or CEOs, out of surgeons, vicars, Major-Generals, golf-professionals or retirement-home matrons. There seems little commonality between the qualities that make for a good judge, police officer or bishop or indeed the systems which they are there to administer. It is by no means evident that institutions which are far from being identical can be regarded as functionally equivalent. Their remits and priorities may have little in common apart from the need for efficient administration and financial accountability, which is mainly what this conformist culture is designed to provide. There may be a shared need to manage resources and foster good relations among those for whom they are responsible, but this hardly defines their principal roles. Whilst it may help hospital administrators, prison governors or law officers to view those who pass through their systems as 'customers', it is doubtful whether the aims of improving healthcare, reducing the rate of recidivism or administering the courts are better served by shoe-horning them into a common mould. The patients, prisoners or defendants are certainly not one whit better off from having this label attached to them.

Corporate language sounds impressive, almost forensic in its complexity, but this is merely a veneer for the simple idea that any organisation needs financial probity, efficiency, and sound, consistent and generally agreed standards. Words, by themselves, contribute nothing to these ends. In fact, the complex terminological tangles to which disagreements about the meaning or use of corporate-speak give rise merely requires more employees to work out what, if anything, these neologisms really mean. It is highly doubtful whether efficiency and accountability are best provided by a one-size-fits-all corporate model.

MANAGEMENT TRAINING

Another raft of disciplines to have emerged (and prospered) on the back of the corporate image culture is that of management training. The perceived need to be forward-looking and generally progressive in any medium-sized or large firm requires having management training built into corporate planning. Managers rarely question the validity or the value of these programmes. If they were they to do so, they would discover much.

Management training is suffused with 'feel-good' nostrums and laden with exotic jargon. It is expensive and glossy but its benefits are largely illusory. It feeds on the proliferation of the kind of 'structures' discussed above, designed to give the impression of worthwhile development, but in reality often leading to inefficiency that impedes progress. Here, common sense has been overtaken by psychology.

There is an important difference between genuine skills-directed training and what is loosely termed self-improvement. The former targets performance in specific, identified techniques—interviewing, employee relations, office management, troubleshooting, etc.—whilst the latter is more diffuse. Pseudo management training usually contains references to enhancing self-esteem, team-building and leadership development, and its literature is stuffed with quasi-scientific jargon to impress potential clients. The less it is understood, the greater it's perceived value. The programmes are often based on basic Skinnerian behaviourist theory and designed to make participants feel appropriately about what they do. This relies on three propositions: first, that to perform effectively, people must feel good about themselves; second, that being positive—about your job, commercial prospects and the corporation—will of itself improve performance; third, that everyone has the potential to perform at a high level and this potential merely requires unlocking.

The key, not surprisingly, is training in general, and the training programme being promoted, in particular.

The purveyors of management training are abetted by the twin disciplines of management consultancy and social / occupational psychology. In order to convince firms that it is worth their while to use their services — to provide the necessary resources and to release their employees for a day or more — they have to assure senior managers that these courses actually work and that the theory behind them is sound. This is achieved by quantifying the 'research' and then dressing it up in pseudo-scientific language. The desired image is that of a fully quantifiable, science-based discipline, of unimpeachable academic respectability. The reality is rather different.

The scientific status of much management training is highly questionable. It is usually couched in imprecise, non-scientific language, which makes it virtually impossible to identify precise, predictive hypotheses. Systems of this type are unscientific in the technical sense that they are neither verifiable nor falsifiable and thus fail Karl Popper's falsifiability test as a defining criterion of science (cf. Karl Popper, *The Logic of Scientific Discovery*, 1959; *Conjectures and Refutations*, 1963). An empirical characteristic of such programmes, which further confirms their non-scientific status, is that when theory collides with a fact that might conceivably falsify it, it is simply amended to accommodate it. This is a characteristic shared with most psychoanalytic and religious systems, which puts management training in exalted company, but even this will not excuse the fundamental weakness.

Notwithstanding their lack of scientific credentials, such systems resort to various forms of pseudo-quantification to give an impression of academic rigour. These usually come in the form of flow-charts, mind maps and decision trees which are in fact qualitative, not quantitative, or as statistical summaries of short-term change in achievement as a result of training — not to be equated with sustainable improvement. This is not just designed to impress potential clients, who are unlikely to spend much time scrutinising the detail of jargon they cannot understand, but also to give participants the impression that they are doing something worthwhile. For them, there seems to be a strong correlation between perceived value and the quantity of buzz words, new concepts and general theoretical psycho-babble such courses contain.

The theories and course stratagems are of various sorts, mainly based either on some kind of psychoanalytic system or on classic stimulus-response theory. Often they are simple parodies of respectable psychological, sociological or evolutionary theories, taking the jargon and conceptual framework of the original and adapting it for a milieu for which it was not intended, and which it does not fit. Psychological mimics include Freudian or Jungian analytics — dealing, for example, with positive and negative motivation and the role of the subconscious in unlocking the hidden potential that new 'personal development' theories postulate us all to possess. Respectable sociology is tapped for structural analysis, which is then mapped on to personality analysis, to identify various corporate 'types' — formers, leaders, delegators, motivators, educators, supporters, etc. Darwinian evolutionary theory contributes 'survival of the fittest' to illustrate and stimulate competitiveness, which has obvious appeal to corporate clients, who understand this kind of language, if not the theory behind it.

At the practical level, work is centred round role and games playing, interlaced with 'feel-good' exercises and strategies. The putative benefits of such training derive from enhancing participants' self esteem. This is based on the contention that self-confidence and self-esteem are self-generated and independent of external validation. The argument is flawed: self-esteem cannot be self-induced. It can only be enhanced by forces external to the individual — by approbation from colleagues or by recognition that something has been well done. There may be a residual 'warm glow' from being told by a trainer that you are of high worth, but this is no more than self-deceit unless that worth is linked to some externally validated standard. As Stephen Williams rightly points out, 'false boosting of self-esteem with group therapy-style sessions' is delusive as 'self esteem can only be derived from shared social standards independent of oneself. Otherwise, it is vanity, egotism or delusion'. (op.cit.)

There is therefore little to support the image management training has of itself. Its theoretical underpinnings appear to be based on discredited Freudian analysis and group-therapy practices which are of questionable relevance to the everyday workplace problems. In particular, there is no evidence for the universal pre-existence of skills necessary for increasing productivity, efficiency and creativity, or for the contention that such skills merely require appropriate stimuli to manifest themselves. This sort of feel-good theory has strong parallels in some sports training systems (for examples: golf, skiing, tennis and athletics) which concentrate on developing appropriate mental processes rather than on learning specific physical skills. As one golf professional describes the trend: 'The current vogue in golf is to improve your game through positive thinking. It is very enticing to think that a simple thought and a positive attitude will improve your swing. This type of "errant" psychology is what I term the "I believe in myself" approach. When sports psychology was first applied to Olympic athletes, a large number of the psychologists were using this approach. It didn't take long for the athletes to realise that just thinking you can do it simply didn't work very well when the competition actually began. The psychology concept that has found lasting success focuses upon the concept of "I understand myself". This approach teaches athletes to understand both their strengths and their weaknesses so they can work within their capabilities ... they (these psychologists) may not be as flamboyant, and they may not sell as many books, but in the long run they are much more effective". (Ralph Mann and Fred Griffin, *Swing Like a Pro*). This applies equally to management training.

If the theory is so much hokum and quackery, one can still ask whether such training delivers anything useful at the practical level. It is perfectly reasonable to suppose that organisations run more effectively if people who work together understand each other and agree upon what they are trying to achieve. It may also help if they are more aware of their own shortcomings and learn to listen more and to be more open-minded. But co-operation on the problems people face in normal working life is not increased by most of the team-building games that constitute the core of such courses, nor by exposing the subliminal psychological undercurrents of meetings or the psychodynamics of decision making, or indeed by categorising people as 'planters', 'shapers', 'fusers', 'finishers', 'developers', etc.

Where these group-bonding sessions excel is in inculcating the feeling that you are part of a co-operative team, working together for the same goals. The after-glow from this corporate feel good factor may have tangential short-term benefits, but is unlikely to make any lasting impact on performance. There is often no systematic follow-up, so the durability of any changes is unaccounted. At the individual level, people probably have neither any clear idea of what they have learned nor how it should be applied. This sort of indoctrination is mainly designed to top-up corporate loyalty and weed out troublemakers. Companies prefer employees who toe the company line, and are committed to its message; hence the emphasis on 'team players' who 'share the company's priorities and goals' and are 'self-motivated'. Whilst short training courses probably enhance these objectives, they offer questionable value for money and are a long way from the practical, goal-directed and skills-related training that are actually needed and would deliver greater long-term benefit to both employees and employers. As Stephen Williams concludes, 'pseudomanagement is essentially a self-defining, self-insulating subculture, whose doctrines and prescriptions are wholly or largely beyond rational evaluation.' (op.cit.)

The halo effect reinforces the perceived value of management training. Those who buy expensive training courses want to believe they work and participants don't criticise the psycho babble because this would make the managers who sent them on the courses in the first place look foolish. So there is strong peer pressure to conform and everyone admires the Emperor's new clothes. What evidence there is suggests that the most effective long-lasting motivator is to ensure that people feel genuinely involved. Perhaps this is the real benefit of management training, but it must be doubtful whether it has any greater or more durable impact than packing people off to the seaside for a traditional, old-style works outing.

MARKETING, CUSTOMER CARE, LOBBYING, CHOICE, ELITES, ACCOLADES, TECHNOLOGY

For the sake of completeness, I mention briefly here other areas in which image influences business and in which, therefore, there is potential for deceit or sharp practice. These are important even if they lack the sheer intellectual interest of CSR, business ethics, corporate culture, and management training.

Marketing

It is undoubtedly in a producer's interests to package its products in the most attractive way. At this important, if superficial, level a refined degree of slick professionalism has evolved since mass advertising really established itself in the 1860s in the USA. Where there is a gap between the image and the reality of the product it is in the consumer's interest to enquire more closely into what exactly is being offered. The advertising industry operates on behalf of business to create an image that will increase sales in the short term and, by enhancing a product line as a brand, will cement brand loyalty for the medium–long term.

The emphasis is no longer selling products on their intrinsic qualities—the purpose for which they were designed—but to tie them in as an essential component of a way of life. Companies and their ad-agencies go to extraordinary lengths to associate a product with a desirable lifestyle. Cars are no longer there to get one efficiently from one place to another. Even the most modest of mass produced vehicles has become a symbol, marketed to project an image of the product (and by association its owner) as stylish, sexy, wealthy, and for the discerning few. Nowadays, soaps, though made from much the same raw materials as their predecessors, have become beauty and skin-care products rather than necessities of personal hygiene. Open reference to reality is considered vulgar, likely to offend people's sensitivities, and well out of touch with the 'desirable object' focus of modern advertising. So, alternative image-enhancing tags must be found.

Classy presentation and skilful marketing lead to a positive image and commercial success, often at the expense of product reality. Where consumers are prepared to ignore the facts behind a product, it can remain successful. Tap water may taste better than bottled water and contain a healthier balance of constituents, yet bottled sales grow apace; cheaper skin creams do not differ in any essential respects from many of the expensive, heavily marketed brands, yet these latter continue to sell at premium prices. Marketing often relies on consumers' unconcern as to whether or not a product offers real value or that quality has been compromised for appearance.

Customer care

Customer service is the major public face of many businesses. They invari-ably boast concern for their customers and devote significant resources to foster an aura of caring, if not always to caring itself. All too often the reality belies the image. Many firms are deluged with complaints of incompetence and impertinence and lack of people skills in their staff from customers whose patience wears thin when their problems fail to be dealt with. This is unsurprising, as those on the public front line are often poorly educated with inadequate linguistic and comprehension skills. If primary care is defi-cient, dealing with the complaints to which it gives rise is often worse still. Many firms have little or no idea how to handle complaints; most encourage their staff to defend them at all costs to, as they see it, 'protect the firm': admit nothing and pay minimum compensation. Companies mistakenly view complaints as a nuisance rather than as opportunities despite over-whelming evidence to suggest that once they change this perspective, client satisfaction, repeat business and average spend increase significantly. A repu-tation for handling genuine complaints brusquely does immense damage to a company's image, but the majority continue to do so, against their own interests. Ecstatic customers, not merely satisfied ones, should be the aim.

This philosophy has been superbly researched and expounded by Chris Daffy in *Once a Customer, Always a Customer* (1996).

Lobbying

Along with straight promotional activity, large companies work hard to establish political influence and to remind governments in the areas where they operate of their presence. They retain political lobbyists to monitor and where possible improve the terms under which they operate in their main markets. Favourable employment legislation (i.e. not unduly restrictive), a helpful tax regime (in particular the tax treatment of capital expenditure), international tariff arrangements etc., can make a considerable difference to profits and thus need constant, expert vigilance.

Choice

Business also likes to be seen as the promoter of choice — an image which is frequently the converse of the reality. In general, major corporations control much of what we consume — in the widest sense — and their activities tend to limit rather than increase choice. They present themselves as consumer champions while pursuing an agenda of market domination. By increasing market share by acquisition, they are able, with judicious use of a few carefully positioned brands, to stifle competition if not eliminating it entirely. Brands in the same ownership may compete against each other, to the benefit of the provider to whom the profits accrue. The appearance of choice is often illusory, as differences between products from the same stable are merely cosmetic and product placement is deliberately designed to reduce the scope for genuine competition. This is true, for example, in the food, drink, entertainment and newspaper sectors. The features that national TV stations or newspapers, for example, have in common are greater than those that differentiate them.

Accolades

In the music and arts business, a popular marketing ploy is the staging of supposedly independent awards. Accolades for 'outstanding contribution to popular/American/ European music' are in reality all about money, being effectively awards for 'outstanding contribution to the popular/American/ European music coffers'. In many cases, these are purely sales–oriented and have little to do with quality or culture. Such awards are driven by celebrity, where what is 'best' equates with what is 'hot'. Reinforcing established celebrity is commercially understandable, but equating such celebrity with quality is deceitful. What is popular is self-sustaining in that it increases its popularity simply by being popular and thus polarises choice and the market. Such antics do nothing to raise artistic standards and merely encourage producers to churn out more of the same. This erodes the distinction between what is good and what is marketable, to the former's disadvantage. There is no point in striving for excellence if you are not saleable. Markets which define 'good' as 'saleable' make it nonsensical to talk of good but unsaleable. The converse is apparent where top quality producers, who have no difficulty selling their wares, see no reason to enter even genuine competitions. This vitiates the results as the competition 'best' is competing against a non-representative, self-selected subset.

Elites

There is a sociological dimension to the image of business. As one commentator noted, 'one of the most striking aspects of our modern mass society is the growing affinities between the aims and methods of big business and those of egalitarian elites ... Egalitarians are happy with a mass culture, business seeks mass markets, and each strives endlessly towards the populist norm'. (George Walden, *The New Elites*, 2000). The image-credibility formula applies as much to business and political entities as to individuals. In many countries political or corporate success is more often than not based upon the ability to project an image of competence rather than upon competence itself. For many enterprises, image is paramount. Thus it is that the system (corporation, organisation, political party) becomes more important than the individual and the message is not 'give them what they want' but 'make them want what we can most profitably give them'. The parallels between business and the populist norm, however, break down when one looks at the media (see Chapter 8). Businesses work mass markets by driving out the competition and then driving out choice with a limited product range. The media barons do all of this, but then add to the mix by concentrating output at the lowest common denominator of audience intelligence leaving niche radio, TV stations and periodicals to cater for the limited market of the better educated. There are also other interesting similarities between big business and egalitarian elites. Both look to a mass market — the distribution of goods and services in the one case, the dissemination of mass culture in the other. Both publicly champion freedom of choice, whilst in reality eroding it. Corporate and egalitarian elites use high-sounding rhetoric to mask realities, whether these are corporate irresponsibility or poor customer service on the one hand, or feigning to flatter shareholders / audiences who are privately derided on the other.

Technology

It is a cliché that the pace of change, rather than change itself, is increasing, and an almost universal perception that technology is seen as delivering all round improvements to quality of life. Time was when 'essentials' were clean air and good water. Now they include—at least in the US bailiff's definition of them—telephone, television, car and microwave oven. There is no doubt that technology can deliver improvements, but wrong to suppose that 'advances' in technology are, *ipso facto*, an unquestionable good. The universal benefit of technological change is a popular belief but not without its detractors. There are instances where technology gives the illusion of progress, while the reality is that it reflects a move backwards. Most children and adults now use calculators and are often incapable of even simple mathematical operations. The internet has undoubtedly unlocked and globalised information but has also created new opportunities for crime and deception, and supplanted creative, intelligent activity in many lives. These are failings, not strengths.

Image is thus central to business activity and superficiality is central to image. It becomes questionable is when it is used to sell products on a false prospectus or to disguise the reality behind a public facade. The trade is not, however, as one-sided as some would have us believe. Those who seek to influence business ethics by creating an image of probity and public accountability which businesses are expected to live up to, are just as manipulative as businesses themselves. Making demands, however widely supported, does not mean that they are justified. There is a strong air of virtue surrounding company CSR and corporate image management. As neither is likely to disappear, change will only come through increased vigilance; this, in turn, will depend on teaching the better educated sectors of the public the benefits of a more sceptical attitude and clearer thinking.

CHAPTER 11

POSTURING POLITICS

'The greatest superstition now entertained by public men is that
hypocrisy is the royal road to success'
Robert C. Ingersoll, Speech Dec 13th 1886

'The Politician is an acrobat; he keeps his balance by saying the opposite
of what he does'
Maurica Barres, Mes Cahiers, 1869–1923

'Politics: A strife of interests masquerading as a contest of principles'
Ambrose Bierce, The Devil's Dictionary, 1881–1991

'No one is exempt from talking nonsense; the misfortune is to do it
solemnly'
Montaigne

Politics is an experienced user of superficiality. It likes obfuscation and routinely resorts to guile and subterfuge to persuade a gullible constituency to
accept an impression of decisiveness, action and progress for the reality of
none. Democratic governments work the media to put across the executive
and its policies in a favourable light. Where democracy is marginal—for
example, in countries under military rule—the relationship between state
and the organs of information is best described as a permissive licensing of
media that are on permanent government probation. Under dictatorships
and other monopolistic regimes the relationship becomes that of master
and servant.

Politicians court the media as their major conduit for dealing with topical
matters that demand immediacy of response and as a resource for public information campaigning on issues requiring more sustained delivery. They employ
carefully chosen language to put across a point of view or policy, to reinforce their self-image and to work debate to their advantage. In developing
public policy, especially in the fields of education, welfare and social affairs,
image manipulation is brought to bear to marginalise awkward information
or to distract voters from unpalatable realities. Political image-making activity
covers a broad spectrum and those involved employ all the available devices
to persuade, retain power and maintain status.

Manipulation of the political surface manifests itself in two notable forms: spin and distortion. The former uses language to alter or put a gloss on perception — negative is turned into positive and positive positively hums with positive resonances. The latter uses selective argument and special pleading to put a case. Economy with the truth is routine, and outright lying — the extreme end of the continuum — not unknown.

Image in the political sphere covers both the perception we (citizens) have of politicians and of the political process, and the image politicians have of themselves. In most western societies, governments like to present themselves as caring and responsible and to convince their electorate that they are decent people and effective managers. The reality is that their principal interest is in preserving power and status, and the interests of their constituents generally come a poor second.

This glowing self-portrait contrasts vividly with the reality that politicians, in many countries, are deeply distrusted by their electorates who perceive them as self-serving, uncaring, ineffective, incompetent and in some cases, corrupt. The poor image may be, in part, because a reactive news media exposes weakness and perfidy more effectively than hitherto. We may not elect politicians primarily for their personal qualities — rather for the appeal of their promises and their party allegiance — and to that extent should not unreasonably reproach them for minor failings. Nonetheless, electorates seek a political process free of corruption and look to politicians to keep their electoral promises and deliver good government. Experience being against this happening and electorates being cynical, the wish rarely amounts to expectation. It is chronic deficiencies in these areas which most engender distrust.

As for the perceptions of politicians themselves, one must distinguish their views on the electorate from their perception of themselves and their role in the political process. On the electorate, they foster an image of an intelligent, discerning public. The reality — generally well hidden and private — is that they regard the electorate as poorly educated and with limited grasp of important political issues. As a result, politicians heed public opinion more as a matter of form than from any belief that it might conceivably change their own. The political elite regards itself as better informed and therefore entitled to ignore public opinion and to substitute more 'enlightened' policies, where they deem it appropriate. The nature of media has ensured that the proclaimed battle for 'hearts and minds' has long abandoned any serious attempt to harness minds and is now a struggle for hearts alone. Success in politics is more likely to be delivered by cultivating the public's instinct rather than convincing it with argument.

Politicians perceive themselves as broadly trustworthy, responsive, progressive and intelligent. In the belief that all public and social ills have a solution and that can be delivered by government, they also consider themselves important. Privately they act to retain power at all costs, both for themselves and for their party, and are adept at concealing (or at least spinning away) failure and incompetence. The recognition that to admit either invariably leads to electoral punishment drives their need for effective mechanisms to deal with any gap between image and reality, for example with patently broken promises or spectacularly failed initiatives.

The pressures of international diplomacy incorporate the need for an element of carefully choreographed schizophrenia. A government with citizens imprisoned or tortured in a foreign country with which it has valuable trading links is often minded to turn a blind eye. On such battle ground does public interest meet public morality and the former generally wins. Torture is routinely condemned by western governments, who unfailingly adopt a public stance of never dealing with terrorists or repatriating people to countries where torture is used. Yet some countries (notably the USA) regularly extradite people to rogue regimes, knowing that they are likely to be mistreated; that they do not expressly intend it provides the convenient justificatory moral loophole. Others (notably France) find that their captured citizens are often mysteriously freed. Then, after a high-profile defiant gesture or two, political and commercial activities continue as before. Here, cynicism meets self-interest—and the latter invariably wins.

Our image of the political process incorporates the delusion that politicians are there to serve their electorates. The reality is that, far from being public servants (except as conduits of access to higher authorities in individual or constituency matters), politicians have never strictly represented those who elected them and public policy is at variance with majority wishes in many key areas. Politicians see themselves as tempering public consensus with a dose of political reality and many are against the sort of populist democracy of, for example, the USA and the UK. In their view, the common man is impulsive, impractical and prone to support dangerous ideas. One only has to have modest acquaintance with the American political process to realise that debate there is no more than superficially driven by genuine concern for issues. It is, more accurately described as a bargaining process between representatives of vested interests. The European Union is no better. Its bureaucracy harbours a deep disdain of its citizens and goes out of its way to avoid the uncertainty of the popular vote. This system produces a strongly elitist political and bureaucratic elite that is heavily distrusted by EU citizens and, indeed, by many of their national parliamentarians.

This is a far cry from classical Athenian society, in which the view of the majority — the *demos* — was considered to be the truth. Modern politicians may be right to have a sceptical image of the public intelligence since much popular opinion is ill-informed and superficial. It is clear that what the majority want is frequently neither right nor even desirable. The common sense which is supposed to infuse public opinion is, whilst common, often far from sensible and, however construed, an inadequate foundation for policy making. Public opinion may have a shrewd nose for chicanery or having the wool pulled over its eyes, but is too often ignorant of practicalities and consequences. As politics is still, at least, the art of the possible — or, as J K Galbraith expressed it 'politics … consists in choosing between the disastrous and the unpalatable' (Ambassador's Journal, 1969), it is the practicable rather than the theoretically desirable that tends to drive governments. It frequently falls to politicians to handle the often conflicting demands of 'common sense' and to fashion these into credible, practicable policies. 'Fortunately, a good deal of foolish [public] opinion cancels out and is finessed by politicians: it is often their main function in a democracy to misunderstand their constituents and to talk sense' (*The Silencing of Society*, Kenneth Minogue).

The representational model of politics has been displaced with the emergence of a new intellectual political elite who see their role as opinion leaders. This harks back to the British political aristocrats of the nineteenth century, who were (nominally) elected by popular (male) franchise but considered themselves as intellectually and morally superior and thus entitled to enact into law whatever they deemed necessary without further consultation of their constituents. Whatever the rightness of that perception of the electorate, this attitude twists the relationship between power and the people. Power should properly come from the people rather than the reverse, in which lawmakers grant liberties to their citizens by virtue of the power vested in them. Liberty should in no sense be at the behest of a governing elite. This is one of the good arguments for entrenching rights and liberties and, indeed, one of the (few) strengths of the American constitution.

To the extent that people's rights and freedoms are constrained by the executive, the political process also distorts the relationship between the citizen and the law. It is felt that, in general, laws should be adapted to people and circumstances, rather than expecting them to fit the laws. This ideal is perhaps not best suited to all societies, particularly those that are violent or chronically lawless, but is a prescription that politicians would be wise to keep in mind.

One might reasonably expect that considerations of image would be of secondary concern to politicians when it comes to providing the good government for which they were elected. However, the immediacy of information has meant that a good image matters more now than it did when the only source of news was the printed media. Technology enables instant transmission of news and views which limits time for reflection and argument. To be a successful politician, therefore, demands media and presentational skills over and above stamina and competence for the job. A good public image is an essential element of both maintaining and exercising political authority, especially important in smaller states where loyalty to government by police forces or armed services cannot be guaranteed. This vests considerable political power in the media as events that compromise an image are disseminated almost instantaneously, offering little opportunity to mount a defence or limit damage. A public persona may be shattered in an instant—the damage is irreversible and swift (even if the broadcast 'facts' eventually turn out to be wrong).

The emergence of *savoir faire* in politicians has been evolutionary and reflects the change in political life from something akin to a vocation to a skills-based job. The aristocrats and upper-class landed gentry who ruled Britain and its Empire during the nineteenth century took time away from their travels and their country estates to devote themselves to politics. They were skilled delegators, leaders and military tacticians and their position and authority came as a matter of right, conferred by inheritance, and from their status as appointees rather than elected representatives. The decline in inherited privilege together with the time-consuming demands of modern politics, have turned vocation into paid employment and with this change came the requirement for greater accountability. This process has brought both benefits and disadvantages. The ability to draw on a range of specialist and professional knowledge in the scrutiny of policy and legislation is welcome; but in non-developed, largely undemocratic countries, the emergence of educated political elites has been an equivocal blessing. Too many have employed their superior intelligence, economic, legal and political cunning to serve their own agendas, rather than looking after their people. Leaders of many smaller countries find in their educational superiority a convenient lever to dominate and rule for personal advantage, and subjugate their people to declining living standards and perpetual poverty, whilst they live luxuriously on stolen money and plundered natural resources. Whether sustained by fear or cunning, their position enables them to perpetuate their tenure of power by usurping control of the media and ruthlessly eliminating opposition. They brush off unwelcome revelations whilst assiduously cultivating an image of benevolent rule over a happy and fortunate citizenry. Dealing effectively with such despots is one of the enduring challenges of modern international polity.

Even in westernised democracies, the image of a compassionate, competent political elite often belies the reality. Surveys repeatedly show that levels of crime and poverty have declined little in decades, whilst health, literacy and numeracy continue to defy attempts at improvement, despite the fact of significant additional expenditure. This often reflects massive waste on managers and computer systems to monitor and administer bloated bureaucracies connected with health, welfare, education and other public programmes.

The overriding need for a polished image drives much modern political activity. The most desirable attributes are 'modern' and 'trustworthy' and both have become image-badges of today's political elites.

MODERNITY: It is essential to political prowess to be seen to be looking forwards which implies an rejection of tradition. This is superficial—a feel-good resonance which has nothing to do with the intrinsic worth of traditional practices, ideas or values. The progressive politician approaches problems and reforms not through the perspective of whether something or other is working as it should, but whether it is appropriately modern. It matters less where you are going than that you are pushing forwards and going somewhere, even if it is turns out to be nowhere useful. Looking backwards is seen as old-fashioned and out of date. In Britain, Margaret Thatcher's call for a return to 'Victorian values', and her successor, John Major's 'Back to Basics' campaign, were both designed to restore a moral consensus in the face of a clear decline in private and public standards. Both failed, not because the ideas were flawed, but because they looked backwards for their inspiration. This well illustrates the influence of superficiality in public life—sound values and virtuous principles are abandoned solely because they are 'Victorian' or 'basic' whilst 'progressive' or 'radical' policies tend to be seen as worthy irrespective of the quality of thinking behind them. More often than not, 'progressiveness' disguises inactivity or pointless process as worthwhile activity. This is chameleon politics, where appearance changes to suit the moment, whilst the animal underneath remains the same.

This is well exemplified by the mindless destruction of tradition which has become a prominent feature of politics, especially in Britain. Centuries old ceremony and ritual, highly symbolic but with no immediately apparent purpose, have being discarded in the name of progress. These changes are presented as essential reform, spun away as modernisation and 'updating'. They are rarely productive as change does not, of itself, create a whit more modern, efficient or better society. Proposals to making court dress informal, with advocates appearing in casual clothes rather than in wigs and gowns which are seen as intimidating or to abolish (or worse to 'modernise') Royal ceremonial are mere cosmetic tinkerings. Changing the trappings changes little or nothing of underlying substance yet, in mistaking the appearance for reality destroys much that is valuable. Tradition is easy prey for progressives who see it as irrelevant and therefore ripe for the populist gesture. Its abolition combines the need to be seen to be doing something with the reality of doing nothing that has any worthwhile impact.

Those who use the abolition of tradition so as to be seen as in tune with the age misconstrue its role, and in seeking to justify it in functional terms mistake its nature. Traditions are not mere forms, but a ritualistic part of the glue that holds societies together providing an element of stability around which they evolve and flourish. Tradition is not the dead hand of the past but rather 'the hand of the gardener which nourishes and elicits tendencies of judgement which would otherwise not be strong enough to emerge on their own. In this respect, tradition is an encouragement to incipient individuality rather than its enemy. It is a stimulant ... rather than an opiate'. (E. Shils, Tradition and Liberty, in S. Crosby (ed) *The Virtue of Civility*, 1997.) Replacing this or that ceremony or ritual may have no obvious detrimental impact, but the cumulative effects of chipping away at tradition do. What the abolitionists fail to appreciate is that tradition represents security and continuity; this is compromised by change which both disturbs people and is not appreciated. Such 'modernisation' is a paradigm of populist, image-driven politics — the Cosmetic Culture, in its finest, if wigless, plumage. As Edward Shils perceptively remarked: "Liberals would sooner see their society ruined than learn something valuable in its preservation from conservatism" (op. cit.).

The cohesive value of tradition is, incidentally, why no British government can touch the Monarchy: its apolitical stance and stabilising presence are a deep-seated component of the national psyche. Republican-inclined administrations therefore content themselves with tinkering at the edges: making the Monarchy more cost-effective and accountable (e.g. paying taxes or travelling by public transport). Such hard-dealing plays well with a public forgetful of the fact that governments squander infinitely greater sums on inefficient arms procurement, badly managed public IT contracts, bloated administration, and countless wasteful bureaucratic projects and agencies. Its advocates also conveniently forget to point out that comparable state figureheads are considerably more costly than the British Monarchy and that experience suggests that the introduction of politics into state office is a recipe for instability, corruption and political opportunism, as many European states convincingly demonstrate. For some years the unappetising candidate selection for the French Presidency has included the racist far right and a series of miscreants; the Italian and German electorate have hardly been much better off. The absence of corruption and political chicanery should be the defining aims of any system of state office, rather than democratisation for its own sake.

Political inertia is frowned upon and activity, however unproductive or senseless, is the essence of modern, image-conscious governments. So it is that administrations embark on futile initiatives and establish scores of committees and quangos to simulate activity. The implication that affairs are somehow progressed by appointing a committee or promulgating a new 'concept' is false. Committees and concepts are not actions, they are substitutes for action.

Such spurious activity extends to the proliferation of unnecessary public sector jobs (the private sector cannot afford them), which aim to reduce headline unemployment. (It may be that the public sector requires two employees for every one in the private sector, but this doesn't destroy the essential point.) Public sector expenditure programmes overseen by governments, whether income or capital based, are generally wasteful and inefficient. Accountability is usually opaque, late and inadequate. The truth of this observation is reinforced time and again by experience: non-delivery, late delivery or inept delivery make a compelling case, despite official spin, that governments should not be trusted to spend significant sums of money on the public's behalf. Removing the public purse-strings from public servants is probably impractical, but as a guiding principle, thoroughly commendable. Better scrutiny of large public contracts would be a good first step.

Government by senseless activism is nothing new. Many will recognise in Dickens' fictional Circumlocution Office parallels with modern departments of state or municipality. Here is a sharply drawn portrayal of a highly efficient public mechanism designed and honed for inefficiency, inactivity and obstruction:

'The Circumlocution Office was (as everybody knows without being told) the most important Department under Government. No public business of any kind could possibly be done at any time without the acquiescence of the Circumlocution Office. Its finger was in the largest public pie, and in the smallest public tart. It was equally impossible to do the plainest right and to undo the plainest wrong without the express authority of the Circumlocution Office. If another Gunpowder Plot had been discovered half an hour before the lighting of the match, nobody would have been justified in saving the parliament until there had been half a score of boards, half a bushel of minutes, several sacks of official memoranda and a family-vault full of ungrammatical correspondence, on the part of the Circumlocution Office. This glorious establishment had been early in the field, when the one sublime principle involving the difficult art of governing a country, was first revealed to statesmen. It had been foremost to study that bright revelation and to carry its shining influence through the whole of the official proceedings. Whatever was required to be done, the Circumlocution Office was beforehand with all the public departments in the art of perceiving—HOW NOT TO DO IT ... It is true that "How not to do it" was the great study and object of all public departments and professional politicians ... that from the moment when a general election was over, every returned man who had been raving on hustings because it hadn't been done ... and had been pledging himself that it should be done, began to devise, How it was not to be done. [Those] who, in slow lapse of time and agony had passed safely through other public departments; who, according to rule, had been bullied in this, over-reached by that, and evaded by the other got referred at last to the Circumlocution Office, and never appeared in the light of day. Boards sat upon them, secretaries minuted upon them, commissioners gabbled about them, clerks registered, entered, checked, and ticked them off, and they melted away." (Charles Dickens, *Little Dorrit*)

Fine satire indeed, but the description rings as true today as it must have done to Dickens in 1857.

The process of government is still bedevilled by Circumlocution Offices. Their names have changed—these days, they are generally 'agencies' for something or other, with smart brand logos, grand offices and trendy acronyms—yet they are all over the place and getting in everywhere to complicate, obfuscate, delay and mismanage public affairs. These over-blown, self-important state bureaucracies emit a semblance of purposeful activity while, in reality, little is achieved and genuinely useful work is often impeded by indecision and an over-developed zeal for regulation.

The implementation is, if anything, even less edifying than the idea. These bureaucracies are manned by legions of practitioners, consultants, monitors and implementers of Quality Assurance, Best Practice, Initiatives, Action Plans and Job Evaluations, and any good they do is perverted by all the management and assessment mumbo-jumbo that accompanies them. The fake jobs created provide employment (often more illusory than real), thus keeping otherwise unemployable people off the unemployment registers and out of benefit queues. Many are poorly educated and thus easily impressed with their important-sounding titles and the mysterious quasi-academic jargon surrounding them. They regard themselves as essential agents of political and social progress; many believe in the meritocratic, anti-elite platform of their superiors, and act in whatever way that they consider will further those ends. The majority are ineffective deskers, driven by a systems-oriented bureaucratic mentality, content to have a job and to sit in an office pushing paper around and compiling endless jargon-ridden reports, with only the most superficial knowledge of the milieu they are supposed to be part of. Many are employed to monitor performance standards set by people of similar ilk, further up the bureaucratic hierarchy, and deliberately talk and write in obscurities to enhance the perceived value of their jobs. There is an institutionalised aversion to contact with members of the public, who tend to ask inconvenient questions and risk exposing their shallow grasp of reality. The general mentality is negative—"I'm afraid I can't help" rather than "How can I help"—and the attitude pettifogging. These self-serving jobsworths represent the lower rungs of the modern power ladder, arrogant, incompetent, financially secure and a massive obstacle to real progress—and perhaps, worst of all, totally incapable of recognising their own irrelevance. This is the new breed of public servants—with neither relish for the public nor any genuine desire to serve.

TRUSTWORTHINESS: The second important attribute for today's politicians is trustworthiness. Indeed this should be essential to any functional political process. If surveys are to be believed, in many countries politicians have squandered much of the public trust they once enjoyed, to the extent that voters no longer see the political process as reputable and worthy of their time. Electoral choices are rendered essentially meaningless by unkept promises and politicians who put the protection of their own interests before those of their electorates. The default attitude to public pronouncements is scepticism and the instinctive reaction is to look behind the words to discover their 'real' import — what is being covered up or left unsaid. If politicians say there is no need to worry about X or panic about Y, the public's first instinct is to worry or panic. This cynicism reflects an habituation to spin and incompetence and frustration at politicians' reluctance to speak truthfully or to address important problems head on. This may well account for a growing tendency for direct action, rather than pursuing grievances through the political process. Despite being among the least trusted of many identifiable occupations, politicians continue to consider themselves as trustworthy.

Distrust may reflect several different perceptions. Politicians are principally distrusted because they don't deliver on their promises. This is not necessarily because of mal-intent but because (political) realities either make those promises naive or impossible to fulfil. Trust is also compromised where non-delivery is seen as deliberate deception — i.e. where promises were made to secure support but with no intention of implementation. It is no less eroded by perceived incompetence — where failed policies are seen as being inappropriate or based on poor choices. Where political decisions or justifications are viewed as reflecting expediency rather than as addressing real problems, resentment usually follows. In general, repeated failures of trust lead to lack of respect — which taints the breed and its image. This, being more durable than trust itself, is less easily reversed.

Cynicism manifests itself in political apathy. This indicates indifference rather than distrust and occurs because (a) there appears to be no significant policy difference between parties, (b) voters are bored with the message ('we've heard it all before'), (c) because they think that their vote is irrelevant, as laws are enacted as expediency dictates, irrespective of policy platforms or public good, or (d) because the public feel excluded by politicians who they see as out of touch and disdainful of their electorates, however much they feign interest. This amounts to scepticism or boredom, but not necessarily distrust.

Words skilfully used can also support an image of progress or obscure the lack of it. People see the political process as conducted in a different language that has no genuine reference to the concerns of those outside it. This is reflected either in the thoughts politicians express or the words they use to express them. Political speeches are full of high-sounding, business-derived rhetoric about 'quality assurance', 'best practice', 'delivering objectives', 'meeting targets' etc. which sits ill with worsening healthcare provision, increasing violent crime and ill-educated children. Meaningless jargon is lifted from business to lend gravitas to public utterances and to persuade people that they have something new to offer. It is as if words have become dissociated from thoughts and taken on a life of their own. What might restore a measure of confidence are fewer words, ones chosen for their meaning, rather than exhausted idiom and tired cliché, and delivery in a manner which might suggest that the speaker has some genuine concern for their import. Nothing corrodes the democratic process more surely than the impression that it is pointless to listen to what politicians say.

At the international political level, the divergence between image and reality is, if anything, worse. Most of the supranational organisations are seen as having little impact on events and, in many cases, are rightly distrusted. For example, the G8 has reneged on most of its international promises and the UN is widely seen as ineffective. We are treated to high-profile declarations of international aid or debt relief, but when the cameras and journalists have gone, the promises are quietly buried. Six months after the Asian tsunami of 26 December 2004, whilst Britain had paid 97% of its pledge, France had only paid 13% and other countries even less. Politicians relish the international acclaim that their media-choreographed pledges attract then find a variety of excuses to avoid paying their dues. Many argue that the massive cost of G8 and similar meetings would be better spent delivering aid or other desirable objectives. The United Nations has repeatedly failed to enforce Security Council resolutions, and there have been well-publicised corruption scandals in some of its agencies. The European Union is wasteful and corrupt and spends a high proportion of its available funding on propping up an outdated farming system. Its bureaucracy is inefficient and expensive to the extent that some 25% of its total budget cannot be properly accounted for and its auditors have refused to sign off its accounts for ten consecutive years. Unsurprisingly, citizens feel traduced, prey to the whims of unelected, overbearing officials and threatened by the tide of EU legislation emanating from a source which they see as remote and as having little understanding of their situation and with which they have little empathy (and vice versa).

International forums are increasingly making policy at the behest of popular pressure. High-profile media campaigns encourage the belief that 'something must be done', even if the effects of what is proposed are pointless or even negative. This exemplifies the attitude that throwing enough money at a problem is bound to do some good which, while superficially attractive, is misguided. Blanket debt reduction or pumping massive aid into poorer African countries gives the developed world a feel-good buzz, but is of questionable benefit. It does nothing to encourage good government or prevent a recurrence of the situation that gave rise to the need for aid in the first place. In such immature countries, aid fuels corruption and stifles democracy. Whilst many crises require a short-term boost in aid, long-term solutions are much more complex and politically involved.

This is politics by media — in this case celebrity and pop concert. It presses hard for the causes it sees as worthy, usually those presented as being in crisis, which inevitably deflects attention and resources from areas that might benefit more from well-targeted aid. Celebrities who become involved in charitable or other aid work gain quasi-political status and politicians find it difficult to resist their appeals, not because they necessarily approve of the cause or the particular use of funds, but because failure to do so would damage their image with that mass of popular support behind the figurehead. Simon Jenkins put the argument pungently in a scathing attack on politics by media and Live Aid / Live 8 promoter Bob Geldof: 'Geldof is a big-time interventionist who claims legitimacy, not by democratic mandate, but by the dubious franchise of rock concert attendances. He was quoted […] as claiming that something must be done even if it doesn't work. For him, doing something useless even if it is harmful is a moral advance on doing nothing. Giving masses of money must work — rather like blanket bombing, something must hit the target. What we see is another chapter in an old story, glibness triumphing over thought and the rich yearning for excuses to impose their values on the poor. We know we cannot "make poverty history". This week we are trying to make it geography. Perhaps, just for once, we should make it economics'. (Simon Jenkins, UK Sunday Times, 3rd July 2005) The development of policy on the basis of what the masses want is a perversion of the democratic process, which is intended to deliver sound decision-making through elected representatives, not to enact laws or develop policy in response to popular demand.

Any sustainable political image must incorporate the policy of inclusivity. In modern society, though many are in fact marginalised in one way or another, no-one must be seen to be excluded. The concept of inclusivity is a product of politicising sentimentality which, like all sentimentalising, ignores reality and exalts feel-good emotion above reason and objectivity. Thus it is that financial benefits are paid indiscriminately rather than on a dispassionate assessment of need; that counselling rather than self-reliance is seen as the solution to the majority of serious personal problems; that 'diversity' and multi-culturalism are allowed to dominate social policy despite their very evident detrimental effects on social cohesion.

Sentimentality is a powerful political weapon, used to make high impact, crowd-pleasing gestures and to avoid having to get to grips with sound policy or difficult issues. It turns serious issue politics into soap opera and invites people to react more like viewers than voters. Thus it was that the British Prime minister, Tony Blair, made much of saving a child's pet calf on a farm in an area where bovine foot-and-mouth disease was spreading and where government policy demanded that all livestock be slaughtered. This deliberate act of compassion was designed to deflect attention from the mass slaughter (unnecessary, as it turned out) of pedigree herds across the country. The emotional impact of widely disseminated pictures of a child and her spared calf rebalanced that of wanton destruction and polished Mr. Blair's image as a caring politician. In practical terms the gesture was futile (even potentially dangerous); in political terms it was a masterstroke.

One negative consequence of inclusiveness has been the gradual emergence of positive discrimination. Inclusivity implies non-discrimination, so to implement a policy of inclusivity requires, to some minds, artificial means to redress imbalances. It has become standard political practice in many countries to promote equality with affirmative action and reverse discrimination. As well as using courts as a form of 'thought police' to correct inappropriate attitudes and utterances, governments require employers to take on, and in some cases, give preferment, to members of identifiable minorities or under-skilled majorities. Thus it is that firms over a certain size are required to employ disabled or gay people and political parties institute 'all women' candidate shortlists to artificially increase the number of elected female politicians. In countries where firms are required to have a stated proportion of black managers, shareholders or board members irrespective of whether the appointees are properly qualified for the job or whether there are more suitable candidates available, the effects have been particularly evident. For example, in one African country the judiciary has suffered from less than competent, fast-tracked judges who have not risen through the usual advocacy practice. Commercial firms finding their case before such a judge tend to regard an adverse outcome as a foregone conclusion and often settle before trial. In such a mistrustful atmosphere, the image of judicial impartiality becomes tarnished and judiciaries risk being politicised.

Positive preferment, which all too often replaces a competent with an incompetent in business or public life on the basis of arbitrary criteria — e.g. colour or disability — is well-intentioned but divisive; you don't end one form of discrimination by instituting another. It also obscures the reality that imposing ethnic or race quotas for jobs — the most widely practised example — doesn't help either those promoted (usually above their merits) or the firms who have to work round the deficiencies of substandard employees. This 'empowerment' may superficially correct imbalances but leads to hardening of attitudes and to a skills drain. One obvious dividend of forced discrimination is that genuinely skilled personnel who find the less able promoted above them become resentful and disillusioned. Many, seeing no future in their companies or even their countries, emigrate, so their training investment and skills are lost. In the long term, distorting markets in this way in furtherance of what must be seen as political correctness can only be counter-productive.

There is no doubt that weak or corrupt leadership succeeds. This is in some measure a dividend of skilful image manipulation. Corruption in many European, Asian and African countries and in supra-national bodies, such as the EU, is well documented. Presidents and Prime Ministers routinely invoke the immunity of their office to avoid prosecution and use crude thuggery to perpetuate their hegemony. The corrupt generally overvalue their status and importance, and consider themselves immune from the rules that govern their society. This convergence of image and reality (both corrupt) is difficult to square with that of an informed electorate. It may be that corruption is all that is on offer, and the franchise boils down to a choice between the staggeringly corrupt and the less corrupt. It may also be that, in some countries, voters prefer politicians who sail close to the ethical wind because it signals that they are tough and cunning enough to preserve their country's interests. In states where the social structures allow political and judicial elite to fraternise freely, corruption can thrive because prosecution of the highest in the land is forestalled by a tame judiciary.

The *zeitgeist* of 21st century politics professes to disdain elites. Aristocratic rule and the inheritance of political power may have gone, but in their place have emerged a new political class—the power elites. These people wield considerable influence but see themselves as simply the superior tier of a mass meritocracy. They do not (in public, at least) regard themselves as anything but ordinary, indeed they are happy to portray themselves as average people who just happened to rise above the crowd—nothing innate in terms of ability or status, just superior in merit, but in other respects entirely unexceptional. They are also avowed egalitarians and are prone to publicly adopt values and opinions that are in fact the opposite of those they really hold, in the belief that this will help cement their populist credentials. This image bears no relation to the reality. As we have seen, these elites scorn the masses, regarding themselves as their intellectual and social superiors. They are assiduous in using all the arts of spin and manipulation to protect their position and interests, and to deflect any disagreeable criticism. They also dislike any form of disloyalty, working hard to keep those below them 'on message'. This is a form of despotic rule, yet comes in the guise of populism, identifying itself (publicly, at least) with the masses and seeking to give them what is considered appropriate for them (thinly disguised as what they want). The reality behind this populist image is not only exploitative, it is also condescending in that it uses its position of power to stifle criticism and to distil policy from popular opinion. Arrogance and contempt are defining markers of today's power elites.

The political elites continue to retain power but now share their authority with media and corporate barons, who also exert considerable influence both directly, on governments and electorates, and indirectly, through economic and social power-bases. This diffusion of actual (as opposed to statutory) power brings politicians into the influence zone of a variety of interest groups and lobbies. Whilst avowing independence from such pressures, the reality is that in the give-and-take of the political process lobbies are an important part of the arrangements. In the USA, political advancement depends entirely on attracting sufficient funding to run a campaign, which, in turn, depends on having policies that attract important donors. If you are anti-gun or pro-abortion or anti-black/Hispanic, then your chances of election are severely reduced. In this environment, politics is much more a matter of squaring influential lobbies than of delivering sensible policies. American politics is diminished by this process which effectively excludes many excellent candidates at the first hurdle.

It is in the misuse of language that politics excels in reality management. In their pursuit of power, politicians and governments need to persuade their electorates that what they are doing is sound and sensible and that their efforts are successful, irrespective of the outcome. They also need to inform the public on matters of national importance and to deal with mistakes and failures. Language is the main medium of information and skill in its use is inseparable from success. What is said, how it is said, when it is said, and in what context it is said are all part of the information process. Change any of these variables and the message changes too.

Much political information is designed to persuade, not to inform. This is particularly true of 'government information' campaigns, which are in reality crude attempts to change behaviour—be it social or sexual behaviour, be it to reduce HIV/Aids or to reform driving habits to improve road safety, or smoking habits to reduce lung cancer. Although providing proof is difficult—how many accidents do you prevent by a road safety campaign?—there is evidence that this kind of social engineering doesn't work, whether or not the views expressed are endorsed by experts. There may be a short-term effect, but it takes more than posters, leaflets and brief television commercials to change ingrained habits. These public campaigns don't merely present the facts; they present a view based upon them. So, one has to ask at what point education becomes propaganda. The reason governments use such methods is that they create an impression of worthwhile activity. The cost-benefit equation is generally less favourable.

Government is also involved in more serious attitudinal engineering. This has come about because of a desire to ensure that people do not behave in a discriminatory fashion. Hence boards and commissions are set up to ensure religious equality, racial equality, non-discrimination on grounds of age, gender, disability, weight, sexual orientation and much besides. This massive effort, under the umbrella of inclusivity, may succeed in stifling overt discriminatory behaviour but does little else. Changing language or nomenclature changes nothing fundamental—certainly not long-held convictions however unpalatable or politically incorrect they may be. On the contrary, it probably entrenches them—people will grudgingly acquiesce in suppressing inappropriate behaviour but will not stomach being told what to think. Putting the lid on highly charged political pressure cookers risks an unpleasant explosion when feelings are provoked or an opportunity arises to protest. At such times, genuine attitudes rather than politically correct ones tend to surface. Pretending that these differences don't exist or are unrelated to social and public life is a fiction employed by governments to appease sensitive minorities which is likely to rebound in the long-term. Positive discrimination is no durable solution to social exclusion, nor is pretending that gross obesity is either normal or beautiful, likely to change the general perception that it is unattractive and abnormal. In many such cases, what governments want to eradicate is the stigma — of colour, obesity disease etc. In fact, it is often stigma and temporary exclusion that change attitudes and behaviour — social disapproval is a normative force, and one that can operate for good.

The effect of Political Correctness, over a wide range of issues, has been to stifle important debate. Nowhere is this more evident that on matters pertaining to race, religion or immigration for example, where the very mention of the subject risks one being branded, racist or anti-minority. The official fiction discounts the evident reality that citizenship and values may not always coincide. For example, immigrants may become U.S. or British citizens by a stamp on a document, but this no more makes them American or British in outlook, values or other essential respects than a Chinaman emigrating to Sudan would become Sudanese overnight. This simple truth is sidelined by governments who expect us not to discriminate between an immigrant and a native. In its truest sense, nationality is earned not legislated, and the longer genuine social integration in terms of language, behaviour, habits, allegiance and custom, is delayed, the greater the scope for racial and religious conflict.

How a policy is presented is critical to its acceptability. Since many policies are likely to be unpopular, presenting them in as palatable a manner as possible is an important element of the art. To avoid negative perceptions, it is often wiser to focus on the consequence rather than the means. Thus, raising prices or taxes may be the policy, but to say so would be counter-productive so the aim is stated as providing sustainable energy or improving healthcare, which helps to sweeten the pill. An international treaty is portrayed in terms of its benefits for the underprivileged in a developing country rather than competition for home industries with a probable loss of jobs as a result of freer trade.

One stratagem for dealing with a difficult policy is to concentrate on the negative aspects of failing to adopt it or, when desperate, to impugn the integrity or motives of its proponents. The argument over Britain's relationship to

Europe is a case in point. The pro-Europeans, who favour further integration, point to the trend to larger political and economic units and portray their opponents as isolationists if they are being polite, or as 'Little Englanders', if not. As they see it, Britain without Europe would be at a disadvantage and this image is used to push the pro-Europe case. They prefer to evoke a doom-laden scenario of isolation and subsequent decline than to face reality — in particular, the fact that whilst the European economies are badly managed and consequently in a mess, the UK economy has outpaced the rest of Europe for many years and seems likely to continue doing so. This has, so far, failed to improve the pro-European position as British people value their independence and see all too clearly and with justified alarm the creeping 'competence' (Eurospeak for 'power') of European institutions. They also contrast the UK's successful economy with the corruption, inefficiency and waste pervading the European Union which signally lacks the political impetus for reform. For the moment, the facts are getting the better of fear, but the balance is fragile. Dripping away at a powerful negative image will in time render it immune to all but the most dramatic counter-evidence, and this is a tactic employed by many whose platforms are less than secure.

The pursuit of populism in politics has accelerated with universal suffrage and lowering of educational standards. The logic is straightforward: in order to maximise public approval with a voting majority at the low end of educational attainment, policies must be presented in terms they can understand, using simple language and popular, persuasive images; it also helps to play on known prejudices. Putting recondite words into a political message is likely to be seen as elitism and may rebound. On the contrary, it is deliberately leaving out a difficult word or concept on the grounds that it would not be understood that is elite and patronising. Accepting that the majority of electorates are of low intelligence also reinforces the need to be seen as populist. In particular, it is politically unwise to denigrate any aspect of popular culture as of low artistic or cultural merit as this would be seen as questioning popular taste. However, governments that push their populism too hard often do themselves harm — for example, Tony Blair's 'Cool Britannia' campaign, which was a spectacular failure.

Governments also have to deal with failures that cannot be finessed away by astute language. The collapse of prominent businesses with the resulting loss of jobs and pensions, failed public expenditure projects, government contracts whose costs balloon out of control etc. — all have to be faced. The usual way out is to blame someone else, or at least to claim that the disaster involved was outside the government's remit. This may work with corporate failures, although the charge then becomes one of inadequate regulation—whether this is interpreted as inadequate regulatory mechanisms or inadequate enforcement of adequate regulatory mechanisms—but won't wash for matters in which governments are directly involved.

It is all too easy to ignore the conventions of straight and honest dealing and thereby deceive the public. Those who 'deal in half-truths and in the bare-faced daily recitation of the unbelievable until it fixes itself in the public mind as if it were true' turn truth on its head, with the result that electorates, however deprived and repressed, believe that government lies as a matter of course. For many politicians, facts are an inconvenience they could well do without; if they meet them face on and don't fit their case, then the facts become flexible. 'It is Orwellian. Words mean what they wish them to mean. Bad news is good. Up is down. Black is white. Fiction is fact. It is no wonder that, to a bewildered public, trust has collapsed.' Governments become so lost to the political black arts that they 'may never be able to find (their) way back to straightforward dealing ... spin doctors have become a byword for underhand behaviour.' (John Major, UK Daily Telegraph comment, 22 February 2005). As another British prime minister, Jim Callaghan commented: 'A lie can be half way round the world before the truth gets its boots on'.

Many of the questions that need to be addressed and often are not—either because they are regarded as politically explosive or else simply fail to be recognised as important—stand above the obvious or immediate issues of politics and economics. There is a marked reluctance to tackle issues of equality, race, cultural integration and morality, even as the image of multiculturalism and virtuous pluralism falls to the reality of ethnic ghettos. The wisdom of transposing democracy from one culture to another is rarely questioned even when international efforts are made to impose it on countries which have functioned tolerably without it for centuries. Universal democracy is considered necessary for the sake of world order rather than imperialistic imposition, and failure to achieve it is regarded as a temporary practical inconvenience rather than a fatal flaw in the idea itself. Oppression may be acceptable if it is in pursuit of what the oppressor sees as a worthy cause.

One would think that the fact that international standards of democracy, human rights or legal process are not accepted in many countries would give some urgency to the question of the sense in which we can be said to 'understand' other cultures or religions and to what extent countries which are undemocratic should be the subject of international reform. It is assumed throughout much of the developed world that the culture and values of western society are good beyond question and that those countries without them are inferior, or worse, primitive. The reality is that little attempt has been made to advance public understanding of societies that reject this model.

Understanding operates on two different levels, intellectual and empathic. The idea that one culture can genuinely understand another at a sensitive level is difficult conceptually and hard to validate empirically, so is given no more than anecdotal weight. On intellectual understanding, which is what the sociologist aims for in describing and interpreting different people and cultures, the principal constraint is that of the culture-boundedness of meaning. In other words, how is it possible to translate meanings and reasons of one culture into the language of another? How, for example, can anyone but a medieval man claim to understand medieval society, if he is not, as *ex hypothesi* he cannot be, part of it. Some would say that, on the contrary, medieval man is himself incapable of understanding medieval society precisely because he lacks the historical perspective and linguistic apparatus available to a modern sociologist. Applying such constraints to our own time clearly puts in question any attempt to analyse or describe social behaviour even in our own society. This is a pertinent debate for those seeking to understand societies, tribes or religions. For example, reading the Qu'ran gives only limited insight into the Islamic world and may enable one to address some of the mischievous misinterpretations put upon it to justify war and slaughter, but this amounts to no more than a superficial understanding of the culture. Where one can observe and evaluate objectively, a measure of understanding is possible. For example, it became clear that communist, centrist economic models didn't work when the political systems based on them in the USSR and elsewhere collapsed; in this light, it is reasonable to predict that China's rapid progress towards capitalism will eventually drag it too out of the communist age. The difficulty of diagnosis, let alone prescription, is compounded by such limits on understanding.

In recognising the need to understand cultures from emotional and cognitive levels, it is also important to ask what it means to explain social or cultural phenomena. In this, we must distinguish interpretative constructions from explanations. Sociology seeks to classify different types of explanation and assess their value to understanding social systems. Traditionally, actions can be explained by reference to intentions or motives, reasons and causes, tradition or emotion or by reference to intrinsic value — be it moral, aesthetic or religious. These are interpretative constructs. Explanations can also be made by reference to social phenomena — myths, conventions, moral tales etc. — which are more often found as grounds for behaviour than as explanations. There is also the difficulty of deciding to what extent an explanatory system can rely on categories used by the explainer, rather than using those familiar to the society or system being assessed. This is particularly important when dealing with other cultures or religions. Whilst it is tempting to try and find a common cross-cultural base for political behaviour or social attitudes, such comparisons fall foul of such limits on understanding and must be treated with a high degree of caution. Those who seek to impose systems or norms on others need to have answers to these problems and then to tread with care — both from an ethical as well as a practical standpoint.

National images

Nations are no less image-conscious than corporations and individuals. Their status in the world and ability to attract inward investment and crisis aid depend, in part, on their standing within the international community. Image also gives an important dimension to international relations: face-saving. No nation, organisation or individual likes to be bested in argument, a deal, diplomacy or conflict. So, the need for face-saving, and the failure to produce satisfactory face-saving formulae, is the cause of much domestic, social and international conflict.

This raises the questions as to what extent images should be fostered for social and domestic harmony, and whether people, corporations or nations should be allowed to live with their flawed images or be required to reconstruct them.

Entrenched ideologies and the need to save face often leave reality behind. For example, the decay of communism and the subsequently slow opening of remaining communist and Arab nations to democratic institutions and international markets can to a large extent be attributed to the unwillingness of their leaders to admit that command economics doesn't work and that they, personally, had let down their citizens. That this has largely not happened has all to do with image, and nothing to do with ideological flaws.

Image polarises actions as language polarises attitudes. Globalisation of trade and industry, once seen as beneficial for many underdeveloped countries, is now widely viewed as a means of exploiting these very same people. In particular, the spread of US culture and values is taken by many non-western governments as an unsubtle attempt to undermine their value systems and to americanise their citizens. After softening them up by media, it is a simple step to introduce American political ideas and consumer goods. The counter-balance to such intrusion is to reinforce traditional national customs and values and, as far as possible, to restrict foreign media output.

One result of globalisation is that human rights are being redefined, especially by the USA, in terms of market forces and free trade. The language of rights has been usurped by those with special agendas eager to carve out territory, and by the proliferation of general rights supported by legal frameworks. Both are, in many cases, contentious. Powerful democracies routinely use the language of human rights to brow-beat countries that resist their own economic or political agendas. By tailoring definitions restrictively to its own image the USA made good capital from such machinations with China and the USSR. Farming out prisoners for 'interrogation' by questionable regimes is apparently acceptable when the needs of democracy are at stake but to be condemned when your opponents are the perpetrators. Much the same can be said of the concept of press freedom — 'feel-good' and generally desirable, except when it acts against one's interests (e.g. Al-Jazeerah and the USA). In this context, rights are only upheld to the extent that they reflect the motives of those exercising them.

It is clear that superficiality pervades political activity. Political credibility is in large part about being seen to be positive, up-beat and progressive, and image manipulation is critical to sustaining that impression. Whether or not your policies are working, it is imperative that you present them as if they are. This requires sensitive, skilful image management, but it also demands spinning failure as success. It is this which forces politicians into 'economy with the truth' and brings them close to lying and deceit. It is possibly good sense to recommend that 'Government should learn to leave lying to properly qualified people. No deception is one thing, self-deception is another. Once a society gets an appetite for lies, it loses the capacity to swallow anything else'. (Frederic Raphael, *After the War*, 1988) Ordinary people accept fallibility — but politicians are denied that luxury. Failure is politically damaging, so politicians understandably strive to limit their mistakes and thus their exposure to sanction. This leads to deviance and strenuous avoidance of the language of apology, which ignorance equates with that of fallibility. Even admission of failure is punished but, as respect for the political class continues to diminish, honesty may yet become the new fashionable coin.

POSTSCRIPT

'Only the mediocre are always at their best'
Yiddish Proverb

'Good sense about trivialities is better than nonsense
about things that matter'
Sir Max Beerbohm

'Oh, what a goodly outside falsehood hath'
William Shakespeare, The Merchant of Venice

This chapter draws together the various threads of those that preceded it and, in doing so, seeks to point up commonalities. It is beyond doubt that superficiality is a powerful influence on many aspects of life — personal, national, social and political. Its effects are not isolated but share a common base in individual and societal attitudes and expectations. Superficiality affects our behaviour and how we look at ourselves and others. It affects what we value and how we value it, our thinking and judgement, and thereby impacts on societies and broader community structures, in particular, those of business and politics. In today's plastic paradise of sentimentality, hype and fad, we chase false illusions of wealth without effort and happiness through consumerism. All too often, it is the superficial rather than reality that governs thought and action. In a contemporary climate increasingly driven by immediacy and constrained by competing demands on our attention, this is hardly surprising.

The resulting damage is both direct and indirect. Directly, shallowness deprives us of much that is intellectually worthwhile and self-indulgence destroys values and compromises virtue. There is a growing belief that character can be grown, as it were, from an armchair, without effort, risk and challenge. Indirectly, we suffer from the consequences of inadequate education and deficient linguistic skills which limit the ability to take full advantage of what life has to offer and lumber societies with many poorly socialised, virtually unemployable citizens who end up as welfare dependents.

Superficiality infects both producers, who resort to the glib, fakes and spin, and consumers who readily accept at face value what is presented to them. It encourages the futile pursuit of idealised images in the expectation of improving self-esteem and social standing. Superficial resemblance is taken for true resemblance and illusion for reality, while a mediocre mind encourages an inflated estimation of the trivial. Thus it is that we idolise, rather than hold in contempt, celebrities who admit proudly that they have never read a book, which they regard as some kind of achievement. This mentality is reinforced by apathy — if the appearance serves, why look further? Shame and disgrace are no longer weapons of social management — freedom is virtually unlimited, as long as the law doesn't catch up with you. The widespread proclivity to judge by appearance means that the externalities come to define the individual to whom they attach. Society increasingly revels in the trivialities of social fashion and celebrates its banality while ignoring the reality that human whim and fancy are capricious and unstable, and moreover, highly unsuitable as a foundation for any code of values.

The ascendancy of individuality and skill over wisdom and the collective interest has eroded standards and led to the de-moralisation of society. It is not just that old morals are rejected or replaced rather that the need for morality itself is questioned. Immoral has become amoral, and individual accountability and community allegiance have been diminished, supported by weak governments more concerned with maintaining a popular image than with running well-ordered societies. These factors, together with an explosion of influential media, have supported the rise of sentimentality which has become an endemic and highly corrosive component of modern life.

This book has been concerned both with the phenomenology of superficiality and its causes. Its power should not be underestimated. For example, much of what is referred to as Political Correctness comprises ideas and opinions which a very few years ago would have been dismissed out of hand as unworthy of notice or comment. Now, these are accepted as reasonable — even self-evident. This is, in part, a symptom of the virus of apathy, but more the result of intellectual insecurity which, in the absence of strong public values, fosters a reluctance to take a stand on any but the least controversial of issues. PC's self-appointed task is to promote social cohesion, and this is taken to imply that no sincerely held belief, however irrational or ill-founded be rejected. For the sake of a veneer of inclusivity, appeasement overtakes good sense. It has been deemed expedient to force equality on societies, which means discounting cultural inheritance and manifest inequalities in individual dispositions, capacities and attainment. The past has been declared disposable wherever its continued existence might conceivably promote inequality and thus, so we are invited to believe, threaten human dignity.

Lack of any collective will to resist nonsense has made it possible for many perverse policies to take hold to the extent that societies' foundations have been undermined. We are now awash with ill-founded ideas which, through a combination of 'feel-good' and constant repetition, have attained the status of incontestable fact. Profound untruths have no difficulty taking hold if they are sufficiently plausible or if they contain sufficient truth to carry conviction. A good example is the so-called 'precautionary principle'—the proposition that future generations have rights, which the present generation is obliged to protect. There is no basis for this whatsoever, beyond a moral obligation for us to behave sensibly (or at least not recklessly) and in ways that avoid inflicting grievous harm on anyone, however removed they may be from us in time and space. That general obligation is no ground for an assertion of specific rights of future generations, but it is portrayed as such and widely used as a basis for restrictions on policy and development.

Political populism leads to unsound argument and makes for bad policies. Where responses were once clear and robust, they are now often indecisive and contentious, especially in areas of ethics, social policy and welfare. This is principally the result of the prevailing climate of moral relativism, a prime factor in the rise of political correctness. Such is the power of PC that the appropriate response to contentious issues (e.g. sanitising children's nursery rhymes or using meaningless job-descriptions to enhance workers' self-esteem) is not to dismiss them as absurd but to bow to the need to consider sensibilities and feelings, however tendentious or over-reactive. This is an inept prescription for restoring genuine consideration and respect for others at a time in which they are in sharp decline.

Reality is, as we have seen, routinely distorted and manipulated for a variety of ends, some more insidious than others. This is a process, not an event, sometimes unwitting, all too often deliberate. We constantly deceive ourselves as well as being manipulated by others intent on deceiving us from social, economic or political motives. Reliable and appropriate governance are at the heart of social and political activity, and there is a demonstrable need to retain a firm grip on reality to ensure their continuance. This grip has loosened markedly in recent years, not least because governments themselves routinely connive at deception.

The aim of much public discourse is the maintenance of a civilised society. 'Civilisation' has an evaluative as well as a descriptive meaning, and determining what is 'civilised' inevitably involves passing judgement on the *mores*, values and practices of other societies and religions. This has the clear implication that some societies and systems are better than others. In times of terrorism, such pronouncements are likely to provoke a belligerent response. The modern tendency is to shirk such controversial judgements and accept all systems as of equal value. This goes against a long tradition of regarding societies and religions as evolutionary systems, where some are seen as more primitive and others more advanced, and replaces it with soft egalitarianism. This extends to toleration, which has gone beyond recognition of social and religious diversity to a stronger position that decrees all creeds to be of equal standing and worth. In doing so, it both debases the notion of value itself and also glosses over the fact that such equality is merely a convenient starting point for dealing with individuals in societies which encourage the expression a variety of personal inequalities, in character, temperament and disposition. The libertarian may counter that diversity itself has rights which are vitiated by hierarchical judgements, but this fails to recognise that societies can only function successfully by retaining their own beliefs and morality. It is these that in a misconceived spirit of 'inclusivity' are progressively being abandoned. The question of the comparative value of one culture or civilisation vis-à-vis another is far from being an idle one as we are invited to integrate minorities from societies whose values and practices differ markedly from what might generally be considered as 'civilised'.

In an increasingly mobile and open world, this is becoming a pressing problem, especially where one system or religion seeks to impose itself on an unwilling recipient and where societies, however corrupt or contemptuous of values, seek to sustain an appropriate public image — tolerance, upholding of individual and collective rights, etc. A willingness to question such images is essential, particularly in a world where one culture and its attendant values aspire to global domination. The American ideal is presented as the only valid framework for political and social affairs whilst others see these same ideals as corrupting and decadent. To the Americans, their values and ideals are *the* values and ideals, and admit of no counter-argument. They are impervious to criticism (and indeed zealous at suppressing it) so there is little genuine debate. You have to agree not only with their selection of values, but where these come into question — for example on democracy or human rights — with their interpretation of them. Any system, particularly one which its proponents see as the single universal model, should attract the most profound scrutiny of its principles and practices.

Whether or not it is desirable to overthrow one system (however bad) in order to replace it with another (however good) raises thorny questions of national sovereignty and the enforcement of international resolutions. What can be said is that standards are under threat from multiculturalism, pluralism and inclusivity, and that fear of reprisal has made governments reluctant to openly criticise dictatorial, repressive or corrupt regimes, especially those which affect their economic interest. Such supine failure to respond effectively to incipient threats is likely to make matters worse.

Although some may not wish to have the debate, it is entirely reasonable to ask where, if anywhere, true civilisation really lies. It is far from obvious that it resides in societies that call themselves 'civilised' or in those with the highest *per capita* GDP. Abundance of material resources cannot be equated with that of moral ones, nor the converse. One sees flashes of civilisation in unexpected places. Children in developing countries relish the opportunity for learning and where it can take them — they rarely truant and are meticulously obedient. In the USA and UK there is widespread truancy and a significant proportion of schoolchildren are argumentative, disruptive and rebellious. Crowds at African football matches applaud the success and sympathise with injuries of either side. In the UK, fans have to be segregated in heavily policed cages. They abuse the opposition and fight rival fans. Sporting pride has become sporting war. Here, in neither case is there any difficulty answering the limited question of which country is more civilised.

All this suggests that there is more than cosmetic appeal in the Law of Reverse Civilisation (Philip Atkinson, www.ourcivilisation.com/reverse.htm, 2000). This, broadly stated, links the fate of a civilisation to the relationship between authority and its charges. 'When a civilisation declines it has stopped getting stronger and cleverer, but has started to become sillier and weaker; it has gone into reverse. This waning is the result of a reversal in the nature of authority; instead of authority ruling its charges, its charges rule authority. A community waxes when parents demand respect from their children; it wanes when parents seek the approval of their children'. In the latter situation, decline is inevitable because 'the reversal of authority has an immediate and crucial impact on the process by which a community constantly renews itself—the way it rears its children.' On this measure, much of western civilisation is heading downhill faster than a greased pig. The obvious deficiency of this 'law' is that it takes no account of differences in religious influence or practice. Repressive societies may have exemplary child rearing and thus be adjudged as highly civilised, but would be rated as uncivilised on other measures. But as a rule of thumb for charting comparative fluctuations in social health it is arguably useful.

A major theme of this book is that societies have inflicted noticeable self-harm by their abandonment of virtue, their failure to uphold ethical standards, and by pandering to a perceived need to indulge the desires and tastes of the masses. These latter, under the influence of libertarianism and as a result of increased affluence and globalisation, have become noticeably more demanding as popular impatience and dissatisfaction have grown in response to a more aggressive individualism and a lessening of respect for authority.

The libertarian ideal has been disastrous for many societies—a fact not diminished by its being based on a falsehood: namely, the equation of liberty with the absence of restraint. Much activism has been directed to the removal of restraints as a route to greater liberty. This, as has been seen, leads inexorably to moral relativism—the shop-shelf 'pick and mix' mentality we have now, which allows almost complete freedom of moral choice in the pursuit of self-interest and hedonism. This extends beyond sexual freedom to interpersonal relations, manners and general social behaviour. There is virtually no moral principle that has not been questioned. Modern morality is seen as a matter individual choice unless it impinges on social or public life; to be ignored if its impact is limited, to be regulated if not, and only in extreme cases to be condemned. In the absence of the stability which comes from community cohesion and shared morality, it is not surprising that people and societies feel increasingly insecure.

Libertarians are able, without much difficulty, to defend their philosophy on the grounds of limited consequence. Does it really matter that people swear or spit in public or have illegitimate children? Some people may feel affected, but "So what?" the argument runs, if there are no materially adverse consequences. Don't people have rights to free speech and freedom of expression and shouldn't these include swearing or spitting? What could be said if, for example, spitting in public were a religious ritual for casting out devils? Those who dislike such practices, it might be argued, should be more tolerant. Stoning people is Nigeria's way of dealing with adulterers, ritual slaughter of animals is required by some religions, and Sharia law demands that thieves have their hands cut off. It is doubtful whether religious tolerance requires Christian or a secular society to accept either these practices or the morality behind them, but it is difficult in a strictly egalitarian libertarian society to pick and choose what is acceptable without inconsistency. (As to practicalities, one might perhaps reflect that social stigma and public humiliation have proved better than moral condemnation or legal restraint in holding societies together.) What is certain is that the drive for tolerance and inclusivity has made dealing with such issues significantly more difficult.

The rooting out of superficiality and distortion involves deciding what is good or bad, worthy or unworthy, acceptable or unacceptable, reasonable or unreasonable. Developing a solid basis upon which to make such decisions is a core requirement in maintaining civilisation. Many libertarians vigorously repudiate this, believing that the modern 'three in one'—equality, tolerance and inclusivity—require the acceptance of all shades of opinion and practice and the prohibition, by law if necessary, of words or actions deemed likely to give offence. The idea of such a wide licence on personal freedom, with its accompanying baggage of group and individual rights, has considerable popular appeal. Together with the 'three in one', these have done much to promote individualism to the extent that the individual is now more important than the community he lives in. Societies must now actively 'include' everyone, however dysfunctional, lazy, abusive, aberrant or anti-social. One result of the ascendancy of political correctness is that genuinely free speech (i.e. plain speaking) has become ever more restricted. In this over-sensitive climate clarity of thought inevitably suffers as rationality is compromised by considerations of avoiding offence.

Considerations of equality also demand that policies are formulated on the basis that no one is better than anyone else, either by birth or merit with the result that social provision is generally designed to be impersonal and structured on the basis that human beings are homogeneous units. This radical liberalism has the advantage of sounding agreeable and is therefore popular, especially in societies which prefer to take their ideas whole, without much preliminary scrutiny. Where social life is driven more by 'feel-good' than by 'think straight', the opportunity for replacing the popular with the rational is greatly diminished.

As we have seen, the unrestrained pursuit of liberty has led to much social, political and cultural misery. We are constantly assailed with demands for toleration and respect, yet live at a time when these have never been in shorter supply. Such raw liberalism has extended toleration to the point at which we no longer seem able to distinguish sense from nonsense or right from wrong. Even where we can, we often lack the confidence to respond robustly, even to extremist activism, such as that which targets essential animal research, kills staff at abortion clinics or preaches hate and vengeance in the name of religion. An effete toleration of failure to deal effectively with those who abuse or undermine society damages its fabric. Such confidence can only come from clear, robust principles and these, as we have seen, have been eroded by the very forces they are needed to combat.

The culture of the individual has developed a heightened sense of personal isolation, in consequence of an over-emphasis on freedom from restraint and the pursuit of personal desires at the expense of those of wider society. Divorcing people from the predictability and stability of close communities has weakened their sense of security and led to tension and anxiety as they search for alternative frameworks for personal identity. Identities are no longer closely linked to membership of a community, rather to an impersonal amalgam of relationships defined more by outside concerns and priorities. Such isolation is reinforced by the impression that the social structures normally relied on (family, school or immediate community) have been altered to the point at which people no longer feel they belong.

This 'freedom' allows a person to see things in personal terms rather than from the perspective of a social community where your place in it and its rules and customs are understood and accepted. As community ethos has traditionally been one of the principal forces in promoting social stability, its weakening well beyond an ability to maintain basic order has accelerated the decline. It is far from clear that this reach for unlimited liberty has paid the dividends predicted by those who championed it. The social account would suggest that it has not and that there is an urgent need to restore to individuals a sense of ownership of their communities and an acceptance of greater responsibility for common welfare.

The loosening of social cohesion has greatly facilitated multiculturalism which — as opposed to multi-ethnicity — is seen as desirable in America, Britain and much of Europe. Given the relaxing of restrictions on international migration, this may be making a virtue of necessity, as many nations adapt to a new world of freer cross-border mobility. Although insufficient thought has been given to the implications of integrating many cultures into one social framework, it should be obvious that this is likely to be problematic without clear ethical and behavioural norms. The demographic reality behind societies which trumpet their multicultural credentials is generally groups of minorities, with their own values and aspirations based on ethnic or religious identity, co-existing in relative cultural isolation at the margins of society and far from being integrated in any meaningful sense. Their values are frequently religion-based and in some cases strongly at variance with those of the host nation, even to the extent of opposing them. In the absence of a receptive and understanding host community, this is a recipe for social division, which is certain to strengthen as time goes on without the political determination to prevent it. In societies enfeebled by Political Correctness and sentimentality this is unlikely to happen.

Any material change will depend on governments' willingness to take a strong moral stance. This was traditionally the province of the Churches but, in the Christian world at least, the Church is no longer regarded as a relevant moral arbiter. Its utterances on secular matters are generally contentious and widely seen as out of touch; this, and a preoccupation with internal divisions, means that it is no longer in a position to exercise moral authority. The abandonment of the doctrine of religious supremacy in Britain and the fragmentation of secular society there and elsewhere have produced a striking deterioration in national self-confidence which has greatly increased the difficulty of maintaining a faith-based social morality. Where other faiths were ignored to the extent that their activities had no obvious public impact, now that their adherents are embedded in significant numbers within western democracies and have to be dealt with at close quarters, as it were, this relationship has become strained. Toleration which once equated to passive acceptance has now taken on an active and more urgent aspect. Some religions, Islam in particular, are regarded with deep suspicion in western countries, especially where they have links with terrorism and also where their doctrines are repressive, intolerant, or anti-libertarian — e.g. advocating oppression of women, arranged marriages, indoctrination of children, *lex talionis*, and willing to denounce (or even kill) opponents or dissenters. Public suspicion and social segregation makes integration at best superficial, at worst a sham. Moral guidance is logically secondary to moral consensus — you cannot have the former without the latter — so, in its absence, in moral and social terms, the state totters.

Culture and social structures often spring from religion and therefore evolve with it. Understanding them falls foul of the usual difficulties of cultural relativism, which means that, in western countries, for example, eastern religions tend to be judged by western standards. Christian social tradition has evolved law based firmly on its principles and reacts strongly to immigrant groups who publicly state their aim as overturning the existing order and establishing an alternative system (e.g. Sharia law). It views the spread of such religions and the force of their extreme elements as a serious threat to public order and a thin cover for political activism rather than a genuine doctrinal background to worship. Such deep divisions soon permeate society at large and a culture of suspicion begets social tension. The image of Islam as a compassionate, peaceful religion contrasts with the reality of some of its public behaviour, a contrast so stark that many, unable to doubt the reality, are forced to question the image.

The fact that people are more self-centered and disengaged from their societies and that immigration has made social ethnic mixes more heterogeneous than ever, has inevitably led to demands for accepting a greater diversity of behaviour and attitude in the name of tolerance, equality and inclusiveness. This not only puts a strain on societies, but makes it increasingly difficult to decide what is acceptable and what is not and to establish norms of behaviour and social priorities. Where these were once clear and largely undisputed they are now matters of debate. The political response is generally to enact laws and regulations which are generally inadequate and, in many instances, unenforceable, so the situation 'on the ground' remains unsatisfactory. Except where a country is under military dictatorship, laws can only reflect religion or morality; where these become unsettled, as in many so-called multi-cultural societies, there is no firm base from which to legislate and the result is uncertainty. The proper quest should be for truth, not tolerance, and that truth should be woven into the social fabric.

An important by-product of the superficial freedom ethic is a search for a risk-free environment—a desire to eliminate adverse outcomes, as far as is possible. This has been discussed in the particular context of the victim culture but has broader resonances for society which is cast in the role of policeman and social catch-all. Risk-freedom is not simply a demand that nothing adverse will befall us or that, if it does, someone else be found to shoulder blame and to compensate, but rather the (false) expectation that the risks themselves are eliminable. One route to achieving this is to compartmentalise responsibilities tightly—the surgeon who specialises in left feet now has a colleague who specialises in right feet. In normal life risk is not eliminable and the marginal cost of reducing it beyond a certain point imposes disproportionate costs on society. The fall out from trading off security against social cost in this way has been increased regulation and legal sanction, which may provide remedy of a kind but does not address the underlying causes. Admitting neither accidents nor uncaused misfortune entrenches the determinist mindset, and with it the blame culture. One only has to look at the increase in medical insurance premiums or the massive explosion of contingency-fee litigation to see how far this mentality has spread. The impression that regulation is an adequate substitute for personal vigilance and responsibility has fed public and media clamour for action across a diverse range of circumstances. In every case, the solution is seen as statutory restraint rather than a looser framework which recognises that true freedom admits accidents. It is a mistake to suppose that the most sophisticated societies are those with the most laws.

The quest to establish 'causes' for most areas of behaviour increases the difficulty of putting personal responsibility at the heart of society. If people believe themselves detached from the causal chain and are encouraged to repudiate their responsibilities in every case then there is little incentive to accept them in any. This attitude extends into organisations, where committees and boards shirk difficult decisions in favour of procedural wrangling, weak compromises and face-saving strategies, which they then finesse as 'collective responsibility'. Failure to sanction bad behaviour effectively has had a further adverse result: namely, that we now blame the cause, not the behaviour. Drugs and depression may contribute to anti-social acts, but to indict them as causes simply takes the agent out of the causal picture and thus out of the way of blame. Modern political practice strives for manipulation and control and sees every defect as requiring a centrally determined remedial policy. Politicians prefer social and attitudinal engineering to the more demanding discipline of exercising authority.

The media have played a crucial role in promoting superficiality. In pursuit of infinite sensation, they have rendered the serious and the trivial indistinguishable, regarding both merely as species of entertainment. They have also made unusual commonplace, which weakens taboos and spreads a general moral anaesthesia. There is little work left for our imaginations. Distorting normal emotional responses in this way makes it less likely that people genuinely care about anything. The media also distort reality by focusing on the least demanding thoughts, which, by their nature, tend to be the most superficial. Since our view of events is largely determined by the media, their obsession with change and triviality make it inevitable that we see the world in terms of constant flux and instability.

I have described the fallout from both abuse and misuse of language. It is plain that language has been devalued both directly as a result of a decrease in overall linguistic and cognitive skills and indirectly by an ethos that puts little value on correct usage and accepts spin and distortion as standard practice. Language is not just a tool for communication; it also makes possible refined expression and detailed argument. Just as a piano can be made to emit noise or to make music, so language allows a spectrum of expressiveness ranging from Eliza Doolittle's coarse grunts to the finest poetry and prose.

Poor education is also a potent facilitator of superficiality. The progressive philosophy which side-lines wisdom in favour of technology and knowledge-based skill and dislikes grading and formal testing, has left people ill-equipped to manage their own affairs let alone to hold corrupt or ineffective institutions to account. Intellectual deficiency reinforces indiscipline, laziness and a willingness to accept mediocrity. As we have seen, educational failings are largely the result of misguided policies and less attributable to inadequate resources, a claim which would be difficult to reconcile with declining attainment despite massive investment. Underdeveloped intellect disinclines people to look beneath the surface and increases their vulnerability to the sharks of society, including those who deal in slogans and sentiment. This promotes the polarisation of political argument whereby 'feel-good' ideas such as freedom, democracy, greater choice, human rights and shorter working hours are accepted as entirely good while their opposites are seen as entirely harmful. Government based on impression-management makes for an ill-informed democracy and allows shallow opinion and bankrupt ideas to pass into the corpus of conventional wisdom unopposed. Once there, they are hard to dislodge. It is not difficult to appreciate that the quality of any society is compromised by poor general intellect.

In such an environment, governments appear increasingly authoritarian, but in reality are constrained within the narrow limits of what public opinion will accept. This means that political and social decisions are dictated by considerations of short-term impact, while genuinely radical options are marginalised and immediacy replaces strategic thinking in both the political and popular mind. In such circumstances, forced brevity is an almost certain guarantee of superficiality.

The tension between the need to bring politics to a mass audience and the need for sound policy-making is palpable in modern societies. Treating policies as consumer products to be 'sold' by PR and marketing machines is perhaps acceptable; making policies as a response to popular opinion is another matter entirely. This provides a genuine difficulty for politicians whose mandate depends on the popular vote, yet whose permanently defensive attitude suggest that they resent sharing intellectual space with others. Not only is such policy-making bad; it would also appear to verge on the monopolistic.

Where the dissemination of ideas is concerned, politicians work on the pragmatic principle that repetition will produce acceptance, if not truth itself. In fact, truth is not cumulative, either as a function of the number of times a proposition is repeated or as a function of the number of people who believe it. Nor, as some clearly suppose, can you 'demonstrate an assertion to be true by brow-beating people into proclaiming it' (Geoffrey Sampson, *Liberty and Language*, 1979).

Superficial minds tend to dismiss anything that surpasses their comprehension—they may see but don't understand, accepting lesser as greater and failing to look beyond what is most readily accessible. Moreover, this facile approach is not invariably neutral, in that in some kinds of naïveté one clearly sees malicious intent. Someone who refuses to condemn a terrorist atrocity on the ground that he 'doesn't do condemnation', or who makes a moral equation between suicide bombers and soldiers fighting a war, is being malevolent as well as evasive.

Free speech and rights have taken over much of the territory formerly occupied by conventional manners and morals. They have come to signify that not only is everyone entitled to their view on any matter, however difficult or technically complex, but also to expect that their opinion will be taken seriously. This aggressive personal assertiveness fuels the crusades of popular journalism. A public wanting guns outlawed or dogs muzzled, irrespective of the efficacy of such measures and often in spite of informed opposition from experts, expects to be heeded. Its demands have a greater chance of being indulged by politicians more concerned with their own popularity than with the wisdom of what they are being asked to enact if they are supported by the popular press.

The image that life is (or should be) easy has made difficulty a serious problem. Nobody much likes difficulty any more and few believe that there is much to be gained by tackling it. Difficult history, philosophy or political theory—gone, as far as the average reader is concerned; the difficulties and mysteries of religion—gone, replaced by happy-clappy brigades of people motivated by 'universal harmony', 'personal growth' and 'self-healing'; personal difficulties—gone to a legion of pseudo-academic disciplines which have sprouted to fill gaps in the need (and to further their own commercial interests). Much of the arts are pitched at the lowest intellectual common denominator of box-office attraction, output diluted for those who dislike, more than anything, having to think for themselves. In too many aspects of life aggressive, arrogant populism takes merit and morality as defined by its own superficial understanding.

Difficulty encompasses discomfort, so there is now an expectation of instant gratification of our desires—and society encourages that mentality. Much of today's youth (and at least one generation of adults) is locked into a permanent, unrealisable personal fantasy, mesmerised by the false glitter of celebrity and the self-assurance associated with rights without risks or responsibilities. Education has failed people who exhibit no vestige of a system of values which takes determination, patience, skill and work as a route to personal fulfilment. Visions of instant celebrity and instant wealth mean that many no longer accept the linkage between reward and effort, so admirably summed up by the golfer Gary Player as "The harder I work, the luckier I get". The commendable search for a better life is not advanced if 'better' is seen exclusively in material terms.

With this illusory freedom have come arrogance and apathy: arrogance in the assertion of individual rights and a decline in respect for those of others, apathy in the avoidance of effort and the search for the short cut or quick fix. Limitless rights, and the victim culture which sustains them, mean that people are now less likely to be penalised for bad actions, wrong decisions, egregious carelessness or even plain stupidity. Not surprisingly, this breeds disillusion and moral laziness.

The erosion of community and values has contributed to increased personal insecurity. The predictability and stability of work, income and a familiar social environment which gave a sense of social place are largely gone—communities lack the cohesion necessary to enforce standards, jobs and income are far from secure, and social mobility has replaced the old fixed order. Whereas people were identified, to a large extent, with their labour, they now have to manufacture and sustain social standing, often embellished by artifice. Why do people feel so keenly insecure? The main symptoms—though not necessarily the causes—are envy, feelings of unworthiness, lack of respect and diminished self-confidence. These are often irrational, reflecting over-sensitivity or simple misinterpretation of others' sentiments. Disillusion now takes its cue from the victim culture—people feel that society has failed them rather than that they have failed themselves. Not only are people less sure of themselves, they are also less sure of their convictions. This lack of confidence has spread to society itself, where what were once clear principles have been blurred by doubt. Now, even the slightest failing in public policy (often more apparent than real) triggers demands for a public enquiry to provide 'independent' validation of what, in many cases, is blindingly obvious. .

The extent of personal disillusion and alienation is evident from the unrestrained cult of celebrity. This exemplifies superficiality at its worst. The world is in thrall to know-nothing stardom, its choice-laden consumerist dreams, and is plagued by its show and seduced by its flash. Cultural heroes include the new elites, whose ideas and behavioural eccentricities are deemed acceptable purely because they emanate from people of perceived high status who are considered trend-setters. The super-rich are feted, lauded and listened to, however odious their personality or immoral their dealings. James Goldsmith said that vulgarity was a necessary concomitant of vigour in society; junk bond king Michael Milliken regarded himself as invincible; Robert Maxwell stole from his companies' pension funds and yet was courted from Moscow to Israel. The new elites exemplify the ethos of an age in which integrity is unfashionable, serial lying or criminal convictions are no longer a bar to high political or social status, mainstream religion is a hobby on a journalistic par with cycling or flower-arranging, and public servants refuse to take a moral stand on anything beyond the flagrantly outrageous or grotesque.

The drive for meritocratic equality has bred ruthless competitiveness which has made image manipulation a routine cover for inadequacy and led to to a rise in aggression as a defence mechanism. People believe—and they are pragmatically correct to do so—that success depends upon a 'thrusting', 'macho' attitude, whatever the deficiencies that lie behind it. The perception is self-reinforcing; all too often, status relies on an illusion of competence rather than on competence itself. Mental and physical aggression are common responses to personal failings, in particular to guilt. If there is a component of guilt involved in social aggression, it is less obviously a response to the promptings of conscience than the product of arrogance or narcissism.

Much arrogance, aggression and self-seeking are the result of deep insecurity. It is easy to forget in today's everlasting social exhibition that real status is earned, not manufactured. When one considers the truly great, these are not businessmen, politicians, celebrities or civic dignitaries but composers, statesmen, artists, writers and occasionally actors and very rarely sportsmen. How remote in sophistication and talent they seem from the loud, aggressive self-promoters who now aspire to take their place.

In business or politics, there is a noticeable tendency for the more self-seeking of those wielding authority to take to themselves the respect that is accorded to their office. The less perspicacious come to believe they are inviolable and beyond the reach of law, and are only brought down to earth when enforcement detaches them from their illusory positional security. It would seem that the bigger people or organisations try to be, the smaller they get.

Superficiality has infected the art world and (temporarily, it is to be hoped) derailed it. In general, and particularly in music, interest is reserved for whoever creates the greatest impression, rather than necessarily who produces the best interpretation or finest quality of work. Modernism is dedicated to show business as much as to merit. The pianist Andras Schiff, commenting on the deterioration in audience behaviour at classical concerts, observed that people, in his view, were less educated; they "go to discos and hear that terrible noise; when they are fifty they will become respected members of society and will start going to concerts, but without the requisite preparation". When they do, what they are likely to be offered is a programme of 'popular classics', designed to suit the prevailing taste for 'easy listening'. This applies across much of the arts where, as so often elsewhere, superficial acquaintance masquerades as knowledge.

Traditional patronage of the arts came from those with both money and passion. Now these have become dissociated and, with rare exceptions, money has gravitated into philistine hands and passion left to those without the resources to indulge it. The new breed of high-profile collectors and patrons employ art to make a social statement to the effect that they have taste, as well as money. Artists are understandably content to bend their craft to these new, generous paymasters, however vulgar their tastes may be. They take little notice either of traditional forms or of public sensibilities and expectations, turning out work designed to shock or confuse. If 'customers' do not understand what they are being offered, they are in no position to criticise or even less condemn it as rubbish thus leaving artists free to continue creating it.

Aggression is an excellent form of self-defence. "Of all sad fate's, the Avant-Garde's is worst; they were going nowhere and they got there first" (*The Meaning of Modernism*, Louis Dudek).

A potent thread through this book has been the damage done by sentimentality. This springs from a deep-seated desire to avoid situations which may cause psychological pain and often appears as much to promote the comfort of the perpetrator as to spare the discomfort of others. The manifestations are widespread—in education, personal, social and political life and particularly evident in the burgeoning victim culture. Sentimentality replaces judgement and blame with a veneer of caring which, in most cases, is unwarranted and by doing so undermines personal morality. In education, the harsh realities of poor achievement or indolence are replaced with contrived optimism, which benefits no one. It is also rife in the field of welfare, where people are 'institutionalised'—not in the sense of being put into institutions but in that of being discussed and handled in a compartmentalised, 'customer'-style manner. We no longer talk much of 'the poor', or try to identify need and poverty, but prefer the language of 'deprivation' and the gloss of rights and entitlements. This is underpinned by a tendency to treat symptoms as causes—someone has no food, so you give them some rather than asking why they are in that situation. Dealing with real causes is challenging and often uncomfortable. Rejecting sentimentality is not to deny the role of appropriate feelings but to highlight the consequences of systematically avoiding facing up to realities.

Another sub-theme of the ascendancy of semblance over sense has been the erosion of respect for the individual, by others, society, governments and the media. Honour and dignity are closely related to respect, as is tolerance. In one sense, toleration and respect may be seen as further facets of sentimentality—permissive qualities which amount to no more than the expedient avoidance of conflict, instead of requiring a deeper recognition of the values, rights and individuality of others. Blanket toleration makes no sense and serves no purpose. True toleration is hierarchical and judgemental and assumes the power to suppress. Respectfulness is a social grace and is equally judgemental, but is neutral as to respect. Dignity, whether as personal conduct or as a cognate of self-esteem, requires behaviour in accordance with acceptable values. If, for example, you strip away superficiality from popular television shows, you often reveal a degenerate value-set, which includes humiliation, bad language and gratuitous offensiveness. Dignity demands that feelings should be clad in a form of manners—suppressed and not always acted upon—which is often not to the taste of those who believe in unlimited freedom of expression. This leads one to wonder whether Darwinism applies to societies as well as to individuals, in respect of selecting groups and social traits that have survival-value. It would be odd indeed if the self-centered aggression that often accompanies individual success might become privileged in heredity in opposition to other traits which promote the long-term survival and well-being of society. We no longer value the community above the individual, and Darwinism makes it no easier to make sense of the complex amalgam of change and persistence that characterise societies or to define the factors determining their continuity.

The desire for unrestricted freedom of expression and the belief in social equality has resulted in a decline in deference. This is generally welcome; the rise in discourtesy is not. Deference has a component of merit that discourtesy lacks — and where a lack of deference is based on perceived incompetence or incapacity, it may be entirely justified. However, there is a sense in which deference has been killed by democracy and been devalued by tolerance. Tolerance is widely misconstrued. It is often opposed to hate, but this is a false antithesis. Intolerance is not invariably connected with hate, nor is tolerance necessarily free of it. Moreover, it does not, as some appear to believe, imply unqualified respect or unquestioning acceptance. The shift in moral emphasis from society to individual has engendered an attitude of aggressive equality and the idea that no one is in any sense better than anyone else, thus removing the main justification for both deference and respect. This is not to condone disrespect or lack of deference, merely to offer a sociological explanation.

The fact of toleration — we tolerate more — does not necessarily mean that we are more tolerant. Toleration is often deployed as a convenient means of excusing anti-social or criminal behaviour, in the recognition that the relentless pursuit of transgressors, especially those from ethnic or other minorities, is all too easily interpreted as persecution by other members of their communities and likely to be portrayed either as racism or as unjustified provocation, irrespective of any actual guilt. To the extent that toleration means not enforcing laws, it is corrosive of civic order and community relations (the opposite of what those involved would probably claim).

True toleration is a limited licence, and implies an element of judgement. Social acceptance of other religions or ideologies does not mean that we approve of or agree with them, merely that we recognise them as having currency and validity. Nor does it mean, as is widely believed, that we are required to accord them equal standing within the existing system. The licence extends to their free-circulation but should not be allowed to undermine the status of the prevailing orthodoxy.

The need for social and international stability in the face of increased aggression and lawlessness has become more urgent. At an individual level, lives are interrupted less and less by the requirements of family or society, from which they have become increasingly separated. Yet, beyond the introduction of greater regulation and more active suppression, thinking has barely progressed. It is part of the distorting focus of superficiality that it is difficult to replace immediate concerns with a broader, even historical, perspective. Regulation and coercion are superficial solutions. An essential element in promoting fundamental social improvement is to discern the forces making for change and stability, which are as much historical as they are topical. A deeper understanding of a society's complexities also requires consideration of which factors are likely to result in conflict and which lead towards consensus. These may be social issues, but they are not necessarily resolved by social engineering.

The evolution of mankind, and its distinctiveness from beasts, is characterised by a broadening range and conception of what amounts to a better life and how to go about achieving it. This constant social aim is far more likely to have contributed to social ills than mere intolerance or increasing individualism. In this, the refinement of behaviour, language and thought have played a central role. As A H Halsey put it, 'what you see and how you learn to see it is rooted in a long procession of human history and cultural achievement' (Reith Lectures, 1977). The shallow image-driven development of modern life trivialises this debate and merely works to providing short-term, and largely ineffective, patches on gaping national and international wounds.

This book has sought to expose what is spurious, shallow, trivial, vacuous and deceitful. In doing so, it has identified the main springs of our relationship with the superficial and suggested that problems reflect the fact that we can no longer be bothered, or in many cases are intellectually ill-equipped, to distinguish authentic from fake, quality from sham, truth from spin, genuine from imitation, relevant from irrelevant, and real from illusory. In too much of our lives, semblance passes for sense.

Why should this matter? People fortunate enough to inhabit a first world country in comparatively affluent circumstances generally consider their standard of living acceptable and discern no obvious harm in the systems and ideas on which their society is conducted, beyond perhaps minor irritations and inconveniences. This superficial perspective increases the likelihood that more serious trends are either not observed, or if they are, their impact is not appreciated. Society, focused on the narrow interest, seems to find nothing amiss in declining literacy, morals and manners (younger generations would undoubtedly question this description), nor in the distortion of language and the erosion of personal moral agency. Exposing the wider implications of such a culture is impossible without appeal to historical perspective and longer-term objectives, both of which fall well beyond the horizons of modern decision-makers and a public dedicated to the here-and-now.

Those who can see the damage being done insist on the serious consequences of allowing these trends to continue. The fault line in modern western societies is no longer demarcated by C.P. Snow's *Two Cultures*, but has shifted and is now characterised by the broadening rift between the educated, law-abiding, useful and competent, and those who are not. It is clear that a large part of societal and national problems come from belligerent minorities whose behaviour and demands take a disproportionate share of available public energy and resources. Unless appropriate measures are taken to close this gap and to involve more people, more intimately, in social affairs, tension, dissent, aggression and anti-social behaviour will continue to worsen. Political and social life will become increasingly difficult as laws are flouted and the rash-scratching regulation designed to ensure a modicum of standards is seen to be ineffective. Establishing what are 'appropriate measures' requires looking beneath the overt social phenomena to identify the underlying causes. This can only be achieved by eschewing sentimentality on such issues as education and personal responsibility, and reforming education and social expectations on the basis of unambiguous standards. Having a majority of well-educated citizens, capable of clear thought and expression and prepared for open debate on tough political and social questions, would do much to correct the current imbalance. The aim of this activity should be [as Bryan Wilson put it] to ensure that 'the unquestionable freedom in Western society for individual or groups to maintain a distinctive, serious and conscientious way of life should not be less than the very evident contemporary freedom to maintain an utterly frivolous and uncaring life'.

That such frivolity is gaining ground, at the expense of the serious and conscientious, cannot be in doubt. What perhaps matters even more is the equally evident failure to distinguish, either in fact or in value, the one from the other. We take the trivial as important and the ephemeral as substantial. Life should be fun, but it cannot be all fun — fun is only fun in contrast to the

serious or more demanding. Fun needs a solid framework of values and expectations around which it can thrive. If we reject this and pretend that everything
is fun, we delude ourselves and create a false society. This is not a matter of
piety or moral asceticism, but recognition of the reality that many modern
ideals — freedom, happiness, self-esteem and indeed fun — are consequences
of something else, not ends attainable in themselves. Chasing inappropriate
ends, or appropriate ends with inappropriate means, is useless — rather like
trying to follow the right route with the wrong map. The fact that civilisations
are frail and come with no guarantee of self-perpetuation should add urgency
to solving these problems. The deterioration in pockets of western civilisation
should deeply concern those who believe that, at its best, it offers an ideal and a
model for others. The more it is corroded by deceit and superficiality, the more
its institutions lose credibility and the greater the difficulty of rehabilitation.

None of this is to deny, or minimise, the improvements in western societies
or to undervalue much in them that is truly excellent. However, the majority
of the progress has come from science and technology — the social hardware,
as it were — while the lubricant of social cohesion — the social software — has
to a large extent disintegrated.

I said at the outset that this book was not intended to provide specific
solutions, but to tease out difficulties — an exercise in diagnosis rather than
prescription. However, elucidating and interpreting does not amount to explanation, let alone to cure. Nor does exposing deficiency equate to discovering
the truth. Error and truth are not opposites. It requires more than analysis to
deal with the phenomena I have sought to describe here. However, deeper
insight into the problems will indicate routes towards their solutions. Ultimately, progress depends upon societies recognising these changes as problems
rather than dismissing them as irrelevant quirks of modern social development
and then acting collectively to tackle them.

What is wanted, above all, is clarity, not cant. It is long overdue to call
"Time!" on superficiality, over-valued mediocrity, political correctness,
sustained incompetence, appetite-driven priorities and inappropriate sentimentality; these have been indulged for too long and are increasingly destabil-
ising societies. It would be refreshing, but ultimately self-deceiving, to imagine
that political will might change to meet the challenges. The more credible
prognosis is that the situation will continue to deteriorate to a point at which
there is an unstoppable demand for action. That, at least, would be a step in
the right direction.